The Age of Ruth and Landis

The Age of
RUTH and LANDIS
The Economics of Baseball during the Roaring Twenties

David George Surdam and Michael J. Haupert

University of Nebraska Press | Lincoln and London

Library of Congress
Cataloging-in-Publication Data
Names: Surdam, David George, author.
Title: The age of Ruth and Landis:
the economics of baseball during the
roaring twenties / David George Surdam,
Michael J. Haupert. Description: Lincoln:
University of Nebraska Press, 2018.
Identifiers: LCCN 2017044997
ISBN 9780803296824 (hardback)
ISBN 9781496205711 (epub)
ISBN 9781496205728 (mobi)
ISBN 9781496205735 (pdf)
Subjects: LCSH: Baseball—Economic
aspects—United States—History—20th
century. | Baseball players—United States—
Economic conditions—20th
century. | Baseball team owners—United
States—Economic conditions—20th
century. | BISAC: SPORTS & RECREATION /
Baseball / History.
Classification: LCC GV880 .S868 2018 | DDC
331.88/11796357—dc23 LC record available at
https://lccn.loc.gov/2017044997

Contents

Tables

Acknowledgments

I was never much of a baseball player. I could hit the ball but without power. I could catch fly balls, but to misquote Will Rogers, I never met a ground ball I didn't boot. What attracted me to baseball were the numbers. I loved the statistics. As a child, I read the first volume of Harold Seymour's trilogy on baseball history and can remember "the triumvirate" (quite a word for a child to mull).

When I was a teenager, Strat-O-Matic Baseball provided hours of fun and numbers. The company created sets for the 1922 New York Giants, 1924 Washington Senators, and 1927 Yankees (later the 1922 St. Louis Browns and 1929 Chicago Cubs would appear); these teams gave me an awareness of the key personnel of the 1920s.

Baseball research has been "berra, berra good to me" as Garrett Morris's Chico Escuela might have said on *Saturday Night Live* if he had been an academic. You meet wonderful and helpful people along the way.

My Robert D. Clark Honors College (University of Oregon) committee (Paul Speckman, Richard Koch, and Edward Diller) allowed me to pursue a baseball topic: baseball run production. Building upon the work of operations-research scholars, I used regression analysis to demonstrate that slugging average and on-base percentage explained 90–95 percent of baseball run production. Unfortunately, I never aggressively pursued this finding.

George Rugg, curator of the Joyce Sports Collection housed at Notre Dame University, has proved to be a good friend and shrewd advisor. His suggestion of using team scorecards was astute. Claudette Burke-Scrafford, manuscript archivist at the Giamatti Research Library at the National Baseball Hall of Fame and Museum, alerted me to the New

York Yankees' financial records on microfilm. These records proved a treasure trove; readers will encounter them throughout this book. While compiling information from the microfilm, I was introduced to Professor Michael Haupert of the University of Wisconsin–La Crosse. He was working with the same data set. We've been friends ever since, and he agreed to write the chapter on the Negro Leagues. Haupert probably knows more about Negro League finances than anyone; in addition his coauthor, Kenneth Winter (also of University of Wisconsin–La Crosse), and he calculated rates of profitability for the New York Yankees. Much of their findings enrich this book.

Professor Kenneth Brown, head of the Missouri State University Economics Department, has been a valued colleague who collaborated on most of the econometric work dealing with the 1920s material. Professor Stanley Engerman, John Munro Professor of Economics of the University of Rochester, has long encouraged me in my work. He read the manuscript and made many useful suggestions.

Two anonymous reviewers gave the manuscript careful consideration and made astute suggestions that will benefit the readers. I, of course, remain responsible for remaining errors.

I also thank the surviving member of my dissertation committee, Professor David Galenson, of the University of Chicago Economics Department. Ruth and Landis are generations removed from my dissertation topic of the Civil War naval blockade, but Professor Galenson has been a steadfast friend and mentor. Nobel Prize–winner Robert W. Fogel and Professor D. Gale Johnson shepherded me through the dissertation process; they are sorely missed.

I received considerable help from the University of Northern Iowa. Farzad Moussavi, former dean of the College of Business Administration, and Fred Abraham, head of the Economics Department, provided support and financial encouragement for this project. Leslie Wilson, dean of the College of Business Administration, generously provided financial support for the index. Beverly Barber, the Department of Economics office administrator, has long provided excellent service in meeting the myriad tasks that I've requested.

Students Kayla Gump and Kayla Darnell looked up and printed articles from the *New York Times* and other sources. Another student, Claire Reinhard, put together note cards that I had typed.

Research is usually a solitary pursuit punctuated by interactions with students in classrooms, office hours, and on racquetball and basketball courts. Along the way, I've had some good students to work with. Andrea Huffman served as copresident of Beta Gamma Sigma and won an economics essay prize. Carsen Anderson was also an excellent student who served as a copresident of Beta Gamma Sigma. He also drained three-point shots with monotony in our pickup basketball games. Paul Van Gorp has become a good friend and worthy racquetball foe. Thomas Cullen worked on a separate project investigating whether Major League Baseball players of the 1920s and 1930s who had college backgrounds fared better in the big leagues. His enthusiasm for research was infectious. Having such sharp, hard-working students reaffirms a professor's faith in teaching.

McFarland & Company graciously granted permission to reprint materials from two articles in *Black Ball*: Michael Haupert, "Ed Bolden: Black Baseball's Great Modernist," *Black Ball* 5, no. 2 (Fall 2012): 61–72 and Haupert and Kenneth Winter, "The Old Fellows and the Colonels: Innovation and Survival in Integrated Baseball," *Black Ball* 1, no. 1 (Spring 2008): 79–92. The Journal of the Economic & Business History Society kindly allowed us to reprint material from Haupert and Winter, "Pay Ball: Estimating the Profitability of the New York Yankees, 1915–1937," *Essays in Economics and Business History* 21, (Spring 2003): 89–102.

The University of Nebraska's staff was a joy to work with, as always. Rob Taylor, senior acquisitions editor; Courtney Ochsner, associate acquisitions editor; and Sabrina Stellrecht, assistant manager had faith in and encouraging words for this manuscript. Ann Baker stepped in and saw the project to its conclusion. Brian King proved a thorough and helpful copy editor; his efforts polished the final product.

Sarah Statz Cords compiled the index to this, our ninth book together. She has been a delight to work with and a good friend.

The Age of Ruth and Landis

Introduction

Major League Baseball owners could be excused for feeling sorry for themselves as 1918 ended. Unlike most Americans, they had endured two wars—one on the baseball fields of the northeastern quadrant of the country and the other on the battlefields of France and the Atlantic Ocean. After successfully thwarting the Federal League, the owners hoped for a return to prosperity. The 1916 season had been reasonably normal, but the declaration of war against Germany in April 1917 disrupted two baseball seasons.

After these serious threats, the owners were warily optimistic regarding the 1919 season. They were uncertain whether fans would return in sufficient numbers. Much to their delight, turnstiles clicked merrily throughout the season. Unfortunately for the owners, they would find peace ephemeral in 1919. Owners found themselves involved in an internecine struggle for power and in a fight against gambling. The much-heralded 1919 World Series promised to put an exclamation point on a successful season, but most baseball fans know the denouement of that encounter. If baseball fans dreamed of reading the sports pages without the intrusion of lawyers and legal terms, such as they endured during the Federal League struggle, they were doomed to disappointment. Organized baseball kept lawyers quite busy during the 1920s.

As the 1919 World Series scandal simmered throughout the 1920 season, tight pennant races drove attendance to new peaks and presaged a decade of general prosperity for the sport. Babe Ruth shattered his own home run record. Along with a growing economy, professional sports ranging from boxing to golf to baseball and collegiate football enjoyed what sportswriters termed "A Golden Age of Sports." The 1920 season heralded a decade of prosperity.

By 1929 Major League Baseball had experienced seismic shifts: the moribund New York Yankees team was now the most glamorous franchise in sports; Judge Kenesaw Mountain Landis was a strong-willed commissioner; the Boston Braves, St. Louis Browns, and Philadelphia Phillies were descending into their chronic mediocrity; and the home run was now the offensive weapon of choice instead of the so-called scientific approach to the game.

Throughout the tumultuous 1920s, Major League Baseball remained a unique mixture of competition and cooperation. During the National League's internecine strife of the early twentieth century, New York Giants owner Andrew Freedman observed, "We are here to-day, with each man trying to clutch his interested partner by the throat and throw him down the baseball abyss as hard and as quick as he can do it. That gets him out of standing in the way of his success with his club and his ambition to win." At the same time, rival owner James Hart of Chicago stated, "We are the only paradoxical business institution in the world. My good is your ill; your good is my ill. We compete for players, we compete for points, we compete for games; it is an antagonistic business from start to finish. If it was not, we would not be in business."[1]

One owner anonymously wrote that organized baseball was "the strongest combination ever formed in this land of the free" because "it has been able to secure an absolute monopoly of flesh and blood" over the players.[2] Whether his fellow owners agreed with him or not, they may well have been aghast at his revelations. Fortunately, the Federal League lawyers did not place this admission into evidence during the antitrust lawsuit.

Sportswriter Hugh Fullerton also recognized this aspect of Major League Baseball: "The peculiar feature of the business is that the owners of the eight clubs are partners, dividing the gate receipts, and each strives to best the other out of games, players, and by beating them to lower their earning power by reducing the gate receipts."[3]

After baseball emerged from its Federal League, wartime, and governance struggles, teams began showing signs of prosperity. The congressional investigation of baseball in 1951 forced owners to provide some financial data regarding profits and losses. The National Baseball Hall of Fame and Museum contains New York Yankees financial records for the 1920s. Between these sources and reported prices paid for franchises, the state of baseball finances between 1919 and 1929 becomes clear. Appendix 1 contains a description of the materials contained in these financial records.

Profitability, of course, depended primarily upon attendance, which in turn presumably depended upon a team's win-loss record, metropolitan population, ticket prices, and schedules. A key aspect of scheduling during the 1920s revolved around whether a team could stage home games on Sundays.

Teams had fluctuating experiences on the field between the 1919 and 1929 seasons. Some teams went into prolonged slumps, while others, such as the St. Louis Cardinals and Philadelphia Athletics, grew stronger as the decade passed. Of course, the Yankees' ascendance was a key development during the decade.

Teams could improve themselves through trades, purchasing Minor League players, or signing untried amateurs. Owners occasionally passed restrictions on player movement, but wealthier teams, such as the Yankees and Giants, with owners both willing and able to expend money could survive more mistakes than teams with limited capital. Competitive balance, as always, was a contentious issue.[4]

Owners also adjusted the game. The 1920s witnessed a surge in slugging and a diminution in base stealing. Owners struggled to provide a better ballpark experience, not only by improving their stadiums but also their fans. Rowdy fans remained a problem. The owners also struggled to adapt (or not to adapt) to new technologies, such as radio, electrical lighting, and air travel. They did not seriously entertain the idea of improving the game by tapping the rich vein of black baseball talent, although they skirted the issue of discrimination by signing Cuban players with darker hues. Entrepreneurs began organizing teams of black players into leagues during the 1920s, and readers will find information on the finances of such entities in this book.

Players and owners had their usual contentious relationship. Owners exerted considerable control over their players; baseball was a lopsided institution with owners having almost all of the advantages. The reserve clause bound players to one team; players moved only at their owner's behest. Players often entertained the idea of forming unions but failed to do so during the 1920s. Owners and their league officials proved willing to crack down on even the biggest stars in the game—Babe Ruth, Rogers Hornsby, and Ty Cobb.

Even the Minor Leagues enjoyed a measure of prosperity during the decade. Since teams in the lowest classifications in the Minors usually played in very small towns, their existence was precarious under any condition.

Baseball during the 1920s, then, enjoyed strife and prosperity, innovation and conservatism. With stars such as the incomparable Ruth, Hornsby, Cobb, Walter Johnson, Tris Speaker, and Eddie Collins, the decade featured an exciting brand of ball.

In order to place baseball in its proper context and truly appreciate its metamorphosis during the decade, we need to examine the state of the American economy during the Roaring Twenties. Baseball didn't operate in a vacuum. Rather, as we shall see, its changes were not all that different in nature from what was going on in the wider world around it.

Overview of the American Economy

It's a bad war that does not bring prosperity for some people. Americans seemingly enjoyed prosperity during the first few years of the Great War. The nation's nominal (unadjusted for changes in the price level) gross national product (GNP), a measure of economic strength, roughly doubled between 1914 and 1918, and GNP continued to increase in the immediate aftermath of the war (table 1). A fairly sharp recession occurred after 1920, before GNP rose through 1929.

These changes in GNP, though, need to be adjusted for changes in the general price level. Americans experienced years of double-digit rates of inflation.[5] The per-capita GNP figures revealed the wartime prosperity to have been partially illusory, as the increases in the price level more than offset the gains in nominal GNP. In fact, real, per capita GNP fell sharply during 1917 and after the war. Although the real, per capita GNP bounced back sharply in 1922 and 1923, the rest of the decade witnessed modest growth. Inflation, at least, stabilized after 1922. Average hourly earnings of production workers, while appearing stable between 1920 and 1930, with a drop through 1922, actually rose in real terms across the decade.

From the vantage point of baseball owners, two facts are salient. First, their patrons' real, per capita GNP peaked in 1918 and only again approached the 1918 level by 1923. The immediate postwar years were abnormal. Second, the 1920–22 period represented a rapid deflation (reduction in the general price level). By 1930 prices had fallen by one-sixth from 1920.

If there was one area of the American economy that boomed during the 1920s, it was the recreation industry. Between 1919 and 1930 expenditures on recreation almost doubled in real terms (table 2). The expenditures on recreation represented 3.6 percent of total personal consumption expenditures in 1919 and 5.4 percent in 1929. Motion-picture theaters and spectator sports did well during the 1920s. The "radio" category requires some explanation. Radio broadcasts only became widespread after 1922; the category includes radios, records, and musical instruments. After 1921 sales of radios, radio equipment, and repairs began to dominate the category, while phonographs, records, and musical instruments lagged.

Overall, though, the economy during the 1920s was capable of sustaining baseball. The Roaring Twenties was a prosperous decade for many Americans. Baseball prospered, but its gains in attendance and revenues were less impressive than those of the motion-picture industry. A key question, then, is why wasn't baseball more prosperous?

1   Baseball's Interminable Wars

Major League Baseball was beset by struggles against the rival Federal League (1914–15) and the Germans (1917–18, with an armistice on November 11, 1918), and also within league ranks. Between 1914 and 1927, peace was elusive.

The Federal League Challenge

The Federal League aspired to Major League status after operating as a minor league in 1913. The league's owners built or acquired leases on ballparks in eight cities. The league competed directly with Major League Baseball (MLB) in Chicago, St. Louis, Pittsburgh, and Brooklyn. Despite two tightly contested pennant races, Federal League owners could not generate large enough crowds to turn a profit. Reporters and historians cited huge losses for the teams, but no one knows with much accuracy how extensive the losses were.

The Major League owners fought hard and sometimes dirty against the Federal League. The rival sets of owners fought over ballparks, players, and fans. The Major Leagues, of course, held an insurmountable advantage through ruthless application of the reserve clause and the blacklist. Players opting to play in the Federal League faced blacklisting from organized baseball for the rest of their careers. The Federal League, therefore, had to pay a premium or offer multiyear contracts to compensate players for the risks they were taking in joining the new endeavor. Small wonder that, in their antitrust lawsuit against Major League Baseball, the Federal League owners identified the reserve clause as one of the anticompetitive measures. Although the Federal League signed a number of current, former, and prospective Major League players, most were older veterans nearing the end of their careers or were very young. Few signees were in the prime of their careers. Benny Kauff, who was the Federal League's batting champion for both 1914 and 1915, was perhaps the best player in the league. When he returned to the New York Giants, his batting average skidded badly.[1]

Owners sued players, and players sued owners over contracts. Some players jumped their reserve clause, having not signed new contracts with their old clubs, but a few jumped their contracts. As other professional sports leagues would discover, under interleague warfare, only the lawyers win unambiguously.

Walter Johnson, tempted by a big contract with the Federal League, eventually decided to trust Clark Griffith's promise of a pay increase from the Senators and to stay put. Ban Johnson (no relation to Walter) persuaded Charles Comiskey to help the Washington Senators placate Walter Johnson's pay demands; Ban Johnson convinced Comiskey that the specter of Walter Johnson hurling for a Chicago Federal League team was well worth avoiding. Griffith did indeed increase Johnson's salary. It rose from $7,000 to $10,000 in 1914 and then to $12,500 in 1915. It remained at that level until 1918 when the war-shortened season depressed player salaries across the league. After Connie Mack lost Chief Bender and Eddie Plank to Federal League teams, Ban Johnson urged Mack to sell Eddie Collins to the Chicago White Sox. The White Sox gave Collins a five-year contract for $15,000 per annum, the longest-term contract in history to that point. In addition, the contract struck the ten-day release clause—the option for the team to curtail the contract at their discretion—and a "no trade" clause that prevented the White Sox from transferring his contract to any other team without his permission.[2]

Major League owners watched their attendance shrivel in 1914 and 1915. The leagues had drawn a combined 6.36 million fans in 1913, but the attendance figures were below 5 million in each of the next two seasons. Attendance rebounded in 1916 before the war in Europe disrupted baseball.

The Federal League owners filed an antitrust lawsuit under the Sherman Antitrust Act against Major League Baseball early in 1915. The lawsuit asked the court to "declare the national agreement illegal, dissolve the alleged combination maintained by that agreement, declare the acts of the national commission void, nullify all contracts made under the national agreement, and order organized baseball to dismiss all injunction suits against Federal League players, and restrain defendants from instituting any more such suits." The hearing raised all sorts of interesting points. Presiding judge Kenesaw Mountain Landis opted to delay issuing a verdict in the hopes that the owners would reach a settlement, thereby earning the gratitude of and eventual employment by Major League Baseball owners.

Major League Baseball justified its behavior as demonstrating its ability to self-police baseball and cast incendiary aspersions at the attorneys for the Baltimore club, comparing them to Lenine [sic] and Trotzky [sic]. "You would have thought that we were on trial in Russia," huffed Ban Johnson, American League president, simultaneously making the ill-timed claim that baseball was successful in "keeping the sport clean and retaining the dignity of the game."[3]

James A. Gilmore, former president of the Federal League, testified that his league bluffed the Major Leagues into settling by instituting a rumor the Federal League was going to place a team in New York. The Federal League enhanced their ruse by taking out a lease on office space in New York City.[4]

The owners reached a settlement. The Federal League's Chicago and St. Louis owners got to buy the Cubs and Browns, while other Federal League teams divided hundreds of thousands of dollars and won the right to sell their more desirable players to organized baseball. Part of the payment to the Federal League owners was for their stadiums in order to ensure that future promoters could not use these facilities. Ineligible players were reinstated.[5]

The Baltimore Federal League club was dissatisfied with the peace settlement, so its owners filed an antitrust suit against Major League Baseball, its officials, and some Federal League officials. The latter were named because they allegedly negotiated a settlement without Baltimore's participation.

Baltimore had a checkered history in organized baseball. The famed Baltimore Orioles of John McGraw and Willie Keeler, while potent on the field, were lackluster in the stands. As soon as land for a stadium was procured in New York City, Ban Johnson quickly relocated the league's Baltimore franchise to the bigger city. In the minds of Major League owners, Baltimore was not a desirable location. During the peace negotiations, Charles Comiskey responded to the Baltimore owners' offer to accept $250,000 for their franchise; he stated that the price was "just the right price for a minor-league franchise," before adding, "Baltimore is a minor league city and not a hell of a good one at that." His fellow owner Charles Ebbets claimed Baltimore was a poor Minor League city because, "you have too many colored population to start with. They are a cheap population when it gets down to paying their money at the gate."[6]

As the court case wended its way up to the Supreme Court, Major League owners occasionally sought to squelch public protest at their practices by suggesting the desirability of a third major league. Reporters, wanting something exciting to write about during the winter months, may have seized on the flimsiest rumors. The proposed third major league usually consisted of taking four teams from the International League and four teams from the American Association, but the proposal went nowhere despite the hopes of Baltimore fans in particular. Jack Dunn worked hard to make his Minor League team a worthy candidate for elevation to Major League status. His team featured several future Major League players.[7] National League president John Tener lent credence to the third-league rumor with a vague statement, "there will be a third major league some day." He cautioned, though, that eight cities with the "necessary public demand" were needed to make any such league a success.[8]

Unlike the Federal League owners, who had to fight to obtain players, a third major league under the auspices of organized baseball would have had easier access to players. If composed of Minor League teams, an exemption from the player draft would have allowed these teams a chance to accumulate sufficient playing talent to be deemed "Major League." Sportswriter H. G. Salsinger, though, demurred. He didn't think there were sufficient numbers of quality players to outfit the sixteen big league teams: "the National League looked as much like a minor circuit as a circuit can look without being officially classed as 'bush.'" Other critics of the third major league contended that some of the current Major League teams should relocate with Detroit being a popular destination (at least in the minds of the pundits). Salsinger dismissed Baltimore as a potential site, while he bemoaned Washington's lack of support for the Senators. He disputed whether Detroit would support two teams, especially given that the Tigers had a big attraction in Ty Cobb.[9]

Baltimore won the first trick in its lawsuit, getting a favorable ruling and an award of $80,000, trebled under the Sherman Act to $240,000. Organized baseball won the second trick, when District of Columbia chief justice Constantine J. Smyth reversed the decision of the lower court. Smyth wrote that baseball was not trade or commerce under the Sherman Act; he also ruled that the reserve clause and blacklists did not directly affect the interstate features of the plaintiff's business. Smyth cited the well-worn defense of the reserve clause, that its absence would lead to wealthier clubs corralling most of the talent and to competitive imbalance. During the lawsuit, Baltimore officials claimed Ban Johnson and other baseball officials had made derogatory statements regarding the Federal League in an attempt to dissuade players from signing with the new league.[10]

Major League counsel George Wharton Pepper, former senator from Pennsylvania, made a weird analogy regarding whether baseball was interstate commerce. Baltimore's attorneys argued that courts had ruled that the white slave traffic constituted interstate commerce, but Pepper argued, "such transportation [of players to game sites was similar] to the sending of a surgeon's tools into another state for use in an operation." Baltimore's attorneys characterized organized baseball owners as "high-waymen" while characterizing players as chattels and slaves. The Baltimore owners and their lawyers lashed out at their former comrades in the Federal League by accusing them of selling out to organized baseball.[11]

Reporters generally rejoiced when the higher court reversed the original court decision. They viewed the decision as wise and as protecting baseball. The reporters, as did almost everyone—even many players—viewed the reserve clause as necessary.[12] The Baltimore club, of course, did not admit defeat, so the case went to the United States Supreme Court.

In the final, winner-take-all Supreme Court decision, Major League Baseball won a big victory. In a unanimous decision, delivered in May of 1922, the court ruled that organized baseball was not interstate commerce, so the Sherman Antitrust Act did not apply. Justice Oliver Wendell Holmes expressed the majority view:

> The business is the giving of exhibitions of baseball which are purely state affairs. It is true that in order to attain for these exhibitions the great popularity they have achieved, competition must be arranged between clubs from different cities and States. But the fact that in order to give an exhibition leagues must induce free persons to cross State lines, and must arrange and pay for their doing so, is not enough to change the character of the business . . . the transport is a mere incident, not the essential. That to which it is incident, the exhibition, although made for money, would not be called trade or commerce in the commonly accepted use of those words.

He went on to compare baseball with, "a firm of lawyers sending out a member to argue a case, or a Chautauqua lecture bureau sending out a lecturer, do not engage in such commerce because the lawyer or lecturer goes to another state."[13]

Although some later legal scholars and justices have questioned the wisdom of the ruling and its key interpretation, there were previous cases that guided the jurists' decision. The E. C. Knight case of 1894 showed that the court did not consider manufacturing as commerce. In *People v. Klaw v. Erlanger* (1907), the court ruled that the theatrical businesses were amusement enterprises and not interstate commerce. In theater as in baseball, performers traveled across state lines to give performances. In another case, involving horse racing, the judge dismissed a charge of antitrust conspiracy on the basis that horse racing was not commerce under the Sherman Antitrust Act.[14]

National League president John Heydler rejoiced and stated, "The Supreme Court's decision will prove a great stimulus to the future development of baseball. . . . All of these basic features of our mode of operation have now been safe-guarded and made more secure. . . . The decision stabilizes the whole structure of American baseball. It insures protection for the owners as well as for the players, and will mean more attractive exhibitions for the public."[15] Had there been a futures market for baseball franchises, the Supreme Court's ruling should have induced a jump in the price, given the strengthened property rights of franchise ownership.

A Real War

Baseball had survived the Spanish-American War of 1898. That war hadn't lasted too long and didn't require a military draft. The Great War of 1914–18, though, required a military draft for the relatively short period of American involvement.

Since owners were still trying to adjust player salaries to pre–Federal League levels, the war seemed a heaven-sent opportunity. Baseball owners undoubtedly gnashed their teeth that American's declaration of war occurred after players had signed their contracts for 1917. Chicago Cubs president Charles Weeghman candidly said that players should have had their salaries reduced because of wartime economy: "It will have to be economy all along the line for the baseball owners." Yankees owner T. L. Huston also cautioned economy, citing a possible reduction in patronage. Huston, however, volunteered for military service, unlike most of the owners (although in fairness to them, many were overage and out of shape).[16]

For most of the 1917 season, players, aside from those who were drafted or who volunteered, saw little change in their lives. At most, they had to participate in rather insipid military drills.[17]

Owners weren't sure what the public response would be to baseball being played during wartime. Some owners, wary of the risks, suggested pooling players and receipts. Apparently Charles Comiskey was the instigator of this idea. Given the White Sox's eventual loss of key players to military service or industrial employment, perhaps Comiskey was prescient; the White Sox fell from world's champions to sixth place in 1918.[18]

After staggering through the 1917 season, owners were understandably perplexed. Would the government allow baseball to operate during 1918? If so would there be restrictions on travel and players lost to military service or to industrial jobs? As early as November 22, 1917, Ban Johnson asked the military authorities to exempt 288 players from the draft. His sense of public opinion failed him miserably; many of the owners repudiated his statement. National League president, John Tener, attacked Johnson's statement: "Baseball is a trifling thing compared to the gaining of liberty for the nations of the world. I cannot state too strongly that the National League has no sympathy with any selfish plan of discrimination in favor of its business or its players. It will not ask special exemption for any of its ballplayers." As it was, many players failed physical examinations, with gnarled fingers (the bane of many a baseball player).[19]

The National League urged its players to offer their services to the military. These owners were angered by Johnson's statements as they had given him no authority to claim they wanted exemptions for their players.[20] Johnson would increasingly issue opinions or statements at odds with some or all of his owners; over the years, these misstatements may have created an accumulation of doubts about his fitness to continue in office.

In a somewhat more astute suggestion, Johnson wanted a war clause included in the 1918 contracts that would absolve clubs of the responsibility of paying players who were drafted or enlisted. Of course, if the player became discharged from the military, he remained bound to his club.[21]

Because of travel restrictions and expenses, many of the big-league teams canceled spring training trips to southern sites. Managers urged their players to begin training on their own for the rigors of the upcoming season.[22]

The 1918 season was harrowing for owners; players and patrons began disappearing. Some owners raised the idea of combining teams and forming an eight-team league, but this radical idea went nowhere. John Tener issued a statement asserting that his league would complete the season, regardless of the "work or fight" order issued by the federal government.[23]

Ban Johnson issued another dubious statement on July 21. He announced that the American League would suspend play as of the next day's games. His premature announcement of the demise of the American League season was repudiated by his owners, most of whom wanted to wait to see what the federal officials ruled.[24] Secretary of War Newton Baker announced that baseball was inessential. Eventually the government ordered baseball to shut down on September 1. The owners split on whether to end the regular season on August 20 or gamble that they could play until September 1 and then stage the World Series.[25]

The World Series was still in doubt, with Tener expressing doubts about its feasibility. Newton Baker, though, gave baseball permission to stage the World Series as he deemed it useful for morale of American troops overseas.[26]

Hostilities ceased on November 11, and with the War Department's announcement on November 19, 1918, that troops would be demobilized as quickly as possible, baseball owners breathed a sigh of relief. They began planning for the fateful 1919 season.[27]

Baseball Looks to Brighter Days

Baseball survived the Great War as it was then known. The world looked forward to peace. Unfortunately for the owners, though, 1919 and 1920 would not be peaceful years for baseball.

2   The Rise of Judge Kenesaw Mountain Landis

The owners apparently were unable to adapt to peace. Although the guns were silent on the Western Front, baseball owners were readying themselves for renewed internecine strife. Their feuds threatened to rend the game asunder, but eventually the owners decided to reorganize Organized Baseball. They selected Judge Kenesaw Mountain Landis as virtual dictator.

A Longtime Governing Structure

The American and National Leagues had declared peace in 1903 after a few seasons of open warfare. The two leagues did not formally merge as rival basketball and football leagues would do decades later. Each league maintained its own constitution and elected its own president. Under the terms of the national agreement, the two league presidents selected someone to preside. Each league maintained its autonomy with regard to intraleague affairs.

Garry Herrmann served as the chairman of the National Commission. Herrmann was one of the owners of the National League's Cincinnati franchise. Although the owners thought it beneficial to have someone who understood the baseball business serve as chairman, Herrmann's selection came with a disadvantage: the possibility of favoritism. Herrmann, in fact, recognized the potential trouble in being perceived as favoring his fellow National League owners' interests; as the years passed, National League owners believed that American League president Bancroft Johnson exerted too large an influence over Herrmann. Some National

League owners viewed Herrmann in a charitable light, believing that the chairman was so concerned about being perceived as equitable that he unconsciously favored the American League owners. Some reporters viewed things differently and openly stated, "The commission has always given the National League two votes and the American League only one and this situation has been the cause of almost continual controversy." National League owners, though, would dispute this description, believing that the two-to-one tally was actually in favor of the American League.[1] Regardless of the truth, the fact that Herrmann was an owner created the potential for suspicion.

Within each league, though, owners bickered and often challenged their respective league presidents. The owners were mostly self-made men who were used to making decisions and getting their way. Riding herd on owners, then, was a contentious assignment. Ban Johnson's savvy and foresight won him loyalty of the original American League owners, but the roster of owners gradually changed. The newer owners often resisted Johnson.

The National Commission was tottering as the war was ending. Johnson was widely perceived as the ultimate power in baseball. National League owners chafed over Garry Herrmann's perceived weakness. A series of disputes over players and some ill-advised statements undermined Ban Johnson and his National Commission members' popularity.

Disputes over Ownership of Players

With the Federal League vanquished, Major League owners could revert to their squabbling ways. Controversies over the rights to players George Sisler and Scott Perry created ill feeling.

The Pittsburgh Pirates signed Sisler to a contract to play for a Minor League team in 1911, but he never played for them. Branch Rickey had scouted Sisler when the player was a collegiate star. Sisler signed the contract with the Pirates when he was but seventeen years old; he later wanted to nullify the contract so he could play baseball at the University of Michigan. Rickey wanted to ensure that the St. Louis Browns, instead of the Pittsburgh Pirates, got Sisler. The Pirates believed they retained the rights to Sisler, but Rickey and the St. Louis Browns claimed the player. Garry Herrmann ruled in favor of the Browns, earning Pittsburgh owner Barney Dreyfuss's enmity.[2] When Pirates owner Barney Dreyfuss strenuously contested Rickey's claim, the Browns threatened to take the matter to civil court, so the National Commission decided in the Browns' favor.[3]

In the Scott Perry case, Philadelphia Athletics owner-manager Connie Mack usurped the Boston Braves' claim to pitcher Scott Perry. Perry was the epitome of a journeyman hurler, but the Athletics and Boston Braves decided he was worth fighting for. When the National Commission ruled in Boston's favor, Johnson urged Connie Mack to disregard this edict and to seek an injunction preventing Boston from getting the pitcher. National League president John Tener was outraged by this breach of baseball etiquette and threatened to resign his presidency unless Johnson and Mack backed down. Johnson waved off Tener's wrath by stating, "The contemplated resignation of President Tener . . . would occasion me no surprise . . . that course is absolutely necessary for the welfare of baseball in view of the fact that he devotes so little attention to the affairs of the game." But these were just warmups to bigger controversies.[4]

One War Ends, Another War Begins

Peace may have descended upon Europe in late 1918, but the 1919 season proved a contentious one for baseball. It started when Red Sox pitcher Carl Mays left the team after being removed from a game. Some accounts suggest he was exasperated by his teammates' errors. Red Sox owner Harry Frazee decided to trade Mays to the Yankees, but Ban Johnson repudiated the trade. Johnson claimed that Mays should have been suspended and therefore could not be traded while suspended. What Johnson and some of the other owners feared was that Mays's example of sulking that led to a trade to a contender would give other players similar ideas.[5]

Harry Frazee and the Yankees' owners Jacob Ruppert and Tillinghast L. Huston became burrs under Johnson's saddle, so to speak. What probably hit Johnson harder, though, was the eventual defection of longtime ally Charles Comiskey. Reporter John Sheridan lamented the rupture between Comiskey and Johnson, attributing much of Johnson's and the American

League's success, "to the fact that he had an intelligent collaborateur [*sic*] in C. Comiskey of Chicago." Sheridan believed "Comiskey inspired the idea [of the American League] and Johnson had the executive power, the punch to put the idea across."[6]

Johnson's charisma and demonstrated competence kept the other five American League owners in line, although Connie Mack and Clark Griffith occasionally bristled at some of his later decisions. Johnson was not an executive to treat rebellious owners with kid gloves. Historian Robert Burk may have slightly exaggerated Johnson's demise when he wrote that the Yankees legal victory in the Carl Mays's case was "the end of the AL president's effective authority over his circuit's club owners," but Johnson remained embattled for the remainder of his tenure as league president.[7]

With the turmoil roiling about Johnson, Herrmann, and National League presidents Tener and John Heydler, rebellious owners floated ideas concerning revamping baseball's governance. Many wanted a prominent American who had no financial interests in baseball to become the head of organized baseball. Among the names broached were former president William Howard Taft, federal judge Kenesaw Mountain Landis, and Judge Charles McDonald. The latter two judges were involved in baseball litigation. Landis had gained favor with owners, because of his dilatory actions in deciding a Federal League lawsuit, while McDonald became prominent for his handling of the Chicago White Sox scandal. Other owners suggested a three-man body. The three-man body, proposed by Albert Lasker of the Chicago Cubs, remained in play up until owners named Judge Landis commissioner of baseball.[8]

The rebellious owners' floating of Taft's name revealed a certain bungling. Frazee and New York Giants president Harry Hempstead approached the former president. They overstated the support the other owners were willing to lend Taft.[9] Taft told reporters he presumed his position would limit him to act only as "a judge of law and fact . . . [but not to] in any way take part in the management of their business." Garry Herrmann characterized the offer as "a huge joke," while Ban Johnson disappeared from public view in order not to have to discuss the matter.[10] Taft eventually discovered that Johnson's loyalists repudiated the offer.

Even putative Taft supporter Jacob Ruppert ruefully admitted to reporters that he regretted the leaking of the proposition to Taft. Taft quickly let reporters know that he was not considering the situation. Johnson had won another trick against his foes.[11]

In the wake of the Taft brouhaha, baseball owners, not entirely learning their lesson, quickly leaked the names of new candidates including Landis and baseball legal advisor John Conway Toole. The *New York Times* reported on September 17, 1919, that owners were going to offer Judge Landis the chairmanship of the National Commission.[12]

After stymieing this threat to his authority, Ban Johnson quickly inserted his foot into his mouth by telling reporters he favored a 154-game schedule for the upcoming 1919 season. His club owners agreed with many National League owners in wanting a 140-game schedule since they were unsure of how many players would be available from the military and of the strength of the public's demand for baseball. Although Johnson proved correct about the desirability of the 154-game schedule, some of his owners chided him for his premature comment.[13]

While simultaneously fighting Taft and defending Herrmann, Ban Johnson spent energy in trying to oust Boston Red Sox owner Harry Frazee from the American League. Frazee clearly did not share many of his fellow American League owners' respect, even awe, of Johnson. Although National League owners had rid themselves of Charles Murphy of the Cubs, that owner received his price for the franchise and left without legal action. Frazee was unlikely to leave peaceably if forced; he maintained he was willing to sell but only at his price.[14] Frazee told reporters, "It has seemed a war of extermination on the part of Mr. Johnson ever since I bought the Boston American League Club," and continued by attributing Johnson's animosity as just, "vent[ing] his spite toward me, simply because I insist on managing my own business, in which my money is invested. . . . It is too bad, that Mr. Johnson could not be as militant toward me when I was in Chicago as he is now when there are a thousand miles between us."[15]

Sportswriters took sides in the feuds. Joe Vila belittled Frazee, writing, "These insects had been telling how Johnson would be forced to abdicate, how Harry Frazee was going to make a monkey of him and how Garry Herrmann, too would be hurled into oblivion. They raved about the expected downfall of big Ban until their eyes bulged like hard boiled eggs." Vila lauded Herrmann for his ability to defeat John Conway Toole's bid for the National League presidency over his (and Johnson's) favorite, John Heydler. By the time Herrmann finished canvassing, the Toole supporters had to tell the candidate that he was not, as earlier announced, the new president.[16] Readers should not weep for Taft or Toole, as President Warren G. Harding selected Taft as Supreme Court chief justice, and Toole became president of the International League.

Frazee and his allies succeeded in launching an investigation of Ban Johnson's handling of American League finances. Charles Comiskey and the New York Yankees' owners filed an injunction to restrain Johnson from paying for the cost of the New York lawsuits with league funds. They cited his financial ties with the Cleveland Indians, claiming that the Cleveland club owed Johnson $50,000 and his decision in the Carl Mays case was animated by Cleveland's and his financial interests and not the best interests of the American League (Cleveland was a contender in 1919 and badly wanted Mays).[17]

After the World Series, owners continued to bicker over the National Commission. In January 1920 the Yankees' owners told reporters they envisioned Judge Landis arbitrating whether Ban Johnson should be allowed to continue as league president. A reporter viewed this as a cynical attempt to shift blame for baseball's interminable feuding: "The thing that impresses one in the alleged peace proposition is that some insurrecto [a rebel fighting in Cuba or the Philippines] has been waking up to the force of public opinion and realizing that the public has no patience with the stand of the minority—therefore an attempt to make it appear the blame for the 'war' is not on the shoulders of the insurrectos."[18]

As this was transpiring, Ban Johnson's authority took a direct hit when the New York supreme court sustained the ruling of Judge Robert Wagner allowing the New York Yankees to restrain Johnson from enforcing the suspension of Carl Mays. Sportswriter Joe Vila believed, "The result is that the authority of the president of the league to enforce baseball discipline is taken out of his hands and put in the hands of the courts, in this particular case at least."[19]

The Crumbling National Commission

Baseball owners next clashed over retaining Garry Herrmann as chairman of the National Commission. American League owners were in favor of Herrmann, but National League owners were opposed to his reelection. One reporter stated, "The opposition of the National League club owners against Herrmann is not that he has ever shown any intentional favoritism in deciding cases, but they believe that in many cases he has tried to be so fair that in order to avoid the suspicion of favoring his own league his decisions have unconsciously favored the American League." The reporter pointed out, "In cases which include both leagues there is rarely any unanimous agreement. So, the National Leaguers say, the cases are really settled by one man anyway, so why not make it a one-man commission."[20]

Herrmann was tiring of the sniping. He had been the chair of the National Commission since 1903. The owners knew he was planning to resign, so the league presidents appointed four owners in early 1919 to compose a search committee for a new chairman. Ban Johnson chose Frank Navin and Jacob Ruppert, the latter being somewhat of a surprise choice, given the Carl Mays controversy. The committee later named Senator James Walker of New York, "Big Bill" Edwards (an Internal Revenue collector of New York), John Conway Toole, Harvey Woodruff (*Chicago Tribune* sports editor), and Landis. Owners voted against Herrmann continuing as chairman by an eleven-to-five count. The search committee was suspended temporarily during the Baltimore Federal League trial.[21]

Garry Herrmann resigned as chairman of the National Commission in early January 1920; his resignation was not a surprise, but his timing was. He agreed to serve another month. Ban Johnson allegedly sought to refuse Herrmann's resignation, forcing the beleaguered executive to remain in office. In the aftermath of Herrmann's announcement, John Heydler told reporters, "Baseball must be kept clean, and the man who heads the commission will have the responsibility of seeing that this is done. Gambling must be stopped." Although Heydler may have been referring to the ongoing Hal Chase saga, his observation proved prophetic.[22]

Adding Fuel to the Fire

Baseball's long-standing difficulties with gambling applied the match to the combustibles gathering about the old National Commission. Baseball's gambling scandals are covered in detail later. The Black Sox scandal would provide the impetus for baseball owners to resolve their governance problems.

The three rebellious American League owners continued to seethe at Ban Johnson's actions. Owners struggled to revitalize the game's governance. Johnson fought the Lasker plan (a three-person commission) and the one-man commissioner plan since either plan would dilute his power; Johnson was loathe to relinquish power. The National League owners and the three American League rebels—Frazee, the Yankees, and Comiskey—floated a plan for a twelve-team league. This plan received much press play but was probably doomed from the start. Many observers recalled the National League's unhappy experience with a twelve-team lineup during the 1890s (baseball missed the gaiety of the "Gay 90s"). The twelfth club was a team "to be named later" as the baseball phrase goes. Frederick Lieb claims that the eleven owners were trying to squeeze Frank Navin of the Tigers in order to get him to defect from Johnson.[23] Other observers, though, said that the eleven owners were willing to see which American League loyalist owner broke ranks first.

Sportswriters believed the public was not in favor of the twelve-team league, especially since the two eight-team leagues setup made for an attractive World Series, more so than matching first- and second-place teams in a twelve-team league would have. Other writers pointed out that the remaining five American League clubs included some of the weaker clubs in terms of finances and stadiums.[24] The five American League clubs that ultimately aligned with Johnson recognized that the twelve-team league was probably a bluff; Garry Herrmann told reporters that "it would be ridiculous to form a league with two clubs in three cities."[25]

Ban Johnson and his allies argued that if the Yankees, White Sox, and Red Sox joined the National League teams, their players would remain as American League property to be distributed among the five remaining teams and to stock three new teams in Chicago, New York, and Boston. White Sox attorney Alfred Austrian dismissed Johnson's claim, saying, "The players belong to the clubs and their contracts are made with the clubs."[26] Johnson also thumbed his nose at the rebels in a verbal way by saying the American League would be better off without the three "undesirable club owners, who have been a detriment because they openly allowed gambling in their baseball parks. . . . The five clubs of the American League which remained with me are the only decent element in the major leagues. They have fought with me to stamp out the gambling evil. I got no assistance whatever from the others."[27]

During the contretemps, Major League owners made overtures to Minor League owners and even to players, hoping to garner their support in the feuds. Big league owners implied that they would expand a new National Commission to five members, including a seat for the Minor Leagues and another for players. The idea of including players in baseball's governance had arisen earlier when owners were trying to maintain player loyalty and to thwart creation of a player union. Ban Johnson reportedly recommended Detroit Tiger player Sam Crawford for a berth on an expanded National Commission as player representative in 1916.[28]

When the big league owners realized they no longer needed these constituencies, they quickly jettisoned Minor League owners and players from involvement in baseball governance. One reporter stated, "The apparent solicitude of Johnson and these club owners for the minor leagues caused many a smile in view of past happenings in baseball. The minors were not so highly regarded by these same persons two years ago when they were making demands." Another reporter, though, argued that, "if the minor leagues stand by Johnson he can make a good deal of trouble."[29]

As the 1919 World Series scandal unfolded during the 1920 season, owners called a special joint meeting. Ban Johnson announced that he would not attend such a meeting before the Cook County grand jury completed its investigation of the scandal. He hinted that he had unrevealed information regarding the scandal.[30] Charles Comiskey blurted that he, "did not see how any one interested in the real welfare of the national game could object to the conference." He further indicated that the search for a new chairman now included Generals John Pershing and Leonard Wood, as well as Judge Landis and former president William Taft, although why Taft, now Supreme Court justice, would condescend to assume duties as baseball's majordome was left unstated. Johnson succeeded, though, in persuading his five loyal club owners to boycott the joint meeting.[31]

Just how far Johnson was prepared to go in maintaining his power can be seen by press reports that Charles Comiskey and his attorney Alfred Austrian knew that the eight White Sox players met and conspired to accept bribe money to fix the World Series. A reporter wrote, "The ace that Johnson and his five supporters hold is this: There is a section in the constitution of the American League that provides for the termination of a membership by a three-fourths vote if a club fails to expel a player or players who are proved guilty of agreeing, conspiring or attempting to lose any ball game. It is President Johnson's contention that the three-fourth vote required to expel means three-fourths of the clubs at a meeting and not three-fourths of the membership of the league." Naturally, the three rebellious clubs disagreed with this interpretation. Johnson's potential tactic was reminiscent of National League owners' actions during the 1902 war between the American and National Leagues. The National League owners were split on selecting a new president. When four owners left the room, the remaining four, claiming "once a quorum, always a quorum," elected Albert Spalding president.[32]

Owners Seek a "Savior"

All these machinations aside, reporters and the public appeared disgusted with Major League Baseball governance. A *New York Times* correspondent lambasted the owners and their officials for their failure "to run down rumors of this scandal," while chiding Ban Johnson, "who was once a brilliant and successful executive, and now seems to think that baseball exists for his greater glory." The writer scorned Johnson's allies: "Of course Johnson and his friends want to keep the game clean as much as the other faction, but they will not consent to measures for keeping the game clean that involve the reduction of Johnson's authority."[33]

Perhaps tiring of the turmoil and recognizing the public clamor for a clear, decisive response to the gambling scandal, the eleven owners in opposition to Johnson, selected Landis as the new chairman of baseball by unanimous vote on November 8, 1920. They offered Landis a seven-year contract with a salary of $50,000, which was much more than top players made.[34] At a later meeting, owners put authority in the hands of one man; fifteen of them voting on November 12 to offer Landis the position. St. Louis Browns owner Phil Ball was the only owner not voting in favor of Landis; he did so out of loyalty to Ban Johnson. Landis held out for an ironclad guarantee of his absolute authority. Since many of his flamboyant judicial decisions were overturned by higher courts, one can understand why Landis demanded such a stipulation. Landis also wanted to retain his federal judgeship; the stampeded owners agreed.[35]

Left unclear was whether the Lasker plan's proposed three-member committee would be implemented. While a majority of owners sought Judge Landis to serve under the Lasker plan, Ban Johnson wanted attorney Henry Killilea for the National Commission.[36] The owners eventually decided not to implement the three-member committee (possibly because of the cost of hiring two more members at tens of thousands of dollars of salary each). Johnson expressed "pleasure" at Landis's selection, claiming, "I am for Judge Landis and I think these club owners have acted wisely . . . I am well satisfied with everything that took place today."[37]

Some baseball observers worried about a sole baseball dictator as early as 1918. They granted that a one-man authority meant "simplification and retrenchment," but how would this authority enforce "the imperial ukases and dictum? Would the one-man commission be given a police force, with secret service attachment?" One author concluded that someone with unassailable reputation, such as Taft or Landis, was required.[38]

In the wake of naming Landis commissioner, owners approved a new agreement covering organized baseball. The key parts of this agreement included a stipulation that no owner could transfer his or her franchise without unanimous consent of the league and majority approval from owners in the other league; an increase in the reserve limit from thirty-five to forty players; a rule stating that no ten-year veteran could be assigned to the Minor Leagues without their consent; and a revision of the waiver rules. Owners enacted explicit rules for blacklisting players, with the notorious article 2, section 17: "Any player who violates his contract or reservation, or who fails to report to his club within 10 days after the opening of the championship season, or who participates in a game with or against a club containing or controlled by ineligible players or a player under indictment for conduct detrimental to the good repute of professional baseball, shall be considered an ineligible player and placed on the ineligible list."[39]

Landis quickly made clear his top priority: "The keynote of the entire newly outlined plan is to rid our great national game of the sinister and oppressive burden of gambling. . . . As for the gamblers, they will be attended to with a firm hand. Action as drastic as may be necessary will be taken to keep them away from the ballparks of all the leagues associated with us, and any other needed measure to prevent them from blighting the game . . . will also be adopted."[40] Landis would discover just how difficult uprooting gambling would be in the years to come.

In retrospect, the owners' selection of Landis may have simply been hastened by the World Series scandal. Landis had long been on the "short list" of candidates, although he played coy. Early in 1920 he announced that he was not a candidate for the chairmanship of the National Commission; if this was a calculated decision to await a more propitious moment, it was astute. Landis, though, may have had a few worrisome moments, as Ban Johnson predicted that Judge Charles A. McDonald would be selected as chairman; John Heydler immediately denied this.[41]

Baseball owners knew they had to revamp the National Commission; Landis's selection was the culmination of two years' consideration. On the other hand, the historical legend that the owners chose Landis in a moment of panic has some merit. Years later, Chicago Cubs owner, Philip K. Wrigley, presumably recalling his father's actions during the scandal, told the congressional committee investigating organized baseball, "As a result of this occurrence [World Series scandal], public confidence in the integrity of the game was severely shaken, to the point where the continued confidence of organized baseball appeared to be in danger. In an effort to make a dramatic move to restore public confidence as well as to prevent a recurrence of a gambling scandal, the idea of having a commissioner was evolved and put into effect. This action was taken in an atmosphere verging on panic on the part of many club owners." Wrigley suggested that the owners wanted a commissioner who would serve as "a symbol of baseball's desire to be honest."[42]

Select in Haste, Repent in Leisure

Whether the owners realized how Landis would seize absolute authority is unclear. As the owners and Landis were finalizing his contract, he recognized a potential loophole that might constrain his authority. He objected to the phrase stipulating that he could "recommend such action as he deemed advisable" and demanded that it be changed to "take such action." He told the owners that they had announced that his powers were to be supreme: "To give me the power merely to 'recommend' takes all power out of my hands."[43] The owners quickly revised the contract.

To explain why he took the post, Landis explained that he was talking with Clark Griffith. He took Griffith to a window conveniently overlooking a group of kids playing ball. As they watched the kids, Landis explained to Griffith that his son had recently discussed baseball; his son said, "Dad, wouldn't it be a shame to have the game of these little kids broken up? Wouldn't it be awful to take baseball away from them?" Landis then told Griffith that he accepted the commissionership in order to "keep baseball on a high standard for the sake of the youngsters," adding, "that's why I took the job, because I want to help."[44]

Although Landis may seem a character in line with Old Testament prophets, some observers believed he was a canny actor who knew how to manipulate his image. Heywood Broun lauded the judge: "His career typifies the heights to which dramatic talent may carry a man in America if only he has the foresight not to go on the stage."[45] The judge was known for issuing bombastic remarks and verdicts; he gained fame for fining Standard Oil $29,400,000 [roughly $720 million in today's dollars] and for advocating the violent suppression of radical labor leaders.[46]

One writer, H. K. Middleton, depicted Landis: "A huge shock of gray hair, allowed to grow to tragedian lengths. Features finely chiseled, upon which rest almost continuously a threateningly serious expression. A high standing collar with a tiny black string tie. An astonishingly heavy cane with a great number of rubber bands wound about the head."[47] Certainly the unruly shock of hair and rumpled clothes created an aura of someone so powerful or so self-assured that he didn't have to give a damn about appearances. Many observers described Landis as stern or severe, but early in his tenure as baseball commissioner, the *Sporting News* ran a stock photo of Landis looking somewhat bemused, even resembling a kindly, if doddering grandfather with a whimsical look, akin to a twinkle, in his eyes.[48]

Landis displayed petulance three years into his tenure: "In a dramatic and acrid speech at the joint meeting of the two major leagues . . . [Landis] told the sixteen club owners and the two league Presidents that he is ready to resign immediately if a majority of the magnates indicate that they are not satisfied with his administration of the commissionership. Apparently some owners had the temerity to express some reservations over some of the commissioner's decisions, although Johnson played a role in the reputed disgruntlement. The owners quickly assured Landis of their fealty."[49]

The *Sporting News* mentioned that Landis criticized the publication for disagreeing with him; Landis reputedly called the periodical's columns "swill." Landis would also excoriate *Baseball Magazine* editor F. C. Lane in subsequent years; Lane claimed Landis was verbally abusive towards him during an interview, with Lane complaining in an editorial that Landis "did [not] have the common decency to insult [him] in private."[50]

Amidst the cheering for Landis's selection, though, some observers raised warnings. Would the owners really accede to the Judge's decisions? One reporter wondered, "The test of their [the owners] good intentions will come later, when they will have to trust him even when he decides that a valuable player belongs to somebody else. If they do that, a great reform has been accomplished. If they will not, baseball is beyond reform."[51]

Landis proved somewhat capricious with his decisions. When acting decisively in suspending the eight White Sox players, along with some other players who apparently knew of the fix, he reaped public acclaim. In his later actions, though, his decisions were questionable. The *Sporting News* editor, J. G. Taylor Spink, began sniping at Landis within a couple of years. Spink referred to the commissioner as "Landis the First" (and hopefully "last"). Spink wanted Landis to weed baseball of incompetent or corrupt owners, improve the Minor Leagues, eliminate gambling, and reduce the commercialism he thought was infecting baseball.[52]

Writer Frank Menke was more critical, accusing Landis of taking too much credit for the Black Sox purge, while allowing Charles Stoneham to remain in baseball. He also derided Landis's decision to evict Benny Kauff from baseball, even though a jury cleared that player of wrongdoing in an auto-theft case.[53]

Various writers in the *Sporting News* covered Stoneham's involvement with a financial investment "bucket shop" that defrauded investors of money before going bankrupt. Stoneham claimed to have been only tangentially related to the people running the operation, but documents unearthed in the various legal hearings reveal his involvement was more than casual. Stoneham testified that he lent "out of the goodness of his heart, and at the solicitation of ex-Sheriff Thomas Foley of Tammany Hall," $137,000 without "demanding any security whatever, or even inquiring as to the firm's solvency."[54] John Heydler proved mealymouthed: "As president, I have only to do with Mr. Stoneham, as a club owner and a league member, and I wish to state that during his more than four years as a member of our organization I have found him a good sportsman, fair and straight, in all his league dealings, standing for the progressive and constructive policies of the league and reasonable in his official dealings with my office."[55] Writer Irving Sanborn pointed out that the national agreement (the agreement reached and revised periodically between the two major leagues in 1903) gave even Landis little scope for punishing

Stoneham, citing the near-helplessness Ban Johnson and Landis faced when dealing with Harry Frazee of the Red Sox.[56]

Stoneham was eventually indicted for conspiracy and using the mails to defraud, although he was later acquitted of these charges in 1925. Other owners said that Stoneham had only been indicted and not been proven guilty, so they would take no action against him; the contrast between an unsavory owner and the White Sox players is interesting: they were acquitted (dubious though the acquittal was) but were still suspended. Certainly the other owners were embarrassed by Stoneham's indictment.[57] Stoneham and John McGraw co-owned a race track in Havana, but despite these questionable ventures, Stoneham retained ownership. His heirs retained ownership of the Giants for decades.

Impeachment of Landis

Some legislators and reporters questioned Landis's decision to retain his federal judgeship. They wondered whether the judge could devote sufficient attention to the duties of two demanding jobs. Sportswriter Paul Eaton raised a salient point, given Landis's previous inaction in ruling on the Federal League lawsuit: "As a judge, it is his duty to abate trusts if they are found to be unlawful; and as commissioner, he is at the head of an institution that is alleged to be a trust by at least one other federal judge."[58]

One writer worried that because of baseball's frequent litigation, "We do not imply that Judge Landis' federal position can in any way prejudice litigation, but it seems to us that there are certain ethical phrases to be considered." Another writer, though, viewed Landis's continued judgeship as an advantage for baseball since "there are avenues of investigation and operation open to him as a federal judge which would not be open to any ordinary baseball officials" and that his legal authority would "cause magnates, players and every one else in the game to feel greater respect and fear for him and his powers." Landis, of course, certain in his rectitude, haughtily dismissed such concerns regarding his ability to handle two demanding jobs and the ethics of his continuing his judgeship.[59]

Chicago attorney Thomas J. Sutherland published an opinion piece regarding Landis's dual positions and concluded that Landis was "acting in violation of the spirit of statutes preventing a Government officer from engaging in remunerative private enterprises." Representative Benjamin Welty of Ohio pressed for a congressional investigation of the judge; he also pushed for a law prohibiting judges to receive compensation for exercising the "duties of an arbitrator, commissioner, or officer of any corporation."[60]

Landis responded to South Carolina senator Nathaniel B. Dial's concerns about his dual position with rudeness. Dial retorted, "He [Landis] shows by his reply to me that he is not constituted by temperament to exercise the duties of a Judge."[61] Landis, though, received support from United States attorney general Alexander Mitchell Palmer, who ruled that Landis was within the law by holding the two positions.[62]

Representative Welty listed five reasons for his impeachment proposal, including Landis's involvement in the Federal League litigation and his lobbying for state and federal laws against gambling on sporting events. Welty pointed out that Major League Baseball hired Landis prior to the Supreme Court's decision in the *Federal Baseball Club of Baltimore v. National League* case, so Landis might have ended up working for an illegal operation. He also noted that Congress had passed a rule barring federal officials from receiving "any salary in connection with his services as such official or employee from any source other than the Government of the United States." He quoted a baseball owner as brazenly stating, "K. M. Landis, lawyer, means nothing to organized baseball, but K. M. Landis, judge of the Federal court of the United States, was worth any price he might wish to ask."[63]

The judiciary committee investigating Landis, while disapproving of his acceptance of the commissionership and characterizing it as a "serious impropriety" and "at least inconsistent with the full and adequate performance of his duties as a United States district judge," made no recommendations and passed the buck to the incoming Congress.[64]

Landis eventually resigned from the federal bench in February 1922; one reporter regretted this: "A few petty-minded persons criticised Judge Landis for maintaining his proposition on the bench while accepting a salary from baseball. Men of Landis' caliber are so scarce that the nation would be better off if they could be induced to accept a dozen different positions that worked for the common good."[65] Given the acclaim the owners' decision received in hiring Landis, the congressional committee may have been wary of repudiating the decision.

Let Us Have Peace

The owners' selection of Landis only temporarily halted the turmoil in baseball governance. With two epic egos in Ban Johnson and Landis, and the various fractious American League owners, peace was fragile. Readers familiar with the old western cliché, "This town ain't big enough for the both of us," might consider an updated version: "This sport isn't big enough for the both of us."

Johnson, however, wasted little time in pursuing his vendetta against Comiskey, Frazee, and the Yankees' owners. The owners rotated serving on the league's board of directors. Frazee, Comiskey, and Ruppert were to serve on the upcoming board with Cleveland's James Dunn, but Johnson selected owners from St. Louis, Washington, and Philadelphia to serve instead of the three rebellious owners. Johnson also wanted to be reimbursed for expenses incurred investigating the Carl Mays situation. Yankees owner Tillinghast L. Huston promptly issued a retort to Johnson's actions, claiming Johnson showed "how very deeply he resents the part which these three clubs had in bringing about the new order of things. Johnson is against any plan that does not originate with him.... The strength of this unholy alliance [Johnson and the other five American League clubs] has made Johnson exceedingly arrogant.... The elimination of Johnson would automatically restore tranquility."[66]

Huston did not relent in the war of words, practically blaming Johnson for the ongoing gambling scandal: "It is due to his failure and cowardice that recent baseball scandals were not averted. Prompt action by him as a member of the National Commission would have resulted in such punishment for Chase and Magee that the members of the White Sox would have been afraid to sell out the World Series [sic] in 1919." His ally, Frazee, with regard to Johnson's choices for board of directors, accused

Johnson of "stating a deliberate falsehood ... which you also know is an absolute lie, and is but one more evidence of your gross stupidity and incompetence to further fill the office you now hold."[67]

Baseball owners claimed that organized baseball (the Major Leagues and Minor Leagues, although the former dominated) did a good job of governing itself. When outsiders made occasional proposals to place baseball under state or federal regulation, the owners were generally lukewarm. The Massachusetts state legislature considered a proposal to license professional ballplayers. Francis Richter, longtime sportswriter, argued against such legislation, and he cited the sorry example of boxing commissions purporting to regulate the sport. Ban Johnson, of all people, commended the licensing scheme, which left Richter perplexed as Heydler and Landis opposed it. Whether Johnson's irritation at losing some of his authority over the game drove him to endorse such proposals in order to deny Landis some of his authority remains unclear.[68]

Baseball was fortunate in having New York governor Alfred E. Smith and New York City mayor James J. Walker leading the opposition to the New York legislature's proposal to place all professional sports in the state under the athletics commission. The commission already regulated boxing and wrestling.[69]

Landis and Heydler acted quickly and decisively in the Jimmy O'Connell and Cozy Dolan scandal (described in greater detail in the next chapter). Ban Johnson expressed his belief that the 1924 World Series should be cancelled because of the scandal, which irritated Washington Senators owner Clark Griffith (this was Washington's first World Series). It should be noted that the National League third-place club owner, Barney Dreyfuss, also thought the Giants should not be allowed to participate, basically implying the series should be cancelled. Johnson also vented some vituperation (including calling Landis a "wild-eyed crazy nut," to which Landis responded, "keep your shirt on") over Landis's handling of the situation. Johnson's outburst embarrassed the American League club owners, and they took the step of issuing a written statement promising Landis that they would "muzzle" Johnson's mouth or force him out of office.[70]

The American League owners recognized Johnson's prior services as president of the league and were unwilling to send him packing in such ignominious circumstances. "It soon became obvious that the American Leaguers not only sought peace and harmony with both the other League and Judge Landis, but that they considered Big Ban as something speaking from the dead past—some one who had once led the procession, but whom the parade had long since passed and abandoned on a corner. . . . Too bad that two such men [Landis and Johnson] should clash, when their influence should have been exerted hand-in-hand for the advancement of the game."[71]

National League owners, eager to display their loyalty to Landis, passed a resolution recommending the extension of his contract for ten additional years, thereby squelching rumors that some of them were dissatisfied with the commissioner. Meanwhile, the American League decided to defer granting such an extension, despite Charles Comiskey's efforts to get the extension approved.[72]

Baseball Magazine editor F. C. Lane took stock of Landis's first four years as commissioner. He noted Landis's success in restoring confidence in the game and creating favorable publicity for baseball. He fought gambling, and baseball prospered during the early 1920s, although Lane was unsure how much credit Landis should get for the prosperity. Lane, though, criticized Landis: "The Judge has a cold, self-centered, merciless strength of purpose entirely lacking in loyalty, gratitude or the more human elements. . . . The Judge has a truly colossal egotism and a personal vanity quite as astonishing. We understand that these characteristics are the usual accompaniment of genius. Napoleon had them. But unfortunately they are not the proof of genius. Many very small men have inflated notions of their own importance in the general scheme of things."[73]

Slow Demise of Ban Johnson

Instead of voting to extend Landis's contract in February 1926, American League owners restored Ban Johnson to his former power and authority in December of that year; they elected Johnson to the Major League

Advisory Board that was being revived. Charles Comiskey was the sole holdout against the restoration.[74] Johnson had little time to savor his return to power. American League owners helped re-elect Landis to a second term in December 1926, granting him a $15,000 per-year raise (30 percent); Johnson made nice and "was the first to extend his congratulations," and the two shook hands. Landis, for his part, apparently had made it known to American League owners that he would not be "displeased" if Johnson was restored to the advisory council.[75]

The very next month, Johnson was stewing in his own verbal juices. He criticized Landis's revelation of the charges against Ty Cobb and Tris Speaker (detailed in the next chapter). American League owners warned Johnson not to discuss the case. The American League president claimed that he had evidence against both players that Landis did not have. Observers quickly predicted Johnson's defeat in the forthcoming showdown, and some even began speculating on who would be Johnson's successor. New York Yankees official Edward Barrow was named as a potential successor, but he denied having interest in the job. Senator George Wharton Pepper, baseball's attorney during the Federal League lawsuit, also refused to accept consideration for the presidency. The most outlandish rumor was that Mayor James J. Walker was offered the presidency at a salary of $100,000, which was more than Landis received.[76]

To the end, Johnson was defiant and refused to resign. The American League owners hit upon the short-term palliative of putting Johnson on a sort of administrative leave, citing the president's health problems. "It would have been an act of inexcusable brutality if the American League had acted otherwise than it did yesterday," according to an unnamed owner, "[It] would have been inhuman [to force Johnson to resign]."[77] The owners expressed their belief that Johnson would remain retired.

Sportswriter John Kieran described how Johnson misread the effect of Swede Risberg and Chick Gandil's resurrection of the 1919 World Series scandal upon Landis. Johnson thought the public disapproved of Landis's handling, and thinking to strike when his foe was vulnerable, Johnson jumped into the fray and attacked Landis's handling of the affair as well as his handling of the Cobb-Speaker case. Kieran felt Landis had no choice but to inform the public of the charges against the two veteran stars, lest the public hear it first from some reporter.[78] Another reporter suggested, "To an unbiased outsider it would seem that Judge Landis was simply freeing himself of a load of dynamite that was likely to explode at any moment. . . . And if the charges had come out prematurely the Judge might easily have been accused of trying to hush them up and thus destroy public faith in his own integrity and that of the game. . . . There is much under the surface which we will probably never know, but the club owners have handled a difficult situation with unexpected tact."[79]

A few months later, though, American League owners discovered that Johnson was not safely retired. As sportswriter James Harrison wrote, "One of the most miraculous recoveries in medical history is that of Byron Bancroft Johnson . . . who spent three months at Hot Springs, Ark. . . . and is now back at his office 'restored to health.'"[80] A week later, Harrison recounted Johnson's greatness: "He has been by far the biggest man in baseball history. The latter-day fan may be inclined to regard him as a pompous, disappointed person. . . . This is unjust to the man who did more than any other to make baseball what it is today." Harrison listed Johnson's efforts to interest women in baseball, to eradicate rowdy behavior at ballparks (although some persisted), to support his umpiring staff, and to eliminate gamblers.[81] Johnson's successor, E. S. Barnard, a capable executive, paled in comparison with Johnson perhaps simply because the American League no longer had the same challenges confronting it and had less need of a strongman.

The owners decided to let sleeping presidents lie, as it were. As long as Johnson kept quiet, they would countenance him continuing in office. The fact that they owed him hundreds of thousands of dollars may have also been a factor. For Johnson, the final straw involved Ty Cobb. Cobb had a minor confrontation with an umpire in a game early in the season. Johnson suspended Cobb for a few games and fined him two hundred dollars. Mild-mannered Connie Mack was outraged at this treatment of his veteran player, and other owners believed the punishment was excessive. Johnson resigned on July 9, 1927. In a characteristic flourish, he refused to accept the balance due him on the remainder of his contract (up to $320,000—a king's ransom in the 1920s): "I will resign, but I insist that my compensation cease with my resignation. I make that stipulation before I will agree to quit."[82]

Johnson later elaborated, "I hope the American League owes me something, but whatever it is, if anything, it couldn't be paid in money. . . . Maybe it's a good thing now that I'll have to play for a while. I hated to let go the reins. Who doesn't hate to leave the work he's given his life to?" Although poignant is not a word many people would associate with Ban Johnson, these comments were. Johnson, however, left with one last defiant shot, "None of them [those he ruled against] can say that Ban Johnson ever shirked his job."[83]

A sportswriter suggested, "What the American League owes Ban Johnson, then, is not money due him under his contract, but an obligation to carry on its affairs as he conducted them, with the same principles he stood for and enforced—as long as he had the authority of enforcement."[84] Comiskey, for one, could not muster the grace to wish Johnson well on his retirement. The other American League owners passed a resolution affirming Johnson's role in making the league a success, but Comiskey refused to endorse this.[85] It is worthwhile to recall that Ban Johnson was one of just two men, Lamar Hunt of the American Football League being the other, to bring his eight-team league intact into parity with an established league. For this alone, he belongs in the first rank of professional sports executives.

With Johnson's resignation, Landis lost his most formidable foe. John Heydler and new American League president E. S. Barnard worked harmoniously and possibly willingly in the commissioner's shadow. Barnard was an interesting choice since he was the president of the Cleveland Indians. Fortunately, Alva Bradley was in the process of purchasing the Indians; upon completion of the sale, Barnard was relieved of his duties with the club. Reporters did not indicate whether Barnard would retain any stock in the club, which, if so, would smack of the same potential trouble as afflicted Garry Herrmann.[86]

Peace in Our Time

The December 1928 meetings were characterized as having "a pleasing absence of the acrimonious debates, the bitter personal animosities, which have stirred similar meeting in by-gone years. In short, the masters of a gigantic industry, represented by the investment of many millions of dollars, met and discussed their business interests quite as business men should do."[87]

By 1929 Commissioner Landis was firmly ensconced as baseball's ruler. Although owners chafed at some of his rulings, none of them made a serious effort at deposing him after the mid 1920s. Baseball's governance was at least stable, and owners could now spend their efforts on more productive endeavors than repeated internecine struggles. A decade and a half of strife ended, just as baseball confronted another serious challenge—the Great Depression, but that is the subject for another book.

3   Baseball's Longstanding Gambling Problem

Simply stated, baseball had a gambling problem. When fans attended a game, the implicit assumption was that all of the players, coaches, and management were trying to win. From the earliest days of the National League, organized baseball struggled with gambling and related vices. Players, owners, and management engaged in ethically dubious activities. The 1919 Chicago White Sox players' malfeasance was simply the most publicized of the nefarious activities.

The owners, several of whom frequented various gambling venues, were not so naive to believe they could stamp out gambling at the ballpark. In fact, they might not have viewed such an outcome as desirable. The owners, instead, might simply have aimed to assure fans that the games were honest, that players, managers, and coaches were always trying to win.

Early History of Gambling in Baseball

Although baseball and gambling were not made for each other, the two activities proved close traveling companions. For many fans, simply rooting for one's favorite team was not sufficient; many fans found that a friendly wager enlivened interest in the proceedings on the field. As early as the end of the National League's second season, the Louisville franchise expelled four of its players from the league because of gambling activities.[1]

Some professional sports, such as the National Basketball Association (NBA), continue to battle perceptions that at times players, coaches, and owners are hoping to lose in order to secure a better draft situation. In the old days of the NBA's coin flip to determine which team would have the first pick in the upcoming draft, fans, owners, and players of a woebegone team may well have desired their team to lose a game, if it meant securing a place in the coin flip. This is one reason why the NBA went to the lottery, with its more gradual increase in odds of securing the top pick. The NBA continues to tinker with its draft lottery to forestall such antics.[2]

Gambling scandals recurred during the next fifty years or so after 1877. During these years, bookies set odds on the outcomes of baseball games. Football and basketball betting, with their higher scores, proved more conducive to point spreads. Gamblers might have had better opportunities in inducing football and basketball players to cooperate: players did not have to throw a game but could merely shave a point here or there. With the bets based on odds of winning the game and not on a point spread, baseball players typically had to throw a game if they conspired with gamblers.

Baseball officials seemed to have a schizophrenic attitude regarding gambling. Some officials, such as those in the Minor League American Association, were actively seeking help from government officials in stamping out gambling, while National League president John Tener delightedly asserted that during his forty years of baseball, "no man can say with a semblance of verisimilitude that a player ever conspired to lose a game."[3] Owners benefited when gamblers bought tickets to ball games, and many gamblers were regular patrons at ballparks. Reporters described widespread betting on National League games in 1918, especially in Cincinnati.[4]

Owner William Wrigley bet his manager, Bill Killefer, $1,000 against a ten-cent cigar during spring training whether the Cubs would win the pennant in 1918. The team won the pennant, and Killefer got himself $1,000.[5] Most fans and baseball personnel presumably smiled when they read the news snippet and considered it an innocent bet.

Fans often bet on the most trivial things at the ballpark during the 1920s, just as they would almost a century later with fantasy sports and legalized betting. They would bet on whether the next pitch would be a ball or a strike, whether the batter would hit a foul ball or a fielder would commit an error, and so forth.

Owners knew that gamblers lurked within their stadiums. In one round up, forty-seven men were arrested for alleged betting at Wrigley Field; they were fined one dollar each and warned to steer clear of the ballpark. Clearly, though, these efforts were missing the big players, the gamblers associated with organized crime.[6]

The absurdity of rounding up small-time bettors was revealed by a magistrate's ruling that a fan was guilty of disorderly conduct because he was "moving about in the stands"; the accused party claimed he was talking with friends. The culprit may well have been guilty of gambling, but the charge of "moving around" seems pretty vague. Many fans move to better seats when it becomes apparent that the occupants are not coming to the game. Indeed, Louis Hirsch, a composer and author of musical comedies, filed a lawsuit for $100,000 against the Yankees over just such an issue. Hirsch and his brother were sitting in the bleachers and changed seats to be upwind of a cigar-smoking fan. Hirsch and an usher got into an argument, and the composer was forcibly removed from the ballpark.[7]

Other sports, too, had problems with gambling. Decades later, NFL commissioner Bert Bell, himself a former racetrack gambler, acknowledged that many fans were going to place small, friendly wagers. His office concentrated on the big-time gamblers; Bell maintained contacts with bookies to determine whether there was an unexplainable shift in odds. He hired former law-enforcement agents to monitor players and gamblers and created the league policy of announcing injuries and player availability. He told reporters, "The gamblers know these things. I want the public to know them too. I don't care if people bet, because people are gonna bet. I just want to be sure they stay away from our ballplayers and don't spread rumors."[8]

The NBA had several gambling scandals in its first decade; some of the scandals originated with players during their collegiate careers and were revealed during their NBA tenure. While baseball had Hal Chase, basketball had Jack Molinas. Gambling accusations hovered over Molinas like low-lying smog, and the league eventually banished him.[9]

In addition to consorting or conspiring with gamblers, Major League Baseball players sometimes held a remarkably loose sense of ethics. Players made payments to opposing players, and a good deal of flippant talk transpired. In the case of St. Louis Browns players, owner Phil Ball accused them of "laying down." The players sued Ball for alleged slander, and the presiding judge ruled, "The construction placed on this expression by the plaintiffs was not forced or unfair and the language complained of was such as might tend to injure the plaintiffs in profession and was therefore actionable."[10]

Players and officials, though, saw nothing wrong with betting on their own teams. Players were also hesitant to inform on any nefarious activities by teammates. Concurrent with the gambling, though, players and baseball officials at times rewarded players on opposing teams for beating pennant rivals. The propriety of such actions was dubious.

Prior to the 1919 World Series gambling scandal, baseball officials had dealt with Hal Chase, a talented first baseman whose integrity was suspected early and often (where there was Chase, there was gambling). Chase allegedly approached New York Giant pitcher Pol Perritt "with some sort of a mysterious proposition or other about a game he was to pitch." Perritt told John McGraw, who reported the situation to league president John Heydler. The owners, worried about adverse fan reaction to gambling situations, tried to suppress information on Chase's alleged gambling incidents.[11]

Although the Cincinnati Reds were the virtuous team in the 1919 World Series, they had recently employed two crooked ballplayers. In February 1920 Lee Magee confessed during his trial to throwing games while playing for the Reds in 1918. Magee implicated the ubiquitous Hal Chase. A couple of months later, Magee filed a lawsuit seeking $9,500 ($4,500 salary and $5,000 for lost World Series pay); baseball officials dismissed the suit with Garry Herrmann saying, "Magee's suit is a joke."[12] Magee apparently conspired with Chase to bet against the Reds when he played for them in 1918 (the Cubs acquired Magee in 1919). Magee told Cubs executive William Veeck that he bet on a game while playing for the Reds and made errant throws, among other actions, to ensure a Reds loss.[13]

The Magee-Chase tale was surreal. The two players went to James Costello's billiard room in Boston and said they wanted to contact some gamblers about "tossing" the next day's game. Costello relayed the information that the gamblers would only be interested if the two players put up some of their own money. The players didn't have any cash on them, but Costello agreed to accept checks (this being before credit cards, so Costello couldn't run the players' cards through a machine). Chase's check cleared, but Magee's check did not. Magee claimed he stopped payment on the check when he learned that Chase used their money to bet *against* the Reds. The next day, Magee threw the ball over the second baseman's head; he also did not obey manager Christy Mathewson's sign to steal, raising Mathewson's suspicions. Magee's actions were rather blatant, especially the failure to steal. An errant throw might have been excusable, and although players missed signs sometimes, Magee's refusal to steal seemed more damning. Chase denied all of Magee's charges and claimed that the National Commission exonerated him of all charges of betting.[14]

An article in the *Sporting News* chastised the National League for its "perfunctory" and secret investigation of the Chase-Magee episode. The owners were obviously afraid of adverse publicity, but because they did not punish Chase, other players may have been inspired to try their own gambling ventures. Another writer, though, admitted that John Heydler had little choice but to leave Chase unpunished. Chase claimed baseball officials exonerated him, but the real verdict was that they undoubtedly thought him guilty but couldn't definitively pin guilt upon him at the time of the hearing. Later evidence unearthed by Ban Johnson might have been sufficient to change the verdict.[15]

Chase's "exoneration" did not protect him for long. After being released by the New York Giants, Chase played in the Pacific Coast League. The league promptly barred him after he approached a Salt Lake pitcher with a "proposition to make some easy money." That Chase was even allowed to play in the league, after all the Major League controversy dogging his career, was a testament to the faith of man in man or willingness to overlook character flaws in favor of talent. Pacific Coast League president William H. McCarthy issued a statement stating that the league had allowed Chase to play because the ballplayer "was repentant and [McCarthy] felt it would be unfair to punish him for sins committed outside of California." But McCarthy added, "This latest episode is enough, however."[16]

Widespread Corruption

Although the Chicago White Sox team earned the most opprobrium for their activities, the New York Giants may well have been baseball's biggest trouble spot. Owner Charles Stoneham was under investigation for shady stock-market practices, and when compared with player misbehavior, Stoneham's behavior was far more outrageous. Stoneham and manager John McGraw had interests in a Havana racetrack. While betting on the horses was not a sin in the eyes of baseball, McGraw and Stoneham knew many big-time gamblers personally. In a telling anecdote, Stoneham responded to a late-night phone call from Arnold Rothstein, widely held to be the bankroller behind the 1919 White Sox gambling scandal. Rothstein needed a large sum of cash to cover his own gambling debts, and Stoneham, without question, withdrew said cash from his safe and delivered it to the gambler. Stoneham, Rothstein, and gambler Abe Attell all used William J. Fallon's legal services.[17]

McGraw testified in the Hal Chase case. McGraw's close friend and former pitcher, Christy Mathewson, who was managing the Cincinnati Reds, was suspicious of Chase's behavior. Mathewson was currently serving in France and could only submit a written statement. Despite Mathewson's and Reds players' testimony, the committee decided there was insufficient evidence to warrant banishing Chase.

McGraw was a witness against Chase but later traded for him. McGraw claimed league president John Heydler exonerated Chase, but this was distorting the truth. McGraw later hired Mathewson as a coach, so Mathewson and Chase were reunited, which must have made for an interesting dugout dynamic. McGraw let Cincinnati hire his coach, Pat Moran, to be their manager, thereby creating a quid pro quo giving McGraw first claim on Chase's services, if the player was cleared.[18]

Chase had the chutzpah to later sue the Reds for salary withheld during his suspension. During the lawsuit, Chase "claims that the huge pile of affidavits collected by the Cincinnati Club were all faked, or the result of exaggerated rumors and spitework, and that he can prove he never placed a bet except to win—a practice which Hal acknowledges was bad and foolish, but which, he contends, shows that he was always trying to win." Chase may have been too cute with his self-justification; then again, he might have made an excellent politician. Mathewson claimed he never had any difficulty or cross words with Chase in Cincinnati: "He says the only charge he ever made against the player was for indifferent playing, something which at one time or another can be made against almost any baseball player." Mathewson's recollection seems odd, given the fact he suspended Chase. Garry Herrmann refused to trade Chase to New York until the player agreed to drop his lawsuit for back pay.[19]

Chase and Heinie Zimmerman became a dubious pair for the Giants, and McGraw and Stoneham later suspended both of them for throwing games. The White Sox scandal exploded during the ensuing investigation despite the attempt by Charles Comiskey and Ban Johnson to cover it up. Hal Chase may have been baseball's poster child for malfeasance, but no one doubted his cleverness.[20] Lee Allen concluded, "Hal Chase's problems were not financial in nature, but were problems of personality."[21]

One reporter said no evidence had been found that Zimmerman consorted with gamblers, although the editorialist concluded, "We hope we are mistaken when we say that Heinie Zim may be disorderly and a general bad actor, but not a crook."[22]

Sportswriter Joe Vila lauded McGraw and the Giants' handling of the gambling scandal, and he quoted McGraw as saying, "I never was more deceived by a player than by Chase. I believed in his innocence when Heydler exonerated him of Matty's charges, which to me appeared to be based upon circumstantial evidence."[23] Vila, usually pro-Giant and anti-Babe Ruth, was demonstrating the extent to which he believed in the Giants. He didn't seem to ask why McGraw believed Chase more than Mathewson—the beloved Matty (and the author is not being ironic here—Mathewson was probably McGraw's favorite player).

During a Cook County grand-jury investigation pitcher Rube Benton described how Chase, Zimmerman, and Buck Herzog offered him a bribe to lose a game. Pitcher Jimmy Ring filed an affidavit stating how Chase approached him about purposely losing a game for a five-hundred-dollar payment; Ring refused and the Reds lost anyway, but Chase gave him fifty dollars. Another Reds player, Alfred "Greasy" Neale also filed an affidavit describing Chase's nefarious activities on the Reds; outfielder Benny Kauff also reported a Chase proposition.[24]

Benton denied winning $3,800 on the 1919 World Series based on advice given by Chase to bet on the Reds. Other players were also accused of making money on the 1919 World Series. President Heydler investigated Brooklyn shortstop Ivan Olson and Philadelphia Phillies infielder Johnny Rawlings (later acquired by John McGraw, who must have relished collecting baseball's "uncollectibles") but found nothing that suggested the two players knew of the fix, although Olson won money by betting on the Reds.[25]

A Fixed World Series

Baseball historians and fans remain transfixed by the 1919 World Series. Readers interested in details of the scandal should consult Eliot Asinof's *Eight Men Out*, but they should also read some of the more recent studies on the situation, including Charles Fountain's *The Betrayal*; Gene Carney's *Burying the Black Sox*; Jacob Pomrenke's *Scandal on the South Side*; William Lamb's *Black Sox in the Courtroom*; and Charles Rivers's *The Black Sox Scandal*. Film director John Sayles's movie version of the scandal, *Eight Men Out*, although entertaining, takes typical Hollywood liberty with accuracy.

The Chicago White Sox, despite an inferior win-loss record (88-52 versus 96-44), were favored to defeat the Cincinnati Reds. The White Sox, with Hall of Fame stars Eddie Collins and Ray Schalk and likely inductee Joe Jackson, have been touted as one of the greatest teams of all time. The club had won the 1917 World Series. The Reds countered with just one eventual Hall of Fame player, Edd Roush. The White Sox, though, were riven with cliques. Many players disdained Eddie Collins, possibly because of his college background and aloof behavior. Collins negotiated a five-year contract in the wake of the Federal League bidding that called for $15,000 a year. According to Warren Tormey, Collins was imbued with a white-collar mindset, although he "grasped the importance of silently staying above the fray."[26] Collins did participate in some of the team's dubious practices, such as rewarding players on other teams for helping the White Sox's pennant chances.

Eliot Asinof argues that the White Sox were poorly paid relative to other teams (an assertion that will be examined). Comiskey certainly was not a cuddly sort of owner. During the 1918 season, when many players opted for jobs in shipbuilding rather than in the military, Comiskey allegedly stated, "there is no room on my club for players who wish to evade the army by entering the employ of ship builders." He later referred to some of his players as "slackers." Comiskey also pinched dollars on players' meal money.[27]

John Sheridan, who knew Comiskey from the American League's earliest days remained supportive of the owner, even in 1921. He claimed Comiskey knew how to increase the drawing power of his ball club, calling him "the greatest manager-owner baseball has ever known." More surprising was Sheridan's characterization of Comiskey: "In his prime he was the soul of hospitality, generosity and good-will. He loved people and people loved him."[28] Certainly Comiskey's players would attest to the owners' generous provision of postgame buffets for reporters, but they would probably dispute Sheridan's description of Comiskey's universal generosity.

White Sox players were upset that the National Commission passed a rule after the 1917 World Series forbidding participants in the World Series from participating in any barnstorming trips at the close of the series. The White Sox players, under Eddie Collins's organization, had been offered $10,000 for such a trip. In order to enforce its prohibition, the National Commission withheld $1,000 from each player's World Series share as a bond, payable on December 1 with interest, incumbent upon the player not going barnstorming.[29]

The players' share of the receipts was also a contentious issue. Owners had earlier agreed upon a 60-40 percent split of the players' pool in place of the existing 75-25 division. The wider division between winners and losers led to players hedging their bets between each other, which may have raised questions of integrity.[30] This change was not as much of an issue for the players as was the commission's unilateral decision to broaden the pool of recipients.

Before the 1919 World Series, the National Commission decided to rearrange splitting the World Series receipts. The players of second- and third-place teams would receive shares of the receipts, leaving the pennant winners with 75 percent of what they normally would have received. The National Commission had tinkered with the division of the shares before the 1918 series too (splitting the receipts among the top four teams in each league, which led to a brief strike by the World Series participants). Some criticized the plan because it was apparent that the receipts generated would likely fall short of recent levels, leaving current participants with little reward.[31] The 1918 Red Sox received $1,108 each, a very low payoff compared with recent series. The resurging popularity of baseball in 1919, though, meant much greater gate receipts; by game five of the 1919 World Series, it was clear that, even with the diluted World Series participants' share, the player's pool would triple or quadruple that of the 1918 series. After the 1921 World Series, the Giants received around $5,200 per player; the Yankees got $3,400 per player.[32]

Associated with discussion of how to divide World Series gate receipts were proposals for other interleague series: second place versus second place down to eighth place versus eighth place. Such an arrangement would shed further light on the relative strengths of the leagues. Some suggested pooling the receipts from these series and then dividing the money. One wonders what the attraction of attending a seventh-place versus seventh-place matchup would have been, to say nothing of last place versus last place. The idea proved stillborn.[33]

Comiskey knew that gamblers frequented his ballpark since a few had been arraigned on charges of gambling. The White Sox management requested detectives to sit in the bleachers, and the detectives arrested four fans. His fellow American League owners too had more than an inkling of widespread gambling on baseball games. On September 17, 1919 (before the World Series), they chided Ban Johnson for not divulging information he claimed to have with regard to gambling in baseball.[34]

Author William Cook makes an implausible claim based on Chicago's depleted starting pitching staff (Urban "Red" Faber, 11-9 in 1919, was unable to pitch—Cook characterizes him a big-game pitcher based solely on his 1917 World Series exploits): "Just considering the inequities of the available pitching between the White Sox and Reds is cause enough to argue emphatically that there was *no way* [italics mine] that Chicago was going to win the 1919 World Series."[35]

Cook's argument that the Reds were certain to win the World Series is nonsense. In a series between two pennant-winning teams, nothing is certain, aside from the fact that one team will certainly win five games in the then best-of-nine World Series. What may surprise fans is how often an inferior team may prevail in a seven- or nine-game series.[36]

Cook's claim that the White Sox's superiority was largely enhanced after the fact is not confirmed by sportswriters in the *Sporting News*. The headline on October 2, 1919, blared: "Joy if Reds Win—But a Shock if They Do."[37] New York sportswriter Joe Vila, as did other writers, hoped the Reds would pull off the upset (some writers did favor the Reds based on their pitching), but the American League had won eight of the previous nine World Series, lending support to the idea that the American League champions, at least, were stronger than their National League counterparts. An analysis of the upcoming series in the *New York Times* suggested, "There is not the slightest doubt that the White Sox will enter the conflict favored by the majority to emerge with the world's baseball championship. . . . But this is due chiefly to the fact that the American League seems to be somewhat stronger this year than the National," before adding that the new, best-of-nine format might favor the Reds with their deeper pitching staff.[38]

The *New York Times* reported a betting line of 10 to 7 against the Reds in the September 27 issue, a few days before the start of the series. Two weeks later the newspaper reported that the White Sox were favored to win Game Eight by 6 to 5 or 11 to 10.[39] A day later Comiskey declared, "he would give $20,000 for a single clew [sic] to lead to evidence that any of his players had deliberately attempted to throw any of the world series games ... he was sure of the fidelity of his players."[40] Christy Mathewson reported that White Sox manager Kid Gleason "tore into his players ... and the remarks he made to them could not be printed. He had felt all along that some of his players were not doing their best. . . . He felt that an influence had developed among the players of the Chicago team which was not good for the winning of the series."[41]

Although sportswriter Hugh Fullerton claimed to have smelled a fix as the World Series transpired, it is questionable whether his highlighting peculiar plays would have stood as evidence in a court of law.[42] Sportswriter Leonard Koppett noted that on-the-field performance was rarely, if ever, used in prosecuting players for malfeasance: "How, then, are fixes detected? By external evidence only. Never by examination of how a game was played. . . . And when is suspicion justified? Never on the basis of an unexpected result. Never. Every imagined fix can easily be a legitimate upset. . . . Again, the basis for suspicion must be external. That external evidence lies within the betting world."[43]

Players seeking to fix a game must either accept a bribe or place a large bet in order to profit from their malfeasance. The bromide "follow the money" holds for professional sports gambling scandals. On the eve of the 1946 National Football League championship game, two Giants players—quarterback Frank Filchock and running back Merle Hapes— admitted to being offered money to keep the Giants from beating the point spread. Based on their testimony, Hapes was not allowed to play in the championship game, but Filchock was allowed to play. Filchock threw six interceptions (which was characteristic of him during the regular season), but few people publicly expressed suspicions about his efforts.[44]

As rumors swirled, White Sox players contended for the 1920 pennant. Opposing players taunted Cicotte and Williams, while fans flocked to White Sox home games, setting a team record for paid attendance.[45] After the 1920 season, White Sox benchwarmers Byrd Lynn and Hervey

McClellan described how some of the Sox players "carefully . . . studied the score board . . . and that they always made errors which lost us the game when Cleveland and New York were losing. If Cleveland won—we won. If Cleveland lost—we lost. The idea was to keep the betting odds, but not to let us win the pennant."[46]

Other teams, too, experienced suspicious activities in 1920. Chicago Cubs president William Veeck Sr. revealed that he received an anonymous tip that a game between the Cubs and the Phillies to be played on August 31, 1920, had been fixed. He ordered his manager, Fred Mitchell, to substitute Grover Alexander for Claude Hendrix, even offering Alexander a bonus for winning the game (which the pitcher was unable to do). Judge Charles McDonald presided over a grand-jury investigation of the August 31, 1920, game between the Cubs and the Phillies.[47] Time was running out for the Chicago White Sox players, as this grand jury investigation led to the revelations accusing them of fixing the 1919 World Series.

The grand-jury investigation in Chicago exploded a bombshell, when Assistant State's Attorney R. A. Replogle announced, "The last World Series between the Chicago White Sox and the Cincinnati Reds was not on the square. From five to seven players on the White Sox are involved."[48] Now the rumors surrounding the series assumed center stage of the baseball world. During the investigation, the foreman of the grand jury, H. H. Brigham, informed reporters that the "name of the man who 'fixed' the 1919 World Series . . . had been given to the Grand Jury. . . . Naturally this evidence cannot be made public, for if the men whom it implicates realized what has been told the jury they would immediately cut off other sources of information. We know they have the power to do this." Brigham was being too cute; presumably, just by mentioning the fact that a name had been dropped should have alerted the gamblers.[49]

Ban Johnson admitted that the gambling scandal touched the current 1920 pennant race, as he had "heard statements that the White Sox would not dare to win the 1920 pennant because the managers of a gambling syndicate, alleged to have certain players in their power, had forbidden it." The gamblers apparently had placed large sums on Cleveland to win the pennant; at the time the White Sox were just a half game behind the

Indians. Johnson then denied that the White Sox deliberately lost games as they won two out of the three allegedly fixed games. The allegations, though, served to cast a pall upon the Indians' splendid season.[50]

From here the tale of the 1919 World Series quickly became publicized, although the veracity of some of the witnesses and participants is questionable. The reader is invited to consult the references cited earlier for greater details. The upshot was that seven players agreed to accept money from gamblers; Buck Weaver apparently sat in on the meeting but declined to get involved. Joe Jackson, Chick Gandil, and Eddie Cicotte received some money, but the amount was a fraction of that promised. After losing the first two games of the World Series, the White Sox rallied around unsung pitcher Dickie Kerr. Cicotte and some of the others claimed they played to win, and the gamblers seemed to confirm this when they complained about being double-crossed. Comiskey and his manager, Kid Gleason, became suspicious from the first game that something wasn't right, and although Comiskey offered a reward for relevant information, he kept his doubts to himself.[51]

Although it would be easy to criticize Comiskey for his hesitance to reveal his suspicions earlier, one should remember that he had hundreds of thousands of dollars tied up in the players, and he might have been liable for slander if he could not prove his charges. He very well may have hoped his enemy Ban Johnson would have to divulge the charges against the players. Once the grand jury indicted the seven players, Comiskey suspended them. Cicotte and Jackson confessed to Comiskey and his attorney Alfred S. Austrian.[52] Throughout the testimony, one wonders why players and gamblers even trusted one another in the first place. The players were charged with "conspiracy to commit an illegal act," which was punishable by up to five years' incarceration or a fine of up to $1,000.

The question of just what law the White Sox players violated was an interesting one; the players were indicted for "conspiracy to do an illegal act," but what illegal act? In later cases involving professional football and basketball players, New York prosecuting attorneys had difficulty finding specific charges to apply to players involved in point shaving. Judge Charles McDonald cited the injury to Comiskey and to the honest teammates who might have lost out on larger World Series shares due to their teammates' corruption. Austrian made a similar argument with respect to Comiskey's economic loss, "which consisted of contracts worth more than $200,000, the drawing power of the team to attract crowds to games and other losses of good-will." The White Sox attendance fell by almost three hundred thousand between 1920 and 1921. Austrian's other point, though, was more interesting: "the public paid admission prices to see honest baseball played . . . and the conspiracy to throw the games thereby cheated the public."[53]

New York City assistant district attorney James Smith informed reporters that gamblers convicted of participating in a fix could be punished for a misdemeanor, with up to three years' jail time. He cited section 988 of the penal law: "any person who by fraud or false pretension, while playing at any game, or having a share in any wager, or while betting on the side of such a play, acquires to himself or any others a sum of money or any other valuable thing, is guilty of a misdemeanor."[54]

It didn't take long for grandstanding politicians to enter the fray. Congressman Nicholas Longworth of Cincinnati was investigating how congressional power could help protect baseball. He favored antigambling legislation; Senator Albert Cummins of Iowa later made a similar proposal.[55]

Brooklyn district attorney Harry Lewis ordered Brooklyn Dodgers players to tell what they knew of the 1919 World Series fix and whether they had made plans to "throw" the coming 1920 World Series with the Cleveland Indians. Lewis had Brooklyn owner Charles Ebbets's permission to do this; Lewis admitted that there had been no evidence suggesting any malfeasance and that the investigation was mostly to reassure the public and to protect the players.[56] Cook County chief prosecuting attorney, Maclay Hoyne, stung by criticism when he had ordered his assistants not to further pursue the baseball inquiry, scrambled and denied he issued any such order and that he was "misquoted."[57] Major League owners wanted legislators to enact laws making it a felony "for a gambler or a representative of a gambling syndicate to attempt to bribe baseball players and . . . also make it a felony for any ball player to accept a bribe to 'throw' a game."[58]

Other commentators criticized baseball officials, from Heydler to Johnson to Comiskey, for not being more aggressive in exposing the scandal; the October 7, 1920, issue of the *Sporting News* contained several pieces on the perceived foot dragging. Baseball governance, as was described previously, was in disarray, as the in-fighting between Ban Johnson, some of his owners, and National League owners left the game without a definite leader.

Hugh Fullerton, though, complimented Charles Comiskey. While castigating National League officials for their handling of the Chase case, which he believed sent a message to players that they would not be punished for dishonest play because the club owners feared adverse publicity, Fullerton wrote, "There was one man who gave more thought to the sport than to the money. He was Charles A. Comiskey, who as ball player, captain, manager and owner, amassed a fortune in the game. His players were accused. He stood to lose more than all the others. Yet he insisted upon proving or disproving the charges against his men."[59] Given Comiskey's actions, Fullerton is at best being charitable. Of course, when he wrote his opinion, he may not have realized that Comiskey knew as the series was being played that something suspicious was happening. The New York Yankees' owners, though, backed Comiskey's claim that he expended no little effort in investigating the series; the Yankees' owners also suggested that Ban Johnson was usurping credit for revealing the scandal. Clearly baseball partisanship took no rest when a juicy scandal was involved.[60]

Some fans' reactions to the White Sox scandal perplexed sportswriters. An editorial in the *Sporting News* expressed surprise that St. Louis fans protested the dismissal of Joe Gedeon, who bet on the Reds with the knowledge that the World Series was fixed. The fans argued that Gedeon had not actually thrown a game and that he had appeared before the Chicago grand jury voluntarily. Many Chicago fans, too, supported their players. In the context of innocent until proven guilty, these fans' support was charitable. Given that Cicotte and Jackson had confessed, though, the fans' actions were less defensible.[61]

With the eight White Sox players, Hal Chase, Heinie Zimmerman, and other banished players, a fair amount of talent was floating around. Baseball owners had long recognized the potential danger of blacklisting too many players. Some entrepreneurs decided it would be a swell idea to hire the Black Sox players to form a team to play independent teams. Organized baseball expressly prohibited its players from playing in games with banished players, so the entrepreneurs would likely have had difficulty scheduling games that would be attractive enough to consistently draw large crowds.[62]

Baseball Magazine heaped scorn on attempts to field a team with Black Sox players: "Branded by their own infamy, writhing under public contempt, let them not presume too far on public forbearance. The only ball club which might cross bats with this ill-favored crew is the ball club of a state penitentiary. And we wouldn't blame a prison ball club from resenting the indignity of such associates."[63]

Baseball got some good news, when the *New York Times* reported that betting on the 1920 World Series was at an ebb. The Dodgers and Indians were listed at even money. The *Times* would continue to publish stories regarding gambling on World Series. In 1923, for instance, the initial odds were 7 to 5 in favor of the Yankees, but injuries to Yankees players reduced the odds to 11 to 10. A Wall Street brokerage firm said that $100,000 had already been wagered on the outcome of the series.[64]

When it appeared the White Sox's roster would be gutted for the final few games of the 1920 season, Yankees owners Ruppert and Huston made a gratuitous offer to help Comiskey, pledging to put the entire Yankees club at Comiskey's disposal. The Yankees' owners may have made the offer because Comiskey had allied with them in the wrangles with Ban Johnson. They had to admit, however, that such an offer was unlikely to be acted upon since American League rules required waivers (and probably prohibited loaning players).[65]

Comiskey gave his remaining players $1,500 each to help compensate them for not getting the winners' share of the 1919 World Series.[66]

Lest readers fear that Comiskey was relinquishing his reputation for penurious treatment of his players, the sad saga of pitcher Dickie Kerr is described later.

Reporter W. A. Phelon pointed out in January 1920 that Comiskey had talked to Hugh Fullerton, who never named the players alleged to be guilty, even though their names were circulating in conjunction with the gamblers. Phelon remarked that some players liked to dissemble with gamblers, spreading false information, just to watch the gamblers lose. An article in the *New York Times* in January 1920, though, suggested that although rumors were widespread, none of the investigations found any evidence that the World Series was tainted. Nevertheless, the writer of the article mentioned the prevalence of gambling at several Major League ballparks, despite owners' efforts to eradicate it. There were numerous other articles on the topic throughout 1920.[67]

Baseball fans who have watched John Sayles's motion picture *Eight Men Out* saw an amusing portrayal of the subsequent trial of the original Chicago eight. Players' confessions mysteriously disappeared (only to reappear later), and other suspicious actions transpired. Gamblers fled to Canada, while Abe Attell had the nerve to tell a subpoena server that he wasn't *the* Abe Attell. There was a theater of the absurd quality to the proceedings. Jackson and Cicotte told presiding Judge William Dever that they had not confessed to a conspiracy when they testified before the baseball grand jury, but they did not deny accepting money to throw games. Other reports claimed that copies of the players' testimony had been sold to New York and Chicago newspapers.[68]

The defense argued that Ban Johnson "had furthered this case in an effort to injure his enemy, Charles A. Comiskey."[69] The defense also claimed that the "players were not under contract for the World Series . . . and that there was nothing in their contracts obliging them to try to win games anyway."[70]

In the end, the Chicago jury acquitted all of the players. The scene with the jury room erupting in cheers may well have reflected sentiment in the city. A Chicago newspaper polled its readers on the question of whether the White Sox players should be punished or the court action dropped. A large majority of the first three hundred votes wanted the case dropped and the players to go unpunished. Many of the voters wanted the players to be restored to the White Sox. Granted, this was a small sample of an unscientific poll, but the *Sporting News*'s editor took it seriously enough to wring his hands: "Is a public that was supposed to be exacting so lenient? Is the effort to give it [the game] one thing clean to be so unappreciated?" Even presiding judge Hugo Friend "congratulated the jury, saying he thought it a just verdict."[71]

The players' celebration was brief, as Landis barred the players on August 3, the day after the jury returned its verdict. He gave a statement: "Regardless of the verdict of juries, no player that throws a ball game; no player that undertakes or promises to throw a ball game; no player that sits in a conference with a bunch of crooked players and gamblers where the ways and means of throwing games are planned and discussed and does not promptly tell his club about it, will ever play professional baseball."[72]

The banished White Sox players would spend years and much effort toward being restored to organized baseball. Some of the players potentially still had a few seasons left in them; others just wanted their names cleared. Some sued for back salary; Buck Weaver appealed directly to Landis. All of the players had their coteries of fans who signed petitions urging restoration. One such movement was launched in New York City to restore Joe Jackson; these fans argued that Jackson hit .375 without an error and that he threw out five men at home plate. This last piece of trivia was untrue, as the *New York Times* of October 10, 1919, shows that Jackson had just one assist during the series.[73] By most accounts, the eight players were not a particularly unpleasant lot, some of them were sympathetic characters. Perhaps it is a fitting irony that Joe Jackson is now more famous than Landis, Charlie Comiskey, or Eddie Collins, and the phrase "Say it ain't so, Joe" has become iconic.

Joe Jackson won a temporary legal victory in 1924. He sued Comiskey for back pay. He claimed the White Sox induced him to sign a contract at terms that he [Jackson] did not understand, due to his inability to read. Jackson's attorney, Raymond Cannon, persuaded a jury in Milwaukee to award the ex-player $18,500, the remaining amount of his contract. The jury went beyond awarding him the back pay by indicating their belief that he was not guilty of conspiring to throw ball games. *Baseball Magazine*'s editor found the jury's decision to be incomprehensible. Unfortunately for Jackson, Judge John Gregory, presiding over the trial, scolded the jury members and set aside their verdict; he argued that Jackson either perjured himself in the original trial or in the current trial.[74]

Further Adventures in Gambling

Gambling on baseball did not end with the jury verdict and Landis's response. After the 1921 World Series, the *New York Times* reported that a New York stock operator hosted a party to celebrate winning his $100,000 bet on the New York Giants and New York Yankees winning their respective pennants.[75]

National League president John Heydler made the dubious statement in October 1920 that there were no more crooks in baseball. He claimed the banishing of Chase, Magee, and Zimmerman now served as a deterrent to any player tempted to throw a game and that everyone understood that "no man is so big in baseball that he will be tolerated for an instant if he becomes a menace to it."[76]

Gamblers did not disappear from ballparks. Barney Dreyfuss vowed to prevent gamblers from entering his stadium. He complained that the police hadn't acted upon his requests to keep gamblers from entering the park in the past. He did not explain how the police or his own officials would recognize gamblers, there being no obvious mark of the gambler. Landis bellowed, "Politics or no politics, we'll put a stop to this gambling," when Dreyfuss informed him of the situation at Forbes Field.[77]

John McGraw prided himself on handling baseball eccentrics. Aside from Chase, McGraw also obtained Bugs Raymond and Phil Douglas. Both players showed promise, but their heavy drinking made them unreliable. McGraw hired a coach to accompany Douglas, but the plan backfired when the coach/sitter began drinking with Douglas. After McGraw had authorities incarcerate Douglas in a mental institution, the pitcher in a pique of anger wrote a letter to his friend Leslie Mann on the Cardinals, stating he would leave the Giants so McGraw and the team would not win the pennant. Douglas did not explicitly state that gamblers were involved in this foolish plan. Landis and McGraw agreed that Douglas would be suspended from baseball. Decades later, John Lardner wrote that McGraw and Landis, knowing of Douglas's problem with alcohol, did not view it as an extenuating circumstance. Landis did tell reporters that Douglas "is more ignorant than anything else—a foolish, simple fellow who is unmoral rather than immoral. He is amazingly credulous and is inexperienced in many sides of human nature—an easy dupe for others." Sportswriter Thomas Rice was equally condescending: "[Douglas] was with [Brooklyn] in 1915 and impressed us as an overgrown man with the mind of a wayward child. His mental processes, as far as we could observe, and he was an interesting study, were those of a child. . . . He is by no means the cold-blooded schemer that Hal Chase, Eddie Cicotte and the like were."[78]

Douglas's attorney attempted to get the pitcher reinstated. He portrayed Douglas as a sick man who was agitated when he wrote the ill-advised letter.[79]

The Giants' woes didn't end with Douglas's ouster. McGraw's expensive Minor League purchase, Jimmy O'Connell, became a tragic figure in baseball. McGraw reputedly spent $75,000 to purchase O'Connell from San Francisco. O'Connell played sparingly, although he was hitting .317 with sixteen runs batted in (with only 104 at bats, suggesting he performed well with runners on base) during the 1924 season. The Giants were struggling to win their unprecedented fourth consecutive pennant. Before a game with the Philadelphia Phillies late in the season with the Giants barely holding off Brooklyn and Pittsburgh, O'Connell approached shortstop Heinie Sand and offered him five hundred dollars to not "bear down too hard." O'Connell knew Sand from their days in the Pacific Coast League. Sand turned down O'Connell's bizarre offer; Sand was hardly a key player on the Phillies, being a light-hitting infielder in his second season. Sand did, however, report the conversation to his manager, who relayed the information to John Heydler and Landis.[80]

O'Connell was suspended after a secret hearing where he implicated coach Cozy Dolan and teammates Frank Frisch, Ross Youngs, and George

Kelly. Landis did not examine John McGraw or Charles Stoneham, yet cleared them of wrongdoing. After the hearing, Landis permanently suspended O'Connell along with Dolan. Landis and the National League handled the matter so adroitly that reporters and the public did not know of the situation until Landis announced his findings. Ban Johnson blasted Landis's handling of the scandal and demanded that the World Series be called off; author Frank Graham believed Johnson was motivated by his hatred of McGraw and Landis. F. C. Lane shared Graham's opinion regarding Johnson's motives.[81]

The O'Connell scandal left many unanswered questions. Few people believed that Dolan and O'Connell concocted the plan on their own. Some people wondered whether Frisch, Youngs, and Kelly had played a practical joke on O'Connell, but if so, why didn't they say so during their testimonies?[82] If McGraw instigated the plan, then he was risking losing a player who had cost him tens of thousands of dollars. Baseball's highest officials, though, did not seem interested in pursuing the case any further. The O'Connell case remains an enigma. O'Connell later refused to return from California to testify without being granted immunity; Dolan received legal representation from Giants' attorney William Fallon. He threatened a lawsuit but later backed off; reporter Joe Vila hinted that rumors circulated that Dolan had been told to keep his mouth shut.[83]

Some people commented on the irony that while O'Connell and Dolan were being vilified, Stoneham and his financial partners were in court listening to government witnesses testify that Stoneham and the E. D. Dier and Company had defrauded them.[84] The *Sporting News* may have come closest to the truth when its editorialist pointed out that baseball officials did not want the case to end up in New York district court, as "there is no telling where it will end."[85]

Ban Johnson may have been right that there was more to the case than what Landis divulged, but he may have been tactically in error if the "more to the case" resulted in exposure of widespread corruption. Presumably Landis knew the stakes involved, and because he was better at keeping quiet than Johnson was, baseball may have been spared yet another scandal to rival the 1919 World Series. On the other hand, if McGraw and Stoneham were culpable, they should have been exposed.

Another case ended favorably for baseball. *Collyer's Eye*, a sporting sheet, claimed that gamblers offered Cincinnati Reds players Pat Duncan and Sammy Bohne $15,000 apiece to throw some key games. John Heydler ordered the players to report to him; after an investigation, Heydler urged the players to sue the publication for defamation in order to defuse the situation. After some delay, *Collyer's Eye* settled out of court. Lee Allen points out that *Collyer's Eye* didn't accuse the players of accepting bribes or throwing games, simply that they had been approached by gamblers. Such an allegation was still potentially damaging, and Heydler's forthright investigation vindicated the two players.[86]

Ban Johnson crusaded against another form of baseball gambling. Gambling syndicates established baseball pools. Fans could bet on how many runs a team would score during a week and other odd bets. Johnson asserted that the syndicates frequently cheated the bettors by not paying off. Left unstated was why bettors would continue to patronize these betting pools if they were being cheated. Although the pools often did not publicize winners, making it difficult to check up on them, presumably people who had won and were cheated would have spoken up and spread the word.[87]

Landis expressed "astonishment" at the prevalence and size of the baseball pools. He, too, issued a warning to baseball fans and sought judicial help in curtailing the practice; at a baseball dinner event, Landis stated, "Vile and unspeakable as he [the professional gambler who corrupts ballplayers], he is by no means the worst of the two menaces. In pure sliminess the baseball pool has no equal. It takes money from those who can least afford to lose it, and my investigations prove that only 10 percent of the total money received is disbursed in the form of prizes."[88]

Landis encouraged newspapers to stop publishing tables showing how many runs teams scored each week as this was one of the primary bets used by the betting pools. Landis seemed pretty naive; if the pools couldn't use weekly runs as a betting focus, they could easily use other baseball statistics.[89]

Irving Sanborn described the typical betting pool: bettors paid fifty cents and wrote the names of four teams in each league they thought would collectively outscore the other four teams during the coming week. "Each slip was signed and filed in the cigar box, and each fan was given a carbon copy to avoid disputes or mistakes." Sanborn noted that from such humble beginnings, the pools proved highly popular, and crooks took over the games and began cheating customers. In a later article, Sanborn detailed that crooked pool operators claimed there were duplicate winners, among other phony devices to avoid paying the promised prize money.[90]

Baseball's Biggest Names Implicated

Landis needed time to eradicate gambling from Major League Baseball. Ultimately, he banned more than just the eight White Sox players. The aftermath of the 1926 season left fans wondering. Ty Cobb and Tris Speaker resigned from their player-manager positions with the Tigers and Indians respectively. Cobb and Speaker were among the first dozen players selected to Baseball's Hall of Fame, and their retirements within a short period caused an uproar. The retirements were puzzling, especially given that Speaker had done an excellent job managing Cleveland to a second-place finish.

Landis announced on December 21, 1926, that Dutch Leonard had accused Cobb and Speaker of involvement in a conspiracy to bet on an alleged "fixed" game on September 25, 1919. Supposedly Cobb, Speaker, Leonard, and Smoky Joe Wood met under the grandstand at Navin Field. Speaker's Indians had already clinched second place. The idea was for the Indians to go easy on the Tigers, so the Tigers would get third-place money (and thereby possibly keep the Yankees from finishing third and getting the money).[91] The players allegedly placed bets on the game, detailing a Detroit clubhouse worker to place the bets. Something went awry, and some of the players reaped little if any financial benefit.

Dutch Leonard and Joe Wood bet $600 against $420 on the Tigers to win. The available evidence did not show that Cobb or Speaker bet on the game. Leonard had letters written by Cobb and Wood that made vague references to an arrangement and betting. Leonard subsequently had contretemps with Cobb when Cobb managed Detroit, including an ugly incident when Cobb left Leonard in to absorb a 12–4 battering from the Philadelphia Athletics (even Connie Mack commented unfavorably on Cobb's action). Leonard jumped to an outlaw team and was put on the ineligible list before Landis allowed him to play with the Tigers again in 1924 and 1925.[92]

Cobb's letter read: "Dear Dutch: Well, old boy, guess you are out in old California by this time and enjoying life. . . . Wood and myself were considerably disappointed in our business proposition, as we had $2,000 to put into it and the other side quoted us $1,400, and when we finally secured that much money it was about 2 o'clock and they refused to deal with us, as they had men in Chicago to take up the matter with and they had no time, so we completely fell down, and of course we felt badly over it." The other letter was one Wood wrote Leonard:

> Dear Friend Dutch: Enclosed please find certified check for sixteen hundred and thirty dollars. The only bet [Fred O.] West [Tigers clubhouse assistant] could get down was $600 against $420 (10 to 7). Cobb did not get up a cent. He told us that and I believed him. Could have put up some at 5 to 2 on Detroit, but did not, as that would make us put up $1,000 to win $400. We won the $420. I gave West $30, leaving $390, or $130 for each of us. . . . If we ever have another chance like this we will know enough to try to get down early.[93]

Ban Johnson's American League attorney, Henry Killilea purchased the incriminating letters from Leonard for a reputed $20,000. He then turned the letters over to Johnson. Johnson then advised the players that he held the letters and persuaded them to leave baseball, lest the news leak out.[94]

Johnson told reporters, once the letters became public knowledge, that in 1919, "this thing of betting on ball games was a common practice previous to the World Series." Reporters recalled that Leonard may have had a grudge against Cobb, but they could not figure out why Leonard sought to besmirch Speaker. The evidence in the letters, though, hardly indicated any wrongdoing on Speaker's part.[95] Reporters, fans, and baseball officials also wondered why Leonard waited so long to divulge this information. Perhaps he was emboldened by an eruption of the 1919 scandal caused by Swede Risberg and Chick Gandil, who alleged that most of their White Sox teammates had paid Detroit pitchers in 1917 after those hurlers beat the Boston Red Sox in a key series. In return, the White Sox took it easy on the Indians in 1919 to assure the latter club a share of the World Series money.

Speaker was already under scrutiny, as the American League and Ban Johnson knew about his fondness for betting on horse races. Johnson didn't refrain from making provocative remarks: "The American League is a business. When our directors found two employees who they didn't think were serving them right, they had to let them go. . . . As long as I am president . . . neither one of them will manage or play on our teams." Johnson then made a confusing remark, "I don't believe Ty Cobb ever played a dishonest game in his life. If that is the exoneration he seeks, I gladly give it to him. But it is from Landis, Cobb should demand an explanation. The American League ousted Cobb, but it was Landis who broadcast the story of his mistakes."[96] In the confrontation between Landis and Johnson, Landis demanded to know who was leaking rumors about the players. Johnson admitted (as Landis already knew) that he had planted the stories and that he had no additional evidence.[97]

The two players had many friends, some of whom were quite influential. They also retained legal counsel and decided to fight Leonard in public. Cobb retorted, "Speaker and I had nothing to hide in connection with this rotten affair. My conscience is clear. I am sure the records of neither Speaker nor myself will suffer in comparison with the action of the officials conducting the present investigation." He went on to tell reporters that he immediately reported to Landis when apprised of the situation.[98] Speaker demonstrated to Landis's satisfaction that he played his usual line-up and made three hits, including two triples. Cobb made only one hit in five at bats. There was no evidence that Speaker was going easy or trying to lose. Cobb had support from Georgia senators and congressional representatives; some senators were openly critical of Landis for divulging the letters.[99]

Landis knew the press was about to break the story, so sitting on the letters was not an option. He did, though, figure out how to handle the situation in a way that put Ban Johnson (with help from Johnson's uncontrollable curse of gab) in a bad light.[100]

Dutch Leonard denied that he had sold the letters to the American League. He claimed that he approached authorities to press a claim against Detroit for loss of salary during the 1922, 1923, and 1924 seasons, when he did not play in baseball. He claimed the money he received was for his back salary and that he had surrendered the letters to the American League authorities because they persuaded him it was the right thing to do. Leonard undermined his credibility by refusing to face Landis, Cobb, and Speaker at a hearing.[101]

Clubhouse worker Fred West later claimed that the bets were for a horse race and not a ball game, but even Speaker's and Cobb's attorneys disputed this interpretation. West stated that Leonard wanted to use the money to bet on the Detroit-Cleveland game, but West put the money on a horse race. His story seems pathetically ridiculous; what if the horse lost—how would he have explained that to the players?[102]

One reporter summarized the situation: "There is no proof yet made public which implicates Speaker in either game-fixing or a betting coup. Cobb admits that he knew Leonard and Wood were betting on the game, and the evidence is that he himself tried to get a bet up, but failed. In all except the betting angle Leonard's charges are uncorroborated, unless Mr. Landis has evidence which he has not disclosed. And it should be remembered that a ball player's betting on a game in 1919 was not considered the grave offense it is now."[103]

John Sheridan may have written what many baseball people thought: "I believe in Cobb. If I don't believe in Cobb, I can't believe in the greatness of Organized Baseball. . . . I am disappointed because Cobb did not tear into Leonard when that worthy first indicated that he desired to dispose of the letter written him by Cobb and insist that the letter be published."[104]

Sheridan came up with the odd argument that if Cobb and Speaker placed bets on the game in question, "Their very ignorance of all written and unwritten laws of betting marks them as innocent as 4-year-old boys." Cobb and Speaker had been described as many things, but "as innocent as 4-year-old-boys" must have struck most readers as ludicrous; Speaker was fond of gambling, and Cobb was financially astute.[105] Cobb and Speaker's attorneys kept the two players silent until they could mount an effective counterattack, making Cleveland and Detroit fans restless— why didn't their heroes confront Leonard publicly?[106]

Other observers questioned Landis's actions. Francis Richter thought Landis had, "by his Scotch verdict, blasted the reputation of two men who have had a million times more to do with making baseball America's best loved sport." Richter found Landis's handling of the Cobb-Speaker affair contradictory to that of the O'Connell-Dolan scandal. In the latter case, he did not press too hard to discern who, if anyone, was behind O'Connell, even though O'Connell said Giants veterans told him to go ahead. In the Cobb-Speaker case, he appeared to accept the testimony of Dutch Leonard and was leaving Cobb and Speaker to twist in the wind. He also thought that Ban Johnson handled the situation better than Landis had.[107]

Landis, however, was about to trump Ban Johnson. The commissioner challenged the American League and Johnson to divulge any additional information they had regarding the Cobb-Speaker case. He arranged a meeting in Chicago. Reporters learned of an unnamed source saying that the two ballplayers would never again be allowed to play or manage in the American League. Johnson made a misstep when he told reporters he had reports on Speaker that Landis would not get outside of a courtroom. He also chastised Landis for conducting the investigation of the Risberg-Gandil charges without getting the approval of the advisory council. He again reiterated his belief in Cobb: "I know Ty Cobb's not a crooked ball player. . . . Tris Speaker is a different type of fellow. For want of a better word I'd call Tris cute."[108]

Johnson couldn't keep quiet; a couple of days later he claimed that Cobb's and Speaker's "incompetency as managers and not alleged crooked dealings was the real reason" for their releases. Johnson cited

Cobb's violent temper and Speaker's fondness for horses as detracting from their managerial abilities; Johnson also denied making insinuations about the Yankees' play during the 1922 World Series.[109] Landis was fortunate to have such a voluble antagonist in Johnson.

Jacob Ruppert may have reflected his fellow American League owners' sentiments, when he told reporters that Johnson was "wrong and unjust if he declared that Landis had 'tarnished' the reputations of Cobb and Speaker by giving out the evidence in their case." He emphatically supported Landis's decision in both the Cobb-Speaker and concurrent Risberg-Gandil cases. "I am going to ask Ban Johnson one question tomorrow. I am going to ask him what he would have done if he had been in Landis's shoes in the Cobb-Speaker case. If Johnson says he would have acted differently from Landis, then he is unfit to be president of the American League."[110]

Landis announced that there wasn't evidence to find Cobb and Speaker guilty. The Tigers and Indians owners, desiring to wash their hands of their high-priced player-managers, refrained from retaining them. Landis granted them their unconditional releases, making them free agents. There was one detail that he did not announce: neither player would be allowed to serve as coach or manager of an American League team.[111]

With Cobb and Speaker free agents, the other American League owners scurried to sign them. There was one unspoken belief: these owners certainly did not want their stars to end up in the National League. There had been rumors that John McGraw was interested in Cobb. Baseball fans can ponder how such a match would have worked, as Cobb would seem to exemplify the McGraw approach to baseball. Then again, they might have clashed and sundered the Giants. Even the Yankees were interested in signing Speaker (although they already had Earle Combs in centerfield). Within a few days, Speaker signed with Washington and Cobb became an Athletic.[112]

American League owners forced Ban Johnson to take a vacation, citing health reasons. They were aghast to discover that Johnson had been leaking "information" and running a bluff against Landis. He had no further evidence regarding the Cobb-Speaker scandal. The owners publicly stated their approval of Landis's actions in handling the case, but they also expressed sympathy for Johnson's ill health, with some reports claiming the president "twice was near collapse . . . having to be helped to his chair. After the meeting he failed to recognize a close friend for almost a full minute."[113] Since Johnson proved remarkably recuperative in the months to come, the owners may have exaggerated Johnson's health status, so as to spare him some humiliation.

During the post mortem, *Baseball Magazine*'s editorialist lambasted Dutch Leonard. He mentioned that Speaker and Cobb had referred to the former pitcher as a "Judas and a Bolshevik." He cited Leonard's refusal to make his accusations in person.[114] In the end, though, he had only two questions: What was Leonard's motivation? Why did he divulge his information years after the fact?

Modern-day readers, not as imbued with fondness or rancor towards Cobb and Speaker or the White Sox and Tigers players of ninety-plus years ago, may well be perplexed by these situations and their outcomes. Why did Cobb write to Leonard? Speaker, at least, didn't appear to be involved, except at the alleged meeting under the grandstand, but he wasn't mentioned in the letters. While there's nothing to suggest that Cobb bet against the Tigers or tried to have his team lose, betting on his team with the possible connivance of a fellow manager was certainly ill-advised.

White Sox Scandal Reprised

Landis was not only investigating the Cobb-Speaker case, he was also handling another eruption of the 1919 World Series scandal. Swede Risberg and Chick Gandil had made new accusations about their teammates and other players. Risberg claimed that his teammates agreed to throw games to Detroit in 1919 in return for Detroit having thrown four games to the White Sox during a crucial series in 1917. Risberg said the White Sox team pooled $1,100 to pay Detroit players for throwing the games in 1917 and that the White Sox manager, Clarence Rowland, engineered the fix. Risberg made the bizarre statement, "They push Ty Cobb and Tris Speaker out on a piker bet. I think it's only fair that the 'white lilies' [*sic*] get the same treatment."[115]

Chick Gandil decided to join his former teammate in spewing lurid charges. Landis arranged for twenty or more ex-teammates and opponents to confront Gandil and Risberg. The two players stood their ground during the inquest, even as witnesses disputed their account of the incident.

Irving Vaughan recalled that White Sox catcher Ray Schalk admitted in 1920 that the club raised a purse to reward Detroit pitchers for their good work in defeating Boston in 1917. Eddie Collins also contributed. Since Schalk and Collins were the "white lilies" whom Risberg scorned, the charges seemed to emanate from spite.[116]

Swede Risberg may not have been a sympathetic figure (nor was Chick Gandil), but he was not intimidated by the legion of former teammates and opponents and "lolled in a near-by chair, a cigarette burning in his fingers, his face sometimes lighted up with a cynical smile" as former teammates and opponents repudiated his version of the thrown games. Former manager Clarence "Pants" Rowland argued that he used his best pitchers to win the four-game series, which he would not have done, if he had known that the Tigers were going to lay down.[117]

All of the other players claimed the purse was not a payment for throwing the games but a reward for beating Boston and that the White Sox had not repaid by purposely losing a couple of games in 1919. Sportswriter James Harrison described Landis as hammering away relentlessly at each witness. At the end of the hearing, not one player provided any support for Risberg's version of events; Risberg remained defiant and did not recant. Risberg's account of the game differed from the *New York Times'* version. Eddie Cicotte was not knocked out of the box, but, rather, pitched just two innings (yielding one run). Risberg and Gandil could not account for all of the money they collected from their teammates.[118]

As reporters, fans, and baseball awaited Landis's decision, one reporter suggested that the consensus was "Judge Landis never does the ordinary thing, and if he thinks there is anything to the Risberg or Gandil charges he will punish mercilessly."[119] This was a pretty good summation of Landis, although one still wonders why he didn't delve more deeply into the O'Connell-Dolan story.

Landis announced, "If the Gandil-Risberg version be correct it was an act of criminality. If the other version be true, it was an act of impropriety, reprehensible and censurable, but not corrupt," before exonerating Risberg and Gandil's White Sox teammates and the Detroit Tigers. Landis accepted the explanation that the money was raised to reward Detroit pitchers for beating Boston. Undoubtedly exasperated by these charges and countercharges regarding past indiscretions and misdemeanors, Landis proclaimed a statute of limitations. He also made it a punishable offense for offering or accepting gifts or rewards between personnel of different teams, as well as clarifying punishments for betting on games.[120]

Baseball Magazine's editorialist asked, "What has happened beyond a deluge of printer's ink and the gossip of startled fandom? Merely this. Baseball has been celebrating a SQUEALER'S HOLIDAY [caps his]. It has measured the height and breadth of the fictions that pure malice could create." The editorialist argued that the Joe Wood letter, "proved that Wood, although willing to wager upon the game, was not willing to take long odds," before dismissing Cobb's and Speaker's actions: "What of it? All this occurred away back in 1917." The writer claimed baseball mores were different then.[121]

As late as 1927, owners still had not formalized punishment for game fixing. Landis suggested a one-year suspension for offering or accepting illicit gifts, but the owners responded by urging a three-year suspension to "anyone found guilty of giving or accepting a bribe or 'going easy' on an opponent. Any attempt to improperly influence an umpire, in turn, would result in permanent blacklisting of both the offerer and the taker of a bribe. Players also would draw permanent banishment for betting on games with a direct connection, and a one-year suspension would follow bets on other contests." The owners approved these punishments on December 15, 1927.[122]

A Good Eye for Hitting, Not for Horses

As these allegations floated, other players got into trouble gambling on other events. Baseball players loved horses and the races they ran. Rogers

Hornsby and Babe Ruth were only the most glamorous ballplayers turned equestrian aficionados. Ruth, by betting on slower horses, owed $7,500 to an Edward J. Callahan. Ruth claimed he had an agreement to repay his debts in all good time, but Callahan was impatient. The spectacle of baseball's highest-paid player being (temporarily) unable to pay a gambling debt was mortifying. Then again, owners sued each other, too, for sleazy shenanigans.[123]

Rogers Hornsby was having gambling problems of his own. Hornsby loved playing the horses (perhaps because he was a native Texan). His eyes were better at hitting baseballs than picking the fastest horses. During January 1927, as charges swirled around Cobb, Speaker, and the White Sox players, Frank Moore, a Cincinnati betting commissioner, claimed that Hornsby owed him $92,000—a large chunk of change for a player making $40,000 a year, although not all of this sum was for gambling. Hornsby's attorney advised the player "not to recognize the $90,000 claim."[124]

Baseball Survives Gambling

Baseball survived its biggest gambling scandal. Whether it was Landis's decisive action in banishing the players, or the game's burgeoning popularity thanks to Babe Ruth, or simply the fans' love of the game, attendance remained strong throughout the decade. Gambling did not end with the 1919 World Series, but by 1921 players knew the potential penalties for betting on games or consorting with gamblers.

There was another aspect to consider. As salaries increased, Jacob Ruppert, for one, believed players would be less willing to jeopardize their careers to get involved in throwing ball games. Higher salaries meant the potential loss for getting caught betting on games was greater and might have tilted the decision towards remaining honest.[125]

4   The Financial Side of the Game

The seasons between 1919 and 1929 were generally prosperous ones for Major League Baseball. The evidence suggests, though, that prosperity was unevenly distributed.

Profits and Losses

Owners were jealous of their financial records. The congressional hearing of 1951 required owners to submit financial records for 1920–50, with detailed information for a handful of seasons. Sometimes court cases forced owners to divulge their profits. For instance, during the settlement of William Yawkey's shares of Detroit Tigers stock, the net earnings for 1914–18 were introduced. The Tigers had positive net earnings for the first four years, but reported a loss of $29,544 in 1918.[1]

During the Brooklyn owners' feuds, court documents showed that Brooklyn made $190,000, $150,000, $146,000, $116,000, and $263,000 between 1920 and 1924; these figures were close to those reported to Congress in 1951, although the 1923 figure differed ($116,000 versus $93,000).[2]

Baseball owners provided "consolidated profit and loss" statements to the congressional committee (table 3). Economists studying the economics of professional team sports are usually stymied by a lack of good profit and loss data, so these data are quite valuable.

The two leagues reported roughly $20 million in profits for the eleven seasons between 1920 and 1930. The combined profits may be slightly overstated since the Boston Red Sox did not report figures for 1920–22. The Red Sox were respectable in 1920–21 but sank to last place in 1922. Attendance fell from 417,000 in 1919 to 230,000 in 1923. Given the team's history of wretched win-loss records and small losses throughout the remainder of the 1920s, whether the team made a small profit or recorded a small loss during the three seasons is difficult to say. The team had not yet relinquished all of its stars during those seasons, so its payrolls may not have diminished by much.

The two leagues had almost equal combined profits. The New York Yankees, though, dominated the American League's profits. Seven American League teams made profits overall during the eleven seasons. Three National League teams made modest profits, but the other five teams made more profits than any American League team outside of the Yankees.

The St. Louis Browns and Cleveland Indians were becoming unprofitable as the decade waned, while Detroit and Chicago also weakened. In the National League, the Cincinnati Reds declined after their 1919 World Series championship. The Boston Braves barely broke even during the decade, but the Philadelphia Phillies, a moribund franchise, at least did not incur heavy losses.

Even in prosperous seasons, some owners still lost money. The National League celebrated a strong season in 1924, but John Heydler bemoaned the fact that St. Louis and Boston lost money, "We have just closed the best years [1923–24] in our history, yet we find that in every one of those years one or more clubs lost money."[3]

Team Profits

Baseball owners realized they faced competition for consumers' discretionary incomes. The 1920s were a period of prosperity, and Americans had more discretionary income than before. They also had many new ways to spend their money on amusement and recreation. Although the owners had little to fear from professional football, other sports such as college football, professional boxing, wrestling, cycling, and track and field provided some competition for fans' money during the 1920s. A major new competitor, though, was motion pictures. The industry was rapidly becoming the choice of entertainment-seeking fans. The quality of motion pictures dramatically improved during the first decades of the twentieth century; films grew in length with well-developed plot lines. In addition, recognizable directors and actors help boost reliability. Technological improvements such as sound and color in the late 1920s and 1930s continued the improvements.

Whether Major League Baseball was interstate commerce had been debated in the Baltimore Federal League court case (along with other cases). Regardless of whether baseball was under the antitrust statutes, owners worried about profits and losses. Although some of them may not have been profit maximizers, most of them were keenly interested in not losing too much money. Some owners, of course, simply could not afford to lose much money.

Baseball officials, as with other professional sports, claimed that the owners were in baseball as "an avocation," as later commissioner Ford Frick testified in 1951: "They are primarily in baseball because they are interested in baseball as a game. They are not dependent upon it for a living and they are well aware that the financial return from baseball does not justify it as an investment."[4] Frick's contention that baseball was not a lucrative investment aside, some owners reported large profits. The Yankees' reported net income of $8.5 million from 1920 to 1950 was more than the combined net income of six of its rival American League teams for that period. The St. Louis Cardinals' net income for the same period was $6 million, which the Congressional committee attributed to its farm system, citing sales of players worth $2 million between 1922 and 1941.[5]

Owners earning profits faced losing well over half of those profits to the federal government. Wartime profit taxes on regular income and capital gains peaked at 77 percent in 1918; the rates both fell to 73 percent between 1919 and 1921. Treasury Secretary Andrew Mellon convinced President Harding and Congress to slash income rates to 58 percent in 1922 and 43.5 percent in 1923. The income-tax rate fell to 25 percent in 1925. The capital gains tax fell more precipitously to 12.5 percent in 1922, where it remained throughout the 1920s. Corporate taxes were roughly 10–13.5 percent between 1919 and 1931. Owners could pay themselves salaries, which reduced profits (since salaries were expenses), but exposed the salaries to income taxes. They could also disburse profits in the form of dividends. The income-tax rates sometimes spurred owners to reinvest any profits into the ball club instead of paying dividends; teams differed on issuing dividends. The increasing prevalence of dividends during the 1920s may have reflected the more favorable income-tax rates.[6]

Several teams did not pay any dividends between 1920 and 1930 (table 4), including the New York Yankees. The Giants paid out most of their reported profits in dividends.

The two St. Louis teams also took different approaches to paying dividends. The Browns paid out about half of their reported profits as dividends, with the team declaring a large dividend after its near-pennant-winning season of 1922. The formerly penurious Cardinals, flush with cash after their first pennant in 1926, reportedly issued a dividend, but the congressional hearing showed the team paying no dividends that year; the team made $359,000 in 1926 (table 3). Primary owner Sam Breadon hoped to use the balance of the profits to improve the team's farm system. Breadon's decision revealed a basic trade-off: paying dividends meant fewer funds to replenish the team's personnel, which, in turn, affected the likelihood of earning enough income in the future to sustain future dividends.[7]

The Washington Senators, fresh off winning their first pennant, issued dividends of $80,000 after the 1924 season. The team reportedly paid $318,000 in dividends out of $409,000 in profits the following year, but the team appeared to have actually paid much more in dividends in 1925.[8]

The Cleveland Indians reported $173,480 in net earnings for 1921, a year after their pennant. By 1925 the earnings dwindled to $13,294. These figures reported in the *New York Times* differed somewhat from those presented to the 1951 congressional committee, but the sharp decrease in earnings appeared in both sources.[9]

An article in *Collier's* (March 1922) implied that a set of investors would have been better off investing somewhere else. The owners were not identified, but it seems reasonable to think they were the Yankees' Jacob Ruppert and T. L. Huston, given that after six years, "we checked up and found we owed ourselves $160,000 . . . but we were close to the pennant." This tallies fairly closely to the Yankees' reported figures. They claimed to have invested $700,000 (but this may have included more than the purchase price of the team). According to Haupert and Winter, the colonels paid $460,000 for the franchise and $100,000 for Ruth. The owner cited an appreciation in the value of the franchise up to 1922, although given the inflation during his ownership, it may have not been an appreciation in real terms.[10] Baseball writer John Sheridan, though, painted a different picture. He claimed, "It is a poor baseball club that does not net 25 percent per annum and the net return for all Organized Baseball must be around 15 percent per annum." Then again, he considered baseball a "very Big Business," when, in fact, it was of modest size. As a comparison, R. H. Macy's planned to renovate and enlarge its Manhattan store at a cost of $5 million in 1922, much more than Yankee Stadium cost. The retailer planned to house ten thousand employees; on busy days, some sixty thousand patrons entered the store. The Lehigh Valley Railroad company's annual report showed revenues of $62 million in 1922, which was a decrease of $12.5 million from 1921. The Yankees, as will be seen, struggled to get $1.2 million a season from all revenue sources during the 1920s.[11]

Success on the field was a key determinant of profitability according to the congressional committee. A team could have a losing record and still earn a profit, with a win-loss mark of .423 being a rough break-even point. Profits rose as a team's record improved. At high levels of success, such as a win-loss record of between .650 and .700, the added gains became modest; a tight pennant seemed to boost league profitability.[12]

Teams finishing last did not necessarily lose large amounts of money. Connie Mack's Athletics finished last year after year, but Mack was able to minimize the team's losses by maintaining a low payroll and selling players to other teams. A surer way to lose large sums appeared to be to spend heavily on buying ballplayers and then to have a disappointing record on the field, as Thomas Yawkey would find with the Boston Red Sox in the 1930s.[13]

The congressional committee noted that gross paid admissions fluctuated fairly closely with the gross national product, concluding, "For every change in the GNP of $16 billion, American League receipts tended to fluctuate $800,000 and National League receipts $700,000. A team's win-loss percentage was strongly correlated with its attendance and fairly correlated with net income. For a given win-loss record, the Yankees and Giants experienced greater attendance and net incomes.[14]

Other Sources of Revenues

For most owners, their primary source of revenue was the gate receipts at home and on the road. Those owners receiving receipts from concessions found this source strictly a secondary one. During the 1920s big league owners did not receive revenues from selling broadcasting rights to radio stations.[15]

Owners who owned their own ballparks could expect revenue from selling concessions. The Chicago Cubs owned the Los Angeles team in the Pacific Coast League. The concessions in Los Angeles provided a valuable secondary income. Having concessions at the ballpark meant that fans leaving work could come directly to the game rather than stopping and eating. The Los Angeles club was renowned for its popcorn. The concessionaire stated that many clubs made the mistake of trying to buy the cheapest ingredients for their hot dogs and popcorn. But the fans at Los Angeles Wrigley Field knew they were getting high-quality food served by well-trained vendors.[16]

In addition to revenues from concessions, owning your own ballpark meant that you could lease it out for other events. Many Negro League teams leased MLB stadiums when the home team was on the road. Outside of the season, popular uses of MLB ballparks were college and professional football games. The Yankees were masters at churning out income from the "House that Ruth Built." A track was constructed inside the stadium and a PA system was located under the infield for use during boxing matches, which were a common and lucrative source of income for the Yankees.

The New York teams leased concessions to the Harry M. Stevens Company for ten years; the concessionaire had to pay at least $40,000 per year. Although this company was competent, it didn't appear to be outstanding, if the quality of its scorecards was any indication.[17]

The 1918 season appeared to be a disaster for the owners. The *New York Times* quoted a baseball official stating that at the winter meetings, "not one major league club showed a profits [*sic*] on its book at the end of last season. In fact, many of them lost so much money that training trips to Southern States in the Spring would be out of the question."[18]

Rising Expenses

Owners faced a variety of expenses. While the player salaries were the most publicized, the costs of transporting and housing teams on the road, equipment (including baseballs), stadium maintenance and overhead, office salaries, spring training, and so on were significant. Another large expense was player replacement, as owners sought new talent to replace aging or failing players. Even baseballs probably cost at least $7,500 per season since National League teams each used roughly five to six hundred dozen balls during the season by the mid 1920s; balls cost fifteen dollars per dozen.[19]

What financial information did sportswriters provide the public? John Sheridan presented a hypothetical club's financial figures after the 1923 season. The club had operating expenses of $437,000, but the largest amount—$175,000—went to "Interest and Sinking fund." Player salaries at $140,000 were the second-largest amount. Traveling expenses amounted to $50,000. The club also incurred expenses for player replacement, which was not part of the operating expenses. One owner estimated $60,000 to $100,000 for buying new players, although some of this was offset by sales of players.[20] The foregone interest was a key item to consider, one that fans and historians often neglected. For an owner investing $1 million, at an interest rate of even just 4 percent, the owner was giving up the opportunity to earn $40,000 on his million dollars.

Team owners worried about transportation costs; teams traveled primarily by railroad during the 1920s. Railroads often charged per mile per person. Pullman accommodations incurred additional charges. Owners therefore scrutinized schedules for the extent of travel, as mileage differed between teams. For instance, during 1923, Brooklyn logged 9,404 miles, while Pittsburgh had 12,980. Some of these miles were incurred in order to play single games in ballparks permitting Sunday ball. Brooklyn and New York were fortunate in that their "road" trips to each other's stadium did not require railroad fare. Teams usually played three or four games in each city during a road trip, but owners sometimes economized by adjusting the schedule. Railroads raised their fares in the years after World War I, probably just enough to match the increases in the general price level.[21]

John Kieran pointed out that spring training trips were a relatively recent introduction to the baseball world. As baseball grew prosperous, some owners figured that the benefits from training where the weather was good exceeded the added expense. Paul Eaton wrote that Washington spent $21,744 for the 1924 spring training, but exhibition games brought in $11,413, reducing the net cost to a little more than $10,000. The Cubs reportedly spent $25,000 on spring training for 1925; since the team trained in California, its travel expense was probably higher than those teams training in Florida.[22]

Teams incurred expenses on the road. Players received $3.00 per day for food when they stayed in European-plan hotels (without meals included). The American-plan hotels included food in the daily room rate, but these plans were disappearing for ball clubs, as the players ate too much. How far did $3.00 a day for meals stretch? Some Chicago restaurants advertised in the Chicago Cubs scorecards during the 1920s. The Beach View Garden boasted a "Tasty Table de Hote Dinner" for $1.25 or an "Extra Special Sunday dinner" for $1.50. The Addison Restaurant, near the ballpark, offered a presumably more modest evening dinner for $0.60. Block's Restaurant and Grill offered "Block's Special Steak with Shoe String Potatoes and Salad" for $1.00. In the 1920s hotels sometimes offered rooms without baths. Patrons desiring such an amenity paid extra for a room with a bath; the Buckingham Hotel in St. Louis charged $1.50 to $2.00 for rooms without baths and $3.00 to $5.00 for rooms with baths.[23]

New York Yankees Finances
Jacob Ruppert and Colonel Tillinghast Huston bought the team on December 31, 1914. Prior to that date, the Yankees had scant success,

finishing out of the second division only four times, as high as second three times, but not since 1910. Ruppert and Huston tried to strengthen their team by purchasing Frank Baker from Connie Mack for $37,500 on February 15, 1916.

The team generated just under $1 million in gate receipts for the new owners in their first four seasons of ownership (tables 5 and 6). After that, gate receipts rose quickly, peaking in 1920 in nominal terms and in 1921 in real terms. Part of the gains in gate receipts was a result of higher gate receipts per attendee, a reflection of increased ticket prices and a greater proportion of fans sitting in more expensive seats. In real terms, the increase in nominal ticket prices in 1920 simply restored the purchasing power of the ticket charges to prewar levels.

The Yankees were likely to have been the best-drawing team on the road after the acquisition of Babe Ruth, thereby boosting their road receipts. The Yankees also received a boost to their exhibition revenues with the acquisition of Ruth. There is no available data on exhibition revenue for other teams, but given the popularity of Ruth, it is likely that the Yankees gained significantly more revenue from this source than other teams. The team earned only small concession revenues until it moved into Yankee Stadium in 1923, but by 1925 such revenue matched and then exceeded exhibition game revenues.

The Yankees payroll in nominal terms rose consistently after 1918. The team's payroll, adjusted for changes in the general price level, however, reached a low in 1918 and then rebounded, although it would not exceed the 1915 real payroll until 1922. The team's ratio of payroll to total revenue was very high in 1915–18, but fell below 25 percent for most of the 1920s, aside from 1925 (when the team went into an unexpected slump) and 1929 (table 7).

Economist Michael Haupert and accountant Kenneth Winter painstakingly pored through the New York Yankees' financial ledgers held at the National Baseball Hall of Fame. They calculated the team's profit on the team, before taxes and depreciation. They also calculated the profit on Yankee Stadium for four years. Their work is shown in table 8. The team consistently earned a profit after World War I and throughout the 1920s.

The team's smallest profit was in 1925, when the team finished seventh. The team was generally more profitable than a similar investment in the Dow Jones Industrial Average.[24]

Rich and Not-So-Rich Owners

Baseball owners were a disparate group of men. Although a few were genuinely rich by 1920s standards, none of the owners of the 1920s would rival today's wealthiest owners (even after adjusting for inflation), such as Paul Allen and Mark Cuban. Jacob Ruppert owned a large brewery, among his other businesses, but he was nowhere near the Rockefeller, Carnegie, or J. P. Morgan class of wealth, nor was Charles Stoneham, despite his reputed $10 million in wealth. Ban Johnson had struggled to rid the game of unsavory owners; Frank Farrell, original owner of the New York Yankees was an ex-saloonkeeper, but he was also politically connected.[25] Some owners were former players turned capitalists: Connie Mack, Charles Comiskey, and Clark Griffith. All too often, though, these players turned owners had slender capital reserves. They may have held an advantage in being more astute judges of talent than owners coming in from other industrial endeavors, but wealthy owners like Ruppert could hire baseball men such as Edward Barrow to counterbalance the player-owners' acumen.

Sports leagues often have stringent rules concerning transfer of ownership. A new owner is a matter of concern for all owners. An owner with unsavory habits can reflect poorly upon the league. An owner with inadequate capital can create financial turmoil.[26]

Co-ownership did not always work. When T. L. Huston sold his half share in the Yankees to his partner, Jacob Ruppert, the overall effect was probably beneficial for the team. Baseball people believed that Ruppert knew more about baseball than did Huston, although the latter's engineering ability proved invaluable during the construction of Yankee Stadium. Huston and Ruppert split over the latter's decision to hire Miller Huggins as manager; Huston favored Brooklyn manager Wilbert Robinson. With Huston gone, Yankee players could no longer pit owner against owner in disputes with Huggins.[27]

The Yankees owners came close to concluding a deal transferring Huston's half interest to Ruppert in December 1922. There were other interested buyers, such as boxing promoter Tex Rickard and circus owner John Ringling, but the co-owners declined any such offers. Huston backed out of the December deal but eventually agreed to all terms; the sticking point had been a clause stipulating that Huston remain out of baseball for ten years. The two reached a final agreement in May 1923, when Huston received $1.25 million for his half ownership of the club; because of the increase in the general price level, though, much of the appreciation in value reflected inflation.[28]

Owning the Yankees club was not devoid of risks. T. L. Huston told reporters, before the Yankees collapsed into a seventh-place finish, "I hate to think what would happen if the Yankees should slump into the second division." After three consecutive pennants, the Yankees became victims of their own newfound success.[29]

American League owners disliked Boston Red Sox owner Harry Frazee almost from the start of his ownership tenure. As early as December 1918, the owners were trying to induce wealthy men to buy the club from Frazee, who was a theater impresario: "the American League desires to be rid of Frazee as an unwelcome man in baseball and a disturbing factor." The reporter speculated that finding a buyer and setting a purchase price "seem to be matters of detail only."[30] St. Louis Browns owner, Phil Ball, referred to Frazee as a "postage stamp" magnate. All of this animosity occurred before Frazee thumbed his nose at Ban Johnson by trading Carl Mays and selling Babe Ruth to the Yankees. Rumors of Frazee's ouster always seemed premature, as Frazee placed a fairly high value on the Red Sox franchise.[31]

An indication of Frazee's precarious finances was the legal wrangle regarding Fenway Park. Since Frazee did not have enough cash to purchase the club outright, former owner Joe Lannin accepted a note for $262,000, "secured by a pledge of the entire issue of the capital stock of the Fenway Realty Trust, subject to mortgage bonds aggregating $25,000." The note came due in November 1919, and Frazee's attorney admitted there were outstanding debts of $60,000. Lannin went to court and obtained an injunction preventing Frazee and an associate from disposing of any stock or from drawing dividends. One can see why Frazee was desperately seeking cash, when he made the Ruth deal.[32]

Frazee was no fool, however. He hired Edward Barrow in January 1918, and Barrow helped him identify and acquire capable players to sustain Boston's pennant drive that season. In 1921 comedian Fred Stone reportedly offered Frazee $756,000 for the franchise, but Frazee denied being contacted by the comedian.[33]

One writer pointed out that at the end of 1918, "The Red Sox, as it stands today, is the greatest collection of baseball talent in either league. . . . Frazee has more trading material than any other club owner in the game. He also has a lot of baseball talent to sell. That is why he is asking such a big price for his club."[34] Frazee eventually sold his club to a group of Columbus, Ohio, businessmen, fronted by Bob Quinn. The sale price was reputed to be $1.25 million. Frazee had bought the Sox for $675,000 in 1916; between 1916 and 1923, the consumer price index increased by 76 percent, so even a price of $1.25 million would have represented a pretty low rate of real return on his investment. Then again, he had stripped the club of most of its assets by 1923. After cautioning Red Sox fans not to expect too much too soon, Quinn assured Boston fans that his ownership group would reward their patience. Quinn had been a savvy baseball executive in the past, but his group could not rejuvenate the Red Sox.[35]

When Frazee sold the Red Sox, one sportswriter was sorry to see him go: "I always liked Mr. Frazee as a magnate, because he frankly admitted that he was a speculator in baseball, and he never wept crocodile tears over the 'good of the game' or pretended that he was a magnate for the sheer disinterested love of the national pastime. Mr. Frazee was anything the Bostonians please but a hypocrite."[36] For American League president Ban Johnson, Huston's exit followed quickly by Harry Frazee's sale of the Red Sox, rid him of two of his staunchest enemies.

Frazee thought his club worth well in excess of $1 million , but the Boston Braves' new owner Judge Emil Fuchs purchased a franchise that some observers believed was worth $1 million. The franchise's previous sales prices lent scant support for this belief.[37]

Some owners developed innovations to improve the game. Charles Ebbets devised the rain check and helped set up the system of rotating holiday playing dates among the ball clubs, thereby ensuring an equal distribution of such lucrative dates while minimizing arguments over them.[38]

When Ebbets died, his will stipulated that his heirs sell the club within ten years. One reporter cited estimates of the club's value of $3 million, since "the Brooklyn club is considered one of the soundest organizations financially in professional baseball . . . [because] the fact that the Brooklyn fans are steady patrons of Ebbets Field and the Robins are able to play nineteen Sunday games [per season]."[39]

What appeared to be a clear-cut transfer proved to be a contentious battle. Ebbets held half the shares in the team; upon his death, Edward McKeever became president of the team. The Ebbets's heirs called a meeting of the board of directors in order to give manager Wilbert Robinson a new contract and to retain him as club president, thereby instigating a long-standing feud between owners in Brooklyn. Ed McKeever quickly succumbed to influenza in late April 1925, not long after Ebbets died on April 18. If you want to talk about baseball curses, this one ranks pretty high. Some people thought T. L. Huston would seek half ownership of the Dodgers.[40]

Thereafter Brooklyn fell into chaos, as the McKeever and Ebbets heirs bickered and fulfilled Abraham Lincoln's observation that a "house divided against itself cannot stand," and the Dodgers continued a string of sixth-place finishes (seven such finishes between 1922 and 1929, including five consecutively). The team had adequate attendance to remain solvent but was a chronic headache for the rest of the National League. The league officials eventually tried to involve Landis in the ownership feud.[41]

William Wrigley applied some of his gum-manufacturing experience to running the Chicago Cubs. Wrigley used advertising to publicize the Cubs. He initially sought to obtain established stars, whether through purchases or trades. The Cubs won the 1918 pennant with newly acquired stars Grover Alexander and catcher William Killefer, but Wrigley gradually realized that buying veteran players was an expensive process due to their tendency to deteriorate quickly. He told reporters in 1922 that he felt the Cubs should develop young players, but this strategy was temporary.

After a last-place finish in 1925, Wrigley announced that he was (again) on a buying spree and was willing to spend a million dollars to provide Cubs fans with a winner. Wrigley had already made an astute hire in William Veeck Sr., father of the later impresario Bill Veeck Jr. Although Veeck Sr. was not as imaginative as his son, he knew how to draw crowds. Even with a purported million dollars to spend, Wrigley found it difficult to buy a pennant. Wrigley made a second strong hire in 1925 when he hired Joe McCarthy to run the Cubs. By the late 1920s, the Cubs would outdraw every team in baseball.[42]

Clark Griffith proved willing to spend money to obtain players during the 1920s. After he took over the Washington Senators, the club's fortunes improved, culminating in three pennants in ten years (1924, 1925, and 1933). Griffith's shallow reserves of capital, though, eventually caught up with him, and the Senators fell back into their accustomed mediocrity after 1933. Griffith was handicapped by playing in a relatively small city. He exemplified the "sportsman" model of ownership: "As long as I can make a living out of baseball, everything else to give Washington a winner." A sportswriter may have exaggerated in stating, "[Griffith] has known the days when he wasn't so sure as to where and when he would eat," but Griffith's pocketbook could not sustain winning teams in Washington. When he got good returns for his spending, he prospered, but his margin for error was slender.[43]

Charles Stoneham was a broker on Wall Street. He was well connected with Tammany Hall, the ruling political machine. Along with McGraw and Francis McQuade, Stoneham acquired control of the New York Giants early in 1919 from John Brush's heirs.[44]

When Tex Rickard was unable to purchase the Yankees, he considered buying the New York Giants. He hoped to own sports arenas in several large northeastern cities so he could avoid having to lease or rent suitable venues for his roster of sporting events. He claimed he had offered the Yankees $2 million for a half interest and $4 million for sole ownership; he also claimed to have offered $2.5 million for 51 percent of Giants stock.[45]

Alva Bradley and a group of investors purchased the Cleveland Indians from James Dunn's family after Dunn died. The rumored price was $950,000.[46] Bradley hadn't owned the Indians very long before he realized just how valuable owning a club was in terms of advertising. He related how he had recently attended a conference of railway associates, and reporters and photographers had ignored the railway executives. He said, when he attended the baseball owners' meetings, "Nearly a hundred of the greatest baseball writers in America were present. A dozen photographers and motion picture camera men 'shot' us three times a day. . . . I was fairly dazed by the importance given baseball by the press."[47]

The St. Louis Cardinals at one time resembled the football Green Bay Packers in one respect: widespread community ownership. Before America's entry into the war in Europe in April 1917, the Cardinal stockholders numbered seven hundred, although plans had been for up to ten thousand. Eventually Sam Breadon began acquiring blocks of stock, and by May 1922, he held a controlling interest.[48]

Jacob Ruppert told reporters that he thought the overall value of all the clubs in Major League Baseball was roughly $50 million. He speculated on the reasons for the escalation in values, recalling that Huston and he had each paid around $250,000 to acquire the Yankees in 1915. Ruppert attributed the growth to "the existence of all other sports. That is, people have become interested in other sports and this has given them interest in baseball." In addition, he cited the number of college players and the better behavior found at the ballpark, both on the field and in the stands. The improved behavior, in turn, encouraged female patrons.[49]

Instead of viewing the influx of new owners with greater wealth, such as Stoneham, Bradley, Ball, and Ruppert, with concerns that such men were interested solely in the bottom lines, one writer argued for the Cleveland owners, at least, "It was civic pride that took them into the American League. . . . They wished to advertise the city of Cleveland."[50]

Detroit was a growing city due to the rapid expansion of the automobile industry. As early as 1929, owners of teams in St. Louis and Cincinnati considered moving their franchises to the Motor City (never mind what the Tigers thought of such trespass). Baseball officials began to realize by the end of the decade that St. Louis was incapable of supporting two Major League teams, and Detroit was an attractive alternative.[51] As evidence, James Gould pointed out that the Browns, even with a fourth-place team, drew fewer people than the last-place Red Sox. He noted that some observers considered the city as "a poor baseball city," but he thought contending teams could draw well there. The fact the two teams shared the same ballpark reduced stadium overhead, but it also meant the two owners had to agree on basic decisions. Agreement wasn't always forthcoming.[52]

Franchise Values

Franchise values should reflect expected future profits, often based in part on past profits. Such expected future profits should also reflect the value of baseball owners' property rights and institutions, such as the reserve clause, territorial rights, Minor League draft, and so on. Changing these property rights could affect franchise values.

The information on franchise sales are suspect. Newspaper accounts sometimes reported erroneous figures. Economists James Quirk and Rodney Fort compiled a list of all sales, based largely on newspaper accounts. Some of the transactions dealt with part ownership, and these sales were adjusted to reflect a full-ownership value. Relatively few owners lost money selling their franchises, although such losses did occur on occasion.

Fans of *The Antique Roadshow* and similar shows are often impressed by a doubling in an antique's price. If you hold an asset for several years, doubling your money may not be as impressive as it sounds. The rule of seventy-two provides a quick way to estimate how long an asset takes to double in value. You simply divide seventy-two by the interest rate. An asset earning 4 percent a year would double in value in eighteen (72 divided by 4) years. Although 4 percent a year is a respectable rate of return, it would not drive viewers of *The Antique Roadshow* into ecstasy.

Owners of professional sports teams have to adjust their capital gains for two factors. The first is the change in the general price level, what most people call inflation. What is important is the change in an asset's real, inflation-adjusted value. With the inflation of the late 1910s, an owner purchasing his team in 1902 and selling in the 1920s might receive a handsome increase in his franchise's nominal value. Taxes are levied on nominal, not inflation-adjusted gains; in addition, capital gains tax rates fell in 1922.[53] After adjusting for changes in the price level, though, his return might not be so handsome and could even be a loss. The other factor is risk. Although owners rarely went bankrupt owning a MLB team, a few owners have required bailouts to stay in business.

According to Quirk and Fort's list, there were nine franchise sales between 1919 and 1929. Three involved the Boston Braves (table 9). Four of the sales occurred in 1919–20, years of rapidly increasing prices. The Detroit Tigers sold for $1 million in 1920; the owner had paid $50,000 for the team in 1903. This appears to be a twenty-fold increase in the franchise's value, but after adjusting for the price level, the franchise's value jumped a still-impressive nine-fold.

Quirk and Fort concluded that franchises were "relatively undervalued in the 1901–1919 period, and relatively overvalued in the 1920s (from hindsight)." Their table 2.8 (not shown) suggests that franchises purchased in the 1920–29 period and sold within that decade entailed a 12.6 annual rate of decrease; if such franchises were held to 1930–39, franchises purchased between 1920 and 1929 had an average decrease of –0.6 percent. The Boston Braves changed hands three times between 1919 and 1925. The team's nominal value rose and fell during those sales. The Cincinnati Reds' franchise increased from $146,000 to $1.2 million between 1902 and 1929, but in real terms the rate of increase was 5.4 percent a year. The Washington Senators sale in 1919 involved a loss in real terms, even though the franchise appreciated in nominal terms. Mike Haupert updated Quirk and Fort's compilation and determined that throughout the twentieth century owning a MLB franchise only returned a negative capital gain to its owners during the Great Depression.[54]

Franchise Sales and Proposed Relocations

Baseball had weak franchises. Philadelphia, Boston, and St. Louis each had difficulty sustaining two Major League teams. In Philadelphia and

Boston, fans had at least recently witnessed World Series in 1914–16, and 1918. St. Louis had never hosted a World Series during the first two decades of the twentieth century.

The Phillies had their moment of glory by winning the pennant in 1915. After that, the franchise deteriorated like a mansion in a Tennessee Williams novel. Owner William Baker struggled to keep his team respectable. By the late 1920s the Baker Bowl was attracting scant crowds.

The St. Louis Cardinals were in dire straits. After her uncle, Stanley Robison, died, Helene Britton inherited the club. She ran the team for six years, becoming the first female owner of a professional sports franchise before selling it in 1917 for $350,000 (ballpark included) to a syndicate of St. Louis businessmen headed by Sam Breadon. By 1918 the team had a multitude of stockholders. The stockholders, though, had scant reserves, and the directors spent part of 1918 figuring out how to generate $50,000 to buy players to bolster the club. A few months later, the officials were begging stockholders to come up with a loan of $90,000 after having recently subscribed $50,000 to defray expenses. The team was clearly hemorrhaging money.[55]

The Boston Braves had fallen on difficult times after their stunning pennant and World Series triumphs in 1914. By 1918 all that glory was in the past, and the unpaid bills were accumulating. Present owners hoped to induce former owner James Gaffney to take over the club; Gaffney retained Braves Field, so it was plausible that he would be interested. The situation was so dire that the other National League owners placed the issue on the agenda for the upcoming meetings.[56]

With the Cardinals and Braves teetering on financial disaster, a Toronto entrepreneur, James McCaffery, was rumored to be making an effort to obtain one of the teams with the intention of moving it to Toronto. National League officials promptly dismissed the rumor, calling it absurd.[57] Toronto had earlier sought the Washington Senators in 1918; the year before, a rumor arose that the Senators would be heading to Brooklyn. Who thought up the latter rumor was never divulged; Ban Johnson denied the story. Braves stockholders had somehow put their financial house back into solvency, and James Gaffney pronounced himself satisfied; the franchise sale rumor swirling around the Braves quieted for a while.[58]

A few weeks later, George Washington Grant, a motion picture and theatrical promoter (shades of Harry Frazee!), purchased the Braves. New York Giants manager-owner John McGraw encouraged Grant to purchase the team. Grant reputedly paid $400,000 for the club and assumed a lease on Braves Field.[59] Because of McGraw's involvement, fans would wonder why he seemed to get most of Boston's best players in years to come. A few years later, Christy Mathewson and some associates purchased the Braves. A *Sporting News* writer pointed out that the chummy relationship between the Giants and the Braves was likely to persist, given that Mathewson was one of McGraw's closest friends; the reporter called on McGraw and Stoneham to issue a statement saying they had no financial ties with the new ownership.[60]

Clark Griffith gained control of the Washington Senators early in 1920. The new ownership group elected him president. The franchise had been mediocre for most of its history, but pitcher Walter Johnson was one of the game's most valuable assets.[61]

A Prosperous Decade?

Baseball teams generally reported profits during the 1919–29 seasons. Franchise values increased rapidly, but the significant hike in the general price level accounted for much of the gains in nominal franchise values. The moribund Boston Braves somehow kept afloat during the decade.

Could the baseball owners have done better? The motion picture industry, for instance, appeared to have grown more rapidly during the decade than baseball.

5   Getting Fans to the Ballpark

Owners worried about generating enough revenue to remain solvent, if not profitable. The key source of revenue during the 1920s remained gate receipts. Owners needed to attract sufficient numbers of fans to their ballparks.

Baseball's Improved Image

Baseball used to have an image problem. Brawling players and fans, dilapidated ballparks, gambling, and other unsavory aspects limited baseball's appeal for potential middle- and upper-class patrons.

By 1920, though, *Baseball Magazine* could tout baseball's hard-won respectability. Its editor pointed out that "to be an owner or a league official has become a distinction, while to be considered a fan is the proper heritage of every American from President Coolidge down."[1]

Social commentators often lauded baseball. The documentary-filmmaker Ken Burns had nothing on these observers with regard to rhapsodizing about baseball. Although juvenile delinquents are more associated with the 1950s, troubled youths have plagued American throughout the country's history. In the 1920s some sociologists discovered that programs promoting baseball among youth paid off in reduced crime statistics.[2]

Of course, many Americans saluted the canard that baseball was open to all, converting the unwashed immigrant into a true-blue American. The wonderful motion picture, *Pride of the Yankees*, depicted this transformation, as the youthful Lou Gehrig's love of baseball was initially dismissed by his immigrant parents. Of course, once they realized Lou's baseball ability (and ability to make good Yankee dollars), they became baseball fans. Irving Sanborn characterized this transformative process as, "a great factor in leveling artificial barriers, either social or economic;" he recounted seeing President William Taft conversing with Nick Altrock, baseball clown.[3]

Organized baseball lacked known descendants of sub-Sahara Africa, but neither was it completely silent on race. The editor of the *Sporting News* wrote, "a tacit understanding [exists] that a player of Ethiopian descent is ineligible—the wisdom of which we will not discuss except to say by such rule some of the greatest players in the game has ever known have been denied their opportunity."[4] Baseball was not at the forefront of civil rights for all, and, given contemporary social mores, it may well be unfair to demand that it should have integrated before Jackie Robinson. The tragedy is that the editor's claim about "some of the greatest players" remains unproven. There is no doubt, based on the experiences of the 1940s and 1950s, that several African American players were capable of rivaling Ruth and Cobb, but which ones?

Baseball Magazine issued its own encomiums about baseball and about itself when its editor wrote it "is a worthwhile periodical in a worthwhile field. It is the clean publicity organ of a clean sport. In these days when the newsstands are cluttered with a veritable epidemic of cheap, flamboyant and trashy periodicals, it should be a source of satisfaction to every father of a growing boy that he can take home to his son a magazine whose text pages are free from emotional rot and whose advertising carries no immoral taint." Whew! One of its reporters, Irving Sanborn, suggested enshrining baseball's sacred records in a library or hall of records, a prototype of a hall of fame.[5]

Not everyone was enamored of baseball's popularity during the 1920s. A college professor was reputed to refer to a baseball crowd as an "assemblage of Morons": "The hoarse shouts of the spectators, their quick anger at umpires' decisions; their wild excitement and childlike joy at what seemed like trivial things, were suggestive to his cynical eye, of undeveloped mentality."[6]

As baseball trumpeted its collegiate alumni, it failed to confront a less-appealing aspect. During the 1920s, baseball had a drug problem: alcohol.

Thanks to Prohibition, it was illegal to *sell* most forms of consumable alcohol. For some ballplayers, being on the road half the time during the baseball season may have proven daunting. Some players disliked big cities or missed their families. Some players were simply vulnerable to alcohol. Baseball prided itself on ridding the image of a group of drunken, carousing players from the public's mind. The focus on alcohol abuse was now concentrated on individual players. Irving Sanborn reflected that players seeking to drink had little difficulty finding such beverages. He worried that the lure of "forbidden fruit" induced some players to drink since he felt they were, by nature, risk seekers and dare-devils. The bootleggers generally served drinks with higher alcohol content than beer, since smuggling shifted the incentives toward stronger drinks.[7]

The game's growing respectability, though, helped to draw large crowds of middle- and upper-class fans.

Population

Using city population figures from U.S. Bureau of the Census, the 1920s witnessed growth in the major cities of America (tables 10 and 11). Of the ten cities having Major League Baseball teams in 1920, Detroit grew the fastest between 1920 and 1930. Chicago and New York also grew rapidly; Boston, Philadelphia, and St. Louis, however, grew at more modest rates. Pittsburgh's suburbs grew faster than the city. Aside from Detroit and Pittsburgh, the three remaining cities with just one team each grew at remarkably similar rates, whether in terms of city or metropolitan population. If city population was more relevant for a team's ability to generate large crowds and revenue, then the population shift augured ill for Boston, Philadelphia, and St. Louis. By the 1950s, these cities would all become one-team cities.

Attendance

The owners misjudged demand for baseball games in 1919. In the aftermath of the war in Europe and the war with the Federal Leagues, the owners could be excused for timidly approaching the 1919 season. They decided to shorten the season by fourteen games. Attendance rebounded strongly from 1918, catching the owners by surprise (table 12). Despite the truncated season and a runaway pennant race in the National League, attendance matched that of 1916. The 1920 season far exceeded the previous MLB attendance high in 1907 (9.1 to 7.1 million).

The New York Yankees became the attendance bellwether for MLB. After obtaining Babe Ruth from the Boston Red Sox prior to the 1920 season, the Yankees typically drew well in excess of one million fans per season. Yankees owner Jacob Ruppert, though, had sobering evidence that New York fans would not support a mediocre Yankees team. The Yankees attendance ranged from 619,000 to 1,289,000 between 1919 and 1929, although the lower figure occurred in 1919. The team's lowest attendance mark during the 1920s was 697,000 in 1925.

After the Yankees left the Polo Grounds, the Giants strained to exceed 900,000 and never attained the million-attendance mark until 1945. The Yankees exceeded each of their American League rivals' attendances figures by more than 2.8 million across the 1919–29 seasons. In the National League, the Giants were less than 600,000 ahead of the Chicago Cubs. The National League had two of the worst-drawing teams in MLB with the Braves and Phillies, while the Red Sox trailed all American League teams.

Owners, though, experienced large fluctuations in attendance. Aside from the New York Giants, all owners had seasons where their attendance was less than half their peak attendance of 1919–29. Some of these owners, though, suffered their weakest attendance in 1919, although in most cases, even the addition of seven home games would still have left the attendance well below half of their best season.

Robert Burk believes that owners boosted the offense in an attempt to jump attendance for 1920. We'll test whether this thesis is true with respect to home runs. He leaves unstated why owners would forego attendance in previous years with limited offense, unless they worried about having to pay players more for higher batting averages and more home runs (offensive statistic illusion). Why they wouldn't offset this by paying "worse-performing" pitchers less was not indicated. Burk is not the only historian who believes this attendance-boosting motive existed.[8]

There is some evidence to back Burk's claim. Regression analysis suggests that home runs had a positive effect upon attendance during the 1920s and 1930s. The effects were on the order of eight to nine hundred more fans per additional home run.[9]

A team's ability to generate large crowds was based partly, of course, on its quality. The other key factor was the team's population base. The Yankees, Giants, and Dodgers held huge advantages over the Pirates and Reds in terms of city or metropolitan population. To some degree, though, New York's advantage was offset by the city's much wider offering of entertainment venues. No other city boasted New York's collection of theaters, music halls, museums, and the like. The congressional committee analyzed attendance data for 1931–50 and discovered that "the paid attendance ranking of 10 of the 16 major-league clubs is identical with the ranking of retail sales in their metropolitan areas." Of the six teams not matching, the Red Sox and Cardinals typically were contenders, while the White Sox, Athletics, and Phillies were losers.[10]

Some teams had a disproportionate number of downtown office workers. The Yankees and Giants were conveniently located to New York's central business area. Many white-collar and clerical workers could leave the office for a weekday afternoon game. Washington DC had a similar advantage.[11]

Weather factors affected attendance, too. Although baseball's 154-game schedule mitigated the weather factor relative to professional football's (whose teams played a handful of home games during the fall; bad weather for any particular home game loomed large in an owner's fears), weather could still exert a significant effect upon season attendance. The loss of a holiday doubleheader, for instance, might send an owner into conniptions. Owners even considered buying rain insurance; such insurance would reduce the risk, but the expense ultimately may have been better borne by the owner.[12]

Baseball attendance rebounded strongly in 1919 and 1920. Peace, prosperity, and Babe Ruth each contributed, no doubt. The *New York Times* featured article after article on fans being turned away from the Polo Grounds and new attendance marks being set. The Yankees with Ruth, of course, were the main attraction in 1920. Record crowds saw the Yankees in Boston and Washington during the first week of July.[13]

In the baseball-mad world of 1920, even an exhibition game featuring Ty Cobb could conjure a crowd of thirty thousand for one game on the West Coast. H. G. Salsinger attributed to what he considered Cobb's superiority, especially in the eyes of baseball cognoscenti: "Ruth is simply a freak, while Cobb is a phenomenal product of a highly developed pastime. Cobb is a super-intellect, Ruth a cave man slugger. Cobb will stand alone as long as baseball is played."[14]

Despite the game's prosperity in 1919 and 1920, owners were worried about the upcoming 1921 season. The residue of the White Sox scandal and concerns about whether the Babe Ruth phenomenon was ephemeral raised doubts. The country's economy proved shaky, too. John Sheridan played Cassandra by doubting that attendance "will be within 30 percent as good as 1920;" there was a decrease in attendance of 500,000 (the White Sox alone accounted for nearly 60 percent of this total). This drop was on the order of 6 or 7 percent not 30, and baseball still enjoyed a good season in 1921. Baseball officials downplayed the decrease in attendance, attributing it to the economic conditions.[15]

The Boston Braves demonstrated that fans were willing to see an improved product. The Braves finished an unaccustomed fourth place in 1921, and the team's attendance almost doubled from that of 1920 (albeit to only 319,000).[16]

Inept teams dreaded September. Unless a contender came to town, attendance at meaningless games dwindled. Thomas Rice described the dreary games at Ebbets Field during the late stages of the 1922 race. He cited attendance of 1,500 to 2,500 per game and noted, "the mental attitude of the fans is that a man does not go to a National League park nowadays, if he has somewhere else to go."[17] But even pennant winners witnessed a sharp drop in attendance once they clinched the pennant. For almost everyone, a runaway pennant race was deleterious. The problem for baseball was that no individual owner had an incentive to restrain himself in acquiring talent."[18]

The New York Yankees' new stadium quickly attracted large crowds, setting records for a single regular-season game (a reported 74,200 for an opening-day game with the Red Sox in 1923).[19] The irony was that the Yankees, despite their new stadium, would fail to draw as many fans as they had during their last two seasons at the Polo Grounds. They would have to wait until after World War II to do so.

The Giants, with their enlarged Polo Grounds, set a single-game attendance record at that venue a month later with 42,000 in attendance. They still badly lagged the Yankees in attendance.[20]

When the Giants and Yankees met for the 1923 World Series, they failed to sell out the games. Only 34,172 fans showed up for one of the games at the Polo Grounds, well below the enlarged stadium's capacity.[21] Part of the reason for the failure to sell all of the tickets was that World Series tickets cost far more than regular-season tickets. Owners were more interested in maximizing revenues and profits than they were in maximizing the number of tickets sold.

The New York teams' repeated success between 1921 and 1924 may have bored fans. Both teams' attendance figures were lower in 1924 than in 1921; the Yankees failed to win the 1924 pennant. Both teams were involved in tough pennant races in 1924. One New York writer speculated, "the city has grown a little blasé and indifferent about a world series. That has come to have too much the air of a family affair. There is a quiet but pervasive feeling that it would be a good thing for baseball if outsiders were to win the pennant."[22]

During the 1920s, attendance figures for individual games were difficult to obtain. The box scores did not list attendance figures until many years later. Although the leagues often issued yearly attendance figures for the league, owners sometimes felt it was better to keep such information secret. Publicizing prosperity could embolden potential interlopers to start up another league; after all, Federal League owners, seeing baseball's prosperity in the prewar years, had decided to get into the industry.[23]

Reporter Irving Sanborn cautioned readers about reported attendance figures. During the American and National League war of the first years of the twentieth century, owners reported bloated figures in order to demonstrate superiority. Players believed these figures and began to believe they were being cheated of World Series receipts; owners showed players the true figures and quelled the unrest. Visiting team officials always inspected the turnstiles and met with home club officials for a settlement; the league also required accurate records, at least in part because league offices were due a percentage of the gate.[24]

Although the Yankees and Giants faltered in 1925, attendance at all Major League games held steady with 1924, even though the Yankees' attendance fell by 350,000. The Philadelphia Athletics and Washington Senators enjoyed banner seasons at the gate.

By 1927, Major League Baseball flirted with the ten-million mark in total attendance. The American League first exceeded five million during the 1924 season, while the National League finally attained this milestone in 1927. Baseball recorded its first ten-million attendance figure in 1930.[25]

The New York Times reported that the Yankees set a new record for home attendance in 1927: 1,264,015. The figure in Total Baseball was 1,164,015. The Yankees reportedly drew 982,081 on the road that season.[26] Fan ennui in the wake of the Yankees' three consecutive pennants between 1926–28 seemed confirmed by the drop in league attendance from 5.2 million in 1925 to 4.2 million in 1928, despite a tight pennant race in the latter year.

Was New York City such a great baseball town? Sportswriters Joe Vila and John Sheridan raised some interesting points. Vila, ever the New York (Giants) partisan, argued that it was best for baseball if both New York clubs were strong since it was by far the largest city in the country. Vila also inferred that all star players wanted to play in New York because they could get more money. Sheridan, though, thought that crowds for Babe Ruth's games at the Polo Grounds were exaggerated. He also pointed out that prior to Ruth's arrival, the Yankees were not a particularly good-drawing club.[27]

After the Yankees' second straight pennant in 1927, some baseball people worried that the seemingly limitless Yankee dollars would relegate the other seven league members to being dwarves to the Yankees Snow White. League president E. S. Barnard begged to differ. He told reporters that the other teams had strengthened themselves and that the 1928 race would be competitive. The race was competitive—for two clubs, at least. The Yankees and Athletics fought down to the last few games, but everyone else was out of the race early on.[28]

As the decade waned, the Chicago Cubs became the pace setters for crowds. The team set an attendance record of 1,485,166 in 1929 (and came close to the same mark in 1930). This mark was well above anything the Yankees had drawn, despite the Cubs having a much smaller stadium capacity. Despite the disparity in the sizes of Yankee Stadium and Wrigley Field, the latter had a much greater number of box seats, enabling the Cubs to generate healthy gate receipts.[29]

The St. Louis Cardinals, even with a pennant-winning team, struggled to get a half million attendees in 1930, a large drop-off from its 1928 team's attendance (761,000). The Cardinals, now one of the National League's top teams, would prove to be a drag upon league attendance during the 1930s. *Baseball Magazine* pointed out that the Cardinals began relying upon Sunday doubleheaders to generate large crowds, while Sam Breadon advertised upcoming games in the newspapers.[30] The moribund Browns were much, much worse at the gate.

Schedules

Schedules mattered. Owners of professional sports teams often fought hard to get favorable schedules, which usually meant home dates on weekends and holidays. Major League teams typically had some of their largest crowds on the holidays and often celebrated with a doubleheader. But these doubleheaders were different than the two-games-for-the-price-of-one affair favored by the fans. Fans paid for the morning contest, and when the game concluded, they filed out the stadium. The second game required a separate admittance. Historian Lee Allen claimed that only after the St. Louis Cardinals began the tradition of a scheduled doubleheader for one admission after 1918, did the old-style double-header disappear. In the past few decades, MLB has, on occasion, used similar separate admission setups for playing two games in the same day. Lucrative holidays, such as Memorial Day, Independence Day, and Labor Day were usually rotated, so that every team received an equal share across the years. The holiday dates were assigned intraregionally. For example, in the American League, New York, Philadelphia, Boston, and Washington always played doubleheaders between the four clubs; the western teams did likewise. William Veeck once suggested revising this, but his proposal appears to have gone nowhere.[31]

Owners restricted doubleheaders during the early part of the season, although only a few wanted to schedule doubleheaders then. Some owners purposely used postponed games to their team's advantage. National League president John Heydler tried to end such chicanery by stipulating that postponed games had to be made up at the first available opportunity rather than at the home owner's discretion.[32]

The length of the season was important. Baseball had scheduled 154 games per season for many years. The difficulty of having the 154-game season was that the beginning of the season and the World Series often ran into poor weather, necessitating postponements and rescheduling. For some teams, September became an ordeal of doubleheaders. In deciding the number of games for 1918, American League and National League owners disagreed, with Charles Comiskey advocating 154 games. The military eventually reduced the number to fewer than 140 games that year. Owners also debated whether to play 140 or 154 games for the 1919 season; they opted for the shorter season since they were unclear as to the state of fan demand and also how many players would be available.[33]

Even with a 154-game schedule, though, teams had open dates during the season. One *Sporting News* editorial lamented that some teams had consecutive days off during September; these open dates were scheduled to allow for making up postponed games. Owners filled the gaps with interleague exhibition games. Owners eventually chose to shorten the season in terms of calendar dates; by finishing the season a week earlier, most of the open dates vanished.[34]

The National League owners let Barney Dreyfuss create its schedule. Dreyfuss, of course, had to coordinate the National League schedule with the American League's, since some teams shared a ballpark and other teams simply sharing a city did not like to be both playing in the city on the same day.[35] Both leagues were split into eastern and western groups of four for the purpose of scheduling. Teams usually played three- or four-games stands, although sometimes they would play a single game to take advantage of an open Sunday date.

By the end of the decade, baseball owners had to confront scheduling conflicts with college and professional football. Baseball owners leasing their stadiums to football teams usually gave priority to baseball, creating headaches for the football schedule maker. The two sports' competition for playing dates would only increase in the years to come.[36]

Ticket Prices

Baseball owners were relatively conservative with respect to setting ticket prices. They maintained three or four different admission prices (bleacher, grandstand or general admission, reserved, and box), and these prices did not change much from year to year. Owners did occasionally reclassify seats, as they did for the 1917 season by reducing the number of bleacher seats, possibly due to the lack of competition from the Federal League. Owners usually set prices in multiples of five cents in order to make change quickly at the ticket booths. The Yankees went further, charging $0.50, $1.00, $1.50, and $2.00 during the 1920s (ignoring the war tax). Their superintendent of Yankee Stadium, Charles McManus, said, "To guard against the possibility that some ticket seller may short change a patron who is in a hurry, we supply the men with half dollars. . . . A ticket purchaser might not miss a dime or even a quarter . . . but he would be likely to notice the loss of a half a dollar."[37]

After maintaining stable prices until World War I, despite the jump in the general price levels (about 84 percent between 1916 and 1920), owners raised ticket prices in 1917. Because the federal government imposed a war tax of 10 percent, the owners decided to tack the tax onto the ticket prices. They declared that the fans would have to pay the tax. Because owners wanted to avoid using pennies, the wartime price increases were denominated in nickel increments.[38] The twenty-five-cent bleacher ticket became thirty cents instead of twenty-eight cents. Owners hesitated to raise prices for 1919, as they were unsure as to the fans' demand for baseball. When the season demonstrated the fans' renewed demand for the sport, owners felt more confident.

Surprisingly, Charles Comiskey asserted that he was against any attempt to raise ticket prices—especially prices for bleacher seats—but he was clearly in the minority. A reader might wonder whether, knowing the owners were going to enact higher ticket prices anyway, he decided to posture for his fans by protesting. Reporters cited the higher salaries but also the new stadiums built in the previous decade with better accommodations.[39]

Owners began to prepare the way for significant hikes in ticket prices. They pointed out that the higher price level forced them to pay their players more. As one reporter noted, "Baseball is the only thing in the line of entertainment—or in any other line . . . which did not advance in prices because of war conditions [aside from the war tax] . . . prices at the major league parks have remained stationary." Owners were not crying wolf regarding rising salaries. By 1920 average MLB salaries had climbed 20 percent from their prewar level of 1917, and they would increase steadily throughout the decade, experiencing double-digit growth each year from 1921–23. By 1926 the average MLB salary had grown from $3,227 in 1917 to $6,434.[40]

Owners also bemoaned the war tax. The *Sporting News* characterized the idea that baseball was a "luxury" and therefore subject to the tax as ludicrous. The editor then became shrill: "A ten percent tax on baseball receipts at this time would mean confiscation practically, and is unthinkable."[41]

After the war, the federal government wanted to impose an additional 10 percent tax, and a *New York Times* reporter noted, "Witnessing a baseball game is merely recreation to most spectators and is something that they will first dispense with in the event of a heavy tax."[42]

Thomas Rice presaged 1970s economist Arthur Laffer's idea on taxation: at high enough rates, people will stop buying the product and tax revenue from the product will dwindle. Rice simply used the "killing the goose that laid the gold egg" motif in suggesting that so many people would stop attending games in the face of a 20 percent tax that there would be little to tax.[43] The government ended the admission-war tax in late June 1928. Many owners correspondingly adjusted prices; for example, $1.65 reserved seats now became $1.50.[44]

The owners voted to increase the actual ticket prices (net of the war tax) on February 11, 1920. They eliminated the $0.25 bleacher seat, with the new price now being $0.50 . Owners were free to adjust the prices of reserve and box seats to meet local demand. For instance, the box seats at the Polo Grounds rose from $0.85 to $1.00. The Giants also reduced the number of $0.50 bleacher seats, opting to charge $0.75 for most of the bleacher section. The Brooklyn team charged $1.00 for general admission and $1.25 for reserved seats; they priced the box seats at $1.65, although they dropped the bleacher price from $0.55 to $0.50.[45]

Comiskey must have been pleased with the ticket price increase. During the Black Sox trial, White Sox records showed that the team's gate receipts rose a whopping 75 percent, from $521,175.75 to $910,206.59 between 1919 and 1920. The increase was due to the closeness of the pennant race in 1920; the addition of seven home games; and the increased ticket prices. The White Sox' 33 percent attendance increase from 627,186 to 833,492 only partially explains the revenue growth. The average ticket price increased from $0.83 to $1.09, indicating the effect of the ticket price increase or a massive move from the bleachers to the higher-priced seats.[46]

The general price level fell after 1920, raising calls to reduce the ticket prices. In addition, the economy went into a recession early in the 1920s. Owners resisted reducing the prices since players were not willing to settle for smaller salaries (in nominal terms of dollars). By 1922 though, prices stabilized for the remainder of the decade.[47]

Pittsburgh owner Barney Dreyfuss was not pleased with the higher admission prices. He told reporters, "low prices are the bone and sinew of all business. Then the patrons of baseball are entitled to the best possible accommodations at the lowest possible prices. I would much prefer to have 10,000 persons at a baseball game with a gross gate of $5,000 than 5,000 persons with a gross gate of $5,000. The greater the number of daily spectators the cheaper we can make the admission fees." Dreyfus wasn't just waxing rhapsodic about a boisterous home crowd. Ten thousand fans will spend a lot more on beer and wieners than will five thousand. Concessions were a nontrivial income source for every team. A few years later, however, Dreyfuss raised the ticket prices for all but the bleacher seats.[48]

Teams were somewhat secretive about their ticket prices. The Yankees were particularly reticent to publish ticket prices. Although the Yankees, Giants, and Dodgers advertised their games in the *New York Times*, only the Giants listed ticket prices during the early 1930s. According to the Yankees' cash books, the team charged the same price for season box-seat tickets: $554.40 for a box of eight seats between 1923 and 1944. The team adjusted the price when the war or amusement tax was in force by tacking on $55.44, making the total price $609.84. The Yankees appeared to charge $0.50 for bleachers, $1.00 for general admission, $1.50 for reserved, and $2.00 for box seats beginning in 1920.[49]

Once owners raised ticket prices in 1920, these prices remained relatively stable for most of the next three decades, although the reinstatement of the war tax (now an amusement tax) in 1932 caused a jump in the overall price of attending a game, as owners once again added the 10 percent tax to the face value of tickets.[50] The Chicago Cubs reduced their prices by 10 percent across the board in 1923, in essence, the club was absorbing the still-extant war tax. The St. Louis Cardinals, on the other hand, raised most of their ticket prices between 1923 and 1925, as advertisements in the *Sporting News* revealed; the Browns charged the same prices for the same stadium as the Cardinals as late as 1927, although it had slightly lower prices in 1926.[51]

Some owners had special children's ticket prices. By 1929 the Chicago Cubs and White Sox allowed school children free admittance to three games a week; for other games, the teams charged twenty-five cents. In other cases, New York City councilors wanted to force teams to provide occasional games with twenty-five-cent tickets for youth. The St. Louis Cardinals pioneered the concept of a "Knot Hole" club, whereby boys could enter games for free.[52]

World Series

Baseball's premier event and priced accordingly, the World Series roughly reflected the prosperity or doldrums of baseball. Although year-to-year gate receipts varied due to the number of games played and the participating teams (with their stadiums' varying capacities), the general trend between 1919 and 1929 was upward.

Baseball officials set much higher ticket prices for World Series games, although they reduced the prices for the 1917 series because of the war. By the 1919 World Series, for games at Cincinnati, box seats were priced at $6.60, reserved seats at $5.50 and $3.30, pavilion (unreserved) at $2.20, and bleachers at $1.10; these prices would prevail at most World Series played during the 1920s. Ticket prices were somewhat lower for games at Chicago, but this may have been due to the White Sox's larger stadium. These prices included the 10 percent war tax.[53]

With these ticket prices, owners faced complaints by fans. Fans disliked the distribution of series tickets, which they claimed all too often ended up in the hands of ticket arbitrageurs (scalpers). They charged favoritism and claimed that casual fans got hold of tickets because they were prominent, whereas regular fans had difficulty affording or obtaining tickets. Since owners sometimes did not know until a few days before the World Series opened that they would be hosting the event, they often had to scramble to sell the tickets. They realized that trying to sell all the tickets on the day of the game was infeasible; the crush of people would have overwhelmed their ticket takers.[54]

In one embarrassing incident, Brooklyn hurler Rube Marquard was arrested in a hotel lobby on charges of ticket scalping. Marquard was allegedly trying to sell his eight box seats for $400.00 (the face value was $52.80). He pleaded guilty and was punished . . . with a fine of $1.00 and court costs; Brooklyn quickly got rid of him. Marquard later claimed he was an inadvertent ticket arbitrageur, since he had purchased the tickets for $275.00 and was asked by a passerby if he would sell them.[55]

Teams usually sold World Series tickets in blocks of three games. The Yankees, for instance, put some seats on sale on the date of the game and, in the hopes of forestalling ticket resale, mandated that people had to immediately enter the ballpark upon purchasing a ticket. New York teams may have faced special challenges as many of the people wanting tickets and willing and able to pay inflated prices were bankers entertaining out-of-town guests and customers.[56]

The Bureau of Internal Revenue sometimes assisted baseball owners in combatting ticket resale. Since many tickets were resold by brokers, the bureau had names and addresses; revenue agents monitored the brokers, but their ability to stop the resale mostly depended upon cutting the supply of tickets.[57]

After World War I, owners set ticket prices for box seats at $6.60 during the World Series, roughly triple the regular-season price. They set similar proportional hikes in the prices of other tickets. Some fans and reporters believed these high prices caused some of the negative feeling about the "commercialization" of the sport: "By cutting down the price of World Series tickets, which would reduce the players' share of the spoils, and by eliminating all teams, excepting the rival pennant winners from cutting into those receipts of the first four games, the public, which pays the bills, would be highly gratified."[58]

Owners had carefully arranged the disbursement of the gate receipts. Some of the money went to the National Commission or to the league treasuries. Some of the money went to the participating players (and sometimes players on second- and third-place teams). Owners, wanting to squelch any suspicions that players purposely lost games in hopes of extending the series and sharing more gate receipts, limited the players' share to the first four games (first five when the series was best of nine). Owners, too, may have felt desirous of extending the series. When the Yankees swept back-to-back series in 1927 and 1928, the owners bemoaned the lost gate receipts. Pittsburgh's Barney Dreyfuss ruefully claimed the Yankees' sweep cost him at least $20,000 in cold cash; his Yankee counterparts had to return $170,000 in checks to refund money paid for a fifth game.[59]

The Yankees rarely sold out Yankee Stadium for World Series games, but the club frequently experienced very large crowds. Handling the crowds was a challenge, especially when disseminating information on the number of available tickets was haphazard. As a late-season series between the Yankees and Athletics demonstrated, things could get ugly. Fans mistakenly thought eighty thousand tickets were for sale when there were only eighteen thousand tickets available. "When the supply became exhausted the disappointed ones rushed and roared, or rather roared and rushed," according to one observer.[60]

For the World Series, teams often offered some tickets on sale on the day of the game. Harry Stevens, caterer at Yankee Stadium, knew he had to have plenty of food available when the gates opened at 10:30 for the fans purchasing tickets on the day of the game. He explained that fans holding reserved seats usually had time to have lunch before coming to the stadium, since they didn't have to wait in line to buy tickets.[61]

The Yankees' 1928 World Series opponents, the St. Louis Cardinals, had to return requests for 75,000 reserved seats. The team still had some general admission, bleacher and pavilion seats left, as well as standing-room-only-tickets, but one can imagine owner Sam Breadon's chagrin at having so many unfulfilled requests. The two games of the 1928 series played at St. Louis drew roughly 75,000, while the two games at Yankee Stadium had over 120,000 in attendance.[62]

Even the federal government won big when the Yankees were in the World Series, as tax revenue generally jumped for games at Yankee Stadium. The government estimated it would collect $80,000 in taxes, even though the series was a four-game sweep for the Yankees. The players, too, came out reasonably well with $6,000 per Yankee and $4,000 per Cardinal.[63]

Sunday Baseball

American workers fought hard to get reduced working hours. At the turn of the twentieth century, a growing number of workers worked only five and a half days a week, getting Saturday afternoons and Sundays off. Daily work schedules were gradually shifting from ten hours per day to eight hours. The rise of leisure time was concurrent with the rising popularity of professional baseball, motion picture theaters, and other commercialized leisure.

Baseball owners were of divided opinion regarding playing baseball on Sundays. Some owners, such as the early National League owners, did not play games on Sundays. The American Association chose to play games on Sunday. Old-line protestants objected to playing ball on the Sabbath, especially if such games were commercial. Throughout the late nineteenth century, a bizarre coalition fought Sunday baseball. The coalition included clergy and their parishioners and saloon owners; both sets of constituents feared that baseball would take away "customers." A reporter for *Sporting Life* wrote in 1897:

> that in opposing Sunday baseball the pastors of a number of [Cleveland] churches and the saloon keepers of the city were unconsciously working hand in hand. The opposition of the saloon keepers to baseball on Sunday is even more pronounced than that of the ministers, for it has assumed an organized form. . . . Their [saloonkeepers] opposition to Sunday games is put on PURELY MERCENARY GROUNDS [all caps in original]. . . . Sunday ball games will simply empty the downtown saloons of the city on that day. Men and boys, instead of LINGERING IN BARROOMS [all caps in original] visiting, playing cards or shaking for drinks will go to the games and spend the 75 cents or a dollar each, they would otherwise leave with us.[64]

Chris Von der Ahe avoided this conflict. As a prominent saloonkeeper in St. Louis in the 1880s, he realized that he could sell beer to a captive audience at a ball game. He owned a team in St. Louis, and although he knew little about baseball, he put a strong team on the field. Whether or not he understood the concept of "synergy," he certainly understood the lucrative relationship between baseball and beer.

The issue of Sunday ball was, to some extent, a clash between cultures. Old-line American protestants were uneasy about the influx of immigrants—Catholic, southern and eastern European, Jewish, and other new groups. Maintaining the Sabbath became a form of social control. Opponents of Sunday ball worried that large, unruly crowds would prove disruptive. The onus of demonstrating that baseball crowds would be peaceful and law abiding fell upon the owners. The press ran recurring articles describing the benign behavior at Sunday games. Reporter Joe Vila explicitly cited conflict between workers, who could only watch ball games on Sundays, and the upper class.[65]

John Sheridan penned a more provocative thesis explaining clergymen's resistance to Sunday ball: "Clergymen are human. They want congregations. They want some money. They want audiences. When a clergyman working for $1,500 or less a year reads of the baseball player [and movie star getting large salaries, due to their ability to attract large audiences] . . . he contrasts his empty church, his meager salary and his humble home . . . well, the man is only human."[66]

St. Louis and Chicago baseball owners took the lead in playing baseball games on Sundays. Owners of teams in the eastern cities faced stiffer opposition. Because local laws dictated which teams could schedule home games on Sundays, competitive balance and scheduling became skewed. Owners believed that Sundays were the best-drawing day of the week. If an owner could not schedule home games on Sunday, he presumably lost out on some gate receipts.

Because some teams could not play games on Sundays, their teams had inconvenient open days. To mitigate this inconvenience, some owners scheduled single games in other cities on Sundays. A sportswriter using the nom de plume, Jim Nasium, claimed that the New York and Washington clubs, having gotten the right to play on Sundays, could now "finish last in either league and show a handsome profit on the increased increment from the high attendance at those Sunday games."[67]

Barney Dreyfuss, Pittsburgh owner, was in an anomalous position. His team could not play Sunday games in Pittsburgh, so the other National League owners allowed him more Saturday games, which were the Pirates' most popular day for attendance. Dreyfuss asserted the idea that Sunday games simply siphoned attendance from the other days of the week. In other words, only so many fans would attend games over the season; the large crowds for Sunday games were, in a sense, a mirage. Large Sunday attendance meant smaller attendance at weekday games. Irving Sanborn made a similar argument, pointing out that prior to Sunday baseball, Mondays were the second-best drawing days, behind Saturdays. Brooklyn also gained from its rivals' inability to stage home games on Sunday. Because the Dodgers did not share their ballpark (unlike the Yankees and Giants until 1923), they could accommodate extra Sunday home games. If the Phillies had an open date on Sunday, they could easily travel to Brooklyn; Washington was in a similar position in the American League.[68]

World War I helped alter people's opinions regarding Sunday ball and other moral issues. Prior to the war, the teams in St. Louis, Chicago, Cleveland, Detroit, and Cincinnati could legally play ball on Sundays; the other nine teams could not stage games on Sunday in their ballparks. Due to wartime exigency, the Washington Senators received permission to play Sunday games. The Yankees, Giants, and Dodgers won the right to play such games in time for the 1919 season. The three Pennsylvania and two Massachusetts teams remained unable to play games on Sundays until the early 1930s.[69]

Owners Connie Mack and Charles Ebbets sometimes found themselves hauled before local magistrates on charges of violating blue laws; Ebbets defended himself by testifying that the neighborhood around Ebbets Field remained peaceable during games played on Sundays. Reporter Thomas Rice characterized Brooklyn as the "City of Churches," but Ebbets and the McKeevers, the other owners of the Brooklyn club, had political clout. The Yankees allied with Ebbets to fight for Sunday ball in the Bronx. The blue law originated in 1787 and read: "All shooting, hunting, fishing, playing, horse racing, gaming, and other public sports, exercises, or shows upon the first day of the week and all noises disturbing the peace of the day are prohibited."[70]

Some liberal clergy began urging rescinding the blue laws, as they recognized the beneficial effects of giving working people some amusements to fill their Sunday leisure time. Colonel T. L. Huston of the Yankees, a veteran of two wars, urged passage of legislation allowing Sunday ball using the argument that soldiers benefited from Sunday benefit games during the war and that "soldiers fight and die on Sunday." Another veteran, Charles Muir (of the Canadian army), made a more impassioned argument: "If you deny this pastime, you should tear down the Statue of Liberty, for you take their [veterans] liberty away. I ask you to pass the bill in memory of the men who will never get back to the diamond, the men who have made the great home run."[71]

New York legislators passed the bill permitting Sunday baseball just prior to the 1919 season, so the New York owners scrambled to shift Monday games to Sundays. The league presidents, urging caution, banned Sunday doubleheaders so as to not antagonize church leaders. The owners also pledged that they would not charge more for tickets on Sundays than they charged for games on other days of the week; they kept this promise for decades. Owners got a quick confirmation of Sunday baseball's popularity, when the Giants and Dodgers got inordinately large crowds for their inaugural Sunday games.[72]

When the New York teams got the right to play Sunday ball for the 1919 season, their owners had a new issue to squabble over: the division of Sunday playing dates. Since the Yankees and Giants shared the Polo Grounds before 1923, this obviously was a potentially divisive issue. Some historians seem to think the division of Sunday playing dates created the animosity between the two teams. In 1920 the Giants had thirteen Sundays and the Yankees had twelve, but the Dodgers had nineteen Sunday games. Sportswriters Tom Rice and Harry Williams analyzed the distribution of Sunday games. They believed that if the Yankees had their own stadium, the Giants and Yankees could enjoy more Sunday dates. Rice wrote, "Six Sundays at the Polo Grounds should be well worth more than $50,000 or $55,000 which the Yankees will pay for the use of the grounds this year. In other words, the six Sundays which the Yankees gain at the expense of the Giants should pay the Yankees' rent, and leave them all of their week days in the season rent free."[73]

Pouring oil on the contretemps revolving around the division of Sunday playing dates between the Giants and Yankees was the latter team's new-found popularity. Colonel Huston of the Yankees was not shy about pointing out that the Yankees had drawn more fans to the Polo Grounds than the Giants did for the previous three seasons prior to the Yankees moving into their new stadium. Huston accused Giants owner Charles Stoneham of "entirely mercenary" motives in the Giants owner's willingness to schedule games on the same day at both the Polo Grounds and Yankee Stadium; the Yankees opposed such a challenge. Stoneham argued that with ten million people in the metropolitan area, both teams should be able to fill their stadiums on any given Sunday. He also claimed that local semipro and amateur baseball clubs attracted crowds numbering in the thousands, before he concluded, "We are in favor of as many conflicting dates as possible, as five dates will mean approximately $100,000 to this club, which we consider is a good and sufficient reason." Huston retorted that Stoneham was trying to recoup the loss of stadium rental that the Yankees used to pay.[74]

Stoneham's National League allies, including President John Heydler and Barney Dreyfuss, agreed with the Giants owner that there was no rule prohibiting conflicting dates, and Dreyfuss said the Yankees had no say in the matter. In the end, the matter was settled peacefully; as more clubs throughout the leagues got Sunday baseball, the potential for conflicting dates diminished, since all teams decided to play, at most, half their Sunday games at home, making it simple to avoid conflicts. By the 1930s such a division of Sunday games was institutionalized. The Yankees and Giants never played on the same date, not even for making up postponed games; the Dodgers and Giants rarely shared playing dates unless, of course, they were playing each other. The Dodgers lucked out, as they could fill more Sundays than the other two New York clubs.[75]

Some church leaders in Washington DC and New York refused to accept the new legislation permitting Sunday ball. These leaders attempted to repeat the laws throughout the 1920s. Their efforts failed, but baseball owners remained leery of antagonizing church leaders and congregations.[76]

Owners of teams in Pennsylvania and Massachusetts, aside from Barney Dreyfuss of Pittsburgh, envied their fellow owners' success at getting Sunday ball. Connie Mack; William Baker of the Phillies; Harry Frazee and, later, Bob Quinn of the Red Sox; and Judge Emil Fuchs of the Braves spent the 1920s trying to persuade legislators to grant their team permission to play Sunday ball. A growing number of protestant clergy gave their assent, with Reverend R. P. Kreitler telling attendees at a National Recreation Congress, "Churches must realize that liberty in the use of Sunday is necessary for recreation of the people spiritually and otherwise."[77]

Editorials in *Baseball Magazine* and the *Sporting News* consistently painted foes of Sunday baseball as bigots, who were stymieing the personal freedom to choose. A typical comment read: "The most determined foe of Sunday baseball . . . is that same resolute, well organized and noisy minority that has assumed the self-appointed task of regulating public conduct, and [to] persons such as these, we have nothing to say. Their self-assurance is absolute, their fanaticism is constitutional, nothing but an electric shock or a charge of dynamite would drive home to them a new idea." The same writer wrote two years later: "Slowly but inevitably the blue background of Puritan tradition softens in the whole light of intelligent publicity. The day when Sunday sport in Massachusetts will triumph over well meaning but misguided conservatism may be delayed. . . . For the pendulum of the twentieth century is swinging inexorably away from the superstitions and prejudices of the Middle Ages."[78]

Connie Mack testified that, in his experience with Sunday baseball in other cities, "The people dress a little bit differently and they also seem to have in mind that it is Sunday and do not reprove the players." His co-owner John Shibe contended that the team lost $20,000 a game by not being able to stage Sunday games in Philadelphia.[79]

The team staged a Sunday game on August 22, 1926, but a light rain constrained fan enthusiasm and only ten to twelve thousand fans attended; the crowd was well behaved, and Mack claimed the game did not detract from church attendance. The Athletics and Phillies, though, faced renewed opposition to Sunday ball and would not get a permanent legal right to play such games until the 1930s. Mack later claimed that he had to break up his vaunted 1929–31 championship club because of flagging attendance, exacerbated by his inability to get Sunday crowds.[80]

Judge Emil Fuchs exerted political pull and cash inducements to get Sunday ball in Boston. He had to wait, however, until 1929 to get such permission and was publicly reprimanded for corrupt practices. Boston city councilors raised one issue that proved to be a straw man: Would the Braves and Red Sox set higher ticket prices for Sunday games? The *Sporting News* reported that no team had ever done so, and that it was unlikely the Boston teams would stray from this tradition.[81] When the Braves won the rights, a reporter waxed cynical: "Sunday baseball will draw well in Boston for a while anyway. Neither the Braves nor yet the Red Sox are what could be called a box office attraction. The more they play the greater grows their supporters' distaste. But until the novelty of some place to go Sunday afternoon wears off Boston will be a good money town."[82] The Red Sox were unable to play Sunday ball in Fenway Park, since the park was located within one thousand feet of a place of worship. The team used Braves Field, which had a much greater capacity than Fenway Park, so no tears should be shed for the Red Sox.[83]

Did Sunday ball matter? The three New York teams and Washington had experiences with Sunday ball that were difficult to gauge. Attendance shot up in 1919 and thereafter from the 1917–18 figures, but the wartime conditions muddied the comparison. The two Boston teams and Pittsburgh experienced increases in attendance in the three years after getting Sunday ball compared to the three previous years. The two Philadelphia teams, though, suffered attendance declines; the Athletics' decline was traceable to a reversal in fortunes on the playing field. The team's attendance decline was not halted by the arrival of Sunday baseball in 1934, but perhaps it cushioned the fall.[84]

Regression analysis indicates that gaining the right to play on Sundays boosted a team's attendance by roughly fifty thousand per season. Teams' net incomes, though, were unaffected by Sunday baseball; this finding was surprising and difficult to explain. One possibility is that teams spent more on player salaries. Of the five teams getting night ball in the early 1930s, four paid more in player salaries in 1933 than in 1929, but in a couple of cases the increase was modest.[85]

Competition from Other Sports

The 1920s were referred to as the "Golden Age of Sports." Golf, boxing, college football, and other sports received front-page newspaper coverage. Golfer Bobby Jones, boxer Jack Dempsey, and football player Red Grange were as famous as Babe Ruth. Americans enjoyed more discretionary income, which allowed them to purchase sporting goods, and the gradually shrinking workweek gave them more time to indulge their leisure pursuits. Baseball players found golf similar to baseball; baseball officials, who often loved to play golf, debated the desirability of allowing players to golf during the season or even in the off-season. Some of them went so far as to insert clauses in individual player contracts prohibiting the playing of golf during the baseball season.[86] Baseball officials were more adamant in their opposition to players engaging in football and basketball, even though George Halas dabbled in baseball before becoming a key figure in the National Football League (NFL). Mickey Cochrane, Frankie Frisch, and Jim Thorpe played football in college, as did other players.

Although college football had its fans, today's football fans would find the game a primitive experience. Forward passing was still in its infancy, and all too often, the game resembled a scrum. College football had one advantage—a built-in fan base of alumni. School spirit blossomed during the 1920s as numerous motion pictures attest. Each season during the 1920s, college football's popularity grew and grew, and a few bold souls began to ask whether the gridiron would surpass baseball in popularity. Sportswriter James Gould disparaged college football for its frequent changes in rules, although baseball rules were hardly written in stone during the 1920s (as witnessed by the continuing revisions as to what constituted home runs, sacrifice flies, or intentional walks).[87] College football, while a tremendously popular spectacle in New York and Chicago, was mostly a medium- and small-city phenomenon. South Bend, New Haven, and most of the teams in the Big Ten Conference played in towns that were not major metropolitan centers.

Comparing college football's popularity with Major League Baseball's was difficult. College teams played a handful of games, enabling them to realistically sell out each game, while baseball played seventy-seven home games each season. College-football crowds, though, had to impress observers: 115,000 for a game between Notre Dame and Navy at Chicago's Soldier Field.[88] As professional football owners could attest, though, the limited number of home games for each club rendered the owners vulnerable to vagaries of the weather to a greater degree than baseball owners. On the other hand, admission prices for football games were higher than for baseball games.

Whether these other sports would eventually siphon off fans from the ballpark perplexed Major League owners. A few ventured to hope that fans enjoying one sport would gravitate to other sports, too. Some baseball owners, however, found football a useful secondary source of income. The two sports' schedules did not overlap as much as they do today. Professional football was more conducive to night ball, since the ball was so much larger and the players more concentrated than on a baseball field.[89]

Although football fields were rectangles, some Major League owners of ballparks were able to fit a football field within their fan-shaped ballparks. Jacob Ruppert and T. L. Huston designed Yankee Stadium with the purpose of being a multisport facility. The Yankees took in revenue from leasing their stadium for college games and some professional games. The Yankees' cash books showed receipts for NFL and college games as well as boxing beginning in fall 1923. The Yankees' owners recognized the growing popularity of college football, and both the Yankees and the

Giants hoped to lease their stadiums for big games on Saturdays. The owners were less enthusiastic about leasing their stadiums to the nascent National Football League, given that sport's shaky structure. College games were lucrative business for stadium owners. By 1923 the Yankees hoped to clear $60,000 before expenses for the upcoming Army-Navy game; near the end of the 1920s, the Yankees were rumored to clear $100,000 from an Army–Notre Dame game.[90]

By 1929 Tex Rickard's Sporting Club paid the Yankees $25,450 for renting the stadium for a bout on September 26, 1929. A week later, they received $14,205 for a football game between New York University and Butler. Perhaps reflecting the parlous nature of NFL football, the Yankees received just $7,229 for a game between the football New York Yankees and the Detroit Lions on October 14, 1928.[91]

Charles Stoneham encouraged fellow owner Garry Herrmann's interest in acquiring an NFL team, with the hopes that Herrmann would schedule games at the Polo Grounds.[92] Stoneham's heirs would maintain ties with the NFL for decades to come.

The astonishing rise of Red Grange from college hero to professional football star spurred some baseball owners to consider obtaining professional football franchises. Grange and his agent C. C. Pyle (sometimes dubbed "Cash and Carry") arranged a barnstorming tour as soon as Grange's University of Illinois football career ended. Playing several games within a few weeks' time, Grange raked in a Ruthian sum of money. The following season, C. C. Pyle went too far and set up a new league featuring Grange; the venture failed. The NFL, too, would struggle to remain solvent even after the burst of publicity gained from Grange's association with professional football.[93]

If football was looming large as a competitor for sports fans' interest, the automobile was changing the sports landscape. Minor League owners found that their patrons now had a wider radius of entertainment options as rural and small-town Americans' automobiles enabled them to drive well beyond the radius of that of wagon or horse travel. Baseball owners had to adapt to the growing diffusion of automobiles, including that most vexing problem of all—providing sufficient parking.[94]

Baseball's Attendance Gains

Baseball's prosperity rested, of course, on its ability to draw large crowds willing to pay reasonable ticket prices to ballparks. The owners may have been complacent in the face of record crowds. Did they exploit new innovations such as radio or electric lighting? The owners' actions to bolster crowds are examined next.

6 Trying to Make the Game More Popular

What steps did Major League owners take to bolster their game's popularity? Owners proved conservative throughout the decade—content, perhaps, to enjoy their prosperity.

The Ballpark Experience

The ballpark experience from today's perspective was primitive. Unless you were a frequent patron, you might have had difficulty recognizing the players. Not until the 1929 season did the New York Yankees and Cleveland Indians inaugurate putting visible numbers on the back of their players' uniforms. The Yankees' numbers were based on the players' places in the batting order, with Ruth wearing number three and Gehrig number four. Previously the St. Louis Cardinals had briefly experimented with six-inch-high numbers on shirt sleeves. Owners had earlier considered suggestions for putting numbers on players in 1923.[1] Without uniform numbers, identifying the players was difficult for novices, although some players, such as Babe Ruth, had an inimitable appearance and style. To assist fans, albeit ineffectually, an announcer with a megaphone roamed the first- and third-base lines announcing the starting lineups.

Fans marking scorecards had difficulties since scoreboards often did not relay information on hits or errors. The official scorer decided whether a play was a base hit or an error, but few stadiums had adequate scoreboards or public-address systems to inform fans of the decision. Owners worried that such controversial information might incite fans or might help gamblers (who often placed bets on outcomes of particular plays). An editorial in the *Sporting News* advised, "Anything that aids the fans aids the magnates . . . innovations should be at least tried until found wanting."[2]

If you were fortunate enough to afford an actual seat instead of the bleachers, you would find yourself confined to a narrower seat than today's fans enjoy. When the Dodgers opened their new stadium in Los Angeles in the early 1960s, team officials boasted about the wider, twenty-inch-wide seats in comparison with Ebbets Field's eighteen-inch-wide seats.[3] Frequent fliers will readily understand the benefits of an extra few inches—what economists denote as the "marginal" (incremental) seat width.

Chicago Cub fans may rue Steve Bartman's ill-fated catch of a foul ball during a National League 2003 play-off game. Bartman, at least, got to keep the ball. During the 1920s, cost-conscious owners sent ushers into the stands to retrieve baseballs. Colonel Huston of the Yankees characterized the now-cherished tradition of keeping balls hit into the stands: "this larceny has become a nuisance. That's all it is, petty larceny. Why should a man carry away an object worth $2.50 just because he gets his hands on it? When people go to a restaurant, do they take the dishes or silverware home for souvenirs?" Since baseballs cost $1.25 each when purchased in bulk, Huston was exaggerating the team's loss, although, in the aggregate, teams might have suffered a few thousand dollars per year in expense.[4]

The owners' determination to literally wrest baseballs from the grips of fans ended after an incident in St. Louis. An overly diligent usher and policeman none too gently dragged a ball-grabbing fan to the club office. The fan "presented an appearance of magnificent disarray. It seems that the patrolman took no care to drag him right side up." Cardinals owner, Sam Breadon, realized what a disaster this incident was and eventually settled with the fan for $1,200 (enough to buy almost one thousand baseballs).[5]

Hungry and thirsty fans might have needed a dime or fifteen cents to obtain soda libations and hot dogs. Chances are, the soda would come in an eight-ounce bottle, and the hot dog was probably a miniversion of today's ballpark franks. There were no nachos or pizzas available.

Baseball owners were not usually aggressive in promoting their games. Many felt that it was sufficient to put a good team on the field. Walter Hapgood, business manager of the Rochester team in the International League, though, suggested that owners promote, promote, promote. He advocated advertising in the newspapers, holding ladies' days, keeping ballparks clean and attractive, keeping player uniforms clean and tidy, and not manipulating ticket prices and seat classifications for short-term gains.[6]

Baseball owners had long encouraged women to enter their parks, but they did not seize upon ladies' day for years. The owners hoped having women in attendance would soothe the aggressiveness of some of their male fans; they may have hoped that women baseball fans would induce their male friends to attend or to attend more frequently.

William Wrigley and William Veeck Sr. were pioneers of ladies' day. Although they did not invent the concept, they quickly seized upon it. The Cubs instituted ladies' days in 1927, designating Friday as days where women were admitted free. In time many women became regular paying customers. Not everyone was a fan of mixing women and baseball; Al DeMaree, former pitcher, complained, "wherever the ladies intrude they usually cause trouble." He cited instances where wives of players started cliques that spilled over into the clubhouse. Players, though, liked ladies' days and kept a lookout for attractive women in the stands. In a passage presaging Jim Bouton's *Ball Four*, DeMaree wrote: "In some parks the players cut peepholes in the back of the dugout to spot the 'knockouts,' and then they send notes to them by the ushers. Some players carry field glasses."[7]

Another commentator wrote, more benignly if chauvinistically, "Get a woman talking about baseball and you have a fine ally. If a man finds that his best girl knows all about baseball . . . he will discover a greater need of outdoor air during the baseball season than if he must take Arabella to a movie."[8]

Phil Wrigley instituted ladies' day at his stadium in Los Angeles, too, but his fellow Pacific Coast League owners were none too pleased and tried to bar the practice. By 1929 several of Wrigley's fellow owners in the western regions hopped aboard the ladies' day bandwagon, but team owners in the east seemed hesitant. Wrigley and some of the owners found the concept almost too successful as women jammed their stadiums, displacing paying customers. The New York Giants broke the ranks of the staid eastern clubs by starting a ladies' day during the 1930s.[9] The Yankees appeared to consider ladies' day beneath them and did not schedule any such events until 1938.

Ladies' day made an indelible impression upon some male fans. Years later, a war veteran recalled a Japanese banzai charge: "They made the weirdest sound as they rush at you, screaming. It sounds like Ladies' Day at Ebbets Field."[10]

Rowdy Fans

Rowdy fans have existed pretty much from the beginning of professional baseball. National League organizer William Hulbert prohibited the sale of alcohol at league games. The National League owners professed outrage at the upstart American Association's enthusiasm for selling beer at the ballpark.[11] "Kill the umpire!" was an Americanism both amusing and appalling.[12] Ban Johnson and the American League owners worked hard to reduce rowdyism at their ballparks, including cracking down on umpire baiting by players and fans.

In our era of plastic bottles, readers may have difficulty envisioning soda pop in glass bottles. These bottles held eight ounces or, at most, twelve ounces (the 7-Eleven Big Gulp was decades away), but an empty glass projectile was a potentially lethal weapon. For some reason, owners delayed selling soda pop in paper cups; since they sold other beverages in such cups, it was not as though they lacked this option.

Umpires and players on the opposing team were the usual target of rowdy fans. New York sportswriters took delight in detailing fan misbehavior in Brooklyn, while the *Sporting News* took fans in cities outside of St. Louis to task (the periodical was published in St. Louis). A game between the Chicago Cubs and Dodgers at Ebbets Field on August 11, 1920, resulted in many bottles hurled at umpire Ernie Quigley but no hits. The *New York Times* reporter laconically stated, "The only reason that the poppies of Flanders were not being strewn on Ernie's final resting place last night was because the Brooklyn bottle hurlers were poor marksmen. When the Robins win, the Flatbush fans throw straw hats, score cards and newspapers. When the Robins lose . . . they throw pop bottles."[13]

Even fans at the Polo Grounds were not immune to the allure of throwing bottles, as two hundred engaged in throwing straw hats and bottles. The reporter, however, described the bottles as "tossed, rather than thrown" and the bottles were not aimed at playing personnel or umpires. Fans did not always throw bottles with impunity. About a week later, the police arrested a fan for disorderly conduct, after the fan threw a bottle at an umpire.[14]

Brooklyn officials became alarmed, when several bottle-throwing incidents during Sunday games threatened the sustainability of playing such games in Brooklyn. Charles Ebbets and John Heydler thought that raising the price of bleacher seats would reduce the ruffians, based on the assumption that such characters only occupied the cheap seats. Sportswriter Francis Richter rose to the defense of bleacher fans and disputed the allegation that rowdy fans necessarily occupied the bleacher seats. He also took Brooklyn and other teams to task for not using some other container instead of bottles. As a last resort, he thought owners might stop selling soda pop entirely. He also advocated removing bottle throwers from the ballpark, although he did not state the obvious: why not arrest the miscreants.[15]

One bottle-throwing incident, though, was tragic. During a crucial game between the New York Yankees and St. Louis Browns in St. Louis, it appeared that a fan threw a pop bottle and hit Yankees outfielder Whitey Witt in the head. The crowd hushed, and Witt was taken to the hospital. Browns players admitted that they lost their spirit after the incident, and the team lost the game and the pennant. Although observers decried the cowardly attack, and baseball offered a reward, the denouement proved bizarre. A fan received the reward after testifying that Witt stepped on a bottle laying in the outfield. The bottle flew up and hit him in the head; the officials accepted this story (which was redolent of a cartoon character stepping on a rake or a *Three Stooges* gag). As late as 1929, a *Sporting News* editorialist was still urging owners to replace soda pop bottles with soft containers.[16]

Aside from bottle-throwing fans, some fans tried to get involved on the field. Today's fans are familiar with fans swarming fields and courts, but baseball took a dim view of such antics during the 1920s. A game in Detroit between the Tigers and Yankees ended when an estimated eighteen thousand spectators stormed the field and rioted. The *New York Times* reporter described the scene: "It was a free-for-all fight, with the police, endeavoring to distinguish rival fighters, only making the fight more complicated and intense."[17] In this case, Ban Johnson suspended two players for their involvement in the riot, and the president fined Babe Ruth for his "frenzied effort to participate in the trouble."[18]

Belying the belief that rowdies occupied the cheap seats, a game in Chicago ended in April 1925, when fans in the grandstands began throwing cushions at the overflow crowd; the overflow crowd returned the cushions. There were forty-four thousand in attendance, the largest crowd at any game in Chicago up to that time. The game was forfeited to Cleveland, which was leading 7–2 in the ninth, anyway.[19]

A more dangerous incident occurred in Boston, when Pirates catcher Earl Smith got into an argument with a Boston fan. After Smith struck the fan a "glancing blow," he was tossed from the game. As he exited towards the visiting team's locker room, another fan threw a chair at him—hitting him—but not seriously injuring him.[20] Smith's situation, of course, reflected one of the common causes for precipitating fan violence. Ty Cobb and other players fought fans in the stands, as fans, then as now, felt compelled to hurl vile insults at players as well as umpires.

Even fans outside of stadiums could erupt in violence. In 1925 an estimated twelve thousand boys, unable to obtain the three hundred available free tickets to that day's Yankees game, stormed two gates in an attempt to gain entrance to the stadium. Thirteen boys of the heretofore lucky three hundred were injured, as one can imagine, given their place between the gate and the surging mass of boys.[21]

Stadiums

Major League Baseball celebrated its prosperity during the early years of the twentieth century by engaging in a stadium construction binge. Whereas stadiums were formerly ramshackle structures built of wood and prone to burning down at inopportune moments, the owners spent much of their newfound wealth in constructing steel and concrete stadiums. Table 13 shows the stadiums and their seating capacities.

A successful ballpark depended not only on a good team to entice patrons but also upon the old real-estate bromide: location, location, location. In Chicago, Charles Murphy disdained the city's north side for a number of years and had the Cubs play at West Side Park. After the Federal League war, when Charles Weeghman purchased the Cubs, he installed them into his ballpark, now revered as Wrigley Field. Cubs fans needed several years to accept the change of venue, and although the war may have precluded any hope that Weeghman would turn a profit in 1918, even with a pennant-winning team, "the general opinion [was] that the desertion of the great West Side, hotbed of baseball, was the chief item in the financial failure."[22]

Major League Baseball rarely sold out their stadiums for regular-season games. Opening day, holiday doubleheaders, and crucial games between contenders in September were usually the best-drawing days. Owners faced a tough decision similar to an inventory problem faced by many businesses. Building a larger stadium or increasing the capacity of existing stadiums cost hundreds of thousands or even millions of dollars. Owners realized they could overbuild and have too much capital tied up in a stadium with thousands of superfluous seats. Maintaining their small stadiums meant missing out on additional revenues when games hit peak attendance. The sight of disappointed fans leaving with money for admission undoubtedly vexed owners. With Babe Ruth as a drawing card, the Yankees' owners suddenly found that they were turning away fans for some games during the 1920 season; this realization was certainly one more spur to build their own stadium.[23]

The phenomenon of excess demand for tickets frequently surfaced during World Series, despite the significant jump in official ticket prices for those contests. When the St. Louis Browns were challenging for the 1922 pennant, American League president Ban Johnson consulted with Browns owner Philip Ball on ways to expand Sportsman's Park's capacity of nineteen thousand by seven thousand.[24] The Senators, too, erected temporary seats in time for the 1924 World Series. The Pirates did likewise in 1925, although the club still had to turn away tens of thousands of requests for reserved seats.[25]

The owners sought new ways to generate revenues from their stadiums. Hosting other sporting events, such as football, boxing, track and field, and cycling, filled some dates. During the First World War, the government paid some owners to store military equipment, but of course this was a unique situation.[26]

During the 1920s, only one team built a new stadium—the New York Yankees and the fabled Yankee Stadium, the aptly dubbed "House That Ruth Built." Other owners quickly realized that the Yankees' revenue potential now dwarfed theirs. The World Series of 1925 revealed the disparity in seating capacity and revenue generation when the Pirates and Senators came nowhere near the attendance of the 1923 World Series between the Yankees and the Giants. Owners of smaller parks tried to meet the surge in demand by constructing temporary stands, but many owners faced the reality that they could not fully exploit a winning team.

The Yankees (Hilltoppers) had played at Hilltop Park until 1912 when they gained a lease to play at Brush Stadium (Polo Grounds). After Jacob Ruppert and T. L. Huston bought the Yankees in 1914, they considered making plans for building a stadium of their own. Although some teams (St. Louis Cardinals and Browns) more-or-less amicably shared stadiums for many years, the Yankees yearned for their own venue. After the war ended, the Giants made it clear that they wanted the Yankees out of the Polo Grounds. The Yankees' surging popularity on the wave of their acquisition of Babe Ruth created the embarrassing spectacle of the Yankees out-drawing the Giants at the Polo Grounds, which undoubtedly nettled John McGraw and Charles Stoneham. The Giants announced that the Yankees would have to vacate the Polo Grounds after the end of the current lease agreement.[27]

From the Yankees' perspective, owning their own stadium meant, in return for tying up a large sum of capital in a stadium, opportunities to gain more revenue from staging other events. As tenants in the Polo Grounds, they received only a fixed amount of concessions revenue. Ruppert owned a brewery, which was not producing beer due to Prohibition, but he could envision being able to eventually sell his product at the ballpark. Chris von der Ahe of the old St. Louis team in the 1880s had done so profitably.[28]

In 1922 the Yankees engaged famed sports promoter Tex Rickard to handle sports events outside of baseball. Rickard was an expert at promoting boxing. The Giants, too, had visions of boxing dollars dancing in their cash boxes, but some of their fellow owners were not enthusiastic about using ballparks for pugilism, citing the sport's unsavory reputation. Ban Johnson claimed the other owners opposed boxing in baseball stadiums, but the Yankees and Giants had already signed contracts for such bouts. Johnson's declaration apparently was futile, as the Yankees again signed contracts to stage boxing matches in 1925.[29]

Getting Yankee Stadium built, though, was a challenge. The Yankees owners initially considered a site housing the Hebrew Orphan Asylum— which was looking to relocate, so the club wasn't evicting orphans—but they eventually purchased a plot between 157th and 161st Streets in the Bronx and across the Harlem River from the Polo Grounds. This site was situated on a subway line connecting with Times Square. Stoneham and McGraw had strong connections with Tammany Hall and may have used their clout to delay the Yankees' construction efforts. Ruppert and Huston also had valuable political connections, so the two sets of owners pitted political muscle against each other.[30]

Even with the delays in getting approval for plans and finalizing the land purchase, the actual construction of the stadium went quickly. Huston's engineering background was a huge asset. Historian Robert Weintraub believes the land and stadium cost about $2.2 million, but the Yankees' records reveal the actual cost to have been $3.1 million.[31]

The Yankees planned to build temporary wooden bleachers around the outfield that would seat thirty thousand. They planned to charge bleacher prices instead of grandstand prices; a reporter found this an interesting experiment: "It has been argued that the day of the bleacherite has passed, that he has, or practically all of him, graduated to the grand stand class."[32]

Fans were enthusiastic about the new stadium. Ed Barrow and his office assistants were busy processing ticket requests for the opening day tilt with the Red Sox. An estimated 10,000 people visited the stadium on a Sunday in late March. Opening day was a rousing success; the team announced attendance of 74,217. In subsequent days, Ed Barrow admitted that the 74,000 figure was an estimate, but the actual figures included 52,000 paid admissions, another 4,000 to 6,000 came in on season passes, and 10,000 or more were invitees. Barrow said the seating capacity was 62,000 not 70,000, although the team could crowd more than 62,000 when accommodating standing-room-only patrons.[33]

When the stadium opened, reporter Joe Vila found fault with some aspects. He thought home plate was too close to the backstop, which would result in too many foul balls going into the stands. He also disliked the cinder path. Overall, though, he applauded it: "barring the few defects I have described, the new home of the New York American League club is a model baseball plant and will prove popular."[34]

Once the Yankees decided to build their own ballpark, Stoneham and McGraw realized that the Polo Grounds' capacity of less than 40,000 was inadequate to match the new Yankee Stadium. They had already made some improvements in late 1919 but planned to enlarge the park to accommodate over 50,000. Stoneham told reporters in 1923 that the enlarged Polo Grounds would be ready by the end of June 1923. The seating capacity would be a National League–best 54,000, with only 5,500 bleachers. The seating capacity would be greater for football games, and 92,000 for prize fights.[35]

Throughout the 1920s, owners who were enjoying success opted to enlarge their seating capacity. Frank Navin expanded Navin Field in 1923, stating, "We've got to make this park big enough to get some people into it on our big days."[36] Clark Griffith sought to enlarge his stadium in time for the 1922 season; he later planned another enlargement a couple of years later, while renaming the ballpark Clark Griffith Stadium. Philip Lowry listed the park's 1921 capacity as 32,000, but Paul Eaton reported a capacity of only 20,000.[37]

The Cubs spent nearly $400,000 to enlarge Wrigley Field to 31,000 seats, of which just 5,000 were bleacher seats. Even the Boston Red Sox's new owners announced they were going to spend $300,000 to improve and expand the seating capacity of Fenway Park. Barney Dreyfuss expanded Forbes Field in time for the 1925 season and the Pirates' first pennant since 1909. He spent $750,000 to increase the capacity to 40,000. Sometimes, though, owners' grandiose plans fell through; the Cincinnati Reds announced plans for a new stadium, but this stadium was never built. The owners settled for expanding Crosley Field in 1927.[38]

The St. Louis Browns and Cardinals disagreed on how to finance an enlargement of Sportsman's Park that they shared (although Philip Ball owned the park). Ball wanted to expand the park by 10,000 seats at a cost of $300,000; he wanted to increase the Cardinals annual rental from $20,000 to $30,000, but Cardinals owner Sam Breadon refused to accept an increase in rent. Ball eventually paid to renovate the ballpark after the 1925 season.[39]

John Sheridan estimated building a park such as Sportsman's Park would require $1,000,000 for land and stadium. The resultant overhead combined with player payroll and team expenses would make it almost impossible for any but an extremely successful team to break even. On the other hand, at least St. Louis had two teams using the existing park; Sheridan thought it wasteful for the Giants and Yankees to have separate stadiums.[40]

As the decade waned, the city of Cleveland considered building a municipal stadium (later dubbed by some wags as "The Mistake by the Lake"). The stadium was not completed until 1932 and proved too large to be feasible for regular use. Of course, the city erected the stadium at an inopportune time—the depths of the Great Depression. The Indians continued to play in a smaller stadium except on Sundays and holidays.[41]

Newspapers, Radio, and Electric Lighting

Baseball owners in the 1870s and 1880s were suspicious of newspapers, worrying that newspaper coverage would erode attendance at the ballpark, but by the twentieth century, owners and newspaper editors realized their mutually beneficial relationship. A writer in the *Literary Digest* observed, "Baseball clubs have an advantage that can be found nowhere else. Newspapers make business for the club owner. He is certain of heavy profits as long as the sporting pages are open to baseball."[42] Aside from the motion-picture and live-theater industries, baseball was one of the few industries to enjoy free continuous publicity in the newspapers. Sportswriters covered the previous day's game while previewing upcoming games. Sports sections featured box scores, league standings, and upcoming slates of games. Baseball, in turn, helped sell newspapers, as baseball fans loved to read about the sport.

The *Chicago Tribune*'s editors, though, decided that enough was enough. The editors decided in 1921 to shift emphasis from professional baseball to amateur sport: "We are getting a little tired of the subject.... The *Tribune* is down to about a half column now for games in which the home teams play, which is justified parochialism, and to a bare statement of vital statistics regarding the other clubs. That is enough. Ten years ago professional baseball was given four, five, and six columns a day."[43] Some newspaper editors agreed with the stance taken by the *Tribune*, although few emulated the *Tribune*'s actions. Chicago, of course, was home for the now Black Sox; the Cubs were not contenders in 1920 or 1921, so interest in the local teams may have flagged.

Radio was the new mass medium of the 1920s. Early radio enthusiasts had to build and maintain their receiving sets; however, by the mid 1920s, manufacturers were producing radios that were convenient to operate. The struggle between commercialized and public broadcast radio lasted throughout the decade, until the formation of the National Broadcasting Company and later the Columbia Broadcasting System established the supremacy of commercialized radio. By the end of the 1920s, millions of American homes had radio.

Prior to radio, some entrepreneurs used telephone and telegraph facilities to update information regarding games. Large baseball diamond facsimiles were erected in large cities, and electric scoreboards kept fans abreast of activities of current games. The result was similar, perhaps, to monitoring games in the twenty-first century via ESPN's "Gamecast." You do not see the action, but the situation is updated frequently. Some owners feared these crude forms of informing the public, worrying that ticker tape transmissions of games might encourage fans to congregate in local watering holes with such machinery instead of going to the ballpark. The rise of Prohibition allayed baseball owners' fears of the deleterious effects of ticker transmissions.[44]

Newspapers and baseball initially viewed radio with suspicion and fear. Would the new medium displace newspaper coverage? If baseball owners permitted live broadcasts of games, would they be harming their attendance and gate receipts? Reasonable arguments could be made to support either side of the debate. Optimists believed that radio broadcasts would create new fans who would eventually visit the ballparks and watch the players and the game they had only heard previously. Pessimists believed that the convenience of staying home and listening to games would suppress attendance. Since gate receipts were the owners' main source of income, their concerns were understandable. The New York Yankees, long a holdout against live broadcasts of home games, worried about the effect on attendance. By the late 1930s, when the Yankees were still refusing to broadcast their home games, even though radio stations were paying for broadcasting rights, the team's board of directors made this debate explicit: Would the proffered broadcasting rights payment offset anticipated reductions in gate receipts?[45]

Giants official James J. Tierney denied erroneous reports that the Giants were going to broadcast home games during 1923: "On the face of it the story is improbable. If a play-by-play account of the games were sent out every afternoon, it would cut into our attendance, besides hurting the newspapers. We want the fans following the game from the grandstand, not from their homes."[46]

If the baseball owners worried about radio, newspapermen were down-right hostile to the new medium, although they likely enjoyed general radio programming in their own homes. Sports reporters and their editors feared that radio broadcasts would displace readership of newspaper sports pages, although some observers believed that fans who perused box scores would not desert newspapers. The Baseball Writers' Association of America informed Commissioner Landis and the two league presidents, "If this [broadcasting *results* of games, not even play by play] is permitted, it will kill circulation of afternoon papers and in the end will result in curtailment of baseball publicity. The Baseball Writers' Association is strongly opposed to allowing any wireless connection with the baseball parks which would allow broadcasting stations to give details while a game is in progress."[47]

According to historian Lowell Smith, Major League Baseball agreed to broadcast World Series and opening day games in the early 1920s. The Chicago Cubs and some of the other clubs located in the western regions of Major League Baseball assented to broadcasts of home games during the 1920s. Many owners, though, resisted broadcasting home games to local audience until the mid 1930s. Owners, enjoying financial prosperity during the 1920s, felt little reason to experiment with a potential revenue source in baseball and decided instead to bar radio broadcasts of regular-season home games. Major League owners professed concerns that broadcasting their games might injure attendance at Minor League contests. Once radio stations began bidding for the exclusive rights to broadcast games, though, the incentives facing the owners changed. An explicit payment promised to offset any decrease in attendance.

Many owners worried about the slump in attendance during the early 1930s, though, and a few decided that radio broadcasts were the culprit for the flagging attendance, never mind the economic upheaval in the general economy. By the late 1930s, the three New York teams were among the few teams that were still refusing to broadcast home games.[48]

The *Sporting News* suggested that the Yankees' and ticket speculators' inability to sell out the stadium for the 1928 World Series was due to the prevalence of "radio parties" in apartments, hotels, and other residences.

Despite the controversy regarding radio broadcasts' effects upon attendance, baseball and radio officials acknowledged that radio created an interest among women in the sport.[49]

Baseball owners may have been unduly insecure regarding attendance at ballparks. Although listening to a game on the radio was a substitute for attending a game, longtime baseball fans likely found radio a rather poor substitute. During the early days of radio, most of the announcers were chosen for their personalities or their voices; knowledge of baseball was strictly optional. Graham McNamee was an early star announcer. His vocal quality and delivery gained him many fans, but baseball fans and sportswriters panned his understanding of baseball and willingness to embellish the action. The *Sporting News* suggested that because radio announcers were so ignorant about baseball, that "the fan is not satisfied with his radio account, but, [is] turning to newspapers for something more complete." The writer suggested that baseball owners make better use of the publicity and free advertising provided by newspapers.[50] Lee Allen points out that until the Cincinnati Reds engaged Red Barber to announce their games, radio broadcasts of their games attracted disappointing radio audiences.[51]

Radio may have indirectly affected demand for other leisure activities. Families purchasing radios, for instance, may have had less discretionary income left for other forms of leisure and recreation. A radio was a durable good that provided entertainment and leisure services over an extended period of time, and consumers could purchase radio sets on installment plans, but the purchase remained a major one. An advertisement in the *Sporting News* in 1925 offered a five-tube radio for $59.85; this amounted to more than a week's wages for a middle-class worker.[52]

Major League owners saw little need for electric lighting and night baseball. The New York teams, especially, relied on a large population of office workers for their patrons; these white-collar workers often had more discretion over their work schedule and could attend weekday afternoon games. During World War I, a few owners tried "twilight" baseball, whereby games started in the late afternoon, but attendance was scanty at the few games offered in the hours before nightfall.[53] Owners in Minor League cities faced smaller population pools. As a result, the idea of staging games at night was more appealing to them. No Minor League owner, though, staged a game under the lights until 1930, and their willingness to do so at that point may have stemmed from an attempt to offset the effects of the economic downturn. The Negro Leagues' Kansas City Monarchs played night games in 1930.[54]

The Owners' Conservatism

Owners tried some methods to improve the ballpark experience, but because the game was prosperous, they may not have felt compelled to make big changes. They would only reluctantly embrace night baseball and widespread radio broadcasts of games in the years to come.

7 Not a Perfect Game

Baseball changed dramatically during the 1920s. For some fans, John McGraw's New York Giants may have represented the old guard, while the parvenu Yankees epitomized the new style. Fans witnessed greater scoring, fewer errors, and more power. Some observers drew analogies between baseball's new exciting brand and the social upheaval during the 1920s, with Babe Ruth exemplifying the modern hero.

Style of Play

What about the game on the field? The 1920s were notable for a dramatic change in playing styles. The offense predicated on home runs was displacing the "scientific" style of baseball. Ty Cobb and Babe Ruth personified two different eras of baseball. Cobb, with his slashing speed and high batting average, relied on guile and intimidation to eke out runs. He had power, though, as he once hit three home runs in a game. Babe Ruth exploded upon the scene. His home run feats overshadowed what might have been a Hall of Fame pitching career. Gavvy Cravath hit twenty-four home runs during the dead-ball era, but Ruth quickly soared to fifty-four and then fifty-nine home runs. Other sluggers began exceeding thirty home runs in a season, and Rogers Hornsby cracked forty plus. It wasn't until 1929 and later that other sluggers began approaching Ruth's single-season home run tallies. Even as gifted a slugger as Lou Gehrig failed to reach the fifty home run level. As late as 1927, Ruth alone had more home runs than any other team in the American League.

Rather than produce runs via stolen bases and sacrifice bunts, Ruth's Yankees relied on three-run home runs. American League teams scored just over 8 runs per game in 1919, but the runs per game jumped to 9.5

in 1920 and did not fall below this level through 1929 (table 14). The National League's run explosion lagged the American League's by a season. The National League's runs-per-game mark exceeded the American League's in 1929, but the American League typically featured slightly higher scoring.

Home runs followed a similar trend as runs scored, with both leagues experiencing a jump in home runs per game by 1921. Both leagues also experienced increases in batting average, on-base percentage, and slugging average during the decade compared with 1919. Triples remained relatively stable, even after the home run binge.

Table 15 shows that coincident with the increased number of home runs, bases on balls increased in both leagues. The National League initially had fewer bases on balls and strikeouts per game than did the American League. The increase in bases on balls in the National League was more dramatic. Strikeouts per game were higher in 1919 than in subsequent years, with a noticeable drop occurring in the 1921 season before bouncing around. Given the jump in home runs, the fact that strikeouts displayed stability and possibly a slight downward trend is surprising. The greater number of bases on balls in the American League for most of the eleven seasons may account for games in the American League taking longer to play, although American League officials blamed manager and player disputes with umpires over balls and strikes and other dillydallying (the officials' argument presumes that American League managers and players argued more frequently or for time than their National League counterparts).[1] Fielding improved and the number of errors committed fell.

Both leagues witnessed a drop in stolen bases per opportunity (table 16). Opportunity was defined as the sum of singles and walks; there were sparse statistics on batters hit by pitches and batters reaching first base via error. The drop in the National League was particularly marked. Reporters, baseball officials, and fans frequently commented on the diminishing role of base stealing.

Baseball Magazine editor F. C. Lane bemoaned the detrimental approach to base stealing in numerous articles, with relatively poor base stealers attempting in his opinion too many stolen bases, while the best base stealers were overly reticent. Certainly the success rate of base stealing in the mid 1920s were not impressive: 56.6 percent in the National League and 55.1 percent in the American League; these success rates were slightly higher than those compiled in 1920 and 1921.[2]

Even John McGraw, presumed exemplar of "scientific" baseball, had his players steal fewer bases. After 1919 his team rarely approached 150 stolen bases in a season and sometimes failed to attain 100 steals in a season, unlike his earlier teams that occasionally pilfered 350 bases in a season and frequently flirted with 300. McGraw's Giants led the National League in home runs for the 1924-25 and 1927-28 seasons, indicating that McGraw, even if he deplored the change in the game, exploited the new style. By the end of the decade, his home run star, Mel Ott, was on his way to setting the National League record for career home runs. The confirmation of the shift in playing styles was clear by 1921; a sportswriter wrote, "Speed no longer is demanded by the managers as it used to be. The highest prices are not offered for the men who are the fastest as they used to be. Nor are the highest salaries paid the swiftest runners."[3]

Reporters sometimes discussed how to evaluate players' worth. Baseball observers realized that not all player statistics were created equal. They noted the differences in park sizes, although few mentioned differences in climatic conditions such as humidity and wind. *Baseball Magazine* occasionally ran articles discussing baseball statistics. In theory, players' salaries depended upon their batting or pitching statistics. Some observers attacked the traditional reliance on batting average for hitters and win-loss records for pitchers. Irving Sanborn argued that the traditional measures were fallacious. He thought measures of "bases advanced" for hitters and earned run average for pitchers were superior. F. C. Lane recognized that fielding averages were, "but moderately expressive of fielding talent and verge off into a twilight zone where they become well-nigh meaningless."[4] Sanborn suggested that a new measure was needed to replace the win-loss record as gauging a pitcher's productivity, while J. C. Koford touted batters' total bases instead of batting average. Modern-day baseball statisticians may be interested to know that as early as 1923, some sportswriters discussed a "getting-to-first-base percentage," which presaged the on-base percentage.[5]

But it was the home run that dominated. Ruth's 29 home runs and attendant popularity in 1919 seemed an aberration, as home runs were not inordinately high in either league. In the seasons just prior to 1918, the National League often out homered the American League by a wide margin. The National League sometimes had over 300 home runs in a season, while the American League usually hovered around 150, with occasional forays over the 200 between 1911 and 1917. The American League experienced a bigger jump in home runs during 1920, but it wasn't until 1921–22 that the trend towards more home runs was firmly established in both leagues.[6] Some teams lagged in joining the home run barrage. The Washington Senators won the 1924 American League pennant despite hitting only 22 home runs.

Ruth demonstrated even greater home run prowess in the subsequent seasons. His home runs were unique. Years later, as Ruth was just passing the peak of his prowess, sportswriter Ed Murray noted that Ruth had developed his revolutionary big swing: "Instead of hitting them on a line a mile a minute, Ruth changed his swing angle. Ruth takes a swing from below his waist-line and winds up about his shoulder. His bat is traveling along at an angle of about 45 degrees." Murray made the interesting observation that Ruth, having started as a pitcher, was allowed to take such an unorthodox swing, "He was still only a pitcher and of course a pitcher was allowed to do anything he wanted to do while at the plate."[7]

Babe Ruth's stupendous 1920 season and attendant pay escalation inspired other hitters to strive for home runs. Other players began to imitate Ruth and swing more freely, rather than pushing or chopping at the ball. Rogers Hornsby, Cy Williams, and Ken Williams began clouting thirty or forty home runs in a season, leading reporters and fans to wonder whence the power source. Julian Curtiss, president of A. G. Spalding and Company, pointed out that players were demanding different styles of bats. The old-fashioned choke bats, "which were thick virtually all the way to the end of the handle" were disappearing. He said, "That style of bat is not meant for making long drives but for placing hits."[8]

Why the Home Run Barrage?

Many historians cited changes in the baseball itself as causing the power surge, although they also acknowledged that the trend may have had several causes. Owners had passed rules against various types of "freak pitching" prior to the 1920 season.[9]

Although pitchers had used spit balls, shine balls, and emery balls— the so-called freak pitches—for decades, Major League officials began to push for their elimination, starting with Pittsburgh Pirates owner Barney Dreyfuss in 1918. After the 1919 season, both leagues legislated against these pitches, effective for the 1921 season. World Series pitchers Eddie Cicotte of the White Sox and Hod Eller of Cincinnati allegedly were key practitioners of the shine ball. Manager-owner Clark Griffith had used such freak pitches during his pitching career, but now he opposed their use. The owners realized that some pitchers' livelihoods were threatened by the abolition of the spit ball and that there simply weren't enough good pitchers around to allow the leagues to jettison some prominent ones over the issue, so the owners eventually granted lifetime exemptions from the prohibition to a number of hurlers using the spit ball after the 1920 season. Sportswriter John Sheridan argued that in conjunction with the more frequent use of new baseballs, the prohibition on freak pitching tilted the scales too far in favor of hitters.[10]

Certainly the canard that the ball was livelier resonated with players, especially pitchers. Baseball officials and suppliers of baseballs denied that they had consciously changed the balls. Manufacturers eventually admitted that postwar factors affected their product. Wartime regulations made it difficult for manufacturers to get high-quality materials and labor. When the war ended, manufacturers gradually resumed making high-quality balls. Julian Curtiss flatly stated: "there has been absolutely no change in the manufacture of the ball in recent years; that the ball is exactly the same in weight, in size and in resiliency."[11]

A professor of chemistry (not physics) Harold Fales of Columbia University tested three baseballs, one made in 1914 and two more recent balls. He claimed the balls varied in weight and size: "The 1925 ball is larger in size, weighs more, and gives the pitcher much less control in that the seam of the ball is much smoother and the thread of same almost completely countersunk so as to be flush with the leather of the seam. The elasticity of the ball for small heights of fall, namely 13.5 feet, is practically the same." Credulous officials and reporters placed some weight on Fales's findings, even though he only tested three balls, one of which had been sitting on a shelf for a decade.[12]

Near the end of the decade, the *Scientific American* conducted a study on 1929 versus 1924 baseballs and concluded, "there is no material structural difference in the two." The study did establish, however, that used baseballs quickly deteriorated and softened up: "Its original structural aspect is changed and it becomes slower. Thus in the old days, when a baseball was used longer in a game than one is today, it became slower and responded less to a smash by the bat."[13]

One baseball umpire, Billy Evans, suggested that concrete stands were responsible for the increase in balls used per game. He said balls hitting concrete often ended with a rough spot. "This rough spot enables a pitcher to cause the ball to take uncanny shoots, if properly delivered."[14]

Owners also became willing to bear the expense of providing more baseballs per game, rather than using a ball until it became discolored and possibly damaged. The National League used almost three times as many balls during the 1924 season as it had during the 1916 season. By 1926 the National League was using 4,179 dozen balls, slightly more than in the previous season.[15]

Thomas Barthel claims that in the wake of the fatal Ray Chapman beaning in 1920, umpires had orders to throw out soiled balls; he attributes the 272 percent increase in number of balls used to this incident, but this doesn't seem plausible as Chapman was beaned three-quarters of the way into the season. More likely, the increase in the number of balls used originated in the rule changes issued before the 1920 season.[16]

Some managers were trying to bolster offensive efficiency by using "platoon" baseball, whereby right-handed hitters played against left-handed pitchers and left-handed hitters played against right-handed pitchers. John McGraw was a pioneer in this tactic, using Jimmy O'Connell and Bill Cunningham in center field. His player, Casey Stengel, proved an apt pupil of McGraw's tactics and used platooning to a greater extent with his New York Yankees clubs of the 1950s. One old-timer reporter groused about platoon baseball: "Spoon-feeding baseball players. Giving them setups. Making things soft for them. Coddling them. Softening them morally, by keeping them alternately on the bench and sending them in only to pick on crippled birds. . . . This habit of shifting players to the pitcher is not a sound one. It ruins teams."[17]

By the mid 1920s, some critics wondered whether batters were hitting too many home runs. *Baseball Magazine* editor, F. C. Lane, claimed, "the public is pretty well fed up on homers."[18] Owners debated possible curbs on home runs, especially in parks with inordinately small distances to inviting walls. Some owners and officials, such as Ban Johnson, Barney Dreyfuss, and Clark Griffith, proposed a rule requiring a minimum distance (such as 250 feet) from home plate in order to qualify for a double or a home run. Griffith's Senators were not a power-hitting ball club, so he was trying to curb the Yankees' competitive edge. Dreyfuss, despite the presence of Pie Traynor and Kiki Cuyler and later the Waner brothers, possessed hitters with high batting averages but relatively few home runs, partly because the club's playing field was relatively large. Dreyfuss believed that part of the home run binge was due to the reduced playing field of five of the National League clubs.[19]

By 1929, a majority of baseball managers "believe[d] the present epidemic of home-run hitting is ruinous to the game and believe something should be done to increase the efficiency of pitchers." The managers of the Yankees, Athletics, Cubs, and Braves were the minority who believed fans preferred home runs; of the four managers, only the manager of the Braves had a team deficient in home run prowess.[20]

As shown in table 15, pitchers began issuing more bases on balls throughout the 1920s, especially in the National League. In order to aid batters and to please fans by letting Babe Ruth and his peers swing away, owners tried to outlaw intentional bases on balls, a chimeric endeavor at best. The *New York Times* described the rule: "The new rule prohibiting the gratis walk provides that if the catcher gets out of his position behind the plate to aid the pitcher in giving an intentional base on balls, the runners on the bases will all be entitled to an extra base." Umpires pointed out that this interpretation conflicted with a catcher's legitimate shift on a pitch out to stymie a base stealer, with the result that the base runner would get the added base. They predicted that, in a close game, such a call would incite home fans. Senators owner Clark Griffith proposed that umpires decide whether a base on balls was intentional or not, but the umpires wanted no part of such an unworkable rule. The attempts to curtail bases on balls may have, at most, moderated their increase, but clearly the rules failed.[21]

An Ill-Timed Suggestion

National League President John Heydler made a revolutionary proposal to create a designated hitter. Such a rule promised to prolong the career of aging sluggers, who were liabilities in the field, as well as sparing fans the specter of inept pitchers taking cuts at the plate. Of course, not all pitchers were futile at the plate (Walter Johnson and Wes Ferrell were excellent hitters, as were pitchers-turned-hitters Babe Ruth, Lefty O'Doul, and Smoky Joe Wood). Heydler proposed this to his club owners in December 1928, which was odd timing. National League hitters were nearing the apogee of their prowess, with the league batting average reaching .304 in 1930. National League owners proved unenthusiastic about Heydler's proposal, and he quietly buried it. American League managers also proved resistant to the idea, with Cleveland Indians' manager Roger Peckinpaugh saying, "The manager would not have a chance to do any master minding."[22] Heydler's idea would lie dormant for decades, until the American League instituted such a rule for the 1973 season. One sportswriter recalled that the nine-player game was not sacrosanct, as early versions of baseball featured a tenth man on the field—a rover between first and second base.[23]

The Age of Ruth

One man was a Colossus during the 1920s. Baseball observers debated Babe Ruth's effect upon the game. The *Sporting News* disputed whether Ruth "saved" baseball in the wake of the Black Sox scandal of 1919–20: "No one man makes baseball. . . . There is no doubt that Ruth will leave behind him a very, very great reputation when he leaves baseball for good, but the game will go on."[24]

Ruth's manager, Miller Huggins, pointed out that Ruth's popularity far surpassed Ty Cobb's. Huggins recounted a mid-season series with the Chicago White Sox. White Sox fans "booed and jeered the Chicago pitchers every time they walked Ruth."[25]

Even Ruth's failures loomed larger than other players' failures. Ruth defied Commissioner Landis and went barnstorming after the 1921 series. His return to the Yankees in 1922 was not smooth; his five weeks' suspension left him out of shape, but at least the team salvaged a hard-fought pennant race with the St. Louis Browns. Ruth had a terrible series in 1922, and observers and fans wondered whether he was overrated and whispers ensued.[26] Ruth's terrible 1925 season, starting with medical problems and ending with a team-imposed suspension, also cast him as less endearing.

Ruth's lavish spending also incited comment. Ruth's youth was poverty personified, although he was fortunate to have some adults concerned about his well-being. From the first, he demonstrated a keen sense of his value and demanded top dollar from owners. For much of the 1920s, Ruth exemplified the Roaring Twenties lifestyle of live fast, spend fast. Ruth's business manager, Christy Walsh, though, cared enough about Ruth to persuade him to begin saving money. Walsh, whose advice would presage that of many of today's financial experts, understood that if Ruth never saw the money, he would not regret saving it. Walsh told Ruth to spend his baseball salary any way he desired, but the auxiliary money earned from promotions, endorsements, and exhibition games went through Walsh's office. Walsh told Ruth he would invest the money, including taking out an annuity insurance policy. The plan worked, and by 1930

Ruth's trust fund exceeded $100,000—a tidy nest egg. Walsh was not alone in helping Ruth become financially secure; Ruth's second wife, Claire, also insisted that he prepare for the future. Ruth paid just $10,250 income tax on his fabled $80,000 a year salary, so the relatively low tax rate helped his efforts to save money.[27]

Baseball Chooses Brawn over Brains

By 1929, Major League Baseball faced a deluge of offense. That Lefty Grove could consistently keep his earned run average below three runs per game demonstrated his prowess. Ruth and his imitators transformed the game on the field, making it more similar to the modern game than the one his predecessors played. Whether fans preferred slugging over stealing seemed an obvious answer, given the twirling turnstiles, but the game's popularity may have been more reflective of the general economic prosperity.

Some owners decided that boosting offense wasn't sufficient to keep a winning and attractive team on the field. They aimed to acquire top sluggers to take advantage of the new style.

8   The Stars Are Realigned

Baseball stars did not always remain stationary. Owners often traded even the biggest stars. What were some of the intriguing player trades of the 1919–29 period? The Babe Ruth sale, of course, is probably baseball's most famous or infamous trade. Red Sox fans still despise Harry Frazee, but there was more to his story than meets the eye. Glenn Stout's *Selling of the Babe* is the most recent discussion of the sale.

Connie Mack's Slow-Burning Fire Sale

Connie Mack knew baseball talent. He built two aggregations of dominant teams. His 1910–14 Athletics won four pennants. Anchored by the "$100,000" infield (which shows the ravages of inflation a hundred years on), the Athletics were the class of the American League.

Mack was no stand-pat owner-manager. He replaced three of his regulars from the 1910 team by 1914 and revamped his pitching staff. When the Boston Braves upset his club in the 1914 World Series, he decided to break up his club. Whether because of the Federal League war or because Philadelphia fans grew tired of a winner, the Athletics' attendance plunged from 572,000 to 347,000 between 1913 and 1914. His players, naturally, demanded more money for being repeat pennant winners, and competition from the Federal League put a cruel squeeze on Mack and owner John Shibe. Mack later reminisced, "[Athletics fans] lost interest when I had the best club, and now they're kicking because I've got the worst one. What's a fellow going to do?"[1]

Although Mack was revered as a kindly, courtly man, he was brimming with self-confidence. He figured he could break up his team, which was quite young for such a long-run powerhouse. Unfortunately for Athletics fans, "He reasoned logically that he had collected the members of this team over a period of a few seasons, with no great effort or expense, and that he could rebuild a new team quite as readily. There he miscalculated."[2]

Federal League dollars lured Eddie Plank and Charles "Chief" Bender. Mack sold Eddie Collins to the Chicago White Sox before the 1915 season because he was unwilling to pay Collins the $15,000 per annum the player demanded. Frank Baker voluntarily retired, although a pay dispute was involved. Mack sold Baker to Ruppert and Huston in 1916 for $37,500.[3]

Mack's acumen failed to resuscitate the team for years. By 1920 a *Sporting News* writer was wondering, "Is [Mack] such a confirmed genius that he can see no good in any player who does not exactly fit into his ideas of how the game should be played in its every move and expression?"[4]

What is not remembered about Mack's dispersal of talent is that the Boston Red Sox under Joe Lannin and then Harry Frazee obtained first baseman Stuffy McInnis, shortstop Jack Barry, outfielder Amos Strunk, catcher Wally Schang, and pitchers Bullet Joe Bush, Herb Pennock, and Weldon Wyckoff from Mack. The early Yankees' pennant-winning teams of 1921 and 1922 were also an echo of Mack's great teams, as Baker, Schang, Bob Shawkey, Bush, and Pennock eventually arrived in New York. Eddie Collins, of course, remained a member of the Chicago White Sox and led them to two pennants. Aside from the 1920 Cleveland Indians, American League pennant winners from 1916 to 1922 featured former Athletics on their rosters, and Shawkey and Pennock appeared in World Series in later years.

Unfortunately for Mack, his fans may have tired of pennant winners, but they disdained last-place teams. Attendance at Athletics games fell below 150,000 in 1915. Mack found it more difficult to find and to obtain quality players than anticipated, and he needed more than a decade to resurrect the club.

The "Curse of the Speaker"?

If Harry Frazee had his Babe Ruth, previous Red Sox owner Joe Lannin had his Tris Speaker. Speaker was one of the most productive players in baseball history. Though he was second banana to Ty Cobb, he was certainly a reasonable facsimile. Speaker helped the Red Sox win World Series titles in 1912 and 1915. Whiny Red Sox fans mumbling about the "Curse of the Bambino," forget that the franchise won its first five World Series (1903, 1912, 1915–16, and 1918).

Although Speaker slumped to .322 in 1915, he wanted more money than owner Joe Lannin was willing to pay. Lannin shipped Speaker to Cleveland for $50,000 or $55,000, pitcher Sad Sam Jones, and Fred Thomas.[5] Jones was then an uninspiring young pitcher, but he eventually blossomed and won over two hundred games.

If the Red Sox really got $55,000, this was close in terms of purchasing power for what they got for Babe Ruth four years later. Red Sox fans were apoplectic at losing Speaker. Fortunately for Lannin, his club retained sufficient talent to capture the pennant and the World Series again in 1916. Attendance fell moderately in 1916. Had the Red Sox fallen into a funk, fans and sportswriters might be talking about the "Curse of the Speaker."[6]

Frazee energetically sought reinforcements during the 1918 season to give Boston another pennant winner. He picked up the aforementioned Schang, Bush, Strunk, and McInnis to bolster his club and to win the pennant in 1918.[7] The Red Sox won, but Frazee may well have taken a financial bath, as the team drew fewer than 250,000 fans. Red Sox fans may not believe this, but according to an article in the *Sporting News* early in 1918, "his methods are immensely gratifying to Boston fans . . . as a favor-winning magnate, Frazee is the equal of Charley Comiskey or any other person who 'shoved in their checkers' and gambled."[8]

Frazee may have concluded two things about Boston. First, he could get rid of a star player, as Lannin had, and still come out okay if he kept the team strong. Second, winning did not guarantee profits. We turn now to Frazee's antics that drew the ire of Ban Johnson and five of his fellow American League owners.

Harry Frazee Strips Boston

The record books show that the New York Yankees finished third in the 1919 pennant race, with the Detroit Tigers a scant half game behind them in fourth place. Never has the difference between third- and fourth-place clubs been so fraught with acrimony. It all began with a trade of a disgruntled pitcher.

Before Frazee sold Babe Ruth, he traded pitcher Carl Mays to the Yankees. Mays was a talented pitcher, using an underhand pitching style while winning 208 games and sporting a .623 win-loss percentage during his career. He is one of the best pitchers never selected to the Hall of Fame.

Mays had a strange personality. He warmed up to few teammates, but he wasn't an ordinarily troublesome player. Writer F. C. Lane described him thusly: "his personal habits are quite above reproach. He does not dissipate and he possesses far more than average intelligence. What has made him a solitary genius, lonely and virtually friendless among the ranks of his fellow players?" Lane thought Mays believed that being aloof was his "opinion of what a pitcher should be."[9] Trouble, however, seemed to follow him. During the 1919 season, he was struggling with a 5-11 record after winning twenty plus games in each of the two previous seasons. His earned run average was a stellar 2.48, the best on the team, but he was, in baseball parlance, a hard-luck pitcher.

One day, he became upset with a teammate's play or misplay. He left the team and allegedly went fishing, or so sportswriter Frederick Lieb recounts. During the later hearing on the Mays case, an attorney claimed that Mays had been hit on the head by a thrown ball and left to seek medical treatment, which was ironic, given Mays's later pitch that killed Cleveland's Ray Chapman. Mays had remained in the game long enough to get a base hit, but his departure surprised Barrow, who had no relief pitcher warming up. When Judge Robert F. Wagner issued his decision in the injunction proceedings initiated later, he cited that "Mays had had family trouble, his home in Pennsylvania had been burned to the ground and all his baseball trophies had been consumed . . . he was not himself and pitched poor ball. He was found sitting in the clubhouse with his head between his hands and crying bitterly." Several teams wanted the moody hurler, including Chicago and Cleveland, and made offers.[10]

After Frazee contacted Mays, the owner traded him to the New York Yankees—the first of the infamous series of transactions between the two clubs. The Yankees sent Allan Russell, Bob McGraw, and $40,000 to Boston on July 29 for Mays.[11] The Yankees, despite leading the league in earned run average, sought an additional pitcher in hopes of landing the franchise's first pennant. Mays went 9-3 for them.

Ban Johnson disapproved of the Mays trade and suspended the pitcher for the remainder of the season, although he had a few weeks to have imposed a suspension before Frazee traded Mays. On the other hand, Johnson had previously warned teams not to try to obtain Mays. He rebuked Boston for merely fining and not suspending the pitcher. He felt that Mays had manipulated the situation so he could leave a mediocre Boston club for a pennant-contending Yankees team. Johnson never explained how Mays could know that his antics would induce Frazee to send him to New York and not to, say, Philadelphia or Washington (the contemporary baseball Siberias). Some baseball observers recalled other players leaving their clubs and then being traded without passing through a suspension.[12]

The Mays brouhaha widened the rift between Johnson, Frazee, and the Yankees' owners. The Yankees and Frazee wondered whether Johnson was discriminating against them. The Detroit club was aggrieved because the Yankees had just slipped by them to claim third place. Cleveland and Chicago fumed because, in the former case, the team coveted Mays as they feared the pitcher would propel the Yankees past them in the pennant race.[13]

Sportswriters spilled a great deal of ink covering the Mays contretemps. Johnson claimed that a suspended player could not be traded, but Frazee had not suspended Mays. Johnson also claimed that five teams in the league requested he suspend Mays to prevent one of the contenders from getting him during a tight pennant race, a rather mealymouthed justification.[14] The Yankees wanted to use their new acquisition and obtained an injunction stopping Johnson from keeping Mays on the sidelines, which was the ultimate slap to Johnson's face. Heretofore, Johnson had complete sway over his owners, including Ruppert and Huston.

The Yankees tried to arrange an informal meeting of American League owners and Johnson, but five clubs refused to attend, and Johnson went into hiding. St. Louis Browns owner Philip Ball returned the invitation with an insulting message: "Your sportsmanship smells to heaven. We decline your invitation." The Yankees eventually accused Johnson of being biased because he had a financial interest in the Cleveland club. Johnson had loaned the club's owners $100,000, of which $50,000 remained unpaid and which apparently had been converted to shares of stock in the club now worth an estimated $58,000; Johnson claimed he received no dividends on his shares. As mentioned earlier, much of the enmity surrounding the National Commission resulted from the Mays case.[15]

The Yankees did not capture the pennant in 1919; they finished third and kept the Detroit Tigers from that position. Since players of third-place teams received shares of World Series gate receipts, the Tigers were understandably miffed. Johnson held up disbursing third-place money to the Yankees players for months. One of the oddities in the case was Charles Comiskey's alliance with the Yankees and Harry Frazee. Comiskey, worried about his pitching depth, had contacted Frazee regarding the pitcher but was unable to offer satisfactory terms.[16]

Judge Robert Wagner ruled against Johnson taking any action to interfere with Mays pitching for the Yankees. He cited the fact that suspending a valuable player such as Mays imposed a financial injury upon the club holding rights to the player: "the President's act was . . . not fortified with that perfect appreciation of the facts which evinces a desire to do equity to all parties concerned." The Yankees filed a lawsuit against Ban Johnson, claiming $500,000 damages and alleging that Johnson was trying to drive Ruppert and Huston out of baseball.[17]

The judge's decision did not end the petty sniping and squabbling, with Johnson remaining defiant and refusing to release third-place player shares of World Series receipts. The *New York Times* reported a rumor that the White Sox, Red Sox, and Yankees were considering breaking away and starting a new major league, an idea that would float for quite some time. The height of Johnson's vendetta may have been his attempt to meddle in the Polo Grounds lease negotiations between the two New York clubs and his denying Frazee, Ruppert, and Comiskey seats on the league's board of directors, even though it was their turns to serve.[18]

As the dispute dragged on, owners realized that the impasse was hindering their taking care of the business necessary to start the 1920 season, including scheduling and the rules committee. They declared peace in February. Johnson acceded to the reinstatement of Carl Mays, and the Yankees dropped all litigation. The owners set up a board of review with Ruppert and Clark Griffith, a stalwart Johnson supporter; in the case of a split vote, the decision would be rendered by a Chicago federal judge.[19]

Mays would win 53 games for New York in 1920 and 1921 but lost his effectiveness thereafter. Although John McGraw expressed an interest in Mays and Mays in the Giants, the Yankees shipped the pitcher to Cincinnati. For once, the Yankees watched their former player rebound as Mays won 20 games in 1924 and 19 games in 1926.[20]

The Mays trade presaged an exodus of Boston players headed south to New York. The Babe Ruth trade will be recounted below as well as an economic analysis of the deal. Frederick Lieb describes the relationship between Frazee and T. L. Huston as chummy; they were drinking pals, and Lieb seems to imply that Huston bamboozled the boozed-up Frazee.[21] In any event, when Frazee needed cash to buttress his rickety finances, the Yankee owners were willing to relinquish the green stuff for ball players to win a pennant.

The list of talented Red Sox players transferred to the Yankees in addition to Ruth and Mays is a long one: Ernie Shore, Duffy Lewis, Sad Sam Jones, Joe Dugan, Wally Schang, Everett Scott, Joe Bush, Waite Hoyt, and Herb Pennock, among others. The Yankees-Athletics trades of the 1950s did not benefit the Yankees as much as these Boston trades did, as the latter-day Yankees' best acquisitions were Roger Maris, Clete Boyer, and Ralph Terry.[22]

The Joe Dugan trade elicited howls of outrage. The Yankees trailed St. Louis by one and a half games at the time of the deal. Contemporaries claim that Dugan was a top-flight player, but the records provide scant support. Dugan was a light-hitting third baseman. He drew 250 walks during his fourteen seasons and hit just .280 during a hitter's decade. The Red Sox had obtained him from Connie Mack via Washington (a three-team trade) before the 1922 season; by mid season he was playing with

New York. The Yankees needed a third baseman since Frank Baker was fading fast. The Yankees gave up reserves Elmer Miller, Chick Fewster, Johnny Mitchell, Lefty O'Doul, and $50,000 for Dugan. At the time, no one realized that O'Doul would prove a formidable hitter.[23]

The Dugan trade was interesting, as other teams claimed they had offered just as much if not more than the Yankees had for the Red Sox player. Such complaints were similar to ones American League teams made in the late 1950s when the Yankees acquired Roger Maris. Left unspoken was a belief that the Yankees got Red Sox players at a "discount," possibly because Frazee was in hock to Ruppert. Frazee blandly ignored fan protests and said, "fans didn't take to him [Dugan] and he hadn't come up to our expectations."[24] Ban Johnson called the Dugan deal "regrettable," but he did nothing to rescind it. He noted that Clark Griffith and other owners were preparing to legislate against such mid-season deals.[25]

National League owners considered a ban on cash trades, but monitoring and enforcing such deals seems quixotic. Pittsburgh and St. Louis appeared to be in favor of such a ban, but the Phillies, Braves, Giants, and Cubs owners may well have preferred the status quo. No one was forcing the Braves and Phillies to sell their players.[26] The *Sporting News* editorialist recognized the inherent futility in such proposals: "The 'evil' complained of, and which is sought to curb, is not one that can be handled by legislation, any more than a prohibition law will destroy a man's craving for booze."[27] President John Heydler suggested setting a maximum price for ball players, but again such a proposal needed monitoring and enforcement mechanisms to work. The proposal was easily surreptitiously circumvented.[28]

Another sportswriter made the salient point, "Having abused club owners for not spending money for players to win pennants, such as Connie Mack, Charles Ebbets, William Baker and a lot of others, we are now abusing the men who do spend money to win pennants." At the time of the firestorm of protest (1922), the Yankees had yet to win their second pennant ever, and the Giants were trying to win just their second pennant since 1917.[29]

After the Yankees ran off another three-year stretch of pennants between 1926 and 1928, fans began the "Break up the Yankees!" cry. The *Sporting News* dismissed such antics, pointing out only one team had ever won four titles in a row, so it was likely that some deterioration in the Yankees would occur naturally. The editor criticized such calls: "When a baseball league gets to be a 'help your neighbor' affair, the whole organization of baseball will need a 'Bill' Hulbert [founder of the National League] to come back and straighten things out."[30] Another writer, after making the point, "championship machines soon wear out . . . three pennants in a row is the accepted limit," asked a more relevant question: "why . . . should clubs like the Phillies and Red Sox remain in the rut year after year?"[31] Years later, when the Yankees had won twenty or so pennants, the complaints about "buying pennants" and gaining important late-season reinforcements may have held more content.

Through all of these deals, Frazee claimed he was going to strengthen his club with the money. Ban Johnson accused Frazee of "being the champion wrecker of the baseball age." Although Frazee stripped his club, he presumably also reduced the value of the franchise, as prospective owners would be willing to pay less for a set of contracts covering mediocre players instead of a world-championship roster. Presumably Frazee had to weigh his cash gains against potential depreciation in his franchise's value.[32] Reporters were dubious about Frazee's assertion that he was building the team and argued, "Until Organized Baseball arms itself with the weapons necessary to punish or eliminate 'undesirable' club owners as expeditiously and effectively as it can curb or expel ball players, the nation's pastime will not recover the full confidence of the public. . . . [Frazee] has wrecked what used to be one of the best and most loyal baseball cities in the world."[33]

Prior to selling his club, Frazee swung a few deals that left some reporters claiming that the Red Sox were truly rebuilding: "[the deal] serves notice on the baseball world that Frazee and [Frank] Chance, Inc., mean business. In less than a fortnight five capable young players have been added to the Boston payroll and two veterans disposed of."[34] The youngsters failed to improve the Red Sox, whose record was almost identical in 1922 and 1923.

The Trade That Shook the Baseball World

One of the most important dates in baseball history, or at least New York Yankees baseball history, was January 5, 1920.[35] On that date they purchased Babe Ruth from the Boston Red Sox for $100,000 (paid in four installments). H. G. Salsinger reported that a bank held notes for $350,000 against the Red Sox to cover debts owed to prior owner Joseph Lannin, including a mortgage obligation on Fenway Park. Frazee had a friend who agreed to renew the note when Frazee was short of cash. The friend left the bank, and the directors told Frazee to pay them. Frazee and Jacob Ruppert agreed to a loan of $300,000 or more. The loan was made through Ruppert's real estate company and, therefore, might be considered outside of baseball.[36]

The relationship between the Yankees and Frazee was eerily similar to that between the Yankees and Arnold Johnson of the Kansas City Athletics—Johnson owned Yankee Stadium—in the 1950s and 1960s. The interlocking relationship between the Yankees and the Red Sox should have been investigated, but Ban Johnson, with his loan to Cleveland, was compromised. Johnson claimed he only heard of the situation from St. Louis Browns owner Philip Ball. Thomas J. Barry, counsel for the Boston club explained that the Fenway Realty Trust company owned Fenway Park and was separate and distinct from the ball club, characterizing the team as "simply a tenant." He claimed that Jacob Ruppert, Inc. was a corporation dealing in real estate and had stockholders and officers distinct from Ruppert the individual: "The Boston American League Baseball Club has nothing to do with this mortgage, nor is the franchise included in the mortgage. There is no connection between the club and either Jacob Ruppert or the Jacob Ruppert Corporation."[37] Reporters certainly found the situation rife with hypocrisy on the part of Johnson, Frazee, and the Yankees.[38]

Sportswriter Frank Graham recounted a different version of the Ruth trade. He recalled that Frazee came to New York (he had an office there because of his Broadway shows) seeking cash. He asked Ruppert to lend him $500,000, but Ruppert suggested selling Ruth for cash and possibly some players. Ed Barrow told him to take the cash: "there aren't any players on that ball club I'd want on mine."[39] Robert Weintraub, however, relates yet another version, implying that Huston instigated the deal for Ruth. As with other players sold for large amounts, Ruth demanded $15,000 of the purchase price from Frazee.[40]

In fairness to Frazee, the Red Sox had slumped badly in 1919. The slump may have been because its rivals had more stars returning from the military than did the patched-up Red Sox, who had won the pennant in 1918. Ruth set a record with 29 home runs and hit .322, but few people would have predicted the monster years he had coming. Ruth's .376 and 54 home runs in 1920 stunned the baseball world. The slugger was also a savvy negotiator; he was an unruly employee in the eyes of the owner; and Frazee had tired of his shenanigans, especially Ruth's demand to renegotiate his current $10,000 salary. The Yankees, too, would struggle to keep Ruth in tow for several seasons, including a celebrated blow-up with manager Miller Huggins (this incident was regrettably portrayed by William Bendix as Ruth in *The Babe Ruth Story*).

Boston observers, including ex-player Fred Tenney lauded the deal, agreeing with Frazee: "he knows his own business best. A team is as strong as its weakest link. A player that fits an organization is of more value than any star not working in harmony with his club." Tenney appeared to have ignored the Chicago White Sox, a bickering bunch, who had displaced the Red Sox as American League champions. Since Red Sox manager Ed Barrow told Frazee he was making a mistake getting rid of Ruth, one can surmise that Ruth was not a clubhouse problem. Frazee, though, said that while Ruth was the greatest hitter in the game, "Ruth had become simply impossible and the Boston Club could no longer put up with his eccentricities." Frazee added that Ruth was "likewise one of the most selfish and inconsiderate men that ever wore a baseball uniform." Other sources, though, claimed that Red Sox players "were just as happy as Babe when the new [home run] mark was finally battered out."[41]

Reporters figured that Ruth's appeal at the box office would more than offset the sale price and Ruth's new $20,000 salary (his contract called for $15,000 per season plus a $5,000 bonus for both seasons; the Red Sox agreed to pay half of the salary increase of $10,000). One wrote, "He should pay for himself in a few years at best, and it is barely possible that in one big year he may cross off the Ruppert-Huston slate the record sum paid for his services." The writer pointed out that the sale demonstrated a growing disparity between teams in smaller cities and larger cities in obtaining top talent.[42]

Thomas Rice analyzed the deal's financial aspects thusly, based on an assumption that a team needed 4,000 attendees per game—home and away—to break even: "If Ruth was bought for $125,000 [sic], he represents 166,667 admissions at 75 cents per [which he considered an overestimate of per-attendee admission price]." Rice made adjustments for Ruth's higher salary than the player he displaced, before reaching the conclusion that the Yankees needed to play before 802,667 fans in 1920 if the per capita price was seventy-five cents, but closer to 1,000,000 in actuality.[43] Given that the Yankees' home attendance alone jumped by 600,000 between 1919 and 1920, Ruth appears to have amply repaid the *actual* $100,000 purchase price and higher salary.

Michael Haupert and Kenneth Winter examined the financial aspects of the Ruth trade. They attributed increased home gate receipts, World Series earnings, and increased road receipts to the acquisition of Ruth.[44]

Babe Ruth transformed the Yankees … with a lag. The team's win-loss record improved somewhat in 1920, but the team finished third again. In his fifteen years with New York, the team won seven pennants. Not until Ruth's fourth season did the Yankees win the World Series (shades of Alex Rodriguez); Ruth had a miserable 1922 series. The Yankees did not sport a winning World Series record until they won the 1932 series (Ruth's last pennant) to become 4-3 in World Series tilts.

In the aftermath, Boston's lackluster 1919 record was almost duplicated in 1920 without Ruth. Team attendance fell by only fifteen thousand in 1920. Reporters claimed that Frazee turned a profit with the

Red Sox in 1919, so aside from liquidity needs he was not economically hard pressed.[45]

The Yankees may not have been content with just getting Ruth. St. Louis Browns official Jimmy Burke claimed that the Yankees offered $200,000 for George Sisler after the 1920 season, but that the Browns refused.[46] If so, the Yankees were certainly willing to spend large sums to capture a pennant.

John McGraw Gets His Man . . . Most of the Time

Boston's other fans, those of the National League Braves, also had reason to lament their rivals in New York City. The New York Giants obtained players from the Braves, sometimes via mid-season deals, to shore up their pennant chances. McGraw got pitcher Art Nehf from Boston during the 1919 campaign for $55,000 (he also obtained catcher Frank Snyder from St. Louis and pitcher Phil Douglas from Chicago); pitcher Hugh McQuillan from the Braves during the 1922 season (for a reputed $100,000); and pitcher Larry Benton in 1927. Benton went 13-6 for the Giants, who finished third, just two games behind Pittsburgh. The Nehf deal occurred concurrently with the aforementioned Carl Mays trade, prompting a writer to point out that these mid-season trades were a new phenomenon. A writer made a distinction between Braves president George Grant's attitude and Harry Frazee's: "Had Grant been sending his best material in a stream to the Giants there would be more bitterness felt. . . . Grant never had a great team and did not dismantle it."[47]

If Boston fans were irate about seeing their stars migrate, pity the poor Philadelphia fans. We've already mentioned Connie Mack's fire sale after 1914, but the Phillies also dismantled their pennant-winning team of 1915. The Phillies had finished second in 1917 before owner William Baker started disbanding his club. By the 1919–21 seasons, both teams finished last each season in their respective leagues. The Phillies started their downward spiral by sending Grover Cleveland Alexander to the Cubs in 1918 and star shortstop Dave Bancroft to New York in 1920; Bancroft cost the Giants $100,000, with two lesser players exchanged in addition.[48]

McGraw obtained outfielders Irish Meusel and Casey Stengel and infielder Johnny Rawlings from the Phillies in 1922. Sportswriter John Wray chastised William Baker as someone "bent on stripping his team of all baseball strength for the purpose of fattening his treasury. Not one move made in two years by Baker has indicated an interest in the building up of his team."[49]

Even pennant contenders, though, sometimes tried to jettison star players who demanded too much money. John McGraw tried to pry Heinie Groh loose from the still-contending Cincinnati Reds in 1921, but Landis prevented the trade until after the season. Landis worried that Groh, having sat out much of the 1921 season, was purposely trying to get traded to the Giants after a salary dispute with Cincinnati; the commissioner did not countenance such a breach of discipline and voided any potential deal involving Groh. Landis characterized McGraw's effort as "commercialism" (buying a pennant) in issuing his decision. McGraw sent George Burns and Mike Gonzales and cash to Cincinnati for Groh in December 1921.[50] McGraw continued acquiring late-season reinforcements; he got pitcher Jack Scott from Cincinnati during the 1922 season; Scott went 8-2 down the stretch.

McGraw set his sights high. We'll discuss his wooing of Rogers Hornsby later. The manager also sought Edd Roush, whom he had owned briefly, after the Federal League folded, but he had sold the player to Cincinnati. He tried for years to retrieve Roush, and when he finally got him in 1927, he offered the player $70,000 for three years. Roush hadn't liked McGraw for years, but the manager promised to not ride the player and remained true to his word.[51]

McGraw's acquisition of such big names as Groh and Roush bore mixed results. They were past their primes. Although Hornsby had a big year in 1927 and capably managed the team when McGraw was incapacitated, the two were only together for one season.

Other "Predatory" Trades

Other teams met Phillies owner William Baker's chronic need for cash, and the owner sold several useful players, including Lee Meadows, who would help lead Pittsburgh to two pennants. Baker's players probably salivated at the thought of being traded to pennant contenders.[52]

Owners such as Ruppert-Huston and Charles Weeghman of the Cubs were not reticent about enticing players on rival teams to become dissatisfied and to press for being traded to clubs flush with cash. Reporters related how Weeghman had $200,000 to obtain players, and the owner wasn't shy about letting people know. Weeghman's tampering with opposing players caused consternation throughout the National League.[53]

The *Sporting News* editor further suggested that owners, such as Weeghman, had to learn to refrain from bombastic statements about his willingness to spend money: "When the magnate learns he not only is hurting his game but making an ass of himself by his bragging . . . either through business sense or shame he will curb his mouthings."[54] The owners passed an amendment imposing a fine of $1,000 or expulsion from the league (for repeated offenses) for tampering with a player on another club. Weeghman did succeed in getting Alexander and his batterymate Bill Killefer, as part of his spending spree; Alexander was unhappy about his contract with the Phillies. Weeghman also offered a large sum of cash for Rogers Hornsby but was rebuffed.[55]

Rogers Hornsby, Travelin' Man

The American League had a plethora of all-time great hitters—Babe Ruth, Ty Cobb, Tris Speaker, Lou Gehrig, and Napoleon Lajoie, and the National League's cupboard seemed rather barren for the first decades of the twentieth century. Honus Wagner fit in the group named above, but other top National League players, such as Edd Roush and Zack Wheat, were nowhere near the luminaries that the American League collection were (and Joe Jackson, Eddie Collins, and George Sisler weren't included above). The National League did boast one hitter worthy of inclusion in the group above: Rogers Hornsby. The hard-hitting right-hander hit for ridiculously high averages and with power. Considering that he was not fully fit in 1930, thereby missing out on a prime hitting season to boost his average (he was at .363 lifetime after the 1929 season), his lifetime

.358 batting average is stunning. His slugging and on-base statistics are equally impressive.

Almost from the beginning, New York Giants manager John McGraw coveted Hornsby. McGraw thought Hornsby would be a box-office draw to match Babe Ruth, although the player's personality hardly endeared him to fans. Year after year, rumors persisted that McGraw offered the St. Louis Cardinals $100,000, then $200,000 for the slugger. When he finally landed Hornsby for the 1927 season, the marriage lasted but one season. Hornsby then began an almost-annual migration about the National League: Boston in 1928, Chicago in 1929, St. Louis Cardinals in 1933, and across town to the Browns in 1933.

Branch Rickey was determined to keep Hornsby, even though some of the Cardinals owners wanted to cash in on the player. Sam Breadon disliked Hornsby's behavior. Rickey staved off McGraw's annual bids for Hornsby, with reporters speculating on ever-higher amounts of money being offered. Bidding allegedly started at $70,000 and four players in 1919; by 1920, the speculated amounts exceeded $200,000, and Rickey claimed in 1924 to have been offered $300,000. Sam Breadon claimed in 1920 that any deal for Hornsby should include good players as well as the reputed $200,000 offered by the Giants. Breadon suggested Frank Frisch for a start.[56]

New York sportswriters assumed that Hornsby was itching to play for New York, with one writing, "Hornsby would like to come to New York, where a star may shine at his brightest."[57] Even after Hornsby and Branch Rickey nearly engaged in fisticuffs in the clubhouse after a tough loss in 1923, the team rebuffed McGraw's entreaties. McGraw, disappointed, told reporters, "I . . . think their demands are too much. I wouldn't trade Frank Frisch even for Hornsby, nor would I again offer to give them $250,000 for their second baseman. The day is passed when Hornsby is worth that much to the Giants."[58]

His remarks aside, John McGraw landed Hornsby after the 1926 season in one of the most bizarre trades ever. Hornsby had just led St. Louis to its first pennant and World Series championship ever. He had, it is true, slumped to .317 with only 11 home runs. St. Louis owner Sam Breadon disliked his player-manager's gambling habits. Hornsby, renowned for not attending movies to prevent eyestrain, spent plenty of time eyeing horses. Hornsby also wanted more money and a three-year contract to continue as player-manager of the Cardinals. Breadon told reporters, "I told Hornsby, that the three-year contract he proposed ran into bigger money than the club's earning power for the past eight years justified, and that one year was as far as I could reasonably see my way to sign." Breadon decided to unload him.[59]

Meanwhile in New York, John McGraw was upset with star second baseman Frankie Frisch. If ever a player should have been a favorite son of McGraw's, Frisch should have been. The smart, speedy, talented Frisch was a do-it-all infielder and another manager on the field. However, he was high strung and apparently tired of McGraw and playing for the Giants; he took ill during the waning days of the 1926 season and sat out several games. He had hit .314, well below his career average.[60]

The Giants and Cardinals therefore traded their stars in a shocking move; the Giants threw in pitcher Jimmy Ring but no cash reportedly changed hands. For John McGraw, the offseason between the 1926 and 1927 season must have been a dream, as he also obtained eventual Hall of Fame player Edd Roush and pitcher Burleigh Grimes. Along with Rogers Hornsby, McGraw got his trio of Hall of Famers for Frankie Frisch, infielder George Kelly, and Butch Henline.[61] It was to no avail; McGraw's team finished second, two games back. A year later, Hornsby and Grimes would be gone, and Roush was injured.

There was an unusual aspect to the Cardinals' trade of Hornsby. Breadon had sold Hornsby 1,167 shares of stock (at forty-three dollars a share) in the club as a reward or in lieu of a stipulated salary. National League president John Heydler promptly ordered Hornsby to divest his shares because playing for one team while having an ownership stake in another team smacked of "syndicate baseball," something baseball assiduously tried to avoid. The Giants and Cardinals claimed that Heydler was exceeding his authority as there were no explicit rules against a player owning stock in another team; the situation apparently had not occurred to the owners when they drafted their rules.[62] Heydler's directive, however, created a "fire sale" aspect and might have diminished the shares' value. Hornsby demanded $105 a share, claiming that he had enlisted an auditor to examine the books and estimated a book value of $150 a share; the player therefore thought demanding $105 a share an eminently fair offer. Breadon disagreed, and the two sparred over the stock valuation for weeks. Heydler said that Hornsby would not be allowed to play until the sale was completed, sending Breadon, McGraw, and other National League owners into a tizzy.

The other owners worried that their gate receipts would suffer without their biggest star on the field; this fear ultimately provided a way out of the conundrum.[63] National League owners agreed to back an offer of $100,000 plus $12,000 legal fees for Hornsby's shares. Breadon paid $86,000, the other seven teams paid $2,000 each, and the Giants an additional $12,000. The owners also passed a law prohibiting players from owning stock in another club as well as preventing club officials from owning stock or lending money to any other club or players of another club.[64]

Despite a good season for the Giants, Hornsby was gone by the next season. The Giants tried to gloss over their trade of Hornsby to the Braves before the 1928 season. They denied that Hornsby's behavior—his potential usurpation of McGraw's authority—had anything to do with the trade. They got Shanty Hogan and Jimmy Welsh in return.[65]

Charles Stoneham apparently disapproved of Hornsby winning his lawsuit against a bookmaker by "pleading that race track betting was illegal, and had no status in court." Hornsby owed the bookmaker $70,000. Since Stoneham and McGraw considered themselves good sportsmen in the betting sense, they scorned Hornsby's reneging on a debt.[66]

Although some observers groused about the relationship between the Giants and the Braves, for once Boston got the better end of a deal. *Baseball Magazine* commented on the unique aspect of the deal: "That [Hornsby] should be traded from the greatest city in the country to a town of lesser magnitude where baseball interest had languished for years, was an amazing act. That he should be traded without cash consideration and for player material of much inferior value was even more amazing."[67] Hornsby had a strong year for Boston, but the team finished seventh again and lost even more games than the year before, even with the addition of George Sisler. Attendance declined to 227,000 from 289,000.

Hornsby next found himself in Chicago with the Cubs; Boston got Socks Seibold, Bruce Cunningham, Percy Jones, Lou Legett, Freddie Maguire, and a reputed $200,000 from the Cubs. With these new players, Boston finished last in 1929. Whether the Cubs really paid $200,000 for Hornsby remains unclear.[68]

F. C. Lane may have captured Hornsby's travails best: "Hornsby has always lacked that colorful personality, that picturesqueness or magnetism or what you choose to call it that inspires the enthusiasm of the fans. . . . but if his personal conduct is singularly free from criticism in many respects, it is vulnerable in others." He, of course, cited Hornsby's penchant for gambling.[69]

Player Trades and Competitive Balance

Baseball owners proved willing to trade big stars still in their primes: Babe Ruth, Grover Cleveland Alexander, Frankie Frisch, and Rogers Hornsby being the biggest names. Player trades, of course, affected competitive balance. The Babe Ruth trade certainly benefited the Yankees at the gate and on the field. Other trades, even of top players, did not always affect competitive balance in anticipated ways. The next chapter discusses competitive balance in baseball during the 1920s.

9 Competitive Balance and Its Discontents

As always, baseball teams waxed and waned. However, one team waxed and remained strong for decades. Although most teams had some success during the 1920s, a few teams languished. Teams competed for players, and owners with greater reserves of cash often held the upper hand. Proposed palliatives for competitive balance, including revenue sharing, were not panaceas.

Measures of Competitive Balance

Every era in professional team sports has its dominant teams and perennial losers. Major League Baseball from 1919 to 1929 was no different. The New York Yankees and Giants boasted the best win-loss records for the eleven seasons, with the two franchises winning ten pennants between them (table 17). The franchises, though, were diverging. The Giants won four consecutive pennants between 1921 and 1924; the Yankees spread their six pennants across the 1921–28 seasons. The National League had two inept franchises in the Boston Braves and Philadelphia Phillies, while the American League had only one perennially sad-sack team—the Boston Red Sox.

The Phillies and Braves, though, had come by their lamentable condition naturally. The two teams had won just two pennants between them, and the 1914 Braves were known as the "Miracle Braves" for good reason. The Phillies won the following season. Whether these surprising pennants were tied to the existence of the Federal League and the accompanying dilution of player talent is an interesting question. The Red Sox, though, had been one of the American League's best franchises until Harry Frazee stripped the team. The Red Sox would be dormant until Thomas Yawkey bought the franchise in the early 1930s.

Aside from Pittsburgh, though, every team suffered at least one losing season. The Phillies and Red Sox did not have any winning seasons during these eleven years. Twelve teams won at least 60 percent of their games in at least one season. Winning 60 percent of the games in a season was no guarantee of a pennant, though, as the Browns and Indians discovered to their chagrin.

The Philadelphia Athletics and St. Louis Cardinals exemplified upward mobility. The Athletics had been the American League pennant winners in four out of five seasons between 1910 and 1914. When Connie Mack proved resistant to granting pay raises to his star players in the face of Federal League offers, his team promptly collapsed from 99-53 in 1914 to 43-109 the following year. Mack was a shrewd operator, but it took him over a decade to rebuild his team. The St. Louis Cardinals had been lackluster from 1903 until Branch Rickey took over as general manager; he had been with the St. Louis Browns, and in a misguided move, the Browns' owner canned him.

Modern-day fans may have difficulty accepting the Washington Senators as a strong franchise. Although the Washington Senators had given inspiration to the deathless jingle, "Washington, first in war, first in peace, last in the American League," Clark Griffith assembled sufficient talent initially around pitching legend Walter Johnson to capture three pennants in ten seasons (1924–33); after he sold his son-in-law, shortstop-manager Joe Cronin, to Boston Red Sox in 1934, his franchise transformed into chronic mediocrity. By the 1950s, a scant two decades later, the Senators' futility would be mocked in the plot line of Broadway play "Damn Yankees." The play's conceit revolved around the idea that the Senators could only win a pennant by making a Faustian bargain with the devil; certainly Clark Griffith's nephew Calvin was unable to resurrect the team in Washington.

The American League had three pennant blowouts in 1923, 1927, and 1929, while the National League races tended to be closer, with a blowout in 1929. Pennant blowouts by more than ten games did not necessarily result in a drop in attendance between seasons, although they may have suppressed any potential gains. Both leagues had last-place teams that were fifty or more games out of first place.

Economists James Quirk and Rodney Fort defined a measure of competitive balance. They calculated the standard deviation in win-loss percentages.[1] They compared the standard deviation with that of an "ideal" standard deviation based on a league with evenly matched teams.

One way to think about this "idealized" standard deviation is to consider a coin-tossing league. Over 154 games, your team would win an expected 77 games, but there would be a spread about the expected mean number of wins. For 154 games, the spread would be .040, or 6.2 games. Two-thirds of the teams in a coin-flipping league would have win-loss records of .460 to .540 (70.8 to 83.2 wins). If the actual standard deviation of a league's standing was .040, then the ratio between the actual to the idealized standard deviation would be .040/.040 or 1. League standings typically featured actual standard deviations well in excess of the idealized standard deviation. A ratio of 2:1 was not uncommon.

Looking at table 18, the American League ratio was low in 1922–24 and peaked in 1919 and 1927. The National League ratio peaked in 1928, but had been low in 1925–26. Quirk and Fort found that the average 1920–29 ratios were lower than in either the previous or following decades.[2]

In terms of pennants won, eleven teams out of sixteen teams won pennants between 1919 and 1929. The St. Louis Browns came within a game of winning a pennant in 1922, while the Red Sox had won the 1918 American League pennant. The Phillies, on the other hand, never got within twenty-seven games of first place.

Some observers thought the National League after World War I lagged badly in comparison with the American League and with previous National League talent. Sportswriter John Sheridan berated the New York Giants in 1922 because the team had to go out and buy some players to fortify its roster in its battle with the Chicago Cubs, a team Sheridan characterized as "a good semi-pro team." He characterized the other contender, the St. Louis Cardinals, as a "uniformed mob" such as the

Cardinals. He claimed that Grover Alexander and Charlie Hollocher were the only Cubs players that could have "won places as substitutes on the Cubs of 1909." He made a further dubious comparison by downgrading the 1922 St. Louis Browns in comparison with the 1886 and 1887 Browns.[3] If Sheridan was falling into the trap of worshipping the ballplayers of one's youth, he was not alone. Other observers worried that the National League did not rate with the American League during the 1920s.

Player Movement

Major League owners saw nothing wrong in trafficking in human beings. They bought and sold, traded, demoted, suspended, and released players—usually for sound business reasons, but sometimes out of pique. Owners often traded players whom they felt demanded too much money, and the owners often exchanged malcontents. Occasionally, an owner would trade a player for moral reasons. On rare occasions, an owner would sign what we recognize today as a "free agent," i.e., a professional ballplayer no longer under contract to a team. Fans were ambivalent regarding trades. Fans of wealthy clubs often had reason to rejoice, while fans of downtrodden franchises knew they would likely bid adieu to promising players. Pundits, fans, and baseball people placed their faith in the reserve clause to promote competitive balance. Some teams remained weak, while other teams remained strong, implying the faith was misplaced. Economists Ronald Coase and Simon Rottenberg developed a powerful theory that suggests the distribution of players would be similar under either free agency or the reserve clause.[4]

Consider Babe Ruth. He has all five attributes that scouts are fond of rating: speed, fielding, hitting for average, hitting for power, and throwing. With the emphasis on statistical analysis (which often borders on overkill), modern day scouts might add "patience," in terms of drawing bases on balls and extending pitch counts. Babe has this attribute, too.

Suppose the St. Louis Browns found Ruth on a sandlot. They sign him for a few hundred dollars bonus and a Minor League contract worth $2,000 a year. After a couple of years of seasoning, Ruth debuts on the Major League stage. Eventually he hits .322 with 29 home runs. On the side, he pitches an occasional game for the club, given his powerful arm. He also draws 100 walks while catching everything hit to him in right field, thereby pleasing the Browns owner. He boosts the Browns' attendance by one hundred thousand a season.

Meanwhile, in Gotham City, as contemporary baseball writers dubbed New York City, the Yankees' owners Ruppert and Huston are enviously eyeing the Babe. "That kid would be worth an extra 350,000 fans at the Polo Grounds." If we make the assumption that each additional fan means an extra $0.75 in gate receipts after the visitors take their share (we will ignore the Yankees' and the Browns' additional road revenue from having Ruth), then Ruth is worth 250,000 (350,000–100,000) times $0.75, or $187,500 more per season to the Yankees than to the Browns. The Browns' and Yankees' owners have an incentive to move Ruth to the more lucrative Yankees; the owners simply have to negotiate splitting the $187,500. The sale price goes to the Browns' owner.

If Ruth had rights to his playing labor, though, then Ruppert and Huston would simply deal directly with Ruth. They would negotiate to split the $187,500 per season. In this case, Ruth would share in the value of his unique talent.

The Coase/Rottenberg insight is that, given well-defined property rights to a player's labor (free agency and the reserve clause are forms of property rights to labor), resources will be distributed efficiently. Players will gravitate toward teams where their ability to generate additional revenue (marginal revenue product in economic lingo) is greatest.

Baseball officials, sportswriters, and fans likely would have disagreed with the two economists' prediction. Thomas Rice painted a dire picture of unlimited trading of stars, even with the reserve clause in force: "In a few years the New York teams would have been all-star aggregations . . . interest in the races would have been killed, and the thousands of people would have been thrown out of work, to say nothing of the club owners, losing all they had sunk in their huge plants."[5] Rice's hysteria echoed for decades, as baseball justified the reserve clause again and again.

Why won't the Yankees end up with all of the best players? Additional star players begin to add smaller increments to a team's win-loss record;

you might end up with more lopsided games but just a few more wins by adding another star to a pennant-winning club. If the team is too strong, it will clinch the pennant race early. There is strong evidence that fans lose interest in attending games that "don't matter" in the sense of determining the pennant winner. When the Yankees blew out their opponents in the late 1930s, few fans bothered attending the remaining games during the last two or three weeks of the season. Therefore, a team owner is unlikely to collect all stars at every position and five or six on his or her (Helene Britton was an owner for a few years) pitching staff.[6]

Baseball owners gradually developed the system of property rights to players embodied in the reserve clause and allowed for trading players without having to release them. Gone were the days when Detroit purchased the Buffalo team in 1886 to acquire the "big four"—Dan Brouthers, Hardy Richardson, Jack Rowe, and Jim White, rather than work out a transaction.[7] Being able to transfer players to where their value was greater benefited the owners. By solidifying their property rights to players, owners could more easily transfer players for cash or for other players.

Many trades involved cash. Sportswriters could usually only guess at how much money changed hands. As H. G. Salsinger admitted, "There are several things in baseball that have done the game a lot of harm. Among them . . . is the reported price paid for a player. Some times these prices are really paid; other times they are simply handed out to gather effect and publicity." There was a danger to issuing reports of inflated prices, as players became emboldened to demand a share of the sales price.[8]

Player movement affected competitive balance. Recognizing this, and the value of having competitive teams in large markets, league presidents did on occasion engineer player sales or trades. Ed Barrow, of all people, recalled with outrage, finding that Ban Johnson had forced a trade involving Kid Elberfeld. Johnson sent Elberfeld to the Highlanders from Barrow's Tigers club in return for Herman Long and Ernie Courtney. Johnson wanted to ensure that the New York club was a strong one, and the team, indeed, finished second in 1904 before slumping into mediocrity.[9] Johnson also engineered the transfer of Napoleon Lajoie from the Athletics to the Indians in the early days of the American League. This move was more about league preservation, given that a restraining order had been placed on Lajoie's participation in games in the state of Pennsylvania during the American League–National League war.

A strange piece of information appeared in the *New York Times*, where an article reported that the Yankees were unable to swing a deal during the 1917 meetings: "the co-operation which the Yankee owners had been promised to strengthen the club was not forthcoming."[10] The Yankees finished sixth in 1917, with a .464 mark, but they had a winning record in 1916, so why they needed cooperation is unclear. A few weeks later, the Yankees sent five players and cash to the St. Louis Browns for Derrill Pratt, a light-hitting second baseman. The Yankees had wanted to acquire George Sisler, too, but the Browns rebuffed their entreaties.[11]

Another set of rules governed player movement; these rules pertained to demoting players. If an owner wanted to demote a player to the Minors, that player had to pass waivers. Each team in the league had a chance to claim the player at the waiver price; the original club had the option of revoking waivers and keeping the player. The waiver system was installed to protect players, to keep them playing in as high a level of baseball as any owner saw fit, and to help weaker teams. By 1923 owners proposed allowing teams lower in the standing to have priority in claiming players off waivers. So many owners, though, had secret agreements or engaged in gentlemen's agreements not to claim certain players that the waiver system's effectiveness in achieving either purpose was in doubt. Lou Gehrig was a prime example of such an agreement. The Yankees wanted to send Gehrig to a farm team so he would get playing time. They spent months to convince the other teams not to claim Gehrig when they placed him on waivers.[12]

Building Pennant-Winning Clubs

The Yankees' ascendance was preceded by the decline of three heretofore powerful American League franchises: Philadelphia, Boston, and Chicago. These teams' declines contributed to the rise of other American League franchises.

After he lost the Black Sox players, Charles Comiskey struggled to replace them. He proclaimed that he had sufficient funds to purchase replacements, but his rivals, while expressing sympathy for his plight, offered no pity. The White Sox finished either fifth or seventh every year between 1921 and 1930, aside from an eighth-place finish in 1924. He introduced pitcher Ted Lyons, as well as high-priced third baseman Willie Kamm, to his remaining veteran core of Eddie Collins, Ray Schalk, and Red Faber, but these acquisitions could not retrieve the club's former glory.[13]

Connie Mack's years in the baseball wilderness, after his divestiture of his 1914 World Series team, gave signs of coming to an end by 1925 when the club not only posted a winning record for the first time in a decade, but finished second. Mack's acquisitions of Ty Cobb, Eddie Collins, and Zack Wheat for the 1927 season did not get the club past the New York Yankees nor did the addition of Tris Speaker allow the Athletics to surmount the Yankees in 1928. Mack also purchased Minor Leaguers Joe Boley and the aptly named Dud Branom. Fans began to grumble that Mack, already old by baseball standards, was obsolete.[14]

Mack's mix of veterans and young stars took time to gel, and in fact, most of the older veterans were gone by 1929. One observer thought that Mack may have erred in having three former managers on his playing roster (Cobb, Collins, and later Speaker)."[15]

If the Red Sox's and White Sox's doldrums plunged two teams to the second division, other teams ascended, if only temporarily. The St. Louis Browns struggled to remain competitive after their splendid 1922 showing. The club finished above .500 three times between 1923 and 1929 before a final plunge into the nether regions of the American League began in 1930. George Sisler, the team's best player, suffered from sinusitis incurred during a bout with influenza after the 1922 season. While some of his later batting averages were impressive, no one thought he was the same player he had been. Owner Philip Ball had financial reserves to spend, but he had difficulty finding and obtaining quality ballplayers.[16]

Yankees owners Jacob Ruppert and T. L. Huston spent several years trying to win a pennant. After acquiring the team, they purchased Lee

Magee, Nick Cullop, Joe Gedeon, Frank Gilhooley, and George Mogridge, some from the folded Federal League. They capped their spending spree by persuading Frank Baker to join them in 1916.[17] The Yankees purchased some big names but continued to fall short. A year before buying Babe Ruth, the club obtained Duffy Lewis, whom a reporter called "the most valuable outfielder who has played under the club banner in many years. . . . It has been the misfortune of the Yankees for several seasons past to be weak in the outfield."[18]

The Yankees' owners then sought the services of Edward Barrow, Frazee's manager. They approached Frazee regarding Barrow and received permission to sign him. The *New York Times* stated, "The acquisition of Barrow gives the Yankees another practical baseball man who knows every angle of the game."[19]

In the long run, this acquisition ranks a close second to acquiring Babe Ruth in transforming the Yankees. Barrow, of course, knew all about Boston's players and undoubtedly helped the Yankees acquire them. Then again, most of the American League owners and managers knew about the Red Sox's remaining talent; a key question is whether Barrow obtained these players at a "discount" from Frazee. The fact that Ruppert held a loan on Boston's Fenway Park could not help but foster suspicion. Although Barrow was now the Yankees' business manager, reporter Joe Vila claimed that Miller Huggins "supervised the deals that landed Combs, Meusel, Koenig, Lazzeri, Moore, Pipgras, Collins, Bengough, Gazaella, Wera and Thomas. He correctly sized up Gehrig . . . and got him for nothing." Vila lauded Huggins for his "brains, patience, diplomacy and temperament, together with a thorough knowledge of the inside game."[20] Whether Huggins and Barrow purposely sought players with more decorum is an interesting question. After the riotous years of the early 1920s, the new Yankees seemed more obedient.

When the Yankees tanked in 1925, they had Tony Lazzeri, Lou Gehrig, and Earle Combs waiting in the wings. At the end of the decade, when the Athletics temporarily displaced the Yankees, the Bronx team had Lefty Gomez and Bill Dickey on deck. In this sense, the Yankees differed from other clubs that ascended, peaked, and then began to tail off; the Yankees usually had reinforcements at hand.

Author Dan Levitt believes that the Yankees relied on superior management to remain successful for decades. Edward Barrow was a canny baseball man, but Jacob Ruppert and he were not especially innovative. The team lagged in installing electric lights for night baseball or negotiating contracts with radio stations for broadcasting rights (and this was while Ruppert was still alive). They lagged the Cardinals in building a farm team, although once they decided to make the plunge, they worked hard to get a good system built and hired George Weiss to oversee it. Levitt may or may not be correct about the Yankees' superior management, but another explanation is that the owner had the resources and the willingness to expend those resources to field a winner; the Yankees could afford more mistakes than many of their rivals could.

Levitt did not identify one intriguing aspect. After the Yankees rebuilt in 1926, the team's offense was now composed of not only slugging prowess but patience at the plate. The Yankees were perennial leaders in slugging average, walks, and on-base percentage, and this does not appear to be solely a factor of Ruth and Gehrig; did Barrow presage the modern-day emphasis on obtaining patient hitters with power?[21]

As if the Yankees' growing prowess on the field wasn't sufficient, they decided to hire the Chicago White Sox's mascot, Eddie Bennett, for the 1921 season. For the superstitious, Bennett was a joy. He performed (or whatever professional mascots do) for the White Sox. The Dodgers signed him after the mascot led the White Sox to the World Series. The Dodgers failed to take him to Cleveland for the final games of the World Series, and the Dodgers lost. Bennett claimed that had he attended the games in Cleveland, Brooklyn would have won the series. The Yankees would, indeed, win the 1921 pennant with Bennett.[22] Since the Brooklyn club went on to lose several more World Series, perhaps Dodgers fans should have ruefully considered the "Curse of the Bennett."

The 1920 World Series featured two teams assembled relatively cheaply. The Brooklyn Dodgers purchased their biggest star, Zack

Wheat, from the Minors, as they had a number of their other players. They obtained Rube Marquard and another player off the waiver list, as well as trading for several others. None of the players required a large expenditure of cash.

The Cleveland Indians won their first pennant in 1920. Some readers may think that the Indians won only because Frazee had stripped Boston, and the White Sox were allegedly throwing games. The Indians proved resilient enough to survive Ray Chapman's death, bringing up Joe Sewell. The team's star pitchers Stan Coveleski and Jim Bagby were "working agreement" players, sent to Cleveland in repayment of Minor League deals. George Uhle was signed as a sandlot player, while Slim Caldwell was a free agent. The Indians had, it is true, paid cash and players for star Tris Speaker, but the money was well spent. The other outfielders had cost a combined $17,500 to acquire. The infielders and catchers were mostly purchased from the Minors. Brooklyn and Cleveland would not return to the winner's circle for decades, though (1941 for the Dodgers and 1948 for the Indians, to be exact).[23]

As the Yankees and Giants attempted to win pennants by obtaining star players, other clubs took alternative, less-publicized routes to building strong teams. Signing promising amateur players, purchasing talented Minor League players, drafting Minor League players, claiming players on waivers, and making astute deals for heretofore obscure players were the tools middle-class clubs used.

Washington owner Clark Griffith relied on acquiring Major League players to accompany Walter Johnson, whom the Senators had signed as a semipro player. Griffith acquired Roger Peckinpaugh and other players for cash in the seasons preceding the team's back-to-back pennants in 1924–25; he also signed several Minor League players, although many failed to prosper in the Major Leagues. Griffith reportedly spent $124,500 for players during 1924. Of these players, Earl McNeely became a starting outfielder, while Walter Ruether won eighteen games in 1925. The Senators reportedly spent $154,750 for players during 1929; Buddy Myer was one of the prominent players. These figures probably did not reflect any players Griffith sold, so the net amount spent on maintaining and improving the team may have been less than reported (even allowing for the usual distortions in the actual amounts transacted).[24]

Although former Cubs owner Charles Weeghman made some splashy purchases of star players, his successor, William Wrigley, opted to let his president, William Veeck, try to build a team through signing young players and by treating the players fairly. Manager William "Bill" Killefer lauded the owner's generosity and how it helped build esprit de corps. The Cubs, though, hovered about the .500 mark for most of the decade, before beginning a string of pennants every third year (1929, 1932, 1935, and 1938).[25]

Reporters marveled at how cheaply the St. Louis Cardinals assembled their 1926 pennant-winning aggregation. Many of the team's players were signed for less than $5,000 each. The Cardinals got Grover Alexander for the waiver price—one of the greatest steals in waiver-rule history. Reporter Harry Neilly said, "The Cardinals engage in baseball on a whole-sale basis, and therein resides the why of how they can get men for such small sums."[26] The impressive thing about the Cardinals was their ability to change their roster and to keep winning pennants. By 1928, many of the 1926 squad were gone, including the great Hornsby; the club obtained veteran players for some of their former starters.[27]

The St. Louis Cardinals, though, were revolutionizing team building. Their farm system began paying dividends by the late 1920s. Before the 1929 season, after the Cardinals won their second pennant in 1928, sportswriter James Gould noted that the team had constantly and rapidly shifted its playing and managerial personnel.[28] We'll examine the Cardinals' farm system later.

Player Movement—A Statistical Analysis

Franchises differed in their ability to identify and to introduce top young talent. Using the Thorn-Palmer Total Baseball Rating (TBR) system (somewhat similar to the more recent Win Shares and other metrics) of the top players debuting between 1919 and 1945, the four teams (including the Yankees, Cardinals, and Giants) in the top quartile brought up

43.1 percent of them (table 19). These players represented 42.0 percent of the total TBRs of the 144 players. The bottom four teams (including the Browns and Reds) brought up a combined eighteen star players who had only 9.4 percent of the total TBRs. The distribution of new talent tightened in the 1946-64 and 1965-95 periods, as more teams created effective farm systems.[29]

Even when they introduced stars, though, some teams, such as the two Philadelphia teams, were unable to retain their star players for their entire career. Although a minority of star players performed for the same team their entire careers, those debuting for the Philadelphia teams were almost guaranteed to move on. The Athletics introduced thirty-four star players and kept only one for his entire career over the twentieth century; two other Athletics stars spent all but the final season or two with the club. Players debuting with the Yankees, Giants, and Senators/Twins had a relatively good chance of remaining with their club throughout their entire career. The Yankees retained eighteen of their star players for their entire careers.[30]

Minor League Player Acquisitions

If an owner wanted to find talent, the Minor Leagues were an obvious choice. Connie Mack rebuilt his Athletics by purchasing Lefty Grove, among other members of his great 1929-31 teams from Minor League teams. The Yankees initially bought established Major League players, but they began buying Minor League players in earnest by the mid 1920s, including Earle Combs and Tony Lazzeri (they signed Lou Gehrig and then optioned him to the Minor Leagues).

Sportswriters and baseball officials bemoaned the escalating prices paid for Minor League talent. They blamed the five Minor Leagues that refused to subject their players to the draft. By doing so, Major League owners had to pay open-market prices for young players. Buying Minor League talent was a highly speculative endeavor. Many Minor League players were called, but relatively few succeeded.

As with player salaries and amounts paid to buy Major League stars, the press reported purchase prices of Minor League players. Some owners, such as Charles Comiskey, refused to divulge details; Comiskey defended his actions by claiming, "I do not think the public is interested in what a ball player costs, so long as he delivers."[31]

Owners worried that stories of fabulous sums paid for Minor League players would inspire such players to demand a cut of the proceeds. Connie Mack later advocated paying Minor League players a share of any purchase price over $10,000, but his idea gained little favor among his peers. The *Sporting News* accused Minor League players of ingratitude for wanting some of the purchase price: "The player should jump at the chance to prove that he may be a man worth a salary of $10,000 as against a salary of $3,500."[32]

Fiorello LaGuardia introduced a player-friendly bill in New York. He called for a 90 percent tax on the sales of professional baseball players, whenever such sales exceeded $5,000, unless the player received the purchase price. LaGuardia argued, possibly erroneously, that baseball was the "only field in which an individual failed to profit through improved ability and transfer of his services."[33]

In any event, these sales prices were probably inaccurately reported, but the general trend of even inaccurate figures may provide a clue. Because of the wartime hike in prices, much of the rise in prices paid for the most desirable Minor League players simply reflected inflation. Ford Sawyer described how Ty Cobb and many top players were purchased for amounts well below $10,000 each, and that pitcher Rube Marquard caused a sensation when John McGraw paid $11,000 for him, but the price level had changed greatly between 1905 and 1923.[34]

During the Federal League war, Pittsburgh reputedly paid $22,500 for Marty O'Toole, a St. Paul pitcher. F. C. Lane described this as, "the most sensational speculation in the flesh and blood of a native athlete in the national history."[35] O'Toole had a brief career in the majors.

After the war, the New York Giants traded seven players and cash to acquire Rochester catcher Earl Smith. Waite Hoyt and George Kelly were among the players, and both would have solid careers in the big leagues. McGraw reacquired Kelly for 1919. Smith was a pretty good catcher with a hefty bat.[36]

The crosstown Yankees purchased Dazzy Vance and Bob Meusel in 1919, along with several other Minor League players. They didn't keep Vance, who went on to a sometimes spectacular career with Brooklyn, while Meusel became Babe Ruth's sidekick in the outfield and in various escapades.[37]

John McGraw was not shy about spending big money to get an object of his affection. He set a new high for purchasing a Minor League player in late 1921 when he bought outfielder Jimmy O'Connell from San Francisco for a reported $75,000 and some unnamed players. Whether McGraw actually paid this much is unknown, but O'Connell was typically referred to as a $75,000 purchase; one reporter did cite a $55,000 figure. Another Major League official, quoted anonymously, claimed the Giants were "stung good and proper" in their purchase, as he characterized O'Connell as "just a fair minor leaguer" with a weak arm.[38] O'Connell hit .337 with some power in 1921. The Giants kept him at San Francisco during 1922. He played for the Giants in 1923 and 1924 before being suspended from baseball, as detailed in the section on gambling. O'Connell got off to a slow start and incurred McGraw's wrath for twice missing hit-and-run signs, resulting in disaster: "Jimmy couldn't get started, yet McGraw stuck to him like glue, always hoping that he would hit the proper gait, but it was not to be."[39]

Rogers Hornsby, not the most sympathetic of men, pointed out the burden of being a high-priced Minor Leaguer: "There's one of the real tragedies of baseball. That fellow was over-advertised, and it has ruined him. Jim [O'Connell] is a good ball player—and given the proper encouragement he would make good. But he's through now. His spirit is broken, and the thing that did it was the weight of that $75,000 which McGraw paid for him."[40]

McGraw's purchase of O'Connell elicited much comment. Some observers were appalled by the large sum paid for an unproven player and wondered what the effects would be on the demands by established Major League stars.[41]

At the time McGraw bought O'Connell, the Detroit Tigers purchased two pitchers from Portland, Herman Pillette and Syl Johnson, for $40,000 and eight players. The Tigers must have liked Pillette's raw ability, because his 13-30 win-loss mark for 1921 was unimpressive.[42] Minor League owners could, if they were lucky, find some gifted players simply by relying on the large numbers of players they got in return for their stars.

Until they built farm systems, Major League owners viewed purchasing Minor League players as a worthwhile endeavor. One anonymous official told a reporter for *Collier's* that only "one out of ten" recruits became successful Major League players. He said the players cost an average of $5,000 each, so if they spent $50,000 to get one good player, "he repays us for all the loss." He believed that teams that developed star players and then sold them were playing "a losing game in the long run."[43]

Guessing which player out of the "ten" would become a good player was difficult. As investors know, past returns do not necessarily indicate future returns; the bromide applied to gaudy Minor League statistics, too. Paul Strand played in the highly competitive Pacific Coast League. In 1923 he hit forty-three home runs and batted .394. He hit .228 with no home runs for the Athletics the next season before Mack pulled the plug on him. Lefty Grove went from a 3.01 ERA in the International League to 4.75 with the Athletics his rookie year. Mack stuck with Grove, though, and was rewarded the next season. Eugene Karst studied figures that showed Minor League hitters lost an average of 30-44 points in their batting averages (with the Pacific Coast League batters losing the most points on average) in the jump to the majors.[44]

Willie Kamm, a third baseman for San Francisco, became the first Minor Leaguer to bring in a reputed $100,000 in 1922. The Chicago White Sox spent the large sum and threw in two players. Kamm played for thirteen seasons in the big leagues and was a sure-handed fielder, although he rarely hit home runs.[45]

The San Francisco team also sold shortstop Jimmy Caveney to Cincinnati in 1922 for $40,000. This made three players—Strand, Kamm, and Caveney—sold for a combined $215,000; even if the amounts were exaggerated by a factor of two, the club picked up $107,500. Of course, they probably weren't so successful selling players every year, but the prospect of doing so undoubtedly imbued owners of Minor League teams with dreams of wealth.[46]

One of the best places to seek quality prospects was Jack Dunn's talented Baltimore Orioles. Dunn wanted to give Baltimore a Major League–caliber ball club. Major League owners wanted several of his players, but Dunn tried to keep his team strong. As early as 1921, Dunn told Cincinnati manager Pat Moran, that he would "not break up his club so suddenly."[47]

Dunn's decision caused much comment, and some baseball officials accused him of retarding his players' advancement to the Major Leagues. They used his club as an example of why the draft of Minor League players was essential. Dunn, of course, was taking a gamble by not selling his stars immediately after they had a big year. He could note the example of pitcher Jakie May. May went 35–9 for Vernon in the Pacific Coast League in 1922, and the Yankees made an offer for him. The Vernon owner demanded more money than the Yankees were willing to pay, so Jakie stayed on the coast. The following season, his win-loss record was 19–22 and his earned run average almost doubled. The Vernon owner lowered his demand, and the Cincinnati Reds bought him for $35,000. May had a few decent years with the Reds.[48]

Not all of Jack Dunn's stars made it big in the Major Leagues. Pitcher Jack Bentley excited several Major League owners. He went 13–2 with a 1.73 ERA in 1922; John McGraw paid $50,000 or $65,000 for the pitcher. The *New York Times* said, "there was a remarkable agreement among the guessers as to the price paid; with few exceptions the sum was put at $50,000, with three players." Two days later, the newspaper quoted a sum of $65,000, showing the reliability of figures reported in the press. Bentley had pitched for the Washington Senators between 1913 and 1916; his ERA was quite respectable for the limited innings he pitched, but he dropped out of the Major Leagues for several seasons. McGraw got three somewhat indifferent seasons from him. Contrary to his reputation, Dunn was willing to sell his players, but he may have set too high a price on them. Joe Vila reports that the previous year, Dunn was willing to sell Bentley and two other players to McGraw for $100,000; McGraw retorted that "he wouldn't give that much money for the whole Baltimore team."[49]

Dunn's shortstop Joe Boley attracted a lot of attention. Branch Rickey apparently offered $50,000 and five players for the player, but Dunn turned him down. Brooklyn offered $100,000 for Boley the following April, but Dunn again refused to sell the shortstop. Dunn told reporters that he would not dispose any of his players before the end of the season, because the Orioles were aiming at a fifth consecutive International League pennant.[50]

Dunn's prize player, though, was pitcher Lefty Grove. Grove put in five seasons with Baltimore and is usually cited as an example of a player languishing in the Minor Leagues. The reality was that Grove had control problems, walking a large number of hitters, even as the hitters had difficulty getting base hits off of him. In 1923 pitcher Rube Benton stated, "Groves [sic], a little less erratic than usual, is doing some real work this season. Slowly he is learning that pitching isn't merely throwing them past the batters. . . . If Lefty could be taught control and get over his habit of having one bad inning per game he would be the nearest to Rube Waddell the game has produced." Grove admitted that he didn't have a curve ball until 1923. When Grove came up to the Athletics in 1925, he had a rough adjustment to the Major Leagues. Presuming 1924 was a season of gaining consistency, it is unclear whether he was held back more than an extra year at most.[51]

Connie Mack usually kept a tight grip on his purse strings since the Athletics were not a wealthy club. After floundering for several seasons, he began buying Minor League stars. One of his first big purchases was Portland third baseman Sammy Hale for a reported $75,000 worth of players and cash (sometimes Major League owners offered their cast-off players or a sum of cash per cast-off, allowing the Minor League owner to choose between cash or players); shortly thereafter, he purchased Paul Strand from Salt Lake City for $35,000 and three players or $50,000 without the players. Mack quickly bought infielder Max Bishop and outfielder Al Simmons after his purchase of Strand. Mack didn't announce financial terms, so reporters were free to make up figures. This time they figured Mack paid $25,000 for Bishop, but they made no estimate for Simmons. Simmons and Bishop would become mainstays of the Athletics.[52]

Mack purchased Lefty Grove after the 1924 season. He paid $100,600. The $600 was to ensure that the amount paid was the largest in baseball history, surpassing the amount paid for Babe Ruth. This assumed that baseball people accepted the actual $100,000 price instead of the more-publicized $125,000. For a man reticent about giving out details of transactions, Mack appeared eager to claim the mantle of having paid the largest sum for a ballplayer. Another spin on the $100,600 price was that the Dodgers and Cubs had also offered $100,000, so Mack decided to up the ante by $600. Jack Dunn and Mack were good friends, though, and often helped each other out; sometimes Mack sent players to Baltimore, and in the case of Grove, Dunn was fulfilling an earlier promise to sell the pitcher to Mack.[53]

Shortly thereafter, Mack bought a battery mate for Grove: Mickey Cochrane. He bought Cochrane from Portland for a reputed $50,000 in cash and players. Mack and the Portland owner had a tight connection, although Portland was not an Athletics farm club. With these two purchases, Mack could lay claim to having the most success with high-priced Minor League player purchases of any owner in the 1920s. One would have difficulty naming a better pitcher-catcher combination than Hall of Famers Grove and Cochrane. Mack later bought pitcher George Earnshaw from Dunn for $50,000 and two pitchers.[54]

Major League owners disliked having to pay large sums to Minor League owners, so they continually sought ways to rig the market. John McGraw suggested in late 1922 that the days of the $75,000 and $100,000 payments were nearing an end, as he said the big league owners had decided to boycott the Minors, unless some changes were made.[55]

Certainly the failure of some costly Minor Leaguers to become regular players, to say nothing of becoming stars, caused Major League owners to hesitate. The Chicago Cubs paid $75,000 to Los Angeles for pitcher Nick Dumovich; they got a 3-8 performance for their money. The White Sox got a 2-3 record from Stubby Mack for their $50,000. On the other hand, Detroit found a hard hitter in Dale Alexander and Cleveland found one, too, in Earl Averill. Detroit supposedly paid $100,000 (there's that figure again) for Alexander and Johnny Prudhomme, while Cleveland paid

$40,000 for Averill. Alexander and Prudhomme interested the Yankees and the Athletics, forcing the Tigers to up their ante.[56] Given these sale prices, McGraw's prediction of a boycott had proven premature.

Paul Waner was another highly sought Minor League player. Pittsburgh eventually purchased Waner along with pitcher Hal Rhyne from San Francisco for $100,000, but only $40,000 of this sum was for Waner and the rest was for Rhyne.[57]

On occasion, owners stumbled upon a gem. Pitcher Dazzy Vance had failed to impress Pittsburgh and the Yankees in brief stints with those clubs. He was languishing in the Minors, when Brooklyn wanted to buy his New Orleans teammate, catcher Hank DeBerry. The New Orleans club said that DeBerry and Vance were an inseparable battery; initially Brooklyn owner Charles Ebbets resisted, as he could have drafted Vance in the past but was unimpressed with the thirty-one-year-old journeyman. Ebbets's scout finally persuaded him that Vance had improved and the deal was completed. Vance became Brooklyn's ace for most of the 1920s.[58]

National League owners considered a rule restricting prices paid for Minor League stars to $25,000. Landis believed that such an agreement between both Major Leagues was not practical, and he may well have been right. All of the owners decided upon an informal agreement to limit prices to $25,000. When Major League owners tried various limits on signing the so-called "bonus babies" in the 1950s, the efforts failed and often created distrust. It was too easy to evade any such limit.[59]

Within a few weeks of the informal agreement, John McGraw went his own way. He purchased pitcher Wayland Dean from Louisville for an estimated $50,000 or more. Louisville had refused an offer of $100,000 for Dean and outfielder Earle Combs, since they hoped to get $150,000 from the Cincinnati Reds for the pair. The Colonels later sold Combs for $50,000, so the estimate on Dean may have been roughly accurate; McGraw also won the rights to pitcher Howard Baldwin after a dispute with Newark. McGraw had to pay $65,000; Once again he paid a high price for a mediocre pitcher.[60]

McGraw later traded his two expensive pitchers to the Phillies. An editor suggested that although Bentley and Dean were disappointments overall, "Bentley helped him win two pennants and with McGraw, present success outweighs all future probabilities. Moreover, in making trades, McGraw rightly ignores the cost of trading material. His sole object is to put a winning ball club in the field."[61]

The Major League owners found that buying Minor League players was an exercise in uncertainty. Then again, even established Major League players endured ups and downs. The real mystery is how such an astute baseball man as John McGraw could repeatedly pay large sums for mediocre pitchers. McGraw obtained good talent throughout the 1920s—Bill Terry, Travis Jackson, Carl Hubbell—so it is not as though he was inept. Although Connie Mack made some dubious purchases, he also built a powerhouse around his collection of pricey youngsters.

In 1926 Commissioner Landis released a list of 175 players eligible for the draft, as they had been sold outright or were under option of recall. Francis Richter said this revealed the big league owners' massive waste in money spent on Minor League talent: "Out of the . . . five millions spent by 16 major league clubs in that time [four seasons], about a score of the minor athletes have made good enough to be kept."[62]

What about the New York Yankees? Daniel Levitt compiled a list of significant Yankee purchases of Minor League players from the team's financial records available at the Baseball Hall of Fame. The Yankees purchased Minor League players throughout the 1919–29 period, including Earle Combs and aging veteran Elmer Smith from the Louisville Colonels in 1924 for $50,000. The Yankees, as with all of their competitors, had mixed success with their purchases. Combs, Mark Koenig, Tony Lazzeri, and Lefty Gomez were successful players. Pat Collins was mostly a backup catcher, and players such as Walter Beall, Julian Wera, Gene Robertson, Fred Heimach, Fay Thomas, and Ivy Andrews proved disappointments.[63]

The biggest expenditure, though, was the Yankees' $125,000 purchase of Oakland infielders Lyn Lary and Jimmy Reese in 1927. Many teams sought the duo, and it is interesting that the Yankees paid so much money when they had, only two years earlier, paid a combined $100,000 for Koenig and Lazzeri. Jacob Ruppert said, "We don't need them now, but if so many clubs are after Lary and Reese they must be good, and in that case the Yanks want them."[64]

Lary was a light-hitting shortstop, but Reese was a bust. Indeed J. Newton Colver pointed out, "No claim is advanced for this brace of players that they are likely to set the Major League afire with their hitting. They did not, indeed, rate exceptionally high, even as infielders, in the Coast League's averages." Most of the Major League teams could not afford to spend $125,000 on reserve players. Years later, Edward Barrow admitted that the purchase of Lary and Reese was the "biggest flop" and that "I've got to be ashamed of it."[65]

In competition for attractive Minor League players, of course, the Yankees and Giants could afford more mistakes than teams with scant capital, such as the Braves or Browns. Spending $50,000 on a single player may well have been too risky for these clubs. The Yankees could absorb some expensive duds. Edward Barrow admitted in 1927 that the Yankees had signed almost a hundred players in recent years, and only a few made good. This despite the team maintaining a widespread scouting system.[66]

Other Sources of Players

Where to find or where to grow good ballplayers was a key question. During the 1920s, leisure and recreation opportunities for young men broadened. Other sports, such as tennis and golf, began making inroads for youngsters' time, as did the automobile. Baseball people worried that there would be fewer good young players available in future years.[67] The owners, of course, did not seriously consider hiring from the pool of the roughly 10 percent of Americans whose hue was darker.

Irving Sanborn believed that the "incubator space" for youngsters was in rural areas rather than municipalities because there was more room for baseball in the country than in the cities and that there was less competition for youth's leisure. Steven Riess presents data suggesting that almost two-thirds of native-born Major League players who were active between 1900 and 1919 had birthplaces in towns of 2,500 or greater. However, just under one-quarter hailed from cities of over one hundred thousand, while 30 percent were born in places with fewer than one thousand inhabitants; these rates, though were similar to the general population.[68]

The odds facing a youngster dreaming of baseball fame were daunting. Sportswriter John Sheridan probably miscalculated when he figured that: "Of some ten million males who are of baseball playing age in America we have 500 men whose skill at the game entitled them to be considered of major class. That means that only one in every 20,000 American men make the majors." A more accurate calculation would consider for each year's cohort of eighteen-year-olds, how many ever made the Majors, but the basic point was correct. Major League players represented the apex of a large pyramid of players.[69]

Although organized baseball did not want to invest much money in amateur baseball, it was fortunate that the American Legion volunteered to run a national youth baseball program. One commentator rhapsodized about the ideals of American Legion baseball: "Their motive is a higher one. For they are convinced that baseball develops in the growing boy those sterling characteristics which are the basis of good citizenship."[70]

President John Heydler of the National League suggested that big league owners establish a training school for promising amateur players. Such a program, staffed by ex–Major League players, would provide excellent teaching and developing.[71]

Major League owners still had not accepted the value of an extensive scouting system. Although wartime conditions prompted some owners' decision, including that of the Chicago Cubs, to eliminate scouting staffs, the decision still seems foolish. *The Sporting News* suggested, "We rather fancy that the clubs which now propose to curtail or abandon the scouting system are those that have been the victims of the counterfeits in the past. We doubt if any real scout who has proved his value will be cut off a payroll."[72]

Then again, many managers had relied on tips from friends, and scouting was often a haphazard endeavor at best. In fairness to baseball, National Football League owners only began to set up scouting systems after World War II, but even a decade after that, teams were drafting players whom they had never seen play in college. The National Basketball Association, too, relied upon an incredibly informal process in selecting players. Red Auerbach recalled that he drafted Sam Jones on a tip from a friend, but that he'd never seen the guard play.[73]

The New York Yankees eventually hired a corps of scouts who became as famous as scouts ever became. Paul Kritchell, Bill Essick, and their peers split up the country trying to discover talented youngsters for the Yankees.[74]

Giving It the Old College Try

There was another source of players available. Connie Mack and John McGraw had signed players from college throughout their managerial careers. Christy Mathewson, Eddie Plank, Eddie Collins, and Frankie Frisch were just the greatest of the collegiate players signed by the Athletics and Giants. Scouting colleges made sense, as baseball players between 1900 and 1920 disproportionately came from white-collar families and were more likely to have attended, if not graduated, from college; these characteristics continued between 1920 and 1940.[75] McGraw told Ford Frick, sportswriter and later commissioner, "Personally I like college ball players. They're smarter. They're more willing to learn. They're higher type citizens. They've got better spirits."[76]

Ascertaining how many players had college backgrounds proved difficult. According to one author, more than one hundred current players in the Major Leagues were ex-collegians in 1929, and eighteen jumped directly from college to the big leagues. The Major League teams signed twenty to twenty-five college players each year. Just before the 1930 season, though, another writer said that the current *Who's Who in Baseball* edition showed forty-six graduates and former students of institutions of higher learning as playing Major League Baseball in 1929.[77]

Several owners decided it was more cost effective to sign college players instead of bidding for top Minor League stars, especially now that many colleges had ex–Major League players as coaches. "I can't see any reason for paying a large sum for an uncertain, untried Minor Leaguer when I can step out to the colleges and get a good looking prospect for virtually nothing," asserted an anonymous manager; of course, signing a college player carried no guarantee that the player would succeed in the Major Leagues, and quite a few of those who signed failed to remain in the big leagues. Even the great Lou Gehrig required a few years of seasoning, despite his obvious raw talent.[78]

There was an added benefit from signing ex-college players. Big league owners, across the professional team-sports world, believed having ex-collegiate players enhanced the image of their sports. NFL and NBA owners bragged about their players being college graduates. In the 1940s and 1950s, most of the former collegiate players were graduates. This cachet possibly elevated their organizations in public opinion, but it came at a price. College-educated Americans were a relatively small proportion of the population until well into the 1950s; college graduates often had greater earnings potential outside of sports than non-college graduates. For professional team sports on the edge of insolvency, such as the NBA during the early 1950s and some NFL teams of the same era, there was little opportunity to cut salaries much, lest their players opt for alternative employment.

Baseball people saw pros and cons of signing collegiate players. The college players were used to strict training by their coaches and were more inured to the attractions of city life than kids off the farm or from small towns. The college player's biggest disadvantage was relative lack of experience. College teams simply did not play as many games per season as Minor League teams. One college coach, though, was critical of college players, stating that college players were spoiled by local publicity, and if they didn't immediately make good in the Major Leagues, they got depressed and quit baseball.[79]

Why did some collegiate players turn down Major League offers? Art Nehf, a successful pitcher, admitted that big league pay offered a chance to "get ahead quickly." But for players with aspirations for careers after baseball, the delay in starting these careers was a disadvantage: "A few more seasons and I'll be through. Then I'll have to start in at the bottom of some new work . . . the chaps who worked along side of me in the laboratory and in the shop are now established. I'm a beginner. So far as my profession is concerned, the ten years I put in baseball are absolutely wasted."[80]

Nehf may have represented the minority view of college players. If a college man played in the Major Leagues for a number of years, given reasonable prudence, he could amass enough savings to buy a business or get started in a profession. As Jacob Ruppert pointed out, "He is still a young man when he is through with the game and has capital enough to step into his more serious work."[81]

Because of the perceived shortage of young players, the Minor League owners sometimes demanded that the Major League owners stop signing college players. Of course, their demand went nowhere, but certainly the competition for talent made Minor League owners nervous.[82]

There appeared to have been a slump in the number of college players signed during the 1920s. A couple of commentators stated that some teams were no longer scouting college players: "College baseball has dropped to such a low degree that major league scouts scarcely give the college games a tumble any more."[83]

Roster Limits

Major League owners sometimes played roster limits like an accordion, expanding and contracting for their own convenience and advantage. The owners testified before Congress that roster limits fostered competitive balance because the limits kept wealthy clubs such as the Yankees and Giants from stockpiling players. Congressional investigators were polite enough not to inquire why an owner would want many extraneous players sitting on the bench. Having quality substitutes served an insurance purpose to be sure, but taking this aspect to extremes undoubtedly redounded against an owners' benefit, as the costs of maintaining quality players on the bench began to exceed any benefits from insuring reinforcements. The congressional hearings, though, revealed evidence supporting the argument, as wealthy teams in 1909, when there were no limits, had twice as many players as poorer teams. Under the new National Agreement of 1921, owners were limited to forty players. The remaining players had to be optioned to the Minor Leagues or released.[84]

Along with the overall player limit, though, was the day-to-day roster limit of active players. Having an explicit rule could help all owners collectively by saving on player salaries, transportation, and hotel expenses. Without a rule, managers would be loath to carry fewer players than rival managers carried. During the war, owners pushed for a limit of eighteen active players. Chicago Cubs president Charles Weeghman argued, "Pennants have been won in the past with only eighteen men." He cited that the limit would allow for six pitchers and twelve hitters. Since pitchers usually pitched complete games, the need for the ten or eleven pitchers held on today's rosters was not present. After the war ended, owners quickly restored the playing roster to twenty-five players.[85]

When the Major Leagues battled the Federal League, increasing the roster limit could have helped prevent the upstarts from getting players. When times were difficult, such as during the real war in 1917–18, owners quickly considered reducing the limit.

Revenue Sharing

One supposed remedy for competitive imbalance was gate sharing. Major League Baseball had gate-sharing policies from the National League's inception. Whether the rationale was to redress differences in drawing power between teams or to compensate good teams for boosting the gate on the road resided in the minds of the owners. Either rationale was plausible, although the former was certainly the one touted by baseball people in public.

Gate sharing was a contentious issue. During the early days of the National League, owners bickered about setting the rate. Eventually, they agreed to a fifty-fifty split on fifty-cent tickets, a practice that persisted for decades, even though ticket prices increased.[86]

The National League's revenue-sharing plan appeared to consist of splitting the first fifty cents of the ticket price. For any price above fifty cents, the home owner kept all of it. The National League presented information to Congress regarding team contributions to the league office. Teams each paid 2.5 percent of gate revenue to the league office. The information covered two seasons: 1920 and 1930 (table 20).[87] The tables showed the home team's and road team's share of the league contribution. The league did not provide revenue-sharing data, but one can surmise how a proportional plan might have worked by proportionally increasing the league shares.

The league shares, though, provide evidence that any revenue-sharing plan was likely to shift revenue from the New York Giants and Brooklyn Dodgers to the Boston Braves, Philadelphia Phillies, and St. Louis Cardinals in 1920. In 1930, the Cubs and Dodgers would have been the biggest donors, while the Giants would have had only a modest loss from any plan. The Phillies, Pirates, and Cardinals would have been the biggest beneficiaries, although the Braves would have also gained.

Multiplying the home payments to the league by forty (1/.025) provides an estimate of revenue. Here there is a conundrum. Using the attendance figures, the per capita revenue per attendee was bunched between forty-seven and fifty cents in 1920. In 1930, all of the teams' per capita revenue was fifty cents. These figures suggest two things. First, the league's shares may have been levied only on the first fifty cents of attendance. Second, there may have been some adjustments made for some teams. The 1930 per capita figures, though, strongly suggest a levy made only on the first fifty cents.

The New York Yankees' financial records enable researchers to reconstruct their experiences with gate sharing. The Yankees' bookkeeper entered the gate receipts for each home game and abroad receipts for each road game. At the end of each series, the bookkeeper issued a check to the visiting team.

Table 21 shows the team's experience with gate sharing between 1915 and 1929. The team was generally a net loser from gate sharing, however, the amounts typically were not large. Aside from 1920–21 and 1923, the team rarely lost more than $50,000 in any season. Although Babe Ruth proved a draw both at home and on the road, the team's road attendance did not begin to match its home attendance until late in the decade. By the team's 1927 season, its losses from revenue sharing was well below $50,000 per season. The team emerged a net beneficiary of gate sharing in 1929.

The Yankees finished seventh in 1925 and destroyed the competition in 1927. In both seasons, the club lost roughly similar amounts due to gate sharing (table 22). In 1927 although the net loss from gate sharing was larger, so were gate receipts. Gate sharing did provide some succor for the weak Boston club; in both years the Red Sox had a net gain in their games with New York. When the Browns slumped in 1927, they gained almost $18,000 from gate sharing with the Yankees. In 1927, though, the Chicago White Sox and Detroit Tigers paid more to the Yankees than they received. Overall, the gate-sharing plan did not redistribute much money from New York to the other teams in the American League.

Some owners were dissatisfied with the existing plan. They suggested revising the visiting team's share to depend upon whether a visiting team was from a small or a large city. The poorer teams thought they should get a higher proportion of gate revenues on the road than, say, the Yankees. The problem with the proposal was that some teams in small cities had reasonably good attendance, while the teams in the large city of Philadelphia often struggled at the gate. This proposal disappeared without a trace.[88] Given the hysteria rampant in America over communism, socialism, or Bolshevism, it is surprising that America's game was considering a movement towards such a step.

Competitive Imbalance Reigns

Throughout the 1920s, the two New York teams dominated at the gate and on the field. The Yankees, with their purchase of Babe Ruth and many of his Red Sox teammates became baseball's marquee franchise. After a disappointing 1925 season, the club revealed a penchant for reloading in a hurry via talented rookies. The Giants relied on rookies and aging veterans. Aside from the Braves, Red Sox, and Phillies, most Major League teams experienced a pennant race and also a slump at least once during the decade. In the race to purchase talented players in the Minors or amateur players from the sandlots, the Giants' and Yankees' owners had deeper pockets, giving them a significant advantage versus financially weak teams. Revenue sharing, too, had, at most, modest effects on competitive balance. Competitive imbalance would increase during the 1930s.

10   Owners versus Players

Players and owners faced common interests in attracting large audiences to games, but they also faced conflicting interests. In cases of conflict, the owners held the upper hand. The struggles between players and owners sometimes flared into open animosity.

Player Rights

Because of the reserve clause and the National Association, ballplayers found that once they signed a contract, they were chattel. The owners could sell, trade, or release them at will. The standard contract typically called for only a ten-day notice on the part of the club; the player had no similar release power. Because the reserve clause bound a player to one team, the player's bargaining leverage was weak relative to that of the owner. Player salaries were artificially suppressed.

The Federal League introduced an element of competition in bidding for players' services. The Federal League owners claimed they did not think the reserve clause was legal (although one wonders whether their tune would have changed had they established their league), so signing players under reserve but not under contract was not an illegal act. During the Federal League lawsuit, William L. Marbury, counsel for the Federal League, characterized organized baseball as a monopoly and the reserve clause as tantamount to slavery. Organized baseball's attorney George Wharton Pepper, made the claim that "part of the salary paid professional ball players was given them in consideration of the reservation the clubs held upon their services for the next season"; his assertion was probably news to ballplayers and owners alike.[1]

A *New York Times* reporter dismissed the players' complaints about the reserve clause being similar to slavery: "they are slaves only because they prefer to play ball instead of going to work. A player under contract can be legally prohibited from playing baseball for other clubs, but he cannot be prohibited from engaging in other occupations less profitable and glorious than his slavery."[2]

Yankees owner T. L. Huston claimed the reserve clause was indispensable since there were not enough quality players. He made the astonishing statement, "If there was a large supply of good players the present type of contract would not be necessary."[3] The surfeit of talented players needed to validate Huston's claim truly boggles the mind.

Player Union

Baseball players recognized that the reserve clause and other rules of organized baseball were rather one sided in favor of the owners. On occasion, accumulated player grievances induced the players to consider unionizing. Many people, some players included, believed that a player union was a contradiction in terms because of the readily discernable differences in their productivity, so some players were hesitant to try unionizing.

Baseball players' biggest revolt was the Players' National League of 1890. John Montgomery Ward organized a league run by the players but backed by capitalists. The league lasted just one season, but its spectacular demise affected baseball for years to come.[4] A decade later after the National and American Leagues declared peace, owners quickly tamped down on player rights. Under the reserve clause, owners could trade, sell, demote, suspend, or release players, usually on scant notice. With peace declared, owners no longer bid competitively for players, so player salaries dropped. This was simple economics.

Players grew restive, and former player Dave Fultz, now an attorney, decided the time was propitious for a new attempt at forming a union. Fultz's timing was astute. The nascent Federal League triggered a bidding war for players, and Major League owners, desperate to keep their players from straying, suggested or feigned interest in a players' organization.[5]

Fultz argued that players wanted an explicit clause in their contract that clubs could not suspend players without pay for injuries incurred while in the service of the club. The owners usually took care of injured players, but they were unwilling to be legally bound to do so. Because the owners usually cared for the players, the issue of an explicit clause gained little traction among the players.

By the end of 1916, commentators were suggesting the Players' Fraternity and David Fultz were, "so hard put for issues—grievances rather—that, in order to make the players who are under [Fultz's] domination think he is on the job for them he has to manufacture one. . . . The only conclusion is that David is working a monumental bluff on the players, attempting to pull the wool over their eyes and confuse them with his palaver into thinking that he really is securing some sort of a reform for their benefit."[6] Although one might ascribe the editorialist's opinion to the *Sporting News'* general disdain for player unionization, Fultz overreached himself a few weeks later in early 1917.

Fultz and other player union organizers realized that getting solidarity among ballplayers at all levels of organized baseball would be an effective bargaining tool. Many Minor League players had signed, and Fultz decided it was time to fight for better working conditions for them. In many ways, the Minor League experience was dismal, as many of the Minor League owners were penurious and the leagues were rickety structures. Throughout January 1917, Fultz tried to whip up enthusiasm among his Major League players on behalf of their downtrodden brothers in the Minors. He even went so far as to threaten a strike on behalf of the Minor League players.

Several Major League players expressed sympathy for their brethren in the Minors; after all, almost all of the big league players had spent time in the Minors, and many knew they would spend more time in the Minors in the future, but they weren't willing to jeopardize their paychecks or careers. Because of the Federal League competition, many big league stars had multiyear contracts, so an edict ordering players not to sign contracts already had leaks. Because Major League players received different salaries, another fissure appeared: highly paid players, facing a bigger sacrifice, grew restless as spring training neared. Other players simply needed to sign a contract, as they were running low on funds. The New York Yankees' financial records frequently showed advances on salaries to players in February and March.

John Tener dismissed the Players' Fraternity's petition, which consisted of four demands. Tener said three of the concessions pertained only to the Minor Leagues, and the fourth—payment of salaries to injured players— was already being done; the owners decided to insert such a clause in the 1917 contracts. There was nothing left to discuss.[7] Fultz went ahead and announced that in the absence of concessions he would urge players to boycott spring training. His action got the owners' attention, although at the same time a few players were beginning to sign contracts.

The owners might have been momentarily stunned, but they quickly regained their sangfroid and professed unconcern. Ed Barrow, then International League president, told reporters that owners in his league "welcomed" a strike of the players, and given the incipient wartime conditions, these owners may have been telling the truth. Ban Johnson boasted that the fraternity and Fultz would be "crushed."[8]

Johnson later made a remarkably silly statement: "If they [the players] want to be unionized, but it will be a unionized proposition throughout. We will unionize our side of the league, too, and this will mean the passing of high baseball salaries and the coming of a system of unionized wages." Johnson, of course, was ignoring that owners were already organized via their cartel. He claimed the owners could institute a fixed pay scale, possibly in hopes of weaning star players from the rank and file, but again, the owners didn't need to "unionize" in order to impose such a plan. Fultz quickly retorted that the owners had already "unionized long ago and now have one of the strongest organizations in the country."[9]

Some owners resorted to calumny, likening the Players' Fraternity to a secret organization. These owners claimed that secret organizations harmed sports and had killed professional cycling and some college athletics. Other owners sent out contracts calling for salary cuts, although Charles Ebbets characterized the cuts as a reversion to "the normal conditions" of 1913 and not Federal League–inspired levels of pay.[10]

For a brief time, Fultz hoped to get backing from the American Federation of Labor (AFL, not to be confused with the American Football League). One player lauded the possibility: "The protection of organized labor would be of great service to ball players. That's what we need."[11] Although AFL president Samuel Gompers gave encouragement, the fraternity's application made little progress. Labor officials debated whether baseball players were entertainers; if so, they needed to ally with the White Rats, the vaudeville union.[12]

The owners and their officials severed relations with the Players' Fraternity in mid January 1917. The outcome of Fultz's bold action depended upon whether players would sign their contracts. Eddie Collins quickly announced his plans to attend spring training, claiming he had let his membership in the fraternity lapse as he "was not enthusiastic about it. I never had a grievance in baseball. The Athletics and Connie Mack always treated me right, and Comiskey is doing the same thing."[13]

As usual, the fans were not sympathetic to the players' demands. Since fans knew ballplayers earned more money than most of them did, many viewed the players as overpaid for "playing a game." A few players' ostentatious displays of wealth also irritated fans.[14] The fact that they, the fans, were paying to watch players who were being economically exploited did not seem to bother them. Owners encouraged fans to believe that paying higher salaries would lead to higher ticket prices, although economists might dispute such a chain of events. Ticket prices are based on fans' demand for games and not on the players' salaries (unless the salaries rise to such a level that the owner goes bankrupt). If fans' demand increases, *then* player salaries may rise.

The Players' Fraternity's threatened strike fizzled as the weather warmed up. Players began signing contracts, and owners trumpeted these defections to the press. Some players adhered to Fultz's declaration, but the owners toughened up by issuing notice that the mailed contracts would be considered null and void if the players did not sign and return them within ten days. As a power play, it was a nifty move. John Tener later amended this threat by saying dilatory players would be sent contracts "with large salary reductions."[15]

Fultz issued a face-saving statement, "A player is not disloyal to the Fraternity because he accepts terms. There is a difference between accepting terms and signing a contract. The pledge the players signed has nothing to do with accepting terms, but only binds the player not to sign."[16]

By early February, American League owners boasted that they had signed 85 percent of their players. Garry Herrmann, emboldened by the weakening union, stated, "The players have no grievances. This baseball union must be exterminated and we have a way to accomplish this end. There will be no compromise with the fraternity. Under the present conditions, I am in favor of reducing the player limit from twenty-two to eighteen players."[17]

Fultz called off the threatened strike on February 8. Owners quickly abrogated their agreement with the players' agreement that dated to January 1914. In the post mortem, some observers cited the threat of real war in Europe as diminishing interest in player rights and in baseball in general; players began expressing dissatisfaction with Fultz and started calling for his resignation or removal.[18]

Those players active in the Players' Fraternity found that some club owners sought vengeance. John Henry, Washington catcher, may have suffered a pay decrease because of the aftermath of the Federal League's demise, as Clark Griffith allegedly offered Henry a contract with a decrease in salary. Ban Johnson, while denying that he said that Henry should "be run out of the American League," indicated that he would step aside if Washington chose to release the player. In fact Johnson offered to reimburse the club for the loss of Henry's services. Washington and the other American League owners eventually waived Henry out of the league; he played the 1918 season with the Boston Braves.[19]

Fultz's failed Players' Fraternity had its echoes. During the 1920s, new labor organizers attempted to raise players' consciousness, to use an anachronistic term. Ray Cannon, another ballplayer turned attorney, made little headway with players in 1922. Owners claimed that Landis made everything just and fair, which was palpably false. President John Heydler blandly asserted, "With Judge Landis at the head of organized baseball, every player knows he can always get a square deal . . . there has never been a time in all baseball history when salaries were higher or players were treated better." Heydler claimed that the Baltimore Federal League lawsuit confirmed the ten-day clause as legal and necessary for the game's conduct.[20]

Baseball owners tried to impugn Cannon's motives by noting he was representing Happy Felsch, former White Sox player. Cannon had to emphasize that there was, as the reporter put it, "absolutely no connection between Ray Cannon, attorney for crooked ball players . . . and Ray Cannon, organizer of a union of players." The mere fact that Cannon had to make such a distinction pretty much undermined his potential effectiveness on behalf of the players.[21]

Cannon claimed to have signed up the full rosters of six National League teams. He also stated that the organization was "not seeking to antagonize the owners. Rather, we seek to work with them to secure a better understanding between the player and the owner. Also the organization is not one which will specialize in individual grievances. We are working or rather aiming to benefit all players."[22]

Since Cannon was trying to ameliorate the reserve clause, salary disputes, and the ten-day clause, his claim of not seeking to antagonize the owners was a moot point. They were already antagonized (not that it took much to do so). In some cases, Cannon seemed to be chasing the players. When nominated as president of the proposed union, Frank Frisch told reporters, "I would not consent to be head of the organization or any other office in it. I have no kick to make against the Giants or Mr. McGraw."[23]

Although Cannon did not mention it, a player pension plan was desirable. Several former players were indigent. Ty Cobb pointed out that ad hoc efforts to help suffering players were ineffective. He suggested a "well-established system for dealing justly with unfortunate ball players," a sort of disability insurance scheme.[24]

Owners eventually created funds to assist indigent ballplayers by the mid 1920s, although they established no rights for such assistance such as a pension or disability insurance. Irving Sanborn suggested a current-player financed sanitarium; others suggested an old-players home.[25]

A few sportswriters thought baseball could resolve holdout situations by resort to an arbitration or appeals process. Landis and the owners did not approve of any such ideas, fearing a reduction in their prerogatives.[26]

Another recurring proposal was player representation in the governance of baseball. Owners occasionally hinted that they were willing to place a player on a committee, but these promises were usually made during periods of duress, such as the Federal League war or the gambling revelations. When the furor passed, owners quietly disregarded their previous pledges.[27]

The Reserve Clause

Baseball may have been as American as Mom, flag, and apple pie, but its labor practices certainly were not. Owners liked the reserve clause and its attendant ten-day release clause. John Tener of the National League said the clause was beneficial: "certainly the public does not desire to see the game played in the major leagues by players who are unfitted in skill and experience to participate with high-class players. There must be this means of replacing a player who has lost his efficiency. The ten days' clause is also a necessary provision in the matter of enforcing discipline on baseball clubs." Tener was probably closer to the mark, when he added, "It [the reserve clause] is the essence of a vast system, for the conservation and protection of investment, for the steady and lucrative employment of a small army of athletic Americans." His belief that the reserve clause aided the, "maintenance of the absolute integrity of the sport" was risible.[28]

Garry Herrmann testified in the Baltimore Federal League case that the reserve clause was a matter of "internal protection within organized baseball." He denied it was used to monopolize the player market. He admitted that if a player could not come to terms on a contract, that the Federal League had the legal right to induce a player to sign a contract. Major League owners fought the Federal League owners in courts over players, but the incumbent owners usually limited their legal claims to players who jumped their contracts and not to players who jumped their reserve.[29]

In one case of a player jumping his contract, the court ruled that the player contract "lacked mutuality of remedy because of the clause which permitted the club to release the player on 10 days' notice." Hal Chase, that lightning rod for nefarious and illegal activities, turned the tables on Charles Comiskey of the White Sox. Chase served the club with ten days' notice that he was canceling his contract; he then signed for a hefty bonus with a Federal League club. The New York supreme court justice Herbert Bissell cited the lack of mutuality in denying Comiskey's injunction against Chase and his new employer.[30] Chase may have been a slippery fellow, but in this case, one may admire his moxie.

Owners had inserted a clause in the 1913 uniform player's contract that read: "The compensation of the party of the second part [the player] stipulated in this contract shall be apportioned as follows: 75 percent thereof for services rendered and 25 percent thereof for and in consideration of the player's covenant to sanction and abide by his reservation by the party of the first part for the season of 1914, unless released before its termination in accordance with the provisions of this contract." The infamous reserve clause read: "the party of the second part agrees and obligates himself to contract with and continue in the services of said party of the first part for the succeeding season at a salary to be determined by the parties to such contract." During the Federal League war, Major League owners altered the contract slightly, by removing the 75-25 percent split and specifying amounts for the salary and for the consideration of the option held by the club. The reserve clause now read, "and the salary to be paid the player in the event of such renewal shall be the same as the total compensation provided for the player in clause 1 hereto, unless it be increased or decreased by mutual agreement."[31]

Robert Burk described these cosmetic changes as being, "made to appear fairer to reservists by designating a specific sum of money as the 'option payment' for the next year's services. Although it did not constitute an actual addition to the next year's salary if the player was kept, it did promise some compensation if the club chose not to exercise its option on the player. In the owners' judgment, it also made the reserve clause less indefinite and more mutual in the eyes of the laws, and therefore less subject to court challenge during the [Federal League] war."[32]

Justice Herbert Bissell did not consider baseball as interstate commerce under the Sherman Antitrust Act, although he did view Major League Baseball as a business conducted for profit. He stated that organized baseball contravened common law by invading the right of labor as a property right, as a right to contract, and "in that it is a combination to restrain and control the exercise of a profession or calling.... The quasi peonage of baseball players under the operations of this plan and agreement is contrary to the spirit of American institutions, and is contrary to the spirit of the constitution of the United States."[33]

Although the owners claimed the Supreme Court's ruling in *Federal Baseball* meant that the reserve clause was beyond legal reproach, they were not in a hurry to test it in the courts. An editorial in the *Sporting News* was astute:

> We cannot share the enthusiasm of some of our baseball contemporaries when they hail the ... [*Federal League* Supreme Court decision] as establishing the legality of the reserve clause.... The court decision only incidentally touches ... upon the reserve clause as it was related to the "conspiracy" contentions of the complaining Federals.... Whether the reserve clause was part of a conspiracy to monopolize baseball might be one thing, and whether or not it interfered with the rights of a free American citizen in seeking and entering employment as an individual might be something else again.

The writer argued the true test would be when an individual player filed suit claiming that unless he signed the standard player contract with its reserve clause binding him indefinitely, he could not play professional baseball.[34]

Sportswriters usually defended the reserve clause, although New York's Joe Vila was more adamant than most: "If a player doesn't sign his contract on or before March 15 let him be suspended for one year. Keep a few of these stick-up gents out of baseball for one whole season and the demands for unreasonable salaries will cease."[35]

Another writer was more sympathetic to the players. While admitting that a reserve clause was necessary, Franklin Wilson pointed out the outrageous aspect of the reserve clause when he posed a hypothetical situation. If Frank Vanderlip, a leading financier, had been signed by a local business and paid a set salary as a young man but forced to remain with that company unless traded to a large financial firm, people would consider this un-American. Wilson advocated some amelioration of the reserve clause, a kinder, gentler reserve clause, although he was rather vague on the specific mechanics.[36]

Major League owners reviewing the reserve clause in 1946 were advised by their counsel that the clause was unenforceable. The perpetuity that the owners claimed was not likely to be accepted by a court. There did not appear to be any considerations given in return for the reserve clause, and "the option and the circumstances under which it is obtained is inequitable, because a provision that the player shall accept a salary fixed by the club is an unreasonable restraint upon a player." At about the same time, NFL owners received similar advice from their legal advisors; the NFL owners redrafted the standard player contract and began boasting that their reserve clause included an option year only and was not in perpetuity (not that it made much difference; free agency was decades off for football players).[37]

The congressional committee investigating baseball in 1951 also viewed the ten-day cancellation clause with skepticism. The committee read a quote from a court case: "we have the spectacle presented of a contract which binds one party for a series of years and the other party for 10 days."[38] Owners found a loophole to assist them. By claiming that a Ty Cobb or Walter Johnson were players with uniquely exceptional talent (and by including in the standard player contract a clause stating the player was a "unique individual, capable of performing services of a special, unusual, and extraordinary character"), owners could argue that losing such a player to a competitor would cause injury to the owner.[39]

Ty Cobb would have been an excellent test case of this doctrine. In 1913 Cobb held out for $15,000 instead of his current $9,000 salary. He had led the American League in batting for the previous six seasons. Owner Frank

Navin refused to budge and told Cobb and reporters that Cobb would play for Detroit or no one else. Cobb, though, had friends in high places (or at least high places in Georgia), and a friendly senator and a friendly representative vowed to open a congressional investigation. Navin and the National Commission backpedaled, and Cobb got $12,000. The owners were churlish losers and reprimanded Cobb for standing up for his rights by fining him $50.[40] To invert a Biblical phrase, what the owners would do to the best of players, what would they do the lowliest journeymen?

The owners' victory in the *Federal League* case carried some warnings. The justices ruled that the telegraphic reports of games across state lines did not make baseball commerce, but some legal experts recognized that network radio broadcasts could result in a reconsideration of whether baseball was commerce or not.[41]

Major League owners proved blatant in using their powers in manifestly unfair ways. During the 1917 season, many Minor Leagues disbanded mid season, as patronage evaporated. The National Commission held that the Minor League owners had to pay the full salary of players' contracts in order to hold players to their reserve clause. The next season, when Major League owners had to pull the plug on the season early in September, these owners, unwilling to pay player salaries for the month of September, hit upon a dandy subterfuge. They granted all of their players their ten-day releases; theoretically all of the players were free agents. The owners, however, agreed to honor each other's reserve clauses and not to poach players.[42] Economists might wonder how such an agreement held; wouldn't some owner, or more likely, all owners be tempted to poach? The owners, repudiating the slightly altered bromide that there was no honor among moguls, did in fact maintain their conspiracy.

Players, naturally, were angered by this sleazy trick to save several thousands of dollars per team (roughly one-sixth of a season's payroll). Jake Daubert, Brooklyn infielder, filed a grievance with the National Commission—surely a futile effort—in September for pay owed him from September 2 until October 14 (the date his contract terminated). No one should be shocked that Garry Herrmann and the two league presidents denied his grievance on the basis, "that the Brooklyn club was forced to suspend as a result of a Government order ending then activities of the club . . . there was nothing to prevent the league of which the Brooklyn club was a member, by appropriate action, cutting the season short."[43]

Ty Cobb, as savvy as any ballplayer regarding finances and legal issues, considered himself a free agent, given that Frank Navin had given him ten days' notice in 1918. Cobb told reporters that he was considering retiring; Cobb may have been engaging in some gamesmanship of his own—and who could blame him. Connie Mack retorted, "I was rather surprised to read about Cobb claiming to be a free agent, for he knows better. The club owners did all they could to carry the game along as far as possible last season, and they only closed when they were forced to do so. It was only natural that we should enter into an agreement to protect our interests, and, of course, we are bound to respect each other's rights."[44]

The owners' problem did not end with this slippery scheme. At the end of the truncated baseball season, there was little reason to assume the war would be over by the next baseball season. Owners worried about renewing their options by January 1 and offering contracts by February 1. If they sent out contracts and player signed them, the owners were liable for the salary, regardless of whether there was baseball in 1919. Naturally, the owners did not want to assume this risk.[45] Fortunately, the war ended in November, in plenty of time to plan for a new season and to send out contracts.

Owners also faced another issue. Some players had jumped their contracts to work in shipyards, often playing baseball for industrial teams in order to avoid military service. The latter aspect was a completely legal option for ballplayers, although many of them and their industrial employers were stretching the intent of the law. Baseball players were not indispensable skilled labor in the shipyards. Some of the Major League owners wanted to punish the players for jumping their contracts.[46]

Occasionally players attained or attempted to gain free agency. Ty Cobb and Tris Speaker were the most celebrated cases of free agency. Commissioner Landis ruled the two stars were free agents in the wake of pitcher Dutch Leonard's allegations involving pitcher Smoky Joe Wood, Cobb, and Speaker in a gambling venture. Landis's edict helped boost the two players' salaries for their remaining seasons in Major League Baseball. In another case, a player bought his release in order to become a free agent. Emil Meusel purchased his release from the New York Giants after the 1926 season; Meusel hoped to sign with a Pacific Coast League team in order to be near a chain of delicatessens he owned out there.[47]

Free agency did not always redound to a player's benefit. Stuffy McInnis signed a three-year contract with the Red Sox and Harry Frazee. McInnis claimed, "When I signed a contract with President Frazee last year I had him give me at the same time a written agreement that I was not to be traded or sold without my consent." Frazee went ahead and traded McInnis to Cleveland. Cleveland had to assume the three-year contract that originated in Boston, but the Indians decided to release McInnis on a ten-day notice. McInnis wanted $10,000 back salary from the Red Sox; he had subsequently signed a contract with the Boston Braves, presumably for less than he was receiving with Boston or Cleveland. Landis denied McInnis's claim and said the player was a free agent upon his release from Cleveland. The commissioner did not hold the written agreement with Frazee as binding or material.[48]

Player Discipline—A Regal Crew

Major League owners and their officials liked their players docile. Owners held the power to suspend players without pay and without recourse, although there were limits, as few owners wanted to completely alienate a valuable player. League presidents and the commissioner also could suspend players, and Landis took this authority to new heights.

Owners liked exercising control over their players. Sometimes their justifications were reasonable. Athletes driving recklessly, barnstorming, getting in fights, gambling to excess, participating in risky endeavors— such as other sports—were threats to an owner's investment (if a player were viewed as property). Owners cautioned against and sometimes even considered banning players owning automobiles because some players were reckless or inattentive drivers. Owners probably disliked their players pulling pranks, especially as some of the pranks were slightly dangerous. By the 1920s, though, such pranks as "badger baiting," snipe hunting, and the like had disappeared as a more serious brand of player came into the game. Other justifications, such as a player's unwillingness to sign a contract, were more dubious.[49]

The eight Chicago White Sox players banished from organized baseball in the wake of the 1919 World Series gambling scandal were, of course, the most notorious suspended players. Babe Ruth and Ty Cobb were also suspended, and so were several other well-known players. In some cases, their suspensions seemed capricious.

With the ascension of Landis to the baseball commissionership, Robert Burk noted that Landis's interventions concerning players, "enhanced rather than undermined management's monopsony power over the player work force."[50] In some cases, Landis's edicts limited players' outside sources of income. Not all of these interventions were inimical to players' interests in general, although they certainly worked to the owners' benefit.

Landis suspended New York Giants outfielder Benny Kauff. Kauff had been indicted for the theft of an automobile. He was later acquitted. Nevertheless, even before the judicial verdict was rendered, Landis rendered his own brand of justice: he declared Kauff ineligible to play in organized baseball, ending his career in the game unless he wanted to participate in the shadowy world of outlaw baseball. Landis admitted that the indictment did not mean that Kauff was guilty, but claimed that under section 2, article 4 of the Major-Minor rules relating to "players under indictment for conduct detrimental to the good repute of baseball," Kauff should be suspended: "An indictment charging felonious misconduct by a player certainly charges conduct detrimental to the good repute of baseball."[51] When Kauff sought reinstatement and filed suit, the judge in the case "held that as Kauff's contract with the New York Giants expired last October he had no cause for action and could not charge that Landis' failure to lift his suspension was what kept him off the Giants."[52]

In a sense, the judge's ruling demonstrated the one-way nature of baseball player's contract; surely the Giants owners would have held Kauff to the terms of the contract, even in the off-season, if they had planned to use him the following season. In a few years, people would wonder why Landis did not banish Giants owner Charles Stoneham for being indicted with stock fraud, a far more serious offense than automobile theft, but Landis was not known for consistency.

Outlaw baseball was baseball that was not under the authority of organized baseball. Any player within organized baseball or any young amateur player who wittingly or unwittingly played with or against an outlaw baseball team or outlaw players was liable to be suspended. The rationale was organized baseball did not want its players to play ball with the likes of, say, the White Sox Eight. The edict cut both ways as it hounded the White Sox players from semipro teams as well as outlaw teams. Presumably the onus was on the unwary player to ascertain whether the other players were outlaws or not. Major League players Jim Vaughn and Dickie Kerr ran afoul of the outlaw baseball edict and were added to the ever-growing ineligible list.[53]

Baseball owners had no hesitation in scheduling exhibition games during the regular seasons. Their players received no extra cash for these games on days when they could have gotten some well-deserved rest. The owners, always jealous of players earning income outside of baseball, frowned upon players barnstorming after the season. Since their contracts covered six months, the players were free to do as they wished during the off-season, although some owners inserted clauses prohibited certain activities, such as reckless driving.

Owners passed a rule stating that participants in the World Series could not engage in barnstorming in the months after the series; these restrictions did not apply to players from teams that did not participate in the most recent World Series. Owners tried to ensure that players were clearly not representing a particular team.

Enter Babe Ruth. Fresh off the 1921 World Series, Ruth and teammates Bob Meusel and second-string pitcher William Piercy embarked on a month-long barnstorming tour. The players realized that they might forfeit their World Series shares, but the tour promised to compensate them well beyond any such loss. When Ruth and Meusel did another barnstorming tour in 1922, Ruth reportedly received $1,000 per game and Meusel got $800 per game. Ruth probably figured that, at most, Landis would fine him the World Series money and possibly a little more; Ruth was half right. Ruth claimed the rule was unfair to players whose teams won the pennant, especially when a player's career was brief. He firmly believed in making money while the opportunities lasted. Many observers and baseball people agreed with Ruth that the rule was unfair; even Landis was willing to entertain such a notion. However, Ruth's blatant violation of the rule forced Landis's hand. He suspended Ruth until May 20 of the upcoming 1922 season.[54]

In the showdown between Ruth and Landis, most reporters sided with Landis, even some New York writers. A *Sporting News* editorial read: "a lesson should be taught the ball player who not only would not obey the rules through which he prospers in fame and fortune, but who had so arrogantly taken the stand that he is right and the rules are all wrong." A week later, though, another writer, Grantland Rice, wrote, "Organized Baseball's mistake came in passing a ridiculous rule that put a premium upon failure—a rule that permitted ball players on 14 major league clubs to earn barnstorming money, but that prevented those on flag-winning teams from having the same privileges."[55]

Thomas Rice was more forceful, explaining that barnstorming drained tired players and made them more susceptible to lackluster or dismal performances: "Any half-wit can follow that line of reasoning and grasp why the rule was passed forbidding men who had already shared in the World Series from jeopardizing the good name of the sport." Rice's argument, though, neglected those irritating exhibition games played during the regular season that may have enervated players more than a barnstorming tour; the St. Louis Cardinals finally recognized this factor and tried to cancel some exhibition games during the 1926 pennant race.[56]

No one should shed tears for the Babe, though, as he thereafter signed a contract at $3,000 per week to appear on the vaudeville circuit. The reviews were good: Ruth "concealed any new nervousness . . . held up his end very well, indeed" and "Ruth's work lacks the polish of the other acts . . . but it is far better than that done in other years by baseball stars. . . . Ruth has good stage presence, a winning smile and he gets away well with the singing part."[57] Ruth proved amusing in screen comedian Harold Lloyd's motion picture *Speedy*.

Sportswriters speculated as to how much Ruth's suspension for thirty-five games would hurt the owners' gate receipts. Ruth ended up missing twenty-three home dates and six road games. In the twenty-three home dates without Ruth, the Yankees collected an average of $10,442 in gate receipts; in the next twenty-five home dates, the club collected an average of $17,211 in gate receipts. The difference of roughly $6,800 per date was probably an upper bound of Ruth's effect upon the gate. On the first two dates of his return, May 20 and 21, the Yankees took in $71,000, but these were weekend games against the second-place Browns (the Yankees went 22-11 without Ruth). The Yankees played six of their American League rivals at Yankee Stadium during Ruth's absence, but they did not play St. Louis until Ruth's return, so the difference in the average was probably skewed upward. The Yankees received smaller visitors' shares on the road for the six dates Ruth was absent, but those dates were against the Red Sox and Athletics, two teams destined for the nether regions of the American League. Ruth's first return to action on the road against Washington did not boost the gate much. One writer estimated that Ruth meant an additional $5,000 at the gate for each game; given the actual gate receipts cited above, the writer's estimate was pretty accurate.[58]

Ruth waited contritely as the days of his suspension ticked off. Landis's secretary, Leslie O'Connor, announced that Ruth would not be automatically reinstated on May 20 but that the player would only be given the privilege of asking reinstatement.[59]

Ruth was duly reinstated but promptly got into an altercation with an umpire and then a fan, but league president Ban Johnson decided to fine him two hundred dollars instead of suspending him. The umpire informed Johnson that his disagreement with Ruth was not as flagrant as initially reported, which helped Ruth's case. Johnson made some pseudo-psychological explanation: "Ruth plainly did not possess the mental strength and stability to brave this sudden reversal of public adoration [the booing and catcalls]. It served to warp his playing ability and for days he has been nervous and irritable." A month later, Ruth was involved in another argument and was suspended for a few days and fined; 1922 was not a good year for him.[60]

Ruth's antics got him suspended at the end of the 1925 season as well. His disrespectful attitude and actions towards manager Miller Huggins reached its climax as Ruth flouted team rules off the field; he also ignored a bunt sign and swung away (one might question the wisdom of having Ruth bunt in any situation, but Huggins was a sharp manager). The manager fined Ruth $5,000 and suspended him indefinitely. Ruth, who used to play T. L. Huston against Huggins and Ruppert, had no one who would countermand the penalties with Huston gone. Ruth could be, most charitably, characterized as an overgrown kid, but he was pushing thirty years old at the time. Ruppert immediately backed his manager publicly. Ruth initially let his petulance run wild and issued an ultimatum: Huggins or him. As with the 1922 suspension, presumably Ruth's absence hurt the Yankees at the gate, but the team was already in the doldrums and was headed towards a seventh-place finish. In the Yankees' four home dates without Ruth, they played the pathetic Red Sox and the pennant-contending Athletics. The games against the Athletics brought in decent gates, but the Red Sox receipts were low. The Red Sox–Yankees game of Sunday, September 13 with Ruth playing attracted gate receipts of $10,145 versus a collective $6,044 for the two earlier September games without Ruth.[61]

Ruth backpedaled on his ultimatum a few days later when he arrived back in New York City. He was "subdued and penitent" and stated, "I made a fool of myself. I don't know what made me talk about Huggins the way I did. I am sorry. I know I was wrong."[62] In the end, Ruth paid the fine and did not play for over a week.[63]

Other players were suspended for even less legitimate reasons than Ruth. Hall of Fame Cincinnati Reds outfielder Edd Roush ran afoul of the owners' edict that any player who had not signed his contract by opening day could be suspended. When Roush held out, the Reds suspended him early in the 1922 season.[64]

Landis suspended Ray Fisher for even flimsier reasons than he had Edd Roush. Fisher played for Cincinnati, but after a mediocre season, decided to coach baseball at the University of Michigan. Since the college season ended well before the Major League season, Fisher sought to rejoin the Reds. There were rumors that a team in an outlaw league approached

Fisher with a contract offer, but Fisher did not accept it. Landis denied Fisher's application for reinstatement and banished the player forever.[65] People's faith in Judge Landis as a fair and balanced arbiter was probably misplaced.

True love did not run smooth in baseball. The St. Louis Browns suspended pitcher Urban Shocker in 1923. Shocker wanted to take his wife on the last trip to the eastern cities, but the team denied his request. Shocker refused to make the trip and was suspended and fined $1,000. Eventually Landis had to intervene and work out a settlement.[66]

On one occasion, Landis cleared a player that a league did not want, aside from one owner. Rube Benton had run afoul of Lee Magee, Hal Chase, and Heinie Zimmermann. He may have been involved or had knowledge of the 1919 World Series fix. In any event, the National League did not want him back in the league when the Cincinnati club tried to sign him from St. Paul. When league president John Heydler refused to render a decision, Landis was forced to do so. He allowed Benton to pitch for Cincinnati.[67]

To curb player misbehavior, some owners resurrected the idea of a twelve-months contract. They hoped this would give them control over their players year-round. Left unsaid was what would happen if an owner released a player, say, in October. Would the player receive the balance of the salary (he had, after all, played an entire season)? Reporter Thomas Rice ignored this possibility and wrote, "The contract would contain provisions that after the regular period of six months the player should be entitled to all he could make in the winter, but that the magnate should have the right to put the ban on certain activities [such as participating in other sports]."[68]

Some legislators suggested licensing professional baseball players. A Massachusetts state representative argued, "each individual [player, not state representative] should pass a thorough examination before he is granted a license. . . . The conduct and habit of a professional player should of necessity be of a high order, as he serves as an example to the young men of our country." Left unsaid was what subjects the licensing examination would cover. Deportment 101? He went on to add that players should not use intoxicating liquor, which was not against the law (only the selling of alcohol was unlawful). Ban Johnson, perhaps revealing more of his increasingly capricious judgment, publicly supported the idea.[69]

One of the saddest suspensions involved some Pittsburgh Pirates players. Barney Dreyfuss let former manager Fred Clarke sit on the bench, purportedly to help manager Bill McKechnie during the 1926 season. McKechnie didn't need the meddling old-timer as he had already guided the team to the 1925 World Series championship. Several players intensely disliked the unpleasant Clarke and took a vote. They asked team captain Max Carey, along with veterans Babe Adams and Carson Bigbee, to present their grievances. At the time of the so-called mutiny, team owner Barney Dreyfuss was vacationing in Europe; he left his son in charge of the team. In the ensuing turmoil, Dreyfuss the younger, released or suspended the three veterans—who had played for the team for a combined forty-eight seasons—for insubordination. John Heydler sustained the suspension after Landis washed his hands of it, stating that it was a league matter. Heydler, in absolving the players of the insubordination charge, said the players displayed "mistaken zeal" in trying to oust Clarke, but added they left the game "with a good name."[70] Brooklyn quickly signed Carey, but Bigbee and Adams were through in baseball.

One wonders what would have happened if cell phones and Skype were available in 1926. Reporter John Sheridan expressed a belief that had Barney Dreyfuss been present, "this unpleasant imbroglio would not have occurred." Sheridan pointed out that appointing two team managers was a foolish move, especially given McKechnie's abilities.[71]

A few days later, future Hall of Fame player Frankie Frisch, the embodiment of a John McGraw–style player, left the team without informing McGraw. Frisch and McGraw had been feuding throughout the season, possibly stemming from Frisch's preseason holdout. The *New York Times* suggested that the breach was so wide that Frisch, "probably has outlived his usefulness as a Giant."[72]

McGraw suspended Frisch; the player responded that he was ill and also depressed. McGraw attempted to be conciliatory, telling reporters, "I will be more than fair to him. Frisch has never been a bad actor and deserves some consideration." Frisch's physician stated that he had a nervous breakdown and would not be able to resume playing that season. The Giants later fined Frisch five hundred dollars for deserting the team.[73]

Ty Cobb was embroiled in several imbroglios during his turbulent career. After being cleared by Landis in the strange case of a 1919 game in which Cobb tried to arrange a bet on the outcome, Cobb landed with Connie Mack. The genteel Mack and the fiery Cobb seemed to be an odd couple. Cobb got into yet another violent clash with an umpire, and Johnson suspended him (and teammate Al Simmons), but Mack vented his wrath at Ban Johnson. Writer Manning Vaughan noted the irony; Mack usually insisted on his players being models of decorum with no profanity: "Connie himself seldom used anything more violent than a simple gee whiz. But evidently the fiery Mr. Cobb changed all this." Mack apparently complained that umpires had too much power, but as Vaughan pointed out, Mack knew that one of Johnson's triumphs had been to minimize rowdyism and umpire baiting.[74]

In addition to suspending players, owners and the leagues sometimes fined players for misbehavior. Club owners decided in 1918 to ensure that the players paid the fines levied by the leagues; owners sometimes had surreptitiously paid fines on behalf of their players.[75]

By 1924 there were fifty-three names on the list of suspended players. Although many of these players were past their playing years, this was a considerable number, representing 13.5 percent of total active Major League Baseball roster spots. An outlaw league might have been able to build three or four teams around, say, forty of the players. The Cubs and White Sox had thirteen players between them on the list, while Cleveland had no suspended players.[76]

The Owners' Iron Grip upon Players

Owners wielded considerable power over the players, allowing them to artificially suppress player salaries. We'll examine player salaries in the next chapter. Owners suspended players on sometimes flimsy grounds. Player attempts to organize a union, though, foundered.

11   Highly Paid but Exploited Players

Major League Baseball players made more money than the average American worker. Many, if not most, Major League Baseball players were economically exploited. These are not contradictory statements.

Why Player Salaries Were Suppressed

As described in the previous chapter, baseball players toiled under the reserve clause that bound them to one team and curtailed their bargaining ability. Players still faced a free market when initially signing a contract with a team in organized baseball; the amateur player draft was decades away. The reserve clause meant that, in the absence of a new league, player salaries were suppressed. Owners often bemoaned rising salaries, but even in the 1920s, player salaries composed well below half of total expenses. In any event, the players were economically exploited in the sense of being paid below-market salaries.

Owners liked their players docile, and they feared players who had outside income-earning opportunities. Owners also enacted rules that enabled them to fine or suspend players who had not signed their contracts before or during spring training and the regular season. Owners claimed that players were sometimes too busy with, "Florida real estate deals, local business transactions, Winter occupations, jury duty, deaths of favorite grandparents and other allegedly spurious reasons."[1]

Major League players earning above $2,500 or $3,000 made more money than did the average American worker. Players could augment their baseball salaries by taking jobs in the off-season. Owners could depend upon the public's envy of baseball players' salaries to temper any sympathy for players holding out for more money. The public, however, often did not reflect on the fact that Major League Baseball players were the acme of their profession. The comparison with average American workers was inapt; a better comparison would have been between Major League players and top professionals in other fields. The Ty Cobbs of the baseball world were unique talent with widespread market appeal. Few would ever associate Mr. Cobb with the word "average." Hundreds of thousands of Americans were willing to proffer their quarters and dollars to see Cobb and his teammates play.

Since players intensely disliked seeing the dollar amount of their contracts cut even if they performed poorly, owners had reason to hesitate in granting large pay increases for an exceptional performance—what went up might come down only with strife and enmity. Owners could try to palliate the risk by giving a player a bonus with the tacit understanding that the bonus was transitory and dependent upon continued productivity. John Sheridan, a longtime writer, suggested that some owners underpaid younger players while promising to generously reward them as veterans. In some professions, such a pay progression may help prevent malfeasance on the part of, say, a judge. The drawback to such a scheme, though, was that the player had to trust the owner not to release them when their economic value fell below their salary.[2]

Economic theory predicts that players will be paid based upon their productivity—such as in how many wins they contribute to the team—and, in special cases, their popularity with fans. Owners are essentially interested in how many extra fans, and those fans' dollars, a player brings to the ballpark. Economists attempt to estimate a player's marginal revenue product (the change in a team's revenue by hiring the player) with varying degrees of success. Due to the reserve clause, the presumption is that star players especially were paid below their marginal revenue product and were therefore economically exploited.

Some newspaper reporters had the temerity to suggest that newspapers boosted players' value through the daily publicity of their prowess (or ineptness) on the playing field. "The player himself seldom wants to admit that he needs write-ups and pictures of himself in various poses in the newspapers in order to get 'the' money, yet the fact is without the newspaper help he would be working for a great deal less. . . . Many a near star is made to look like a wonder in print. . . . Newspapers in catering to the demands of the hungry fans are often forced to make the player look an exalted being."[3]

Newspaper Accounts of Salaries

Player salaries fascinated reporters and fans. Newspaper articles frequently mentioned what players made, and news of holdouts made the front of the sporting pages. Salary figures quoted in the press, though, need to be viewed with skepticism. Given the relatively small amounts actually paid, though, any distortion was likely to be a few thousand dollars in either direction. The *New York Times* generally reported Babe Ruth's salary with the Yankees with unerring accuracy, but Ruth was a special case. The Yankees' owners may have thought it wonderful publicity to have the highest-paid player under contract.

As an example of newspaper distortion of player salaries, one reporter stated that Clark Griffith offered Walter Johnson a three-year contract worth $100,000 for the 1925–27 seasons. The Baseball Hall of Fame's collection of salary information shows Johnson making $20,000 per season for 1925–27. When newspaper accounts of salaries are present, the data from the Baseball Hall of Fame collection will be shown within brackets (appendix 2 details the collection).[4]

Sportswriter Bert Walker advised fans, "This much is certain—if a ball player tells you what his salary is he is not giving himself the worst of it. The paymaster might laugh in his sleeve when he hears or reads extravagant statements regarding salaries, but he would be foolish to correct an error in this regard if he can pay a player $5,000 a year and get credit for paying him $20,000, that is fair enough. He is regarded as a big-hearted boss without having the big heart and it helps his business."[5] Walker's advice, though, may not have been savvy; owners worried that inflated salaries reported in the press would trigger envy among other players and spur holdouts. *Baseball Magazine* editorialized, "Salaries paid to ball players are mainly guess work on the part of enterprising scribes. And as there is no law to curb the imagination of a sport writer, there

are no limits to the salaries which he can bestow upon leading diamond celebrities in his own column."[6]

Sportswriters may have been imbued with envy. Many of them considered players overpaid, although they sometimes expressed contradictory ideas regarding player salaries. Hugh Fullerton, made famous by the book and movie versions of *Eight Men Out*, wrote: "Big pay, short hours, easy work, mostly play. Loaf half the year. All expenses paid while traveling. Jobs always open for right men." He used this as a hypothetical advertisement for ballplayers. He suggested players save some of their money because they wouldn't find earning a living outside of baseball very easy.[7] Reporters were not objective observers and often had reason not to antagonize owners. Owners paid reporters for various services; owners also provided lavish buffets for reporters.

The War and Player Salaries

The Federal League and the resulting competition for players drove salaries up. Such stars as Ty Cobb, Walter Johnson, Eddie Collins, and others signed multiyear contracts at hefty increases. Some players—such as Joe Jackson—were not as adept at getting favorable contracts, so their salaries remained below $10,000 per annum. After the Federal League disbanded, Major League owners sought to reduce salaries. The owners came out with their usual hand-wringing. Barney Dreyfuss of the Pirates told reporters in January 1917, "if the major leagues expect to continue business they must cut down the players' salaries."[8] These complaints occurred even after attendance rebounded to pre–Federal League levels in 1916. Dreyfuss claimed the sixteen teams spent a combined $2 million in salaries, or $125,000 each in 1916, before he urged owners to cut team payrolls to $100,000 each. To help owners pressure the players into signing, Ban Johnson advocated suspending players without pay if they did not sign a contract before a specified date. Johnson's National League counterpart, John Tener, phrased the salary cuts as: "a readjustment . . . because some players received salaries greatly out of proportion to their real value. This readjustment is necessary not only to bring about a return to normal conditions, but also in justice to the other players [presumably those who did not negotiate contracts with the Federal League or use such bargaining as leverage to get better, multiyear contracts from the Major Leagues]." Another article, though, claimed that owners paid only $1.5 million in player salaries in 1916.[9]

Throughout January and February 1917, when baseball news was typically sparse, the *New York Times* printed article after article describing the owners' efforts to tamp down salaries. A few players, such as Grover Cleveland Alexander, in the midst of winning 120 games in four seasons, received pay raises; Alexander moved past Christy Mathewson with his $12,500 salary. Mathewson was nearing the end of his brilliance and received $10,000. John McGraw, too, received a pay raise and shares of stocks in the New York Giants.[10]

Although owners manipulated baseball salaries during 1918 with its shortened season, some owners and sportswriters urged efforts to carry fewer players on their rosters. Other owners were not reticent in using the war to make players seeking pay increases or avoiding pay decreases to look greedy, especially with the war going on: "The public attitude toward baseball players who are holding out for more money, will be much the same . . . as their attitude toward striking employes [*sic*] in other occupations." For the owners, then, it was an ill war that brought no benefit. Red Sox owner Harry Frazee told players that if they did not sign their contract before spring training, they would have to pay their own way down south.[11] When the owners cut the schedule from 154 to 140 games, they claimed they needed to pay the players only five months' salary instead of six. The owners' math was, perhaps, purposely faulty; the schedule reduction was one-eleventh of the games, while the proposed salary cut was one-sixth.[12]

Owners also foisted penny-ante economies upon the players when the National League owners adopted a set of rules for travel during the 1918 season. Players now had to transfer their personal baggage to and from the station, meal allowances on trains were cut (as well as the hours qualifying players for team-paid meals), and players could not use taxicabs at team expense. No wonder players were cranky.[13]

Players did get a break, however, when firms engaged in shipbuilding hired players as painters at fancy salaries, reportedly as much as $500 per month. The players' duties for these companies entailed some painting but also some ball playing on behalf of the company. Some of the shipbuilding companies maintained baseball teams even after the war. A want ad in the *Sporting News* promised "big salaries" for players with Major League experience, who were free agents.[14]

After the war, the National League tried to establish a salary limit of $11,000 a month for each club (presumably $66,000 per year). The owners of the wealthier New York and Chicago clubs, naturally, were against the proposition. President John Heydler was empowered to monitor and to punish owners who violated the measure (the penalty was a $5,000 fine). Unless owners granted Heydler access to their financial records, how he could detect cheating was left unstated; the National League owners' attempt was stillborn, as American League owners refused to join them.[15]

The Early Postwar Period

Because of the uncertainty surrounding the 1919 season, owners sought to slash salaries. They were aided in this attempt by the fact that all of the large salaries paid under contracts dating to the Federal League period were expiring. An editorial in the *Sporting News* observed that there was a limit to salary cutting; too low a salary, and Major League players might opt for jobs in industry or playing with semiprofessional industrial teams.[16]

The New York Giants announced before the 1920 season that they would *increase* salaries for all of their players. President Charles Stoneham commented that the league's prosperity in 1919 and the promise of the upcoming season persuaded the club officials to grant such pay raises. Stoneham left unsaid the wartime and postwar increases in the price level. Stoneham's fellow owners, though, may have felt chagrined over the Giants' action.[17]

In discussing player salaries during the 1920s, one should recall that the general price level rose sharply during World War I and into 1920; there was a decrease in the price level after 1920, and prices stabilized after 1922. The postwar jump in the general price level gave owners some cover; they could raise the dollar amounts they paid the players but still end up paying less in terms of purchasing power. When the price level fell for a couple of years, maintaining the same dollar salaries meant paying more in purchasing power. By 1929 in comparison with 1918, owners could pay players 10 percent more dollars and still be paying the same amount in purchasing power.

Ty Cobb, Tris Speaker, Eddie Collins, and Walter Johnson were among the highest-paid players in the American League prior to World War I. They continued to rank high in player salaries throughout most of the 1920s. National League stars Rogers Hornsby, Zack Wheat, Grover Alexander, and Edd Roush were some of the best-paid players in that league. Wheat and Roush became perennial holdouts, although Roush later admitted he held out, in part, to skip spring training that he did not need or desire.

White Sox Players' Salaries

One of the alleged reasons for the Chicago White Sox players' decision to accept money from gamblers was owner Charles Comiskey's tight-fisted ways. White Sox official Harry Grabiner noted the team's salaries for 1918. The *New York Times* reported that during the Black Sox trial, defense attorneys entered into evidence salary figures for the eight players. Table 23 shows these reports of the eight Sox players' salaries and also includes their actual salaries as per the Baseball Hall of Fame data. Star Eddie Collins was getting $15,000 a year for five years; this figure was confirmed by a statement Ban Johnson made in 1917. Joe Jackson was perhaps the most underpaid player, as his 1918 salary was $6,000. Eddie Cicotte was coming off his best season in 1917, but he earned just $5,000 plus $2,000 for signing for the 1918 season. Bill Veeck snidely remarked that Comiskey was being "cute" in giving Cicotte a bonus without making it part of his salary, but other owners did the same with bonuses.[18] Given the reserve clause, Comiskey and his fellow owners undoubtedly paid their stars less than such players would have earned under competitive bidding; relative to the 1914–15 salaries, the 1918–19 salaries were low both in terms of dollars and in terms of purchasing power.

Several of the White Sox players received significant pay increases after the 1919 season. The defense attorneys pointed out that Comiskey paid his players, separate from the players' World Series receipts shares, for the extra days played during the series because their contracts expired at the end of the regular season. If Comiskey did so, this may have been a unique act; for instance, the Yankees never paid players' salaries for the World Series.[19]

Some observers believe Comiskey's pay raises to the seven players were "hush money," but if all of the players—dishonest and honest—received pay raises, this argument seems dubious. The White Sox attendance went from 195,000 in 1918 to 627,000 in 1919 (although it had been 685,000 in 1917, with seven additional home dates). Francis Richter claimed that during Joe Jackson's lawsuit with Comiskey, Comiskey was "forced to sign Jackson at $8,000 a year for three years," an increase of $3,000, and also sign Felsch and Risberg at increased salaries. Richter did not explain why Comiskey was "forced" to sign these players at significant raises.[20] Robert Burk suggests that Comiskey was not particularly stingy with player salaries, as other teams paid similar amounts to their players. Comiskey, though, was a genius at antagonizing his players; for instance, Burk claims Comiskey charged them to clean their uniforms.[21]

While rebuilding his White Sox, Comiskey obtained outfielder Harry Hooper. Hooper was holding out for $15,000 from Harry Frazee and the Boston Red Sox, but he wanted to get off to a good start with Comiskey and filled in the blank three-year contract proffered by Comiskey with $13,250. A few years later, Comiskey cut his salary to $7,000. (Hooper's memory conflicts with the Haupert's Professional Baseball Salary Database, which shows the player earning $14,250 under the three-year contract and $10,000 on the subsequent contract.) When Hooper reminded Comiskey of his reasonableness in filling the blank contract, "[Comiskey] wrote back that he never heard of anyone getting a guarantee of anything in this business, and sent me my release along with the letter."[22]

White Sox pitcher Dick Kerr won two games in the ill-fated 1919 World Series. Comiskey signed Kerr to a two-year contract covering 1920 and 1921 for a reputed $6,500 [$4,500] per year; Kerr had a good year in 1920, and with the release of Ed Cicotte and Lefty Williams, was facing additional work for the upcoming 1921 season. He asked for a new contract, which Comiskey denied. Kerr, not signing before the deadline, was placed on the ineligible list. When he later played a game with a semipro team against some blacklisted players, he was banished for a year from organized baseball—truly an ironic turn of events for a stalwart pitcher.[23]

Owners Reassert Their Bargaining Power

As baseball experienced prosperity during the early 1920s, players began demanding more dollars. Players knew the turnstiles were clicking at a rapid rate even though patrons were paying higher prices for tickets. The Major League owners' willingness to pay tens of thousands of dollars for Minor League players also inspired big league players in their demands for more money. Amid this prosperity, though, owners were pleading poverty. Connie Mack, who may well have been facing financial woes with his equally woeful Athletics, warned owners that they had to do something about the salary problem; he proposed a salary limit.[24]

Ty Cobb, despite being the American League's top hitter for years, struggled to get more than $20,000 per season. Cobb had received a raise in 1914 in the wake of the Federal League bidding, but Frank Navin, owner of the Tigers, did not raise the player's salary again until 1920 when Cobb finally got the $20,000 a year. Navin eventually camouflaged pay increases for Cobb by designating him as player-manager. Cobb reportedly signed for $30,000 [$25,000] for the upcoming 1921 season, but one reporter, Dan Daniel, suggested this was not enough: "But is it high for a man of Cobb's drawing power and abilities? . . . Here we have $30,000 for a whole season's labor and worry causing surprise, while we accept [boxer] Jack Dempsey's $100,000 for less than 35 minutes or more or less action last Tuesday night without batting an eyelash."[25]

In the wake of the Ty Cobb–Tris Speaker scandal that broke in late 1926, Cobb and Speaker became free agents. Cobb signed for a reputed

$75,000 with the Philadelphia Athletics, but, in actuality he received $50,000 in 1927 and $35,000 in 1928, with no bonuses for either season. John Kieran thought Cobb well worth $75,000 because, "the unproved [Dutch] Leonard charges made Ty Cobb a greater attraction than ever." Kieran thought this reputed payment created pressure upon the Yankees to boost Ruth's 1927 salary above the $52,000 he made for the previous three season; Ruth stated he was seeking $100,000 for 1927.[26] According to reporters, Connie Mack and Clark Griffith, who had signed Speaker, found that the two aging stars were not the gate attractions they had hoped for.[27]

Other owners did not take kindly to overly aggressive negotiating on the players' part. One editor joked, "Hold up Barney Dreyfuss and he will trade you," and he cited Dreyfuss's trade of pitcher Burleigh Grimes after the 1929 season (despite Grimes's winning forty-two games the previous two seasons).[28]

Another famous holdout involved Cincinnati Reds third baseman Heinie Groh. Groh held out and eventually signed a contract with the Reds with the stipulation that he be traded. He wanted to go to New York, where manager John McGraw was waiting with open arms; after a delay, he got his wish. Groh reportedly received $15,000 [$12,500] a year for three years, plus a potential bonus if the Giants had won the 1922 pennant. The joke was on the Giants, though, as Groh's productivity tailed off with them.[29]

Outfielder Edd Roush of the Cincinnati Reds was a frequent holdout; early in his career, he had cast his lot with the Federal League. As early as 1922, he was seeking a three-year contract at $18,000 annually. One of Roush's annual holdouts boomeranged against the Cincinnati Reds. Roush's 1922 holdout resulted in his suspension. Roush played in only forty-nine games, and his absence contributed to the Reds' failure to win the pennant that season. One reporter calculated that Roush's absence cost the club far more—he estimated at least $100,000—than the amount of money the player was holding out for, suggesting a penny-wise, pennant-foolish managerial decision.[30]

A year later, a Cincinnati merchant suggested raising a fund to make up the difference between Roush's salary demands and the Reds' offer, but nothing came of this odd proposal. The next year, Roush was still haggling with the Reds' ownership; this time he asked for $16,000 for three years, but the team owners refused to pay him more than $15,000, which the player finally accepted. Roush did win one point: the team agreed not to collect the fine of $50 a day for missing training.[31] According to the Baseball Hall of Fame data, Roush earned $19,000 annually for the 1924–26 seasons; for once the press appears to have underestimated his salary.

Roush's outfield peer, Zack Wheat of Brooklyn, fought to get a $500 raise to his 1922 salary of $8,800 after hitting .335 with 16 home runs. He even offered to play again for $8,800, if owner Charles Ebbets would give him a two-year contract. Ebbets refused at first, but later relented to the $500 raise. An anonymous *New York Times* writer stated, "It would belittle Mr. Ebbets to call him a tightwad. He stands alone as the most economical person in the United States; no name has yet been devised that properly describes his extreme aversion to parting with money."[32]

Two weeks later, another columnist explained that Ebbets's initial refusal to grant Wheat the $500 raise was based on, "other considerations [that] necessarily influence club owners. They have to weigh such matters as the validity of contracts, the needed discipline in the club, the annoyance of temporary 'hold-outs,' the desirability of team play and faithful service. . . . Such attempts [to holdout] have to be met, as Mr. Ebbets met them, in the interest not only of good business and efficient organization, but of the game itself."[33]

If Ebbets seems tightfisted, his fellow Boston Braves owner, George Washington Grant, might have surpassed him. Grant told reporters that Walter Holke was one of his highest-paid players in 1922; Holke got $6,000 in salary. Then again, the Braves finished last in 1922 with a 53-100 record, so Grant may have been justified in paying such low salaries (according to the Baseball Hall of Fame data, the Braves' payroll may have been below $100,000).[34]

Rogers Hornsby was perhaps the National League's biggest star during the 1920s. Hornsby was renowned for acerbic, blunt talk. After his 1916 season, he demanded $6,000 instead of the $3,000 offered. Before the

1922 season, Hornsby wanted an increase in his salary from $11,000 to $25,000, and he wanted a three-year contract. In the midst of a five-season run, where he hit better than .400, Hornsby struggled to get his salary above $20,000 per season [$17,500 for 1922–24].[35]

Hornsby had reason to be aggrieved with the Cardinals' management. The team named him manager midway through the 1925 season. Hornsby managed the team to its first pennant and world's championship in 1926, but the club did not pay him for being the manager. Hornsby held out for more money to compensate him for his managerial duties, but to no avail. After the Cardinals traded him to the Giants, Hornsby reportedly agreed to a two-year contract for $40,000 a year. Later in his career, Hornsby supposedly settled for a three-year contract with the Boston Braves also calling for $40,000 a year. He was not going to manage the team, but he was appointed team captain. This honor netted him $600 a year, so his contract was for $121,800. Hornsby actually received $30,000 a season for 1925–28. He did receive the $600 payment from the Braves.[36]

When the Giants announced that Frank Frisch was getting $18,000 a year, reporters thought that Frisch's success would inspire more college players to turn pro: "Perhaps 50 college stars were offered contracts in the big show but only a scattered few accepted—and these very few likely will be found in the minors next summer." A year later, Frisch wanted a $7,000 raise, based on his .328 batting average.[37] Frisch earned $16,000 a year for 1924–26; he received $18,000 for 1927–28.

Paul Waner recalled how Barney Dreyfuss would flip-flop in negotiations across the years. When Waner hit for a particularly high average, Dreyfuss complained about the hitter's lack of home runs. Waner aimed for the fences and hit more home runs; Dreyfuss then balked at giving a pay raise, because Waner's average had fallen. Waner concluded, though, "Barney didn't treat me badly, though. . . . After I hit .380 that second year, the old man boosted me to $11,500. That was a pretty big pay raise in those days."[38] Paul and his brother Lloyd both held out after the 1928 season. They demanded $35,000 between them, about half of Babe Ruth's income. The Waners were popular in Pittsburgh, but they certainly were not the attraction Babe Ruth was, and sportswriters did not fail to point that out; plus the brothers had not been in the Major Leagues very many years, having debuted in 1926 and 1927.[39]

Lou Gehrig may have been the closest facsimile to Babe Ruth in terms of production. He, however, lacked Ruth's flamboyance and was not as effective a draw at the gate. Some reporters wondered what Gehrig would command in his next contract since he was out-hitting and out-homering Ruth in 1927 (until Ruth's magnificent September in 1927 where he hit seventeen home runs to surpass Gehrig and to set his record of sixty home runs).[40] The Yankees did boost his salary to $25,000 per year after his great 1927 season, a tripling of his previous salary. Gehrig was not an aggressive negotiator, and the Yankees' action is difficult to explain. Despite season after season of great productivity, Gehrig's nominal salary thereafter rose slowly (of course, the deflation of the early 1930s boosted the purchasing power of his earnings). Gehrig held out before the 1935 season and got his salary increased from $23,000 to $31,000. Jacob Ruppert reportedly said, possibly patronizingly, "That Gehrig is getting to be a real man."[41]

While top hitters usually made more than top pitchers, some pitchers earned in excess of $20,000. A sterling record might not reap as much of a benefit if a pitcher did not perform for a wealthy and generous owner. Pitcher Dazzy Vance of the Dodgers held out for $25,000 after the 1928 season, a reported $5,000 raise over his 1928 salary. He had a win-loss record of 22-10 and led the National League in strikeouts and earned run average. The Dodgers finished in sixth place, although the team had a winning record. The club's attendance was just above the league average, and one reporter commented, "The [Brooklyn] club has been no great money maker.... What Dazzy might be worth to the New York Giants or to the Yankees is quite a different proposition." The Dodgers eventually acceded to Vance's demand.[42] Vance had earlier attempted to get the ten-day release clause stricken from any contract he might sign, but Charles Ebbets refused. President John Heydler backed Ebbets in his refusal.[43]

After the 1929 season, owners again decided to scale back salaries. Although no one foresaw the severity and longevity of the oncoming Great Depression, owners worried that the salary escalation of the 1920s had gone too far. Connie Mack's World Series champion Philadelphia Athletics were a case in point. Mack's club, now composed of veterans, had a payroll (including coaches) of roughly $250,000 in 1929. A reporter listed the salaries of key players Lefty Grove, Al Simmons, Mickey Cochrane, Max Bishop, Joe Boley, Jimmy Dykes, Rube Walberg, Jimmy Foxx, and George Earnshaw; these players reportedly earned $123,000 (presumably for 1929) [in actuality only $92,500]. Mack had trimmed the large salaries he paid to Ty Cobb, Zack Wheat, and Tris Speaker, though, so he should have had sufficient slack in his payroll. Perhaps Mack foresaw the dwindling attendance at Athletics games in the coming years; attendance peaked in 1929 and plunged thereafter. According to the Baseball Hall of Fame information, twenty-four players earned a combined $188,000 in 1929, well below the $227,962 paid twenty-six players in 1928.[44]

After the 1929 season, owners still hesitated to grant significant salary increases to players. Lefty O'Doul hit .398 in 1929 and received a $500 raise, to his $8,000 [$7,500] salary. A few years later, he led the National League in hitting and had his salary cut by $1,000, but this was during the worst of the Great Depression.[45]

Some Minor League owners paid salaries that matched those of lower-paid Major League players. Jack Dunn of the wildly successful (on the field, at least) Baltimore Orioles, paid several of his players more than $5,000 per season. He believed that paying good salaries motivated his players and prevented disgruntlement.[46] Lefty Grove reminisced that Dunn took good care of his players: "we were satisfied to stay there [Baltimore]. We were getting bigger salaries down there in Baltimore . . . than lots of clubs were paying in the big leagues. So why leave? We couldn't get $750 to $1,000 a month in the big leagues in those days." Grove recalled that Dunn shared exhibition-game receipts with the players; the players also received money from the Little World Series.[47]

Babe Ruth's Salary Gains

Babe Ruth became the bellwether for player salaries. Between his prodigious productivity as a player and his magnetism as a crowd attraction, Ruth commanded high salaries once he started playing for the Yankees.

Although not a highly educated man, Ruth had a shrewd sense of his value. He also hired some advisors to arrange off-the-field revenue. Ruth showed signs early on of being a savvy negotiator. After his first home run title in 1918 (with the grand total of eleven) and thirteen wins as a pitcher, Ruth planned to ask for a large increase in salary, initially to $20,000 a year and later to a three-year contract at $10,000 per season. Ruth, quickly seizing upon his twenty-nine home run season of 1919, demanded a new contract. The editor of the *Sporting News* took the Babe to task, "It is a plain case of hold-up by a player either absolutely ignorant and unprincipled or misguided. There can be no sympathy for Ruth. He is trying to repudiate a contract he made in good faith."[48] Ruth's actions may have contributed to Frazee's eventual determination to sell the slugger.

Reporter Bert Walker explained why Ruth earned his big salaries and the Yankees were not over-paying him: "Most of the money paid for Ruth may be charged off to advertising. . . . Judged merely for his worth in winning ball games no player was ever worth $50,000 a year. As Ruth draws big crowds in every game the Yankees play, he easily earns the $50,000 he is reputed to draw down."[49]

As Ruth's career progressed and his salary soared, other players not only tried to emulate his free-swinging approach on the field but also his efforts at negotiations. An editorial writer suggested, "His attitude vitally affects the attitude of scores of other prominent players . . . many a less talented fellow player has striven to follow in his footsteps." The editor said players making such comparisons missed the main point: "Babe Ruth is literally in a class by himself. His value is mainly in his enormous drawing power."[50] John Sheridan, though, pointed out that "Ruth would not be worth $100,000, or $50,000, or $25,000 to the Red Sox or Phillies." He believed that the Yankees' ability to draw large crowds meant they could out-bid other teams for the services of top players such as Ruth.[51]

Another writer compared Ruth's salary with athletes in other sports. The author believed that golfer Walter Hagen earned more money than Ruth, while Gertrude Ederle, the first woman to swim across the English

Channel, earned $75,000 a year for swimming exhibitions. The author pointed out that Ruth's $70,000 per season salary meant the slugger earned $500 a game, which "is not a high price for the star performer of any public troupe, and a baseball team has exactly the same relation to the public as an opera company or a vaudeville act.... When Caruso sang at the metropolitan in the days of his glory, the house was sold out. For each one of Caruso's appearances he drew between $3,000 and $5,000."[52] During the 1920s, top boxers and wrestlers, though, earned more money than almost any ballplayer.[53]

Ruth signed a contract calling for $80,000 a year for the 1930 and 1931 season, giving rise to his famous quip about having had a better year than President Herbert Hoover.[54] Ruth had lucrative opportunities outside of baseball. He appeared on the vaudeville circuit for several seasons. After the 1926 season, he signed a contract reputedly worth $100,000 to perform in vaudeville. Ruth later appeared in motion pictures and endorsed various products.[55]

Babe Ruth wasn't the only baseball player turned vaudevillian. Paul and Lloyd Waner played vaudeville after the 1927 season; they made $2,100 a week, which far surpassed their baseball salaries.[56]

As late as the 1970s, baseball players often had jobs in the off-season, although some moonlighted during the regular season. Fictional character Henry Wiggen in Mark Harris's *Bang the Drum Slowly* was establishing his insurance business, but his activities mirrored that of actual players, as F. C. Lane cited insurance selling as a common off-season activity for some players. As Babe Ruth was barnstorming, doing vaudeville, and appearing in movies, his teammates Waite Hoyt (mortician) and Gehrig (real estate) were earning extra income in the off-season. Many players owned farms.[57]

Not all observers were pleased with baseball player's outside interests. Jake Daubert, though, admitted that he thought being involved in outside business interests while an active player had been a mistake; he found himself distracted, although he added that family situations also contributed to the distraction.[58]

Player Salary Data

Owners disliked their players making money outside of baseball. One stockholder in a big league club complained, "Two or three of these fellows [with outside interests] can break up a strong ball team. . . . The best remedy is to cut down salaries all along the line so that playing to get a slice of the World Series melon will be something worth while [*sic*]." A reporter echoed this stockholder's complaint: "We would suggest that the ball players stick to the diamond while they are good and real players, and attempt their commercial flyers when they are no longer active on the field. If they don't, salaries will soon be dropping."[59]

The 1951 congressional hearings into organized baseball revealed that Major League Baseball paid out little more than $4 million in salaries to players, coaches, and managers in 1929, or roughly $250,000 per team. The Yankees had the largest payroll, which was more than double the Boston Red Sox's payroll; a similar disparity held between the Chicago Cubs and Pittsburgh Pirates, the top and bottom salaried teams in the National League.[60]

The disparities in salaries between teams was not as pronounced in 1929 as disparities during the 1990s; according to data presented to the Commissioner's Blue Ribbon Panel, the New York Yankees often had more than five times and sometimes as much as nine times the team salaries of the team with the smallest payroll.[61]

Player salaries as a proportion of revenue or expenses generally fell throughout the first seventy-five years of the twentieth century. The 1929 figures showed that team salaries (that included coaches' and managers' salaries) were 35.3 percent of Major League expenses; by the 1950s, team salaries represented less than 25 percent and often less than 20 percent of club expenses. The Commissioner's Blue Ribbon Panel found that during the free agency era, player salaries composed more than 50 percent of team revenues during the 1995–99 seasons (or an even higher proportion of expenses, assuming teams earned profits). Historian Robert Burk makes the point that the 35.3 percent ratio was one of the lowest ratios in American business, but this seems difficult to prove; baseball teams had other labor costs in addition to the player's salaries, such as office staff, ushers, ticket takers, grounds crew, and scouts.[62]

In a study of New York Yankees' player salaries between 1919 and 1941, researchers found that the team's management based player salaries, in part, on their productivity and number of years in the Major Leagues but also on the team's attendance and revenue from the previous season. The evidence also strongly indicated that they were not paid their marginal revenue product. Therefore the players were economically exploited. During the deflation of 1929–33, the Yankees cut nominal salaries but not so deep as to match the reduction in the general price levels. In that sense, the players weathered the trough years of the Great Depression better than many Americans.[63]

Additions to Salaries

Some owners offered bonuses to their players. The bonuses took the form of performance bonuses (such as winning twenty games or hitting .300, for instance), signing bonuses, and, what could be termed, "behavioral" bonuses (payable at the manager's behest for good behavior). Yankees Bob Meusel received such a bonus. The Yankees once balked at giving Meusel a multiyear contract, because they worried that the player "would take things too easy during the first year of a two-year service."[64]

Most reporters and baseball officials disliked performance bonuses, believing that players should not get extra rewards for posting individual statistics or for hustling. Commissioner Landis, for instance, also worried that bonuses bred "disloyalty and even corruption."[65]

Reporters claimed that Babe Ruth's contract called for him to collect $500 for each of his home runs, but the Yankees' records show a bonus of just $50 per home run and this only for the 1921 season. Yankees owner Jacob Ruppert denied the home run bonus rumor, but the rumor recurred. The sportswriters speculated that such a bonus could cause trouble as they thought rival pitchers might groove one for the Babe to hit, if a game was not on the line.[66] Owners with less wealth feared that bonus payments exacerbated the disparities between teams' abilities to pay players; National League owners voted in 1924 to ban most incentive clauses, aside from clauses predicated upon good behavior.[67]

Some owners even disputed the wisdom of awarding most-valuable-player awards, claiming that it emboldened awardees to demand more money in the next round of salary negotiations. For a number of years, therefore, no such awards were officially made.[68]

Owners sometimes instituted profit-sharing plans. The Minor League American Association implemented a plan whereby a penny from every ticket sold was collected into a fund for distribution among the players of the first seven (of eight) teams in the league, with players on the pennant-winning team getting the most. The owners thought the scheme would motivate players to hustle more on the field, but they were disappointed. Connie Mack considered implementing some form of profit sharing for the 1918 season but decided against it.[69]

Pirates owner Barney Dreyfuss also tried a profit-sharing scheme. He told his players during spring training that he would offer them some of whatever profit the team earned during 1921. His plan failed to motivate his players to win the pennant, and Dreyfuss later expressed disappointment that his players flagged during the pennant race.[70]

Barnstorming

Major League players played in exhibition games before and during the season. Often the preseason exhibition games would be against another Major League team, as pairs of teams worked their way to the northeast and their home stadiums. Owners hoped to recoup spring training expenses in this fashion, but they were often disappointed.[71] Sometimes the big league teams played college teams. If there was a break in the regular-season schedule, owners often scheduled their players for exhibition games in smaller towns and cities. These games brought a few more dollars for the owner, while the players received nothing aside from, perhaps, per diem.

Some players earned a supplemental income by barnstorming. They would enlist a few teammates or friends from other teams and schedule some games in October. Because the players' contracts were not year-round, they were free to set up barnstorming tours during the off-season. Owners disliked these tours for a variety of reasons, but the primary reason was that the sometimes quite lucrative income made players less reliant upon the salaries the owner paid them. Owners worried about injuries, players losing to inferior competition, or generating ill will if players goofed off or didn't appear at scheduled barnstorming games.

Owners particularly worried about players from pennant-winning teams going on barnstorming tours. By 1903 of course, the two big leagues had pretty much established their superiority in organized baseball. Aside from the possibility that the top black teams might have provided stiff competition, no white teams were likely to prevail in an extended series with a Major League club. If an entire team or a preponderance of its key players from the World Series went on the road and lost to some cross-roads baseball team, it would be embarrassing for organized baseball.

A few of the owners may have recalled the National League's early days in the late 1870s, when it was not obvious that the league's teams were the acme of professional baseball. Both the NBA and NFL owners struggled for years to prove their teams were stronger than college teams and other professional teams; during the late 1940s, the Harlem Globe-trotters gave the Minneapolis Lakers spirited competition. The owners, therefore, had reason to worry about a collection of World Series players getting beaten by some sandlot team.

In addition, owners were worried that their players might lose to a team with black players, an unforgivable sin in the owners' eyes. The owners feared that if the white players lost, it besmirched baseball. The standard line "it was only an exhibition game" was not effective in parrying the disturbing thought that perhaps black players were competitive with Major Leaguers. Ban Johnson baldly stated, "We want no makeshift Club calling themselves the Athletics to go to Cuba to be beaten by colored teams."[72]

The Babe Ruth barnstorming tour of 1921 raised owners' hackles. Ruth wasn't the first player to run afoul of the owners' strictures on World Series participants. After the 1918 season, some of his Red Sox teammates played some games under the name of "Red Sox." The owners considered pun-ishing them.[73] A year later, when Ruth was punished by Commissioner

Landis, he complained that the rule was unfair, since players receiving World Series money (second- and third-place finishers in each league), such as George Sisler, got to embark on barnstorming tours.[74]

Owners claimed they were worried about gamblers cozying up to players away from the scrutiny of stadium officials. A year after Ruth's ill-fated barnstorming tour, owners debated ending the barnstorming practice but not the exhibition games during the regular season. An editorial claimed, "It has become more and more apparent that the ball player himself can't be trusted very far when it comes to upholding the integrity of the game . . . he seems to have a very hazy idea of what is 'ethical' when it comes to playing a game that he regards as a mere exhibition and 'don't count.'"[75] The "mere exhibition" aspect applied to owner-arranged exhibition games, as the *Sporting News* described some incidents where patrons of such games left disenchanted with the Major League players and teams, citing loafing players and indifferent play.[76]

A *Sporting News* editorialist issued a nonsensical comment regarding barnstorming players when he argued that players needed to acquiesce to the will of Kenesaw M. Landis: "It will make some ball players with Bolshevik tendencies hesitate, probably in their hinted intentions of definite and organized attempts to violate the rules."[77] Calling the players Bolsheviks seems backward—they seemed more like free-market entrepreneurs.

The historian Thomas Barthel suggests that barnstorming subsided during the 1920s because of rising player salaries and the death of one of the key promoters of barnstorming. A lucrative opportunity for some players disappeared with the waning of barnstorming.[78]

Players Share in 1920s Prosperity

The owners chose to raise their players' salaries significantly during the 1920s; with increased ticket prices and greater attendance, the owners certainly had the financial wherewithal to do so. The gains, though, probably continued to fall short of matching players' true worth. Even Babe Ruth at $80,000 a season was likely to have fallen short of his market value.

12 Hang On, the Minor Leagues' Bumpy Ride

Today's baseball fan often thinks of Minor League baseball as a fun experience. The players are well cared for and usually play in well-kept ballparks. Back in the 1920s, though, Minor League Baseball was a tenuous industry, highly vulnerable to the whims of the general economy.

Minors' Parlous Existence

The Minor Leagues were baseball's weak link. One writer described the minors' plight: "Year after year local capital would grimly dig down into its jeans and pay its debts and come back for more with a smile on its face the following year. . . . and when, because of bad weather or worse ball players, the treasury would become depleted in midseason, a subscription taken among local business men favorably provided [*sic*] the means to keep the teams, or the leagues intact." This writer viewed the gradual infiltration of Minor League Baseball by Major League clubs as a good thing, as big league owners provided financial stability.[1]

The war in Europe sapped demand for Minor League Baseball and reduced the supply of ballplayers. Stuck between two adverse forces, many Minor League owners closed down for the war years. Even teams in the top leagues, such as the International League, struggled during the 1918 season, and some Minor League owners began looking for Major League sugar daddies for subsidies and players.[2]

The Minors' volatility preceded World War I. There were forty-seven leagues in 1912, but only thirty-six finished the season. Rare was the season when all of the Minor Leagues completed their season. From the peak in 1912, the number of leagues fell to twenty-four in 1916 and twenty in 1917, of which only twelve completed the season. In 1918, nine leagues started, but only one completed its season. The number of leagues gradually grew to thirty-one in 1923 (twenty-eight leagues finished) before receding to twenty-five in 1925. The number of leagues peaked again in 1928 to thirty before falling throughout the early 1930s to a low of fourteen in 1933 (but all finished the season). The Minor Leagues were clearly unstable.[3]

After the economy rebounded, Minor League teams rejuvenated, even in small towns. Sportswriter John Sheridan claimed that a Class D in a town of five thousand could survive, if they did not attempt to compete with cities of larger size and if they observed salary limits, but he may have been too optimistic.[4]

Robert Burk points out that a disproportionate number of Minor Leagues, especially at the lower classifications, were in southern states. He attributes this to the region's low-cost environment, although he adds that southern leagues composed of small towns had high franchise mortality rates. He did not attribute this regional distribution of Minor Leagues to weather factors, but surely this must have played a role, as witness today's college baseball world where southern teams dominate. The absence of any Major League Baseball teams south of St. Louis, Cincinnati, and Washington DC left the region open for Minor League teams.[5]

Proposed Solutions for the Minors' Doldrums

The proposed solutions for the Minors' doldrums centered around salary limits, although some more radical ideas surfaced. The salary-limit proposals proved difficult to enforce. Other Minor League owners hoped that representation on the National Commission would help, but this proposal went unheeded. Many Minor League owners thought that eliminating the draft of their players would help them gain larger prices for promising players and restore prosperity. The American Association considered pooling receipts and paying disbursements from a common fund. Any excess would be divided among the clubs. Such a socialistic plan, of course, was more palatable for leagues composed of cities with rough parity in drawing power.[6]

Teams in Nebraska chose to pool their revenues and agreed to disburse expense money through a central office; while the Nebraska State League had a sporadic history, the league, even in the 1950s, had some of the most radical gate-sharing arrangements in all of organized baseball. The league also shared receipts from selling players. A New Orleans club owner made a similar suggestion to that of the Nebraska State League back in 1920, but nothing came of his idea. The Virginia League went the opposite direction and eliminated gate sharing altogether.[7]

Minor League owners took other steps to economize in addition to the usual calls for salary limits. M. H. Sexton, president of the National Association of Minor Leagues, called upon owners to eliminate the double umpire system "wherever possible," reduce the number of baseballs used, put players in cheaper motels, forego Pullmans and use tourist sleepers instead, and even to get rid of spring training trips.[8]

Sexton shared some financial data regarding the Minors. He discovered that Class A clubs (the second-highest tier in the minors during the 1920s) had an average of $101,000 yearly operating expenses per team. Class B teams averaged $43,000 per team, while Class D expenses were between $22,500 and $39,000. Sexton made the odd remark that one-third of the cost of operation was in money paid out to the visiting teams; these payments would, for the league, be a collective wash. Years later, a big league owner seeking to purchase a Minor League team was aghast after looking at the financial ledgers. He told reporters that the players were receiving as much as $1,000 a month (comparable to many big league players), and he argued that the owners in the Minors needed to cut back.[9]

Many expenses rose during the 1920s. Railroads raised their per-mile rates, while hotels increased room rates. Some owners sought hotels that threw meals in with the room rate. Otherwise, owners faced at least two dollars per diem for each player.[10]

Al Tearney, president of two Minor Leagues, suggested that owners reduce admission prices. Many Minor League owners had raised admission prices during 1919 and 1920; other observers felt any proposed admission price reduction would prove injurious.[11]

Despite these drawbacks, Minor League franchises commanded a few hundred thousand dollars from prospective buyers. Even the moribund Jersey City franchise, which was often aided by the rival Baltimore Orioles, sought $95,000 in 1922. By 1925 an owner paid $200,000 for St. Paul, while star pitcher Walter Johnson and associates offered $385,000 for Oakland in the Pacific Coast League. A newspaper publisher, Paul Block, purchased the Newark club in 1927 for $360,000 at a receiver's sale, which was comparable to what the Boston Braves fetched in 1925; Block also agreed to assume team liabilities of almost $150,000.[12]

A Case of Too Much Success

Jack Dunn, one of the very few owners who could plausibly boast to having put together a team capable of competing with the worst Major League teams, found that he was too successful on the field. In the midst of his team's seven-year run as International League pennant winners, Dunn suffered declining attendance while facing rising player salaries (the downside of keeping his best players). Some of his rival International League owners, rather than improve their own teams, cried "Break up the Orioles" and insisted that Dunn sell some of his players. He sold a few after the 1922 season, but his team kept winning. After the 1924 season, Dunn admitted that attendance was down 100,000 in 1924 compared with 1923, although the team remained a top attraction on the road.[13]

An interesting possibility of Dunn's success would have been relegation and promotion, as practiced by European soccer teams. The idea is that the bottom team or teams in the top level fall to the next-highest level, while the top teams in the next-highest level move up to the top level. Although it is unlikely that Dunn's Orioles would have performed better than Mack's Athletics, the process would have been interesting. Had such a system been in place, Mack and the Boston Red Sox would have been scrambling to secure better players to avoid relegation, which was the point of the system.[14]

Minor League Draft—For Whose Benefit?

Major League owners worried about having a reliable supply of players available. The Minor Leagues were the major source of new talent, although some Major League teams also signed collegiate and sandlot players. These players, though, often required seasoning in the Minor Leagues.

Minor League owners often failed to generate enough gate receipts to turn a profit. There was a limit to how low they could cut player salaries, given the possibility of players opting for industrial semipro teams and jobs outside of baseball. For many Minor League owners finding and later selling a talented player was the difference between turning a profit or losing money.[15]

Major League owners claimed that a draft of promising Minor League players was necessary to ensure that players had the opportunity to advance throughout the Minors and up to the Majors. Commissioner Ford Frick told a congressional committee in 1951 that the draft had: "the avowed purpose of protecting the players' interests," as well as facilitating movement of players.[16]

A more likely reason for the draft's appeal, though, was that big league owners wanted to be able to obtain players on the cheap by paying a set price based on the level of Minor League the player was from. The draft ostensibly achieved both purposes, although the draft sometimes worked indirectly by inducing Minor League owners with promising players to put them on the market ahead of the draft. Congressman A. S. Herlong, a former Minor League president, testified: "If a ballplayer is good enough to be drafted, some club is going to go in and offer a little more money than the draft price for him." The congressional report contained a table showing that the numbers of draftees were very low during the early 1920s. Major League teams drafted 117 players in 1907, but this number fell to an average of 78 per year in 1912–13. By 1922 the number was 21 and remained low in 1923 and 1924. As a comparison, Major League teams drafted an average of 22 players per year between 1948 and 1951.[17]

Major League owners also claimed that the draft improved competitive balance, especially after these owners approved Charles Ebbets's suggestion to make the draft a reverse-order one. In other words, the last would be first for purposes of the draft. The congressional report on organized baseball recognized that the draft's and waiver rules' abilities to improve competitive balance were curbed by various exceptions and determinations of which players were eligible to be drafted.[18]

Minor League teams could draft players from teams in lower classifications. The lowest classification, the D level, of course, had no one to draft from.

Before World War I, organized baseball operated with a universal draft, but owners kept modifying the draft. Irving Sanborn believed, "When it was universal and not choked up with all the dampers which have been inserted, the draft provided the youngster a practically sure way to soar as high as his own ability would carry him, and to rise as fast as his talent was developed. . . . The universal draft kept any club owner from abusing his power over the players." Sanborn concluded, "The result [of the universal draft] was that players generally did not reach the Majors too soon and seldom did they get that far up unless they gave considerable promise of possessing Big League qualifications."[19]

For years Major and Minor League owners argued over who was eligible for the draft and what the draft prices should be. The Major League owners wanted low draft prices, while the Minor League owners wanted high draft prices.[20] Minor League owners in the highest classification, say, AA (the AAA classification came decades later) had the keenest interest in this matter since they usually had the most players sought by the Major Leagues.

The Minor League players drafted by the Major Leagues in October 1923 were an undistinguished bunch, and reporters said the recent decision of five Minor Leagues to opt out of the draft hurt the talent pool. The next year, big league owners selected twenty-four players (the number differs from that given in the congressional report). The Yankees, Giants, and Tigers did not draft any players. Almost one-half of the players had previous Major League trials, and one-quarter were twenty-eight years old or older.[21]

A similar story recurred in 1925, as half the players drafted had previous Major League experience. This draft, though, featured Hack Wilson, who was drafted by the Cubs. As long as Joe McCarthy managed the Cubs, Wilson was an exceptional player; McCarthy seemed to understand and to coax the best from Wilson. The 1926 draft consisted of twenty-five players; the two World Series participants—the Cardinals and the Yankees—did not draft any players, and again, several of the players were Major League retreads.[22]

Owners complained that by paying high prices for Minor League players, they demoralized the youngsters. The owners claimed that a youth, upon being purchased by a Major League team, assumed he was headed directly to the big time, but the team often farmed him out for additional experience. Irving Sanborn wrote, "To an ambitious youngster that means suddenly raising his hopes too high only to dash them before he is given what he thinks is half a chance. Very often this has resulted in killing all his ambition." After the system had been in place for a few years, though, players, even young ones, would presumably understand that this was all part of the process. Sanborn's argument requires a chronic naïveté on the part of the players.[23]

Owners sometimes manipulated the draft system to protect certain players. The Brooklyn club tried to draft Jimmy Pattison from its own farm at Macon. Landis put the kibosh on such stunts: "Selection of a player from a club's own farm is wholly inconsistent with the draft.... The club can buy any players before Sept. 15 if it wants them."[24]

Nettlesome Issue of the Player Draft

Minor League owners, especially in the higher categories, chafed at the draft rules. As soon as the war ended in November 1918, the Minor Leagues pressed for an elimination of the draft.[25] Eliminating the draft cut both ways for most Minor League owners. Although they could retain their players until they were willing to put them up for sale without fear of losing such players, they would have greater difficulty obtaining players from teams in lower classifications without a draft. This argument, commonly used by commentators, ignored the fact that the rules limited the number of players a team could lose via the draft in any year.

Major League officials quickly disavowed any willingness to eliminate the draft. John Heydler claimed such an elimination would, "tie the players hand and foot and would keep them at a standstill instead of offering an opportunity for advancement."[26]

Heydler, though, did not demonstrate that many players were held up in the Minor Leagues. If a player was more valuable to a team in a higher classification, an obstinate owner would be giving up the opportunity to reap the higher value if he kept the player. Jack Dunn, perhaps the best example of this alleged phenomenon, eventually sold his best players. He may have held them longer than the player desired, but he usually did this in the hopes of getting a higher price for the player or to bolster his Orioles' chances of winning yet another pennant. Sportswriter Charles Foreman cited the turnover in Dunn's clubs, as he disposed of at least a half dozen players every season.[27]

Some Major League owners professed indifference regarding the elimination of the draft. They renewed their scouting efforts to find players themselves.[28]

The *Sporting News*, hardly a bastion of advocating player rights, argued that, "So long as Organized Baseball maintains a system of reserve rights by which when a player signs a contract he is bound practically for the entire period of his playing career, then the draft must be. If it is abolished then the reserve system must be abandoned or modified, for the player in justice can not [sic] be sentenced for life to serve in a league of lower class regardless of what talents he may develop." The editorialist went on to criticize the current draft system because the highest classifications had opted out of the draft. In the same issue, a writer thought the elimination of the draft was unfair to Minor League players, because, in addition to possibly being prevented from advancing, the player remained in leagues where the salaries were low.[29]

At the January 1919 meetings, Minor League owners decided to issue an ultimatum to their big brothers in the Majors: accept the Minors' demands or the Minor Leagues would exit organized baseball. The Minors' key demand was the elimination of the player draft. Teams in AA leagues told their fans that elimination of the draft would enable these teams to stockpile sufficient talent to provide Major League–caliber quality. Jack Dunn of Baltimore lived up to this promise, but his colleagues generally reverted to selling top players, often during a pennant race. The Minors' big gamble was that they could sell enough players at high enough prices to the Majors to remain independent of Organized Baseball and the big leagues' often high-handed treatment.[30]

Some observers believed the Minors were doomed to failure if they tried to exit organized baseball; they cited the likelihood that Major League teams would sign enough sandlot and college players to disregard the Minors, although where these new players would play was left unanswered (unless the Major League owners decided to increase the active player roster limits).[31] The agreement between Major and Minor Leagues lapsed during the 1919 season.

By the end of the 1919 season, although owners of teams in the top leagues sold enough players to the Majors to make maintaining the boycott attractive, owners of Minor League clubs in smaller cities were growing dissatisfied with the boycott of the draft. Outside of the AA and the next lower level of Minor League Baseball, a vast majority of owners wanted to revive an agreement with the Majors.[32]

At the winter meetings of December 1920, organized baseball reached a new agreement. Draft prices started at $1,000 for Class D and rose to $5,000 for AA players. The AA and A classification teams could lose but one player per year, but the other leagues could lose any number of players. The Major League teams could "option out" up to eight players for up to two years with right of recall (without fear of drafting by another team).[33]

The American Association and International League refused to subject their players to the draft. There was tension within these Minor Leagues, as not all of their owners wanted to opt out; Jack Dunn of the International League was dead set against the draft, but some of his peers with few high-quality players to sell worried about the inability to sign replacement players from the lower classifications. Owners in the Pacific Coast League were evenly split on the question. Dunn later relaxed his opposition to the draft late in 1924; one cynic suggested, "the fact that Dunn had pruned his championship tree so closely in recent months that he was facing dry rot along with the others."[34]

The Pacific Coast League decided to use a different ploy in trying to get the player draft permanently eliminated. The league's owners threatened to "consider itself a major league in the general acceptance of the term" if they were subjected to the draft. The implication of the league's threat was that a "major" league could not be subject to the draft. A few of the league's teams played in large cities and might have had some reasonable expectations to support a Major League team, but several of the teams played in rather small cities. The other two Class AA leagues had similar aspirations or delusions.[35]

In January 1923 the Major League owners decided not to farm out any players to the Minor Leagues unless they could be recalled later through the draft process. The Minor Leagues quickly retorted that any such arrangement was a violation of the National Agreement. Landis sided with the big league owners and their action in increasing the number of players an owner could option from eight to fifteen. The Major League owners eventually decided to increase the draft prices, especially for Class AA players. They agreed to boost the price from $5,000 to $7,500, but the three Class AA leagues still opposed the draft.[36]

The American Association and the Pacific Coast League agreed to a modified form of draft during the December 1923 winter meetings. The Major League owners considered but rejected an increase in the draft price for a player plucked from AA ball from $7,500 to $10,000. The Major Leagues agreed to drop their right to draft Class C and Class D players, while the Class A A clubs could draft one player from Class A, three from B and any number from C and D levels.[37]

Rickey and the Farm System

The enduring controversy regarding the draft of Minor League players spurred some Major League owners and managers to scour the sandlots and colleges for promising players. A spate of articles featured hand-wringing over the perceived diminution in the supply of quality players, and various cures were suggested. Branch Rickey's farm system concept was one response; John Heydler urged his owners to create baseball academies for training youngsters. Opinions differed regarding whether colleges were destined to become a primary source of players.[38]

Branch Rickey quickly became known as an astute judge of player talent through his work with both the St. Louis Browns and the Cardinals. Rickey and the St. Louis Cardinals realized that whenever they expressed an interest in and made an offer for a promising Minor Leaguer, the player's owner would contact other Major League teams and see whether he could obtain a higher price. Other big league owners, knowing of Rickey's acumen, would often out-bid the St. Louis team. Rickey was able to sign pitcher Jess Haines in 1919; author Arthur Mann claims Haines was the last player the Cardinals purchased outside their organization for the next quarter century.[39]

Rickey wasn't the first baseball official to round up some farm teams in the Minors. Lee Hedges, owner of the St. Louis Browns and Rickey's former boss, had suggested owning several teams in the Minors. Teams, such as Cleveland and Brooklyn, purchased Minor League teams before 1920; these owners were ordered to divest by 1914. Other big league owners had close ties with certain Minor League teams and were often given first opportunity to buy a player; sometimes these were formalized into "working agreements," whereby the Major League sent its excess players to a Minor League team in return for that team's most promising youngsters not currently owned by the big league club. Another approach was an option sale, whereby a Major League team sold a player to a Minor

League team, but the big league team retained an option to repurchase the player, usually at a nominal price. Many Minor League owners disliked the option sale.[40]

Rickey testified before the congressional committee in 1951 that he had tired of selling his top players to keep the Cardinals solvent. When the club got some capital, he decided to buy interests in the Fort Smith, Arkansas, and Houston teams. He quickly added Syracuse and later Rochester. He claimed this was the only way a poorer team could compete with the New York and Chicago clubs, especially when the top five Minor Leagues opted out of the player draft, meaning open bidding for top talent.[41] Ultimately, these ownership and working-agreement tactics allowed the St. Louis Cardinals and teams with similar systems to control more than the permitted number of players.

Many of Rickey's peers believed that his plan was doomed to financial failure. Throughout the mid 1920s, several Major League owners denied they were interested in buying farm clubs. Fans of Minor League teams disliked the system, believing that the Major League club cared little for their interests. If the big league team needed help, it called up a top player from its Minor League team, thereby injuring that team's chances of winning its pennant. Writer John Sheridan observed, "To June 20, 1925, the 'chain store' idea did not appear to have done the Cardinals a mite of good. They were in last place. In October 1926, the same Cardinals were the world's champions. What made the Cardinals champions? Automatic operation of the 'chain store' system or a certain pitcher-killer and man-buster, one Rogers Hornsby?"[42] He admitted that former farm hands on the champion Cardinals' team were worth $215,000, acquired through seven years' effort on the system. Sheridan offered a slightly different opinion in a later piece. In this piece, he did not believe the Cardinals' farm system developed enough replacements to justify the expenditures.[43]

By 1928 Sheridan was touting the Cardinal system: "I cannot see how the rest of the major league clubs can avoid following, to preserve their standing, the 'chain store' system of the Cardinals, and acquiring for themselves an assorted lot of minor clubs, for how else are they going to get needed replacements." John Kieran suggested that the real proof of the farm system's sustainability was: "There must be something financially sound in this scheme, because other progressive clubs are edging into the same business."[44]

The 1926 St. Louis Cardinals featured thirteen players who made their debuts with the Cardinals, although not all could be considered farm hands. Rogers Hornsby, for instance, had been purchased before the team started its system. The Cardinals had acquired Grover Alexander off the waiver list. The real proof of the Cardinals' success with the farm system could be seen in the team's 1928 and 1930 clubs. The Cardinals had three-quarters of a new infield, a new catcher, and a new outfielder by 1928. The 1930 team had several new ballplayers, too. By 1934 the team's turnover was almost complete. Only three of the regulars had not debuted with the Cardinals, and the top four pitchers, unlike in previous pennant-winning seasons, had all made their debuts with the Cardinals. By 1934, then, the farm system was reliably churning out sufficient talent that Branch Rickey could sell or trade veterans before their market value diminished.[45]

It was a good thing the Cardinals had excess players to sell, as attendance at Sportsman's Park never put them in the top three with respect to attendance in the National League even when they won a pennant. The team's attendance during pennant-winning seasons badly lagged Pittsburgh's attendance during its two pennant-winning seasons, to say nothing of New York's and Chicago's attendance figures.

John Sheridan recognized one interesting aspect of the Cardinals' farm system. Since the Cardinals owned several Minor League teams, the organization internalized any gains and benefits from transactions within it. If the Cardinals chose to promote a promising player on its AA club in mid season, then it would absorb the losses in gate receipts for that AA club, while reaping the benefits of any increase in gate receipts in St. Louis. He concluded that the financial gains to the Cardinals from winning the pennant outweighed the collective gains if each of its six farms clubs won pennants but the parent club did not. When Major League owners simply purchased a player from a Minor League in which they had no financial ties, this aspect did not occur; in addition, these unaffiliated owners incurred the costs of making transactions. Economists would argue that this internalization was one way to improve the efficiency of producing players.[46]

Several Major League owners began buying Minor League clubs and building farm systems, but they faced a disadvantage. They did not have Rickey's acumen either in organizing a system or in recognizing talent. What worked for Rickey might not have worked for many of his rivals.[47]

Landis disliked farm systems, because he felt these systems could retard young players' progress to the Majors and let teams control more players than the player limits allowed. The circumvention of the rules, which had existed in the past via gentlemen's agreements, were formalized in the various relationships between Major and Minor League clubs. Landis's long-time secretary, Leslie O'Connor, told the congressional committee in 1951 that Landis consulted Barney Dreyfuss and Frank Navin regarding the burgeoning farm systems; these owners believed that "he need have no worries about it because it was financially destructive to a club to undertake to operate minor league clubs, and that the thing would fall of its own weight."[48]

The two owners failed to realize the true genius of Rickey's plan. Rickey was first to see the full potential of a farm system. He believed the system would work if the owner was able to be a net seller of players rather than a buyer, even if his team was rarely a top-drawing club at the gate.

At the 1927 winter meetings, Landis polled the sixteen owners; the owners had a total of eighteen farm clubs; two-thirds were owned by National League clubs. Some owners advocated limiting Major League clubs to owning no more than two Minor League teams, but this suggestion would not eliminate the "working agreements" that enabled Major League owners to circumvent rules on controlling players. When Landis uncovered chicanery, he stepped in and "freed" Minor League players, including several players in 1929; these players—including Claude Jonnard, Guy Cantrell, and Melburn Simons—would have scant impact upon Major League Baseball.[49]

Owners of other teams, such as Washington and the Boston Braves, had difficulty competing in building farm systems. Ed Barrow reflected that the Yankees didn't need a farm system to sustain their success, although by 1929 he began acquiring such teams for the Yankees and eventually hired George Weiss to run the system. As early as 1929, the *Sporting News* suggested that the farm system would "give undue advantages to a few clubs. Four or five rich clubs would buy up and control all the most valuable sources of recruiting ball teams."[50] Ultimately, the richer clubs would come to reap great benefits from owning farm systems.

Advocates for the farm systems claimed that Minor League Baseball survived to the extent it did because of Major League ownership and subsidization. Minor League teams affiliated with Major League clubs tended to fare better on the field and on the ledger.[51] The congressional committee of 1951, though, considered evidence that "the share of major-league receipts which has subsidized the minor leagues has remained substantially unchanged over the past 40 years. Only the method of subsidization has changed." Given that the Major Leagues' receipts increased between 1909 and 1946, if the proportion remained constant, the amount of dollars paid in subsidies undoubtedly increased.[52]

Organized Baseball's Weaker Link

The Minor Leagues were usually the most volatile elements in organized baseball, especially those teams in the lower classifications. Most teams in the lower classifications played in small towns barely able to sustain professional baseball. Some Minor League owners thought their bottom lines would be improved by shedding the draft, while other owners worried that elimination of the draft would make it more difficult to obtain qualified players. The Major League owners sometimes used a divide and conquer strategy to keep the Minor League owners in line. Major League subsidization or ownership of Minor League teams provided financial benefits and stability for affiliated teams.

13   Baseball and Ethnic Diversity

Not every American male could aspire to play in the big leagues during the 1920s. Organized Baseball maintained an informal, though effective, color line.

You Can't Play in Our Game

The 1920s witnessed integration in baseball—of white ethnic and Cuban players. Baseball officials loved to pontificate about how baseball was emblematic of America, with opportunities for all. An editorial in the *Sporting News* revealed the prevailing attitudes, unintentionally ironic, toward America's immigrants and children of immigrants: "No nation in the world has developed a national sport of such universal and gripping interest. Our so-called aliens, hyphenates, unnaturalized immigrants, take to baseball before they take out their citizenship papers. . . . At the opening games the advance guard of this polyglot multitude got together at ballparks, forgot their war feelings forgot their nationalities, forgot their bigotries and their feuds and shouted their loudest in cheers for the athletic feats of the ball players. The American idea of racial assimilation, of amiable mutuality, of equal opportunity, is epitomized and illustrated in the game."[1] The editor appeared to be a few ethnicities shy of a rainbow coalition in his encomium.

Of course, for those Americans who had a black parent, grandparent or even great-grandparent, the game was informally off-limits. Blacks could pay their money and attend games, but they could not participate in games. Given African Americans' relatively low incomes, their patronage, even in the northern cities with burgeoning black populations, was not likely to be large.

Some New Faces on the Playing Field

Native-born, protestant Americans, especially those whose ancestors hailed from the British Isles, spent much of the century between the Battle of Waterloo and the outbreak of the Great War worrying about, first, the influx of Irish Catholic and then eastern and southern European immigrants. On the West Coast, they worried about the Chinese laborers (while eradicating or sequestering tribes of Native Americans). The Great War, however, cast together individuals of various European ethnicities. Movies such as the *Fighting 69th*, featured small units of Americans soldiers with soon-to-be stock characters: the wiseacre from the Bronx or Brooklyn, the "hillbilly" from Tennessee, the quiet literate soldier from a large Midwestern city, the Texan, and others. Priests, rabbis, and ministers were shown administering rites to all of the men in the unit. African American troops, though, remained in segregated units, mostly doing menial work despite their willingness to fight.

The cities with Major League teams often had huge populations of immigrants and immigrant children. New York City, with its large Jewish population, was simply the phenomenon writ large. Anti-Semitism was rampant in the America of the 1920s, with the Ku Klux Klan adding Jewish and Catholic Americans to their list of hated peoples. Henry Ford was a noted anti-Semite, who used his newspaper, the *Dearborn Independent*, to publish notorious diatribes. The editor of the *Sporting News*, who was a foe of racial integration in baseball, took Ford to task. The editor responded to Ford's and other people's allegations that the gamblers involved in the 1919 World Series fix were Jewish (Arnold Rothstein) by retorting that a few Jewish criminals did not reflect discredit upon a whole ethnicity before he lapsed into some provocative comments of his own: "It is not an indictment of Jewry in toto, any more than the fact that a bunch of Irish might be indicted for graft in a sewer contract would be an indictment of the whole Irish race, or the round-up of a bunch of Dago hootch makers would be an indictment of Italians."[2]

To attract Jewish patrons, John McGraw openly sought a talented Jewish player for his Giants. He purchased Moses Solomon for the proverbial

$100,000 in 1923. He also purchased Andrew Cohen. Solomon retired with a .375 career batting average (albeit it in only eight at bats), while Cohen never quite made the cut. McGraw passed on Hank Greenberg but, in fairness to McGraw, Greenberg was pretty raw early on.[3]

McGraw may have sought talented Jewish players for gate appeal, but he held some broad notions about them. He was not alone; according to John Wray, quoted in the *Sporting News*, Jewish players, caring about money (which players of any ethnicity did not?), sought the more lucrative sports such as boxing.[4] During the 1920s, professional basketball barnstorming teams featured quite a few Jewish players, repudiating the old canard that Jewish people were not athletic. Although McGraw's and Wray's attitudes may seem unenlightened, sportswriters, too, did not hesitate to ascribe general characteristics to other ethnicities. The highly respected writer Frederick Lieb penned, "Slugging strength seems to be characteristic of the German element in professional baseball, while the Irish players usually are faster and think quicker. There are exceptions of course."[5]

Baseball officials hoped to introduce the sport to people around the world. Outside of Japan and Latin America, baseball's efforts faltered upon the shoals of indifference. English spectators already had cricket and football (soccer). American teams and players toured Japan in the 1920s and 1930s; one observer went so far as to predict that "a properly managed . . . professional ball league would prosper . . . and produce clubs of a caliber to make a real annual challenge for the now so-called World's championship."[6] No one in the 1920s seemed to consider the possibility of Asian players performing in MLB.

The sport appealed to the Japanese, although during World War II, the Japanese knowledge of baseball took a bizarre twist. Japanese troops reportedly hurled slurs against Babe Ruth while attacking American troops. The game, though, proved enduringly popular, although it would not be until the 1960s that a Japanese player appeared in the Major Leagues.

Baseball Finesses the Color Line

The Cincinnati Reds manager, Clark Griffith, signed Armando Marsans in 1911, while the Boston Braves signed Dolf Luque for 1914 (although he earned most of his glory with the Reds). These owners tread a fine line, however, as they had to finesse the race issue. Owners often asserted that their Latin players were white, white, white. Although we properly admire Jackie Robinson for being the first African American player to reintegrate organized baseball in 1946 at Montreal and 1947 with Brooklyn, the likelihood that players with some sub-Saharan African ancestry performed in the Major Leagues during the first half of the twentieth century is a near certainty.[7] Given the racial mores of the time, when even one African American great-great-grandparent was enough to certify a person as black in some locales, there may have even been many "white" players who were wittingly or unwittingly breaking the color line. The irony to modern sensibilities, is that Tiger Woods, who has more Asian than African ancestry is generally perceived and lauded for being African American. A century ago, though, Woods and a legion of other talented athletes would have been denied the opportunity to prove themselves in professional sports.[8]

The Untapped Talent Pool

White Major League owners could hardly plead ignorance regarding talented African American players. Some owners rented their stadiums to African American teams, or their players played exhibition games with black players. The owners emphasized the "exhibition" aspect of these games. Reporter Oliver Arata, while showing some of the prevailing racial attitudes of the times (he saw nothing wrong with segregation), stated, "[Willie Wells] is generally considered by competent observers the peer of any in the Major Leagues both in hitting and fielding. . . . Although professional white teams do not allow negro members, they occasionally play negro teams, and these contests are anything but a walkover for the more famous Major Leaguers."[9]

Andy Lawson, a promoter of third major leagues, claimed that his Continental League would give black players a chance to play. An editorial written in 1921 appearing in *Baseball Magazine* applauded his "evidently sincere attempt."[10] Nothing came of Lawson's efforts, so official integration remained years away.

Baseball Remains Off-Limits

Established Major League owners evinced no interest in overtly flouting the color line during the 1920s. Owners were satisfied to diversify among white ethnics and Hispanics. Given the game's relative prosperity during the 1920s, the owners' complacency is understandable if not laudable. African American players would continue to seek employment on baseball teams existing outside of organized baseball.

In the next chapter, economic historian Michael Haupert provides a case study of one of the more successful teams in Negro League Baseball.

14   Hilldale and the Negro Leagues in the 1920s

Beginning in 1885 African American baseball players were banned from working in what would become known as Major League Baseball. With that decision, employment at all levels of organized baseball was closed to blacks until Jackie Robinson took the field in 1946 for the Montreal Royals, a Minor League affiliate of the Brooklyn Dodgers. The only sources of employment for professional baseball players of African American descent were teams and leagues organized exclusively for black ball-players. Such leagues first emerged in the late nineteenth century and lasted until 1963, though they dwindled considerably during the decade after the integration of Major League Baseball.

The rise of black baseball paralleled the expansion of African American business activity in general during the first two decades of the twentieth century. Like other parts of the economy, baseball was segregated. Not only were black players barred from MLB, so were executives and owners. They even had trouble in that capacity in their own leagues due to the lack of ballparks owned by African Americans. They often had to lease from or take on white businessmen as partners in order to have access to a ballpark. Access to acceptable parks was perhaps the greatest hurdle black baseball owners faced.[1]

Ed Bolden: Baseball Entrepreneur

In 1927 a reporter for the *Pittsburgh Courier* asked noted black baseball pioneer and historian Sol White whom he considered to be the greatest figures in colored baseball. White listed six individuals whom he referred to as the great modernists—those who propelled the colored game into the twentieth century. That list included Edward W. Bolden and Rube Foster; C. I. Taylor (longtime manager and vice president of the Negro National League from 1920 until his death in 1922); Jess and Eddie McMahon (white businessmen and sports promoters who owned two New York City–based black ball clubs in the teens); and Jim Keenan (owner and secretary-treasurer of the Eastern Colored League).[2]

Each of these men exerted an extraordinary impact on the black game, but Rube Foster, elected to the Hall of Fame in 1981, is the most famous. He was a player, manager, and executive over a long and storied career. He founded the Negro National League in 1920, and in this capacity interacted frequently with Ed Bolden. Despite Foster's fame, we actually know more about Bolden's Hilldale (outside Philadelphia) club through the Cash-Thompson archives at the African American Museum in Philadelphia. These include a collection of primary documents, including a large collection of game logs, team minutes, and financial records covering the period from 1914 to 1932. A study of Bolden and Hilldale provides a window into the operation of black baseball in the 1920s.

Ed Bolden was a twenty-eight-year-old postal clerk in 1910 when he joined the Hilldale baseball club as a volunteer scorekeeper. He eventually rose to president, and under his leadership the club grew from a local amateur organization to a professional powerhouse, flourishing financially until brought down by the Great Depression. During his two decades in charge, Bolden built some of the best black ball clubs in the east. From 1923 to 1928 he also headed the Eastern Colored League (ECL), of which Hilldale was a charter member.

Bolden was a tireless and brash promoter, unafraid to play the race card. He heavily marketed the fact that Hilldale was black owned. It paid off, playing a role in the team's ability to land top-quality talent and schedule attractive opponents. It also made him a local hero of sorts in the African American community of Darby (west of Philadelphia). But while he promoted Hilldale as a "race institution," he was not afraid to do business with white men when he found it profitable. Despite his willingness to deal with businessmen regardless of color, he remained devoted to black business and causes.[3]

Perhaps his greatest stroke of marketing genius was the construction in 1914 of a ballpark known as Darby Field, or Hilldale Park. The ballpark was a continuous work in progress over the next several years, serving as the home field for Hilldale as well as a source of advertising and rental income. The location of the park was convenient for his neighborhood fan base, but Bolden was not content with that. He assured that the park would also be easy to reach from anywhere in Philadelphia by arranging to have a streetcar line run straight to his ballpark with extra cars during games.[4]

The convenient location of Darby, with its low cost of transportation to major black baseball hubs in New York, Baltimore, and Washington DC made Hilldale an attractive destination for all the top teams on the East Coast. The fact that the stadium was owned by Hilldale eliminated the problems of finding quality dates and negotiating profitable lease terms for stadiums owned by white men. Bolden combined these advantages with his marketing skills, ensuring the financial success of the Hilldale franchise.

As he would continue to do throughout his career, Bolden improved his roster by signing players away from other squads. Unlike Major League Baseball, there was no reserve clause in the Negro Leagues. When Hilldale was an amateur team, he recruited players from other sandlot teams, sometimes advertising in the papers for open tryouts, or in "classified" ads seeking specific players.[5] Later on he signed players from other teams, often earning the enmity of other owners as a result. This practice led to his long-running public feud with Rube Foster, a vocal critic of contract jumping.

Discrimination, in one way, was a powerful weapon for the owners of the black clubs. The color line gave them a version of the reserve clause. While they could not easily prevent players from jumping to other colored teams, they did not have to compete with the deep pockets of MLB. Hilldale's salaries were a tiny fraction of those paid by MLB teams, but there was no chance that stars like future Hall of Famer Judy Johnson would be lured to play for the Yankees. Discrimination also limited the other economic choices of the players so that baseball was an attractive occupation despite the low wages (see table 24). The color barrier in baseball and discrimination in society allowed Hilldale to get great players at low wages.

Perhaps the best alternative the players had was to go play in the Caribbean or Cuban leagues, which many of them did, especially during the winter months. Barnstorming was another option, but only the best players, such as Satchel Paige, could make a steady living barnstorming. The average player was not in great enough demand to survive on barnstorming paychecks. As a result, the economic options of black players were limited.

Hilldale Turns Pro

The Hilldale Daisies, as they were frequently known in the press, officially incorporated as the Hilldale Baseball and Exhibition Company in January 1917.[6] The October 22 minutes laid out a plan to incorporate with capital of $10,000. The incorporation was the first step to becoming a professional club. Signing Otto Briggs as the club's first paid player was the second. Bolden proved to be a pioneer in the black baseball business. The club was a charter member of the Eastern Colored League and went on to play in the first two Colored World Series. In order to cover the costs of running a professional team, the park was upgraded, a grandstand was built, and admission was fixed at twenty-five cents, half what the cheapest MLB tickets fetched.[7]

Otto Briggs and Spottswood Poles became the first salaried players for Hilldale in 1917. Briggs was paid $273 for the season and Poles earned $448. To put these salaries in perspective, the average MLB player earned $3,227 that year. Briggs and Poles were the first players to earn a fixed salary instead of taking a share of the gate. Briggs returned the loyalty, sticking with the team for the next thirteen seasons.

Another example of Bolden's creativity was his effort to build a team concession business.[8] Hilldale sold the standard peanuts and soft drinks from the beginning and added ice cream and cigarettes in 1917. Along with regular monthly salaries came the scheduling of games on a greater scale, which meant increased travel and a host of additional details that needed to be coordinated, including meals and lodging, negotiating terms with scheduled opponents, and hiring umpires and game-day staff plus generating publicity before the game and reporting results to the newspapers afterwards.

Hilldale scheduled most of their games individually. Even when they were in a league, they played a substantial number of nonleague games each season. This involved lining up an opponent, a date, time, place, and umpires for each game, as well as negotiating a payment or division of the gate. If it was a home game then game-day staff also needed to be scheduled. For an away game, travel arrangements had to be made as well as scheduling additional games in the area to help pay for the trip. Hilldale had to negotiate each game contract individually, most of which were for a single game rather than a multigame series. Hilldale ran their own concessions (as opposed to contracting them out, as did some MLB teams), scouting, marketing, and field maintenance.

The decision to turn professional was financially risky, but paid off immediately both on the field (23-15-1 record) and off ($2,915 profit, which was nearly three times as much as the previous three years combined). The bottom line was helped by several postseason exhibitions that Bolden lined up against Major Leaguers. To beef up the squad for these games he added stars Smokey Joe Williams, Louis Santop, and Dick Lundy to the lineup. Santop, another future Hall of Famer, remained with Hilldale for several seasons and was instrumental in leading them to the Colored World Series in 1924.

Before joining an organized league for the first time in 1920, a typical game day for Hilldale began with a trip to the bank. The treasurer withdrew enough money to make all of the expected payments associated with each game. At the conclusion of the game everyone (the opposition, the players, the workers) was paid in cash. The day's receipts were then deposited in the bank. If the balance at the end of the day exceeded that at the beginning, it was a profitable venture.[9]

Hilldale's initial experience was that teams would not play for a share of the gate. Opposition teams would generally only agree to play for a cash-on-the-barrelhead guarantee. This could be risky because it put all the pressure of generating a large crowd on Hilldale. Bolden took on the risk because the scheduling of these exhibition games was necessary for the financial survival of the franchise, as was the case for most black ball clubs.

The cash-guarantee system presented a challenge for Hilldale in scheduling. The team had to decide who to schedule, when to schedule them, and how much to pay them. These business decisions were crucial because of the thin margin on which the team operated. Sunday and holiday games could generate big profits with the right competition at the right price, but the loss of even one such lucrative payday could spell the difference between profit and loss for the year.

Bolden's success drew the attention of Nat Strong, a white booking agent from New York. Strong was the longtime president of the Intercity Baseball Association, a white semiprofessional organization that operated as a booking agent in New York City for local clubs. Negro League scholar Michael Lomax believed Strong also had Tammany connections, or it would have been difficult for a relative small-time operator like him to gain control over so many baseball parks in the New York City environs.[10]

Strong coveted Hilldale for his booking agency. When Bolden rebuffed his advances, Strong threatened to drive him out of business by locating a competing team across the street from Darby Field.[11] Bolden responded promptly and publicly to this threat by taking out an ad in the Philadelphia *Tribune* to state his case: "The race people of Philadelphia and vicinity are proud to proclaim Hilldale the biggest thing in the baseball world owned, fostered, and controlled by race men. . . . We are proud to be in a position to give Darby citizens the most beautiful park in Delaware County, a team that is second to none and playing the best attractions available. To affiliate ourselves with other than race men would be a mark against our name that could never be eradicated."[12]

Bolden's public-relations coup and his skills at signing top talent diffused Strong's threat and contributed to the rise of Hilldale to the top of the eastern colored circuits. He earned a reputation as a clean, upstanding owner who did not tolerate rowdiness and umpire baiting. He advocated "clean" ball and gentlemanly behavior on the field and expected the same from the fans. He employed security guards at every home game to ensure the safety and comfort of the players, umpires, and fans. His attention to fan comfort and safety was not novel. This approach to expanding the market for baseball was first broached by William Hulbert when he formed the National League in 1876, and then copied by Ban Johnson's American League at the turn of the century.[13]

Bolden understood the need for the stability of a league but also recognized the profit potential of a well-marketed exhibition game. Despite several seasons of league membership, Hilldale seldom had as many as half its games scheduled as part of a league. In 1920 he secured a lease on a second park in Camden, New Jersey, expanding his market, and securing a site for Sunday games, thereby skirting Pennsylvania's blue laws.

Comparing Hilldale with the New York Yankees

It is worth comparing the operation of the Hilldale club to that of another franchise for which we have intimate financial knowledge, the New York Yankees. Though they followed similar paths, the two clubs have very different stories to tell because of the leagues in which they played. The Yankees played in the American League, a model of stability. The Yankees had been the last team to move, coming from Baltimore in 1903. No other American League franchise would move until the Browns fled St. Louis for Baltimore in 1954. Beginning in 1904 until the league expanded in 1961, the Yankees played at least 148 games every year versus the seven other American League teams (except for the 1918 and 1919 seasons).[14] Other than the World Series, they played no other meaningful games during that span.

Hilldale operated in a completely different environment, much closer to a free market. Even after the club paid five hundred dollars for an associate membership in the National Association of Colored Professional Baseball Clubs (NACPBC) in December 1920, the ability of the league to discipline either the players or the clubs was very limited.[15] Hilldale, or any other team, could, and often did, play any team that would agree with them on price and place to play. In a given year they would play up to two-thirds of their schedule as nonleague games, the majority of those against white teams.[16] The Negro Leagues were also much less stable than either the National or American League. Teams frequently reneged on their obligation to play league games if they could engage a more lucrative opponent in an exhibition match. This behavior, along with shaky finances of some franchises, resulted in teams coming and going from the league on a regular basis, sometimes in mid season, and leagues forming and disbanding in short order.[17]

A great financial divide separated the Negro Leagues from the Major Leagues. The Yankees had two great financial initiatives. The first was their purchase of Babe Ruth in January of 1920 at a cost of $100,000. The second was Yankee Stadium, opened in 1923 at a cost to the Yankees of $3.1 million.[18] It was a great financial investment, but not for the reasons that might seem obvious. Yankee Stadium was not a boon to Yankee attendance and, in fact, was not much larger than the Polo Grounds, which they had been leasing since abandoning Hilltop Park in 1913.[19] The Yankees set their all-time attendance record in the Polo Grounds in 1920 and did not break that record until after World War II. More than serving as a magnet for larger crowds, Yankee Stadium was a highly profitable investment because it provided new streams of income for the team. Some of this was from baseball, mostly in the form of concessions and more frequent Sunday home dates. Yankee concession income increased more than tenfold from a high of $8,000 in 1921 to an average of more than $94,000 a year over the first five years in Yankee Stadium.

The Stadium produced lucrative sources of income beyond MLB games. It was built with an electronic infrastructure buried under the infield to facilitate the staging of boxing matches, which proved to be phenomenally profitable. The Yankees cleared as much as $50,000 for a single evening of matches. This was equal to 5 percent of total home attendance revenue in an average year at Yankee Stadium.[20]

College football was another profitable venture. From the inaugural contest in 1923 through the rest of the decade, more than forty college games were played at Yankee Stadium, every one of which was pure profit for the Yankees.[21] The fledgling National Football League, and what the Yankee ledgers referred to as "colored baseball" also served as occasional tenants.

Bolden also constructed a park, but had to do it with annual improvements out of the team's operating budget. As a result, their park was a modest and continual work in progress. The steel and concrete edifice of Yankee Stadium stood in stark contrast to the wooden bleachers of Darby Field. Whereas Yankee Stadium had a seating capacity of 58,000 when it opened, Hilldale could seat only a few thousand. The verdant pasture of the Yankee Stadium outfield stands in stark contrast to the tree-stump pocked outfield in Darby Field when it first opened.

As an example of the different magnitudes of their budgets, Hilldale sometimes bought baseballs one at a time, and in 1915 they scheduled an extra game just so the pitchers could receive an extra share. The Yankees, on the other hand, spent $12,000 on advertising in 1921 and $2600 hiring detectives to trail their players the following year.

Financial Performance

Hilldale had essentially no assets other than a bank account and a grandstand worth at most a couple of thousand dollars. Thus, an analysis of their cash basis is a good indication of their financial condition. The increase in their cash balance each year approximates their profits. This measure indicates a very profitable enterprise, especially relative to the modest size of the initial investment, and certainly comparable to the alternative. Average salaries for black workers were modest, and job opportunities were restricted relative to what was available to white workers. While race-based wage data are hard to come by, some wage samples are available, and they can be used to estimate opportunity costs to black players (table 24).[22]

Reported team profit figures are reduced by distributions to owners. As the owners often worked for the club, at least some of these distributions can be considered wages, thus this cash basis provides a lower bound estimate for profits; that is, some of the distribution to owners is a return for their work and some is a return on capital. If no explicit salaries for owners are recorded, then there is no way of separating the two amounts. We make the profit-minimizing assumption that all transfers to the owners are salary, not dividends on their investment. This decreases reported profits because salaries are costs, which decrease profits, while dividends are paid out to owners from profits. This further depresses the calculated return to capital, once again biasing it downward.

Profit is one measure of the financial success of a baseball franchise, but it is insufficient because it does not take into account the resources needed to generate the profit. Return on investment provides a superior measure of the effectiveness of an entity. A simple method of calculating an owner's return on investment is to simply divide profit by investment.

If we use the $10,000 figure for Hilldale's capital and assume all distributions to owners for salary, the returns range from 13 percent to 89 percent in the six years for which we have complete data, and a loss in 1922 (see table 25). It appears the investors made a good business decision to go professional.[23] The decision was bolstered by good management. The team continued to make good business decisions about which opponents to schedule, who to employ, and what to sell. They were innovative in marketing and in their pursuit of complementary sources of income. Itemized expenditures on game days included straws and ice for the soft drinks they hawked. Pampering the customers with cold drinks was one way to attract fans during a hot and dusty Philadelphia summer. Another clever marketing approach was used to get around the Sunday blue laws by admitting fans to the ballpark free, provided they purchased a program. The programs were generally profitable for the club since they sold advertising to cover the printing costs.[24]

As a humble cooperative club, Hilldale's financial accounts were approved by the audit committee (consisting of a few players) at the conclusion of each season, and the resources were distributed among the players. The October 15, 1916, minutes describe the move from a town team to a professional team. The "old fellows," as the ownership group referred to itself, left their share in the treasury while the "new fellows" were paid and discharged.[25] The October 22 minutes laid out a plan to incorporate with capital of $10,000.

They earned additional income by leasing out their stadium beginning in 1917. That same year they began to sell advertising in the park to help pay bonuses to big name players like Spottswood Poles and Otto Briggs, who presumably were bigger draws than the likes of George Johnson, Nap Cummings, or McKinley Downs, regulars on the Hilldale roster in the early years of the franchise.

By using $10,000 as the basis for calculating the rate of return on the investment in the Hilldale club, we are biasing our estimates downward. While the minutes reflect a decision by the owners to capitalize the team at $10,000, there is no evidence that they actually put this money into the team. If they actually tied up less capital, then the rate of return they earned on their investment would be greater than we calculate. Because we cannot determine the precise amount of capital invested, we make our calculations based on the $10,000 amount noted in the minutes. Except for 1922, the year Hilldale appears to have lost money, the return on that investment also outperformed the stock market. When compared to the more conservative returns of the bond market (Moody AAA and Moody BAA rated bonds), the gains look even more impressive (table 25).

No Negro League ever had complete control over its franchises. MLB teams had territorial exclusivity and knew that they would have 154 games scheduled against teams and players that fans could not see any other way. Hilldale never had as many as half its games scheduled as part of a league, and even those games were subject to the whim of cancellation if a better opportunity came along. Hilldale needed to work to schedule their exhibition games. They could only hope that the other league teams would stay out of their territory, which unlike MLB, was not protected from invasion by other teams.

The Negro Leagues

No black league had any surviving power until Rube Foster formed the Negro National League (NNL) in 1920. Foster was already an established pitching star, manager, and successful owner of the Chicago American Giants. He convinced clubs from Dayton, Detroit, Indianapolis, Kansas

City, and St. Louis to join his club in the circuit, which operated until 1931. The league membership was anything but stable, however. Twenty-five different franchises joined the league at one time or another, and only two lasted the entire twelve-year run of the league, with eleven of them lasting but a single season; such a record was similar to that of the white National League's early years.[26]

Foster began his efforts to form a league in the late fall of 1919. He attempted to organize the owners of black clubs in the East and the Midwest. Ultimately he proceeded with the midwestern teams, and the league began the following spring. In January of 1919 Sol White had unsuccessfully attempted to organize a league. White had been out of baseball for nearly a decade at the time. His selling point for the league was economic cooperation, the same theme African Americans employed in the development of business enterprises in general.

Despite a successful inaugural season, Foster believed improvements were necessary. He saw the lack of reliable access to ballparks and contract jumping as the biggest obstacles to success, followed closely by image problems due to on-field discipline issues, which led to instances of games ending prematurely because one team would quit in protest over a disputed umpire ruling. Without being able to ensure moral respectability the league could not attract the middle-class spectators who would be necessary for long-run success. The hiring of African American umpires was also a problem.[27]

After the 1920 season the NNL owners met and made some changes to the constitution, among them: club owners and players would be fined for ungentlemanly conduct that would damage the game's reputation; managers were banned from taking their team off the field to protest a call; and a prohibition on players accepting advances on their contracts. Abuses of this had led to many instances of players accepting an advance from one team and then jumping to another team. Again, none of these were innovations. All had been put into practice at one time or another by either the National or American Leagues.

Besides Foster's NNL and Bolden's Eastern Colored League, which operated from 1923 to 1928, five more black leagues would be created by the end of the 1930s. The American Negro League was in existence for only the 1929 season. In 1932 the East-West League was formed, but failed to complete the season. The Negro Southern League ran only in 1932. A new Negro National League, this one formed by Gus Greenlee, debuted in 1933 and lasted through 1948. It was joined in 1937 by the Negro American League, which survived until 1960, though in diminishing stature after MLB integrated.

In 1920 Bolden paid five hundred dollars for an associate membership in the National Association of Colored Professional Baseball Clubs (NACPBC). The advantage of joining the league was a regular slate of games and a central authority governing the teams in the league. Unfortunately, the ability of the league to discipline either the players or the clubs proved to be very limited. Hilldale, like other teams, could, and often did, play any team that would agree with them on price and place to play, bypassing a scheduled league game when the alternative seemed more profitable.

In December of 1920 Bolden left the NACPBC and joined Rube Foster's Negro National League as an associate member for a $1000 deposit. The membership provided him protection from player raids from other league members. The following year he made one of his most lucrative investments, purchasing Judy Johnson from the Madison Stars for $100. Johnson was a fixture in the Hilldale lineup for the next decade, leading the team with a .341 average during the 1924 Colored World Series and managing the team in 1931 and 1932. His outstanding career was recognized with his election to the Hall of Fame in 1975.

Foster had established the NNL as the final step in an evolution that saw him go from dominant pitcher to highly regarded manager to innovative executive to league president. Before he established the league, Foster cut his teeth as a booking agent. He dominated black baseball team bookings in the Midwest, much as Nat Strong did in the New York area. Foster profited by keeping Schorling Park's turnstiles spinning whether or not his Chicago American Giants were home. If they were on the road, he rented the park out to other teams. Sometimes as many as three different games in a day were booked there.[28]

By 1922 Bolden was no longer satisfied with his membership in the NNL. While he was protected from player raids, he had lost lucrative dates against eastern clubs on the NNL outlaw list. The list included clubs boycotted by the league for their refusal to recognize NNL contracts. Foster forbade NNL members from playing these teams in an effort to punish the outlaws by denying them the potential lucrative dates against quality western opponents.

The travel costs associated with league play were another sore point for Bolden. During the 1921 and 1922 seasons, only four western teams came to Hilldale for games. Bolden sought to withdraw from the league after the 1921 season and requested a refund of his deposit, which Foster refused. The two threatened to raid each other's rosters, but ultimately Hilldale retained its associate membership in the league for a second season in 1922.[29] The western road trip that year was a financial bust for Hilldale, and Bolden lost interest in the league.

After the 1922 season Hilldale resigned from the NNL for the second time. Foster still refused to refund his money, citing a recent change in league bylaws preventing it.[30] Foster's refusal to refund Bolden's deposit was a symptom of the mistrust the two executives had for each other. Bolden struck back by forming a rival league, the Mutual Association of Eastern Colored Baseball Clubs, popularly known as the Eastern Colored League (ECL), to begin play in 1923. Unlike the NNL, which was governed by Foster, the ECL had no president but was run by a commission composed of one representative from each club. Bolden was elected chairman of the commission.[31]

The formation of the league set off a public-relations war with Foster and the other members of the NNL. Their chief criticism was that some of the owners of ECL teams were white. Of particular concern to Foster was Bolden's inclusion of Nat Strong. From Bolden's perspective, Strong's tight control of the New York market made it necessary to do business with him, especially since Sunday ball was still prohibited in Philadelphia, but not in New York. Bolden countered that most of the NNL teams rented parks from white owners, and rent on these parks ran to 25 percent of gross receipts.[32] In contrast, several of the ECL parks were controlled by black owners.

An example of how difficult it was for black teams to secure ball fields was exemplified by the experience of the St. Louis Giants. Phil Ball, owner of the Federal League Terriers, did not want the Giants to use the park when his lease expired. When he learned the owner of the Giants had signed a lease on the park beginning the day after Ball's lease expired, he had all the seats in the grandstand area removed.[33]

In his typical fashion Bolden strengthened his team by raiding NNL rosters, resulting in Hilldale dominating the early years of the league. They won the first three league titles in 1923, 1924, and 1925, appeared in the first two Colored World Series in 1924 and 1925, and won the series in 1925. Of course, the signing of NNL players did not enhance his popularity with NNL owners.

Foster's NNL and Bolden's ECL maintained frosty relations throughout the 1923 season and into 1924. But in September, the two executives met in New York and resolved their differences, agreeing to stage a Colored World Series and "respect the sanctity of their inter-relationship" between the two leagues.[34]

The first Colored World Series featured the powerful Kansas City Monarchs as Hilldale's opponent. Kansas City won the crown 5 games to 4, but the series was a financial disappointment, with total attendance for ten games (one ended in a tie) only 45,857. One series game, played on a neutral site in Baltimore, drew only 584 fans, another in Chicago drew 1,549. Hilldale players each took home the losers' share of $193. The Monarchs earned $308 each. Despite the low attendance, Bolden and Foster were happy with the outcome because the series helped to focus national attention on professional black baseball. Unlike regular-season games, the series was acknowledged by the white press in many cities.

In December 1924 Bolden was the primary author of a national agreement, patterned after its MLB namesake, which was ratified by the two leagues. The agreement divided geographic territory between the two leagues, standardized player contracts, and formally inserted a reserve clause into player contracts.[35] Both Bolden and Foster felt the agreement would provide the stability necessary to insure the financial success of their respective leagues.

Despite the peace agreement and national-championship game negotiated with Foster, black baseball leagues struggled. Bolden had difficulty administering the ECL. The commission setup made it hard to govern because each team had a vote, and all owners were very much interested in promoting their own interests. Thus, they were wont to abandon league games for more lucrative exhibitions, especially if the league games meant a road trip. As a result, it was difficult to enforce the league schedule.

In 1925, in an attempt to improve the quality of umpiring, Bolden abolished the home umpire system in which the home team hired the umpires in favor of league-hired umpires rotated between cities. Bolden fell out of favor over his rotating umpire plan when he hired a white man, Bill Dallas, as supervisor of umpires. He claimed there were no qualified blacks for the position, which only inflamed the criticism from the black community. In addition, the system did not solve the umpire problems, and Dallas's lackadaisical approach to the job was blamed. Bolden became the target for criticism as the focal point of the league's discipline and scheduling problems. The black press was against him as well, because he restricted their access at league meetings, and they advocated for his ouster as commissioner.[36]

Hilldale won the second World Series in 1925, but it too was a financial disaster. Attendance averaged fewer than 3000 per game for the six-game series and players received less than one hundred dollars for their participation.[37] By way of comparison, Hilldale drew as many as 5,500 for their games at Darby Field.

The weaknesses in the league, and Bolden's overextended life (he not only ran the team and the league, but throughout he maintained a full-time job with the U.S. Post Office) eventually caught up with him. The ECL responded to the numerous critics who pointed out the conflict of interest Bolden faced as commission chair and owner, and before the 1927 season he was replaced with a league president unaffiliated with any team. In September of 1927 Bolden suffered a nervous breakdown, resigned his position on the ECL commission, and stepped down as president of Hilldale.

Rube Foster had suffered a similar fate the previous year. He had begun to exhibit erratic behavior, was replaced by his second in command, and then suffered a nervous breakdown, which led to his commitment in the state asylum in Kankakee, where he died four years later.

Unlike Foster, Bolden made a comeback. In February of 1928 he was reelected secretary-treasurer of the ECL, and the following month regained the presidency of Hilldale. One week later he announced that Hilldale had withdrawn from the ECL. Two other teams withdrew before opening day, dealing a mortal blow to the league, which did not finish the season. Hilldale went 15-12 that year as an independent team. Though he was the founder of the ECL, by 1928 he no longer found membership profitable, and abandoned the league. He estimated that the team lost $18,000 in 1927 and could do better as an independent team.

Just one year later Bolden changed his mind about league membership. He assembled five of the six original ECL franchises and formed the American Negro League in time for the 1929 season. He learned from some of his past mistakes when constructing the new league. For one thing, the league was more welcoming to the press, which they invited to league meetings, something the ECL never did. It helped that Bolden appointed Rollo Wilson, a respected reporter in the black press, as league secretary.

Neither the team nor the league fared well in 1929, however. Hilldale had a poor season despite being the highest-salaried club in franchise history, featuring future Hall of Famers Oscar Charleston, Martin Dihigo, Biz Mackey, and Judy Johnson. The league itself was dissolved after the season. Bolden bore the brunt of the criticism from the fans.

Umpiring was once again a problem. And once again the flashpoint was race. Bolden was unable to field an all-black umpire roster for home games. That aggravated the local black community, which was hurting economically. Bolden defended his use of white umpires by arguing that there was a shortage of experienced black umpires and that quality trumped race in his hiring decisions.[38] While it might have been true, it did not soothe the wrath of the black community in which he operated.

The American economy began to slow down by 1930, and it soured even more quickly for African Americans. Jobs were disappearing, and the economy was plunging into what would become the Great Depression, wreaking financial havoc on black baseball. In response to the difficult times faced by the high-salaried Hilldale franchise, Bolden attempted to dissolve the corporation in 1930. He quietly made plans for a new team he planned to organize with the financial backing of white promoter Harry Passon. The rest of Hilldale's board had other ideas, however. They blocked his attempt and bought him out of the corporation. Ed Bolden was no longer a part of the legacy he had created in Hilldale.[39]

John Drew, a black politician who earned his fortune operating a successful bus line in Philadelphia, ran the Hilldale club after Bolden's 1930 ouster until it collapsed midway through the 1932 season. His refusal to deal with white booking agents made it difficult to line up quality opponents in 1930 and 1931 when there was no organized black league in the East. In 1930 he was able to schedule only twenty-two home games, which drew an average of 650 fans, barely half the crowd Hilldale averaged the previous four seasons. The 1931 season wasn't much better. Despite a gaudy 42-13 record, the fans stayed away. Hilldale averaged 840 fans a game and drew fewer than 100 paid admissions on three occasions.[40]

In a desperate attempt to survive, Hilldale joined the newly formed East-West League for the 1932 season. Neither the league nor the franchise was able to weather the worsening economy, however, and both were disbanded in July of 1932. Hilldale had played to a 27-17 record under the guidance of manager Judy Johnson, but the depressed economy simply could not support the team. Hilldale sold fewer than fifty tickets eight times in twenty home games.[41]

Hilldale's misfortunes were exemplified by the change in its method of paying players. They went from fixed salaries averaging more than $700 a season in 1929 to sharing the gate in 1932. In the waning days of their existence, the team played games in which their share of the gate was less than $100. After paying for expenses, the players were left with a couple of dollars apiece.

The Fate of the NNL

The league Rube Foster struggled to create, fought to maintain, but ultimately failed to stabilize faded into history a few months after his death in December of 1930. The NNL fell victim to the Great Depression two years after the collapse of the ECL. The Kansas City Monarchs and St. Louis Stars withdrew from the league early in 1931. The league president resigned in October, and the league was finished.

By the time the NNL collapsed it faced multiple problems: rowdiness, scheduling issues, umpires, and incessant infighting. The underlying problem with the NNL was that the owners were not united in their interest in the success of the league. The league was a collection of individual franchises, not a collective of franchises. They were self-interested, not selfless, unwilling to cede control to a league president who would have the power to suspend and fine players and owners for fighting and refusing to play scheduled games. Teams continued to skip league games in favor of more lucrative exhibition games, but the most profitable of those games, against white semipro teams, had begun to dry up. Thus the league was more dependent on black patronage for their economic survival, a major problem given the disproportionate burden of the Great Depression they bore.

Epilogue   *The Roaring Twenties and Major League Baseball*

Organized baseball prospered during the 1920s, although some teams in the Majors and many Minor League teams struggled to remain solvent. The game on the field changed, as Babe Ruth and a legion of sluggers relegated base stealing to secondary importance.

Baseball owners were generally conservative. They resisted radio broadcasts, electric lighting, putting numbers on uniforms, integration, and a variety of other proposed improvements. Some owners hesitated to create farm systems. Their prosperity allowed the owners to ignore innovation. William Wrigley was one of the more innovative owners, and by 1929 his club excelled at the gate and on the field. His fellow owners' conservatism persisted into the next decade, when even economic distress failed to move most of them to innovate.

The game, therefore, remained relatively backward with regard to communications technology and may have therefore limited its reach. Whether more adventurous owners would have enjoyed greater prosperity during the decade by innovating is an intriguing question.

For some owners, the 1920s afforded an opportunity to resurrect moribund franchises. Connie Mack and Clark Griffith built strong teams during the decade. The New York Yankees, of course, were the paramount example of a team enjoying prosperity and success. Their intracity rivals, the New York Giants, while not lapsing into mediocrity, failed to replicate their success of 1921–24, while the Chicago Cubs ended the era as a huge success at the gate and even on the field.

Along with Babe Ruth and the Yankees, Landis and the new form of baseball governance dominated the decade. Although baseball enjoyed peace, it came at a price. The commissioner was an unruly arbiter, and his high-handed methods eventually became irksome. Whether base-ball would have rebounded in 1921 without Landis is another intriguing question. If Landis's commissionership was the main reason for baseball being saved, then his contribution to the game peaked at the beginning and diminished throughout the remainder of his regime.

The decade, therefore, was prosperous for big league owners and players, but baseball's prosperity paled beside that of the motion picture industry. Given the economic upheaval of the next decade, though, owners and players had reason to look back fondly on the 1920s.

Ed Bolden, Rube Foster, and other owners of African American teams provided a stark contrast to MLB. African American teams labored under stringent conditions, thanks in part to the white owners' control of ballparks. Lacking stadiums, widespread publicity in major newspapers, and fans with plentiful dollars in their pockets, Bolden and his peers persevered, if only temporarily, in an environment not conducive to prosperity. Lest MLB owners of the 1920s feel smugly superior, the Negro Leagues' experiences resembled the white National League's trials of 1876–1903.

Tables

TABLE 1. U.S. economic indicators, 1916–30

	$GNP[1]	$PC[2]	$RPC[3]	%Δ GNP[4]	CPI[5]	%Δ CPI[6]	$Ave. Earn[7]
1916	48.3	473	1,317	—	32.7	—	N/A[8]
1917	60.4	585	1,310	-0.5	38.4	17.4	N/A
1918	76.4	740	1,471	12.3	45.1	17.4	N/A
1919	84.0	804	1,401	-4.8	51.8	14.9	0.47
1920	91.5	860	1,315	-6.1	60.0	15.8	0.55
1921	69.6	641	1,177	-10.5	53.6	-10.7	0.51
1922	74.1	673	1,345	14.3	50.2	-6.3	0.48
1923	85.1	760	1,482	10.2	51.1	1.8	0.52
1924	84.7	742	1,450	-2.2	51.2	0.2	0.54
1925	93.1	804	1,549	6.8	52.5	2.5	0.54
1926	97.0	826	1,619	4.5	53.0	1.0	0.54
1927	94.9	797	1,594	-1.5	52.0	-1.9	0.54
1928	97.0	805	1,584	-0.6	51.3	-1.3	0.56
1929	103.1	847	1,671	5.5	51.3	0.0	0.56
1930	90.4	734	1,490	-10.8	50.0	-2.5	0.55

Source: U.S. Department of Commerce, *Historical Statistics*, part 1, 169, 169–70, 211, 224.

[1] $GNP: $billions of GNP (in current prices).
[2] $PC: $GNP per capita (in current prices).
[3] $RPC: real $GNP per capita (using 1958 prices),
[4] %Δ GNP: percent change in real per capita GNP from previous year.
[5] CPI: consumer price index "All Items" (1957=100).
[6] %Δ CPI: percent change in CPI from previous year.
[7] $Ave. Earn: average hourly earnings of production workers in manufacturing (not adjusted for changes in CPI).
[8] N/A: not available.

TABLE 2. Personal consumption and recreation
expenditures ($000,000s), 1919-30

	Rec.[1]	Radio[2]	MPT[3]	SS[4]	Consum.[5]
1919	2,189	667	336	N/A	60,573
1921	2,055	439	301	30	55,766
1923	2,620	637	336	46	66,594
1925	2,835	739	367	47	71,750
1927	3,120	713	526	48	74,569
1929	4,331	1012	720	66	77,222[6]
1930	3,900	921	732	65	69,880

Source: U.S. Department of Commerce, *Historical Statistics*, part 1, 319-20, 401.

[1] Rec.: $s on personal consumption expenditures on recreation.
[2] Radio: $s expended on radio, records, and musical instruments.
For 1919-27, includes radio repairs (usually 2 percent of total).
[3] MPT: $s expended on motion picture theaters. For 1919, includes
theater entertainment.
[4] SS: $s expended on spectator sports. No figure for 1919.
[5] Consum.: $s total personal consumption expenditures.
[6] The original series ends in 1929. New series shown for 1929 and 1930.
The original series lists 1929 as $80,761.

TABLE 3. Consolidated profit and loss ($000s),[1] 1920-30

AMERICAN LEAGUE

	BOS	CHI	CLE	DET	NY	PHI	STL	WAS	LEAGUE
1920	N/A[2]	156	315	112	374	63	126	154	1,299
1921	N/A	93	289	121	226	43	64	133	969
1922	N/A	112	66	240	294	64	260	74	1,112
1923	-37	90	126	214	451	46	80	33	1,004
1924	-16	102	66	297	289	19	163	231	1,151
1925	3	200	69	205	69	313	193	409	1,459
1926	-56	140	88	194	472	139	50	96	1,121
1927	-41	20	-73	151	532	-8	-1	90	670
1928	-59	101	-127	-85	294	89	-127	33	119
1929	-35	11	-23	123	271	276	5	-44	585
1930	8	15	28	75	244	163	-87	57	503
Total	-235	1,041	824	1,646	3,517	1,207	726	1,267	9,993

NATIONAL LEAGUE

	BOS	BKN	CHI	CIN	NY	PHI	PIT	STL	LEAGUE
1920	-1	190	88	121	297	84	156	37	973
1921	90	152	5	75	263	21	249	200	1,055
1922	79	146	181	76	-14	-7	174	137	773
1923	-89	93	44	104	186	-18	143	-14	449
1924	-34	264	70	47	257	36	254	-49	845
1925	62	4	-20	-1	170	8	341	79	644
1926	-39	136	134	137	218	15	286	359	1,247
1927	-61	148	227	-8	183	1	467	235	1,194
1928	-24	62	305	-23	112	-32	90	445	934
1929	20	124	427	-203	161	25	147	51	751
1930	22	427	524	-17	151	28	95	231	1,462
Total	27	1,746	1,985	308	1,983	160	2,404	1,712	10,325

Source: U.S. House of Representatives, OB: *Hearing*, 1599–1600.

[1] In $000s, not adjusted for changes in CPI.
[2] N/A: not available.

TABLE 4. Dividends ($000s),[1] 1920–30

AMERICAN LEAGUE

	BOS	CHI	CLE	DET	NY	PHI	STL	WAS	LEAGUE
1920	N/A[2]	0	186	100	0	0	0	20	306
1921	N/A	0	124	50	0	0	0	10	184
1922	N/A	0	0	50	0	100	240	20	410
1923	0	0	99	50	0	50	40	0	239
1924	0	0	60	50	0	50	40	80	280
1925	0	0	50	100	0	0	42	318	509
1926	0	0	99	100	0	50	0	40	289
1927	0	0	0	100	0	0	0	79	179
1928	0	0	0	0	0	50	0	20	70
1929	0	0	0	150	0	50	0	0	200
1930	0	0	0	50	0	0	0	39	89
Total	0	0	619	800	0	350	362	625	2,756

	BOS	BKN	CHI	CIN	NY	PHI	PIT	STL	LEAGUE
1920	N/A	N/A	0	N/A	0	0	17	0	17
1921	N/A	N/A	70	N/A	25	30	17	0	142
1922	0	N/A	24	N/A	25	30	27	0	106
1923	0	40	48	N/A	0	0	52	28	168
1924	0	80	0	N/A	125	0	30	0	235
1925	0	50	0	N/A	125	20	167	0	362
1926	0	100	100	N/A	625	20	112	0	957
1927	0	225	0	N/A	125	0	171	28	549
1928	0	125	100	0	100	0	96	51	471
1929	0	184	100	0	125	0	20	0	429
1930	0	175	160	0	313	0	20	51	718
Total	0	979	602	0	1,588	100	729	158	4,155

Source: U.S. House of Representatives, OB: *Hearing*, 1600–1601.

[1] In $000s, not adjusted for changes in CPI.

[2] N/A: not available.

TABLE 5. New York Yankees nominal revenue sources ($000s), 1915–29

	Road W-L[1]	Att.[2]	Gate rec.[3]	$ Per att.[4]	Ex.[5]	Road rev.[6]	Con.[7]	Total rev.[8]
1915	.454	256	188	0.73	7	59	6	188
1916	.519	469	354	0.75	10	81	4	324
1917	.464	330	241	0.73	6	73	8	239
1918	.488	282	215	0.76	5	43	4	190
1919	.576	619	500	0.81	10	92	6	441
1920	.617	1,289	1,287	1.00	41	273	6	1,184
1921	.641	1,231	1,268	1.03	79	231	8	1,179
1922	.610	1,026	1,056	1.03	66	253	8	1,043
1923	.645	1,007	1,096	1.09	64	220	94	1,054
1924	.586	1,054	909	0.86	55	259	86	897
1925	.448	697	830	1.19	41	180	71	818
1926	.591	1,027	1,144	1.11	58	243	107	1,130
1927	.714	1,164	1,239	1.06	69	285	115	1,255
1928	.656	1,072	1,096	1.02	86	260	127	1,205
1929	.571	960	965	1.00	85	291	91	1,139

Sources: Thorn, Palmer, and Gershman, *Total Baseball*, for attendance and win-loss (75-76, 2,114-43); New York Yankees Base Ball Club cash books and general ledger for all other data.

[1] Road w-l: win-loss percentage for road games.
[2] Att.: attendance (000s).
[3] Gate rec.: gate receipts before gate sharing ($000s).
[4] $ Per att.: gate receipts per attendee.
[5] Ex.: exhibition and training games receipts ($000s).
[6] Road rev.: road receipts ($000s).
[7] Con.: concessions revenue ($000s).
[8] Total rev.: total revenue, after gate sharing ($000s).

TABLE 6. New York Yankees real revenue sources ($000s), 1915-29

	W-L[1]	Att.[2]	Gate rec.[3]	$ per att.[4]	Ex.[5]	Road rev.[6]	Con.[7]	Total rev.[8]
1915	.454	256	309	1.21	11	96	10	309
1916	.519	469	541	1.15	16	124	6	495
1917	.464	330	314	0.95	8	95	10	312
1918	.488	282	239	0.85	5	48	4	211
1919	.576	619	483	0.78	10	89	6	426
1920	.617	1,289	1,073	0.83	34	228	5	986
1921	.641	1,231	1,183	0.96	74	215	7	1,100
1922	.610	1,026	1,052	1.03	66	252	8	1,039
1923	.645	1,007	1,073	1.07	62	215	92	1,031
1924	.586	1,054	888	0.84	54	253	84	856
1925	.448	697	790	1.13	39	171	67	779
1926	.591	1,027	1,079	1.05	55	229	101	1,066
1927	.714	1,164	1,191	1.02	66	274	110	1,207
1928	.656	1,072	1,069	1.00	84	254	124	1,174
1929	.571	960	940	0.98	83	284	89	1,111

Sources: Thorn, Palmer, and Gershman, *Total Baseball*, for attendance and win-loss (75-76, 2,114-43); New York Yankees Base Ball Club, Cash books and general ledger for all other data; U.S. Department of Commerce, *Historical Statistics* 1:210-11 for Consumer Price Index (1930=100).

[1] w-l: win-loss percentage.
[2] Att.: attendance (000s).
[3] Gate rec.: gate receipts before gate sharing ($000s).
[4] $ per att.: gate receipts per attendee.
[5] Ex.: exhibition and training games receipts ($000s).
[6] Road rev.: road receipts ($000s).
[7] Con.: concessions revenue ($000s).
[8] Total rev.: total revenue, after gate sharing ($000s).

TABLE 7. New York Yankees player payrolls, nominal and real ($000s), 1915-29

Year	Nominal payroll[1]	Real payroll[2]	Payroll/tot. rev.[3]
1915	97	160	0.517
1916	95	146	0.294
1917	87	113	0.363
1918	53	58	0.277
1919	86	83	0.196
1920	114	95	0.097
1921	157	147	0.133
1922	184	183	0.176
1923	208	203	0.197
1924	216	211	0.241
1925	224	213	0.274
1926	210	198	0.186
1927	252	242	0.201
1928	286	279	0.238
1929	290	282	0.254

Sources: Thorn, Palmer, and Gershman, *Total Baseball*, for attendance and win-loss (75-76, 2,114-43); New York Yankees Base Ball Club, Cash books and general ledger for all other data; U.S. Department of Commerce, *Historical Statistics* 1:210-11 for Consumer Price Index (1930=100).

[1] Nominal payroll: $000s.
[2] Real payroll: nominal payroll deflated by CPI (1930=100).
[3] Payroll/tot. rev.: payroll/total revenue.

TABLE 8. New York Yankees profits ($s), 1915-29

	Profit on team	Team profit before taxes and depreciation	Team profit before taxes	Profit on stadium
1915	-73,362	-73,362	-73,362	
1916	40,995	40,995	40,995	
1917	-58,036	-57,847	-58,036	
1918	-46,651	-46,481	-46,651	
1919	106,971	106,971	106,971	
1920	374,079	666,343	666,353	

1921	176,502	340,517	339,984	
1922	270,875	316,029	315,420	
1923	494,071	595,972	532,139	
1924	351,695	441,640	363,279	
1925	77,624	156,250	77,165	
1926	393,272	624,226	554,124	
1927	567,664	682,484	601,351	191,990
1928	297,060	422,057	333,326	-209,149
1929	229,919	355,791	259,195	110,343

Source: Haupert and Winter, "Pay Ball: Estimating the Profitability," 94.

TABLE 9. Team franchise sales($s), 1919–29

	Year	Price[1]	Real price[2]	Year	Price[3]	Real price[4]
Boston Braves	1919	400	386	1911	187	334
Boston Braves	1923	500	489	1919	400	386
Boston Braves	1925	388	370	1923	500	489
Cincinnati Reds	1929	1,200	1,170	1902	146	281
New York Giants	1919	1,820	1,757	1903	125	231
Cleveland Indians	1927	1,000	962	1916	500	765
Detroit Tigers	1920	1,000	833	1903	50	93
New York Yankees	1922	3,000	2,988	1914	400	664
Washington Senators	1919	363	350	1912	270	466

Sources: Quirk and Fort, *Pay Dirt*, 51–53; deflated by CPI (1930=100) taken from U.S. Department of Commerce, *Historical Statistics* 1:210–11.

[1] Sale price in $000s.
[2] Sale price deflated by CPI (1930=100).
[3] Sale price in $000s.
[4] Sale price deflated by CPI (1930=100).

TABLE 10. City population, 1910, 1920, and 1930 (000s)

	1910	1920	1930	Growth[1]	Att.[2]	Per capita[3]
Boston	671	748	781	1.04	6,413	8.39
Chicago	2,185	2,702	3,376	1.25	15,440	5.08
Cincinnati	364	401	451	1.12	5,320	12.48
Cleveland	561	797	900	1.13	6,100	7.19
Detroit	466	994	1,569	1.58	8,323	6.50
New York	4,767	5,620[4]	6,930	1.23	27,302	4.35
Philadelphia	1,549	1,824	1,951	1.07	8,978	4.76
Pittsburgh	534	588	670	1.14	6,738	10.71
St. Louis	687	773	822	1.06	9,427	11.82
Washington	331	433	487	1.13	5,031	10.94

OTHER LARGE CITIES

	1910	1920	1930	Growth[1]	Att.[2]	Per capita[3]
Baltimore	558	734	805	1.10		
Buffalo	424	507	573	1.13		
Kansas City	248	324	400	1.23		
Los Angeles	319	577	1,238	2.15		
Milwaukee	374	457	578	1.26		
Minneapolis	301	381	464	1.22		
New Orleans	339	387	459	1.18		
Newark	347	415	442	1.07		
San Francisco	417	507	634	1.25		

Sources: Dodd, *Historical Statistics of the United States*, 443–61; Thorn, Palmer, and Gershman, *Total Baseball*, 75–76.

[1] Growth: 1930/1920 population ratio.
[2] Att.: total attendance, 1919–29 seasons.
[3] Per capita: 1919–29 attendance/average of 1920 and 1930 metropolitan population.
[4] 1930 NY: 1930 New York population/city population.

TABLE 11. Metropolitan population, 1910, 1920, and 1930 (000s)

	1910	1920	1930	Growth[1]	Att.[2]	Per capita[3]
Boston	1,531	1,772	2,308	1.30	6,413	3.14
Chicago	2,456	3,179	4,365	1.37	15,440	4.09
Cincinnati	568	607	759	1.25	5,320	7.79
Cleveland	623	926	1,195	1.29	6,100	5.75
Detroit	514	1,165	2,105	1.81	8,323	5.09
New York	6,567	7,910	10,901[4]	1.38	27,302	2.90
Philadelphia	1,983	2,407	2,847	1.18	8,978	3.42
Pittsburgh	1,033	1,208	1,954	1.62	6,738	4.26
St. Louis	829	952	1,294	1.36	9,427	8.40
Washington	381	507	621	1.23	5,031	8.92

OTHER LARGE CITIES

	1910	1920	1930	Growth[1]	Att.[2]	Per capita[3]
Baltimore	664	787	949	1.21		
Buffalo	493	603	821	1.36		
Kansas City	396	477	608	1.27		
Los Angeles	465	879	2,319	2.64		
Milwaukee	431	538	743	1.38		
Minneapolis	526	629	832	1.32		
San Francisco	687	891	1,290	1.45		

Sources: U.S. House of Representatives, OB: *Report*, 191; Thorn, Palmer, and Gershman, *Total Baseball*, 75-76.

[1] Growth: 1930/1920 population ratio.

[2] Att.: total attendance, 1919-29 seasons.

[3] Per capita: 1919-29 attendance/average of 1920 and 1930 population.

[4] 1930 NY: 1930 New York population/city population.

TABLE 12. Major League attendance (000's), 1919–29

	BOS	CHI	CLE	DET	NY	PHI	STL	WAS	LEAGUE
1919	417	627	538	644	619	225	349	234	3,654
1920	402	833	913	580	1,289	288	419	359	5,084
1921	279	544	749	662	1,231	344	356	456	4,620
1922	259	603	528	861	1,026	425	713	459	4,874
1923	230	574	559	911	1,007	534	430	357	4,603
1924	449	607	482	1,015	1,054	532	533	584	5,255
1925	268	832	419	821	697	870	463	817	5,187
1926	285	710	627	712	1,028	715	284	552	4,913
1927	305	614	373	774	1,164	606	248	529	4,613
1928	397	494	376	474	1,072	690	339	379	4,221
1929	395	427	536	869	960	839	281	356	4,662
Total	3,686	6,866	6,100	8,323	11,147	6,068	4,416	5,081	51,686

NATIONAL LEAGUE

	BOS	BKN	CHI	CIN	NY	PHI	PIT	STL	LEAGUE
1919	167	361	424	533	709	240	277	167	2,878
1920	162	809	481	568	930	331	429	327	4,037
1921	319	613	410	311	973	274	702	385	3,987
1922	168	499	542	494	946	232	524	537	3,942
1923	228	565	704	575	821	228	611	339	4,070
1924	177	819	717	474	844	300	737	273	4,341
1925	314	659	623	465	779	305	804	405	4,354
1926	304	651	885	673	700	241	799	668	4,920
1927	289	637	1,159	442	858	305	870	749	5,310
1928	227	665	1,144	490	916	182	495	762	4,881
1929	372	732	1,485	295	869	281	491	400	4,926
Total	2,727	7,009	8,574	5,320	9,345	2,920	6,738	5,011	47,646

MAJOR LEAGUE BASEBALL

Year	Attendance
1919	6,532
1920	9,121
1921	8,607
1922	8,816

1923	8,672
1924	9,596
1925	9,541
1926	9,833
1927	9,923
1928	9,102
1929	9,588

Source: Thorn, Palmer, and Gershman, *Total Baseball*, 75–76.

TABLE 13. Major League stadiums, 1919–29

NATIONAL LEAGUE

	Built	Capacity	Improved	Capacity
Boston	1915	40,000	1928	46,000
Brooklyn	1913	18,000	1924–26	28,000
Chicago	1914	14,000	1923–28	40,000
Cincinnati	1912	25,000	1927	30,000
New York	1911	16,000	1917–26	55,000[1]
Philadelphia	1895	18,000	1929	20,000
Pittsburgh	1909	23,000	1925	41,000
St. Louis	Shared with St. Louis (AL)			

AMERICAN LEAGUE

	Built	Capacity	Improved	Capacity
Boston	1912	35,000	1947	35,500
Chicago	1910	28,800	1952	52,000
Cleveland	1910	21,000	1939	22,500
Detroit	1912	23,000	1923	29,000
New York	1923	58,000	1926–29	62,000[2]
Philadelphia	1909	20,000	1925–29	30,000[3]
St. Louis	1909	17,000	1921–29	34,000[4]
Washington	1911	Not listed	1921	32,000

Source: Lowry, *Green Cathedrals*, 22, 27, 40, 60, 110, 117, 131, 138, 143, 195, 207, 210, 216, 228.

[1] Went from 39,000 in 1917 to 55,000 by 1926.
[2] Fluctuated between 62,000 to 82,000 between 1926 and 1929.
[3] Fluctuated between 33,500 and 30,000 between 1925 and 1929.
[4] Shared with St. Louis Cardinals mid-1920 on.

TABLE 14. Offensive and pitching statistics, 1919–29

AMERICAN LEAGUE

	Rns[1]	HR[2]	BAVE[3]	OBP[4]	SAVE[5]	ERA[6]
1919	8.2	0.4	.269	.334	.359	3.23
1920	9.5	0.6	.284	.348	.388	3.79
1921	10.2	0.8	.293	.357	.409	4.29
1922	9.5	0.8	.285	.349	.398	4.04
1923	9.6	0.7	.283	.351	.389	3.99
1924	9.9	0.6	.290	.359	.397	4.23
1925	10.4	0.9	.292	.361	.408	4.40
1926	9.5	0.7	.282	.352	.392	4.02
1927	9.8	0.7	.286	.352	.400	4.14
1928	9.5	0.8	.281	.344	.307	4.04
1929	10.0	1.0	.284	.350	.408	4.24

NATIONAL LEAGUE

	Rns[1]	HR[2]	BAVE[3]	OBP[4]	SAVE[5]	ERA[6]
1919	7.3	0.4	.258	.311	.338	2.91
1920	7.9	0.4	.270	.323	.357	3.14
1921	9.2	0.8	.290	.339	.398	3.78
1922	10.0	0.9	.293	.349	.405	4.10
1923	9.7	0.9	.286	.343	.395	4.00
1924	9.1	0.8	.283	.337	.392	3.87
1925	10.1	1.0	.292	.348	.415	4.27
1926	9.1	0.7	.280	.339	.386	3.83
1927	9.2	0.8	.282	.339	.387	3.92
1928	9.4	1.0	.282	.345	.397	4.00
1929	10.7	1.2	.295	.357	.428	4.72

Source: Thorn, Palmer, and Gershman, *Total Baseball*, 2,122–43.

[1] Rns: runs per game, both teams.
[2] HR: home runs per game, both teams.
[3] BAVE: batting average.
[4] OBP: on-base percentage.
[5] SAVE: slugging average.
[6] ERA: earned run average.

TABLE 15. Other measures, 1919-29

AMERICAN LEAGUE

	BB[1]	SO[2]	SB[3]	FLDG[4]	ER[5]
1919	6.01	6.36	1.63	0.966	2.88
1920	6.18	5.92	1.22	0.967	2.79
1921	6.44	5.82	1.11	0.966	2.84
1922	6.14	5.78	1.13	0.970	2.49
1923	6.64	5.86	1.21	0.969	2.60
1924	6.70	5.27	1.21	0.970	2.47
1925	6.96	5.37	1.16	0.968	2.63
1926	6.87	5.62	1.08	0.970	2.47
1927	6.49	5.40	1.27	0.968	2.65
1928	6.20	6.03	1.13	0.969	2.50
1929	6.61	5.84	1.03	0.969	2.48

NATIONAL LEAGUE

	BB[1]	SO[2]	SB[3]	FLDG[4]	ER[5]
1919	4.69	5.89	2.09	0.967	2.82
1920	4.89	5.89	1.57	0.967	2.88
1921	4.74	5.51	1.31	0.968	2.71
1922	5.57	5.45	1.22	0.967	2.70
1923	5.66	5.52	1.34	0.966	2.82
1924	5.24	5.55	1.23	0.970	2.49
1925	5.65	5.51	1.10	0.967	2.73
1926	5.62	5.44	0.98	0.968	2.61
1927	5.53	5.66	1.05	0.969	2.54
1928	6.27	5.55	0.93	0.971	2.36
1929	6.43	5.63	1.12	0.972	2.30

Source: Thorn, Palmer, and Gershman, *Total Baseball*, 2,122-43.

[1] BB: bases on balls per game, both teams.
[2] SO: strikeouts per game, both teams.
[3] SB: stolen bases per game, both teams.
[4] FLDG: fielding average.
[5] ER: errors per game, both teams.

TABLE 16. Decline of the stolen base, 1919-29

AMERICAN LEAGUE

	Hits[1]	2B[2]	3B[3]	HR[4]	BB[5]	SB[6]	SIN+BB[7]	SB/SIN+BB[8]
1919	10,021	1,607	531	240	3,367	912	11,010	0.082
1920	11,902	2,007	620	369	3,811	751	12,717	0.059
1921	12,525	2,140	694	477	3,965	684	13,179	0.052
1922	12,041	2,032	585	525	3,797	696	12,696	0.055
1923	11,676	2,010	553	442	4,002	743	12,673	0.059
1924	12,253	2,197	551	397	4,136	747	13,244	0.056
1925	12,418	2,218	557	533	4,289	716	13,399	0.053
1926	11,750	2,195	568	424	4,232	667	12,795	0.052
1927	12,024	2,261	610	439	4,018	788	12,732	0.062
1928	11,831	2,200	620	483	3,828	697	12,356	0.056
1929	11,976	2,229	599	595	4,054	634	12,607	0.050

NATIONAL LEAGUE

	Hits[1]	2B[2]	3B[3]	HR[4]	BB[5]	SB[6]	SIN+BB[7]	SB/SIN+BB[8]
1919	9,603	1,315	517	207	2,615	1,165	10,179	0.114
1920	11,376	1,604	644	261	3,016	969	11,883	0.082
1921	12,266	1,839	670	460	2,906	803	12,203	0.066
1922	12,579	1,911	662	530	3,455	755	12,931	0.058
1923	12,348	1,912	588	538	3,494	824	12,804	0.064
1924	12,009	1,881	622	499	3,216	754	12,223	0.062
1925	12,495	2,120	614	636	3,460	672	12,585	0.053
1926	11,755	1,948	589	439	3,473	608	12,252	0.050
1927	11,935	1,888	540	483	3,413	649	12,437	0.052
1928	11,901	2,021	518	610	3,848	568	12,600	0.045
1929	12,668	2,253	569	754	3,961	692	13,053	0.053

Source: Thorn, Palmer, and Gershman, *Total Baseball*, 2,122-43.

[1] Hits: base hits.
[2] 2B: doubles.
[3] 3B: triples.
[4] HR: home runs.
[5] BB: bases on balls.
[6] SB: stolen bases.
[7] SIN+BB: singles + bases on balls.
[8] SB/SIN+BB: stolen bases per (singles + bases on balls).

TABLE 17. Franchise win-loss records, 1919–29

NATIONAL LEAGUE

	W-L[1]	P[2]	Att.[3]	High W-L pct.[4]	Low W-L pct.[5]	High att.[6]	Low att.[7]
Boston	.395	0	2,727	.516	.327	372	162
Brooklyn	.499	1	7,009	.604	.425	819	361[8]
Chicago	.520	1	8,574	.645	.418	1,485	410
Cincinnati	.534	1	5,320	.686	.429	673	295
New York	.585	4	9,345	.621	.490	946	700
Philadelphia	.368	0	2,920	.464	.283	331	182
Pittsburgh	.567	2	6,738	.621	.511	870	277[8]
St. Louis	.524	2	5,011	.617	.394	762	167[8]

AMERICAN LEAGUE

	W-L[1]	P[2]	Att.[3]	High W-L pct.[4]	Low W-L pct.[5]	High att.[6]	Low att.[7]
Boston	.396	0	3,686	.487	.301	449	230
Chicago	.489	1	6,866	.629	.388	833	427
Cleveland	.520	1	6,100	.636	.403	913	373
Detroit	.501	0	8,323	.571	.396	1,015	474
New York	.605	6	11,147	.714	.448	1,289	619[8]
Philadelphia	.484	1	6,068	.693	.257	870	225[8]
St. Louis	.496	0	4,416	.604	.386	713	248
Washington	.509	2	5,081	.636	.400	817	234[8]

Source: Thorn, Palmer, Gershman, *Total Baseball*, 75–76, 2,122–43.

[1] W-L: win-loss percentage for 1919–29.

[2] P: pennants won.

[3] Att.: Attendance in 000s for 1919–29.

[4] High W-L pct.: highest win-loss percentage for 1919–29.

[5] Low W-L pct.: lowest win-loss percentage for 1919–29.

[6] High att.: highest seasonal attendance for 1919–29 in 000s.

[7] Low att.: lowest seasonal attendance for 1919–29 in 000s.

[8] Lowest attendance in 1919 (140 games instead of 154).

TABLE 18. Measures of competitive balance in Major League Baseball, 1919-29

AMERICAN LEAGUE

	W-L[1]	GA[2]	GB last[3]	St. dev.[4]	Att.[5]
1919	.629	3.5	52.0	2.94	3,654
1920	.636	2.0	50.0	2.93	5,084
1921	.641	4.5	45.0	2.44	4,620
1922	.610	1.0	33.0	1.94	4,874
1923	.645	16.0	37.0	1.84	4,603
1924	.597	2.0	25.5	1.74	5,255
1925	.636	8.5	49.5	2.45	5,187
1926	.591	3.0	44.5	2.45	4,913
1927	.714	19.0	59.0	3.06	4,613
1928	.656	2.5	43.5	2.60	4,221
1929	.693	18.0	48.0	2.54	4,662

NATIONAL LEAGUE

	W-L.[1]	GA[2]	GB last[3]	St. dev.[4]	Att.[5]
1919	.686	9.0	47.5	2.75	2,878
1920	.604	7.0	30.5	1.72	4,037
1921	.614	4.0	43.5	2.35	3,987
1922	.604	7.0	39.5	2.30	3,942
1923	.621	4.5	45.5	2.69	4,070
1924	.608	1.5	40.0	2.65	4,341
1925	.621	8.5	27.5	1.65	4,354
1926	.578	2.0	29.5	1.70	4,920
1927	.610	1.5	43.0	2.68	5,310
1928	.617	2.0	51.0	3.16	4,881
1929	.645	10.5	43.0	2.23	4,926

Source: Thorn, Palmer, and Gershman, *Total Baseball*, 75–76, 2,122–43.

[1] W-L: win-loss percentage of pennant-winning team.
[2] GA: games ahead of runner-up.
[3] GB Last: games ahead of last-place team.
[4] St. dev.: ratio of standard deviation of win-loss percentage of all eight teams to ideal standard deviation.
[5] Att.: league attendance in 000s.

TABLE 19. Introduction and movement of top players, 1919-41

AMERICAN LEAGUE

	Number[1]	Total rating[2]	All[3]	All but 2[4]	% all[5]	% all but 2[6]
Boston	7	194.4	4	4	57.1	57.1
Chicago	3	91.0	2	2	66.7	66.7
Cleveland	14	274.7	2	4	14.3	28.6
Detroit	11	264.2	3	6	27.3	54.5
New York	19	379.9	8	11	42.1	57.9
Philadelphia	8	261.7	1	0	12.5	12.5
St. Louis	5	71.8	0	0	0.0	0.0
Washington	5	76.1	1	1	20.0	20.0

NATIONAL LEAGUE

	Number[1]	Total rating[2]	All[3]	All but 2[4]	% all[5]	% all but 2[6]
Boston	2	29.8	0	0	0.0	0.0
Brooklyn	6	99.7	1	1	16.7	16.7
Chicago	7	159.4	1	2	14.3	28.3
Cincinnati	3	30.2	0	0	0.0	0.0
New York	11	289.4	5	5	45.5	45.5
Philadelphia	5	89.1	1	1	20.0	20.0
Pittsburgh	10	244.6	1	1	10.0	10.0
St. Louis	13	292.5	2	4	15.4	30.8
Total	129	2848.5	32	43	24.8	33.3

Source: Thorn, Palmer, Gershman, and Pietrusza, *Total Baseball*, 656-1,383, 1,387-902.

[1] Number: number of hitters with total baseball ratings of 7.1 or higher or pitchers with TBR of 8.9 or higher making major league debut with the team between 1919 and 1941.

[2] Total rating: combined ratings of players and pitchers.

[3] All: Played entire Major League career with the team.

[4] All but 2: played entire Major League career except the last one or two years with the team.

[5] % all: percentage of players spending entire Major League career with the team.

[6] % all but 2: percentage of players spending all but last one or two years with the team.

TABLE 20. National League revenue sharing, 1920 and 1930

1920

	Home[1]	Road[2]	H-R[3]	Est. rev.[4]	Att.[5]	Per capita[6]	W-L pct.[7]
Boston	2,010	6,202	-4,191	80	162	0.49	.408
Brooklyn	9,972	5,381	4,591	399	809	0.49	.604
Chicago	5,879	6,354	-475	235	481	0.49	.487
Cincinnati	6,990	6,946	44	280	568	0.49	.536
New York	11,620	6,837	4,783	465	930	0.50	.558
Philadelphia	3,957	5,618	-1,661	158	331	0.48	.405
Pittsburgh	5,329	5,957	-628	213	429	0.50	.513
St. Louis	3,853	6,315	-2,462	154	327	0.47	.487
League	49,610	49,610		1,984	4,037	0.49	

1930

	Home[1]	Road[2]	H-R[3]	Est. rev.[4]	Att.[5]	Per capita[6]	W-L pct.[7]
Boston	5,810	6,949	-1,139	232	465	0.50	.455
Brooklyn	13,717	8,837	4,880	549	1,097	0.50	.558
Chicago	18,295	8,189	10,106	732	1,464	0.50	.584
Cincinnati	4,834	6,993	-2,159	193	387	0.50	.383
New York	10,859	10,575	284	434	869	0.50	.565
Philadelphia	3,738	7,915	-4,177	149	299	0.50	.338
Pittsburgh	4,472	9,264	-4,792	179	358	0.50	.519
St. Louis	6,356	9,358	-3,002	254	509	0.50	.597
League	68,081	68,081		2,723	5,447	0.50	

Sources: U.S. House of Representatives, OB: *Hearings*, 1,326–29; Thorn, Palmer, and Gershman, *Total Baseball*, 75–76, 2,123–44.

[1] Home: 2.5 percent of home revenue (in $s).
[2] Road: 2.5 percent of road revenue (in $s).
[3] H-R: home-road revenue.
[4] Est. Rev.: home x 40 (in $000s).
[5] Att.: home attendance.
[6] Per capita: Est. Rev./Attendance (in $s).
[7] W-L pct.: Win-loss percentage.

TABLE 21. New York Yankees' gate sharing ($000s), 1915-29

Year	W-L[1]	Att.[2]	NOMINAL Visit. share[3]	NOMINAL Road rev.[4]	NOMINAL Net[5]	REAL Visit. share[6]	REAL Road rev.[7]	REAL Net[8]
1915	.454	256	59	59	0	97	96	0
1916	.519	469	110	81	-29	168	124	-44
1917	.464	330	73	73	0	95	95	0
1918	.488	282	66	43	-23	73	48	-25
1919	.576	619	146	92	-53	140	89	-51
1920	.617	1,289	385	273	-112	321	228	-94
1921	.641	1,231	368	231	-137	343	215	-128
1922	.610	1,026	306	253	-53	305	252	-53
1923	.645	1,007	301	220	-81	294	215	-79
1924	.586	1,054	315	259	-56	307	253	-55
1925	.448	697	208	180	-28	198	171	-27
1926	.591	1,027	289	243	-46	273	229	-44
1927	.714	1,164	319	285	-34	307	274	-32
1928	.656	1,072	294	260	-34	287	254	-33
1929	.571	960	265	291	26	258	284	25

Sources: New York Yankees Base Ball Club, Cash books and general ledger for all other data; U.S. Department of Commerce, *Historical Statistics* 1:210-11 for Consumer Price Index (1930=100).

[1] W-L: win-loss percentage.

[2] Att.: attendance (000s).

[3] Visit. share: visitor's share of gate receipts for NY home games ($000s).

[4] Road rev.: Yankees' receipts from road games ($000s).

[5] Net: road revenue – visitor's share ($000s); negative amount means Yankees were net losers from revenue sharing. May differ because of rounding.

[6] Visit. share: visitor's share of gate receipts for NY home games ($000s), deflated by CPI (1930=100).

[7] Road rev.: Yankees' receipts from road games ($000s), deflated by CPI (1930=100).

[8] Net: road revenue – visitor's share ($000s); negative amount means Yankees were net losers from revenue sharing. Deflated by CPI (1930=100). May differ because of rounding.

TABLE 22. New York Yankees' gate-sharing ($s), 1925 and 1927

1925

	Paid to[1]	Received from[2]	Received – Paid[3]	W-L[4]
Boston	20,879	11,505	-9,373	0.309
Chicago	23,384	25,017	1,633	0.513
Cleveland	25,651	15,291	-10,360	0.455
Detroit	33,829	28,505	-5,324	0.52
Philadelphia	37,530	35,996	-1,534	0.579
St. Louis	24,919	20,300	-4,619	0.536
Washington	41,675	43,241	1,566	0.631
Total	207,866	179,854	-28,012	

1927

	Paid to[1]	Received from[2]	Received – Paid[3]	W-L pct.[4]
Boston	35,930	28,954	-6,976	0.331
Chicago	48,868	57,004	8,136	0.458
Cleveland	39,376	28,839	-10,537	0.431
Detroit	39,025	46,730	7,705	0.538
Philadelphia	76,483	61,761	-14,722	0.591
St. Louis	36,231	18,444	-17,787	0.388
Washington	43,085	43,611	526	0.552
Total	318,998	285,343	-33,655	

Sources: New York Yankees Base Ball Club, Cash books.

[1] Amount Yankees paid to visiting clubs.

[2] Amount Yankees received on the road.

[3] Received – Paid: negative indicates Yankees paid more than they received.

[4] W-L: win-loss percentage.

TABLE 23. Chicago "Black Sox" players' salaries ($s), 1918–20

	1918	1919	1920 NYT	1920 Haupert
Cicotte, Eddie	5,000[1]	5,700[2]	10,000	10,000
Felsch, Oscar "Happy"	3,750	4,300[3]	10,000	7,000
Gandil, Chick	4,000	4,000	DNP	DNP
Jackson, Joe	6,000	6,000	8,000	8,000
McMullin, Fred	2,750	3,000	3,600	3,600
Risberg, Swede	2,500	3,250	3,250	3,250
Weaver, Buck	6,000	7,250	7,250	7,250
Williams, Claude "Lefty"	3,000	3,000[4]	6,000	N/A[5]

Sources: Harry Grabiner figures for 1918 in Veeck, *Hustler's Handbook*, 256–57; for 1919 and 1920, "Stars May Testify at Baseball Trial," *NYT*, July 8, 1921, 15; for 1920, Haupert, Baseball Salary Database).

[1] Received a bonus of $2,000 in 1918 and $3,000 in 1919.
[2] Received a bonus of $3,000. Grabiner lists $3,750, but NYT lists $4,300.
[3] DNP: did not play.
[4] Received bonuses of $375 and $500.
[5] N/A: not available.

TABLE 24. Average Major League Baseball and Negro League salaries ($s), 1917–29

	Average wage[1] (annual)	Ave. MLB[2] salary (6 months)	Ave. MLB salary (baseball season)	Ave. black salary[3] (annual)	Ave. black salary (6 months)	Ave. Negro[4] (baseball season)
1917	887	444	3,227	283	170	217
1918	1,115	558	3,431	364	218	304
1919	1,272	636	3,423	554	333	N/A[5]
1920	1,489	745	3,877	722	433	N/A
1921	1,349	675	4,300	392	235	331
1922	1,305	653	4,957	346	207	N/A
1923	1,393	697	5,166	416	249	N/A
1924	1,402	701	5,548	450	270	N/A
1925	1,434	717	6,033	410	246	N/A
1926	1,473	737	6,434	401	241	299
1927	1,487	744	6,738	409	245	464
1928	1,490	745	6,971	418	251	279
1929	1,534	767	6,932	428	257	738

Sources: Haupert, Baseball Salary Database; Wright, *Old South, New South*, table 5.9, 149; table 6.8, 184.

[1] Average wage all industries excluding farm labor.
[2] Average Major League Baseball salary.
[3] Average salary black textile mill workers.
[4] Average Negro League salary.
[5] N/A: not available

TABLE 25. Profitability of Hilldale and
New York Yankee franchises, 1917–29

					NEW YORK YANKEES		
	DJIA[1]	Moody AA[2]	Moody BAA[3]	Hilldale profit[4]	RTC[5]	Profit[4]	RTC[5]
1917	-2.44	N/A	N/A	1,916	19.2	-58,136	-12.6
1918	-22.35	N/A	N/A	1,339	13.4	-46,651	-10.1
1919	10.15	5.35	7.12	2,413	24.1	106,972	23.3
1920	32.02	5.75	7.78	8,948	89.5	374,079	81.3
1921	-33.24	6.14	8.50	6,510	65.1	176,502	38.4
1922	8.57	5.34	7.70	-3,366	-33.7	270,875	58.9
1923	24.28	5.04	6.98	6,107	61.1	494,071	107.4
1924	-1.55	5.09	7.24	N/A[6]	N/A	351,695	76.5
1925	23.74	4.95	6.44	N/A	N/A	77,624	16.9
1926	32.89	4.82	6.09	N/A	N/A	393,272	85.5
1927	-2.26	4.66	5.61	N/A	N/A	567,664	78.7
1928	31.19	4.46	5.35	N/A	N/A	297,060	34.1
1929	46.25	4.62	5.63	N/A	N/A	229,919	42.5

Source: Haupert and Winter, "Old Fellows and the Colonels," table 2, 90.

[1] DJIA: annual growth rate of Dow-Jones Industrial Average (%).

[2] Moody AA: Moody's seasoned AA corporate bond yield (%).

[3] Moody BAA: Moody's seasoned BAA corporate bond yield (%).

[4] Profit: Profit in nominal terms (in $s).

[5] RTC Return to capital (%).

[6] N/A: not available

Appendix 1   *New York Yankees Financial Records*

The National Baseball Hall of Fame library in Cooperstown, New York, has a unique set of financial records for the New York Yankees covering the years 1914–42. These records allow for a fascinating behind-the-scenes look at how a Major League Baseball franchise was financed. The archives consist of journals, cashbooks, and ledgers covering the operation of the Yankees and several of their Minor League affiliates. While no single type of book is available in a continuous run for the entire period, enough information is available from various books to allow for the reconstruction of annual income statements for most of the period and year-end profits for every year.

Among the interesting tidbits to be found include the amounts the Yankees spent on hiring detectives to trail their players and report on their nocturnal activities, travel costs, fines, and the annual laundry bill for player uniforms. Among the more substantial data contained in the records is individual payroll information, annual profit-and-loss statements, and the financial details concerning the cost and revenues associated with the construction of Yankee Stadium.

The Yankee ledgers are the largest known set of publicly available financial records of a professional baseball team. They arrived in Cooperstown in 1974 courtesy of Clifford Kachline, who at the time was the Hall of Fame's historian, a position which he held from 1969 to 1982. Kachline had received a call from an associate working for the Yankees. He was informed that the team was looking to do some housecleaning in preparation for the upcoming renovation of Yankee Stadium. New owner George Steinbrenner was not eager to pay relocation and storage costs for unneeded material, so Kachline was invited to come to Yankee Stadium to review some of the records that were on the disposal list to see if the Hall of Fame might want them. He recognized the importance of the material and agreed to accept it for the Hall. There they languished for more than a quarter century. Until the summer of 2002, they were not even fully catalogued.[1]

What makes these records so important is their rarity. Because MLB teams are private corporations that are not publicly traded, they are not obligated to reveal their financial records. As a result, obtaining financial data at any level of detail or with any degree of certainty is extremely difficult, if not impossible. Only odd bits of financial information for any professional baseball team exist, and nothing to the extent or duration of the Yankee ledgers has surfaced to date.

The financial ledgers contain a lot of what one would expect from such a beast: routine accounting of monthly bills for such standard items as salaries, office rent, utilities, and postage, as well as occasional purchases of stationery, baseballs, and office furniture. On the revenue side, there are entries covering ticket sales, advertising revenue, concession sales, and after 1923 rental of Yankee stadium. There were also the occasional items that stood out on the page for historical reasons (the $100,000 entry for the purchase of Babe Ruth) or because they seemed odd or unusual for a baseball team.

One unexpected cost item was the length and expense the team went to in order to keep tabs on their players. The Yankees regularly employed the Burns Detective Agency to provide security services for the team's home games. It turns out that they also hired the agency to do a little bit of undercover work. Under account 217, labeled "Investigating Players," the team recorded regular payments. The most intriguing entry for this account was made in October of 1922 when the team paid Burns $259.50 to cover the cost of the "Ruth matter." Unfortunately, no specific details are available to say exactly which "Ruth matter" was being paid for, but 1922 provided plenty of opportunities upon which to speculate.

Ruth began the 1922 season with a thirty-day suspension, a result of his having thumbed his nose the previous fall at baseball's prohibition on World Series participants joining postseason barnstorming tours. He had also engaged the services of Christy Walsh as his agent. During his lackluster 1922 season, he was suspended four times for a total of forty-four games, displayed erratic behavior, and failed to control his volatile temper, the source of his suspensions.[2] His home life changed as well. He and his first wife Helen were experiencing marital difficulties, not the least of which involved the birth of his daughter Dorothy, widely suspected to be the child from one of Ruth's many adulterous affairs. So there were plenty of potential "matters" for detectives to pursue. Most likely enough to keep an entire agency busy around the clock.

Several instances of unusual compensation cropped up in the biweekly salary-payment entries. In November of 1939 the Yankees paid $300 to William and Mary College for payment of tuition for Vic Raschi for the 1939–40 academic year. In 1921 Mrs. Annie Bodie, wife of reserve outfielder Frank "Ping" Bodie, received a check for $150 each pay period—approximately one-third of Frank's salary. Apparently Frank couldn't be relied upon to see to it that his wife received enough money to run the household, so he prearranged to have part of his check garnished by his wife. In 1922 the team purchased four separate life-insurance policies from three different companies for Babe Ruth. There is no indication as to whether the team or Ruth's wife was the beneficiary, but the Yankees were set back a total of $1,850 for the policies.

Sometimes the salary entry stood out not in the way it was paid, but in the way it was *not* paid. One particular example was the May 1937 entry noting a payment of $260 to Dr. G. F. Oberrander with a note to charge the amount against the salary of one Joseph DiMaggio. This was not a baseball-related injury, because there is no evidence to suggest that players were routinely charged for their medical care. A check of the *New York Times* during the spring of 1937 reveals that DiMaggio had his tonsils and adenoids removed on April 16 by Oberrander, Ruppert's personal physician. While it was nice of Ruppert to recommend his personal physician for DiMaggio, he didn't pick up the tab. A quick check of the records shows that DiMaggio's salary was indeed docked for medical expenses. DiMaggio was, however, paid his salary during the two weeks he was out of the lineup.

Interesting patterns sometimes emerged when analyzing the data. For example, players were issued their uniforms at the beginning of the season and then had their pay docked for a thirty-dollar deposit to be refunded when said uniforms were returned in October. When a player was to be released, the Yankees would issue a refund of the uniform deposit. Therefore, one of the worst things that could happen to a player was to be handed a check for thirty dollars. Inevitably the next thing he was handed was a train ticket out of town.

Ticket prices rose rapidly as the fortunes of the team rose. In 1915 a season box sold for $300. Twenty years and seven pennants later that same box would set you back a shade over $900—and that was in the midst of the Great Depression. Of course, the cost of putting that higher-quality team on the field was going up as well. The total Yankee payroll more than doubled over that same twenty-year period from $116,000 to $260,000.

In 1915 the team bought a round-trip steamer ticket from Manhattan to Savannah, Georgia, for a young scribe named Fred Lieb to accompany the team to spring training. He must have pleased Ruppert and Huston with his stories because he was eventually hired as their official scorer, earning one thousand dollars per season, which was more than many benchwarmers were making at the time. Lieb became an accomplished author and reporter, eventually honored by the Hall of Fame with the J. G. Taylor Spink Award in 1972.

In December of 1921, almost two years to the day after the famous Ruth purchase, the Yankees and Red Sox hooked up in another $100,000 deal. This one, while not nearly as famous (or infamous, depending on your rooting allegiance), was a much larger deal. The Yankees sent the cash along with team captain Roger Peckinpaugh, Jack Quinn, Rip Collins, and Bill Piercy to Boston for Everett Scott, Joe Bush, and Sam Jones.

The Yankee ledgers tell us nothing new about batting averages, winning percentages, or fielding averages. They don't reveal anything about pitching rotations or late-inning strategies, and they certainly aren't as exciting as a game-winning hit. Yet in their own way, they are as important to the game as any of these. Baseball is now, and always has been, a business. The Yankee ledgers allow us to view this grand old game from another vantage point, adding yet another piece to the tapestry of America's national pastime.

Appendix 2   *Salary Data Sources*

At first blush it seems that a reliable source of salary information should be either the employee who receives the salary or the employer who pays it. After all, who better to know the actual salary? However, three types of problems occur when asking an employee or employer to reveal a salary (aside from issues of legality that may prevent employers from providing such information). Those issues are faulty memory (or "misremembering" as Roger Clemens would say), generalizations, and self-interest.

How reliable is our memory? Empirical evidence indicates it isn't as reliable as we would like to think it is.[1] What kind of things do I need to remember and what can I afford to forget? I need to remember my spouse's birthday, where I live, and my child's peanut allergy. But do I need to remember how much I was paid ten years ago? After all, if I need to know, I could dig up my old tax records. More likely I do not remember all those details, but I have an idea of a range in which I might have been paid. It's not that *nobody* remembers, just that lots of folks don't, and we have no way of knowing who those folks are. And the longer the gap in time between the pay date in question and today, the less likely my memory is accurate.

Remembering approximately how much I earned is one example of the generalization problem. Maybe what I remember is not how much my salary was, but how much I earned that year from salary and bonus and miscellaneous sources. Maybe I remember an average, or my salary from a year later. Maybe I remember what I asked for, but forgot that I didn't get that whole raise. Maybe I remember what I was promised, including a bonus, but didn't earn, because I failed to meet all the criteria. Or maybe I remember approximately what I earned, but not the exact amount. Regardless of the issue, the result is the same: the number I come up with may or not be what I actually earned. And if it is an actual amount that I earned, it may or may not have all been salary (a distinction that is important if one is conducting research on salaries). And finally, even if I do actually recall my salary, it may or may not have been earned in the year in question.

Maybe I remember exactly. Perhaps I have the contract here in front of me while I talk to you on the phone. But for a host of reasons I may not want to tell you exactly what I earned. A player may want to overstate his actual salary to inflate his importance, to match a story somebody else told, or to brag. Or he may want to underreport it to emphasize a story about a penurious owner or unfair treatment. Owners, as well, have lots of reasons for not being straightforward about salaries. Overstating a salary makes the owner look more generous, and the player more greedy. Understating a salary may protect the owner from accusations of overpaying a player, especially one who had a bad year. It may also serve to emphasize an argument that the team is low on finances or to discourage teammates from asking for more. Understating a salary may also be a strategic move given ongoing negotiations with a teammate.

Whatever the case, salary testimonies given by employees and employers cannot be considered reliable sources of information. The primary sources—the actual contract or the accounting records of the firm—are the most reliable. The additional advantage of relying on these primary sources is that they also often provide additional detail that is valuable in studying labor issues.

Prior to the availability of a large selection of contract cards of MLB players, there was no way to verify most salary claims. Short of a player or owner actually providing a contract, we had no reliable information. The MLB Player Transaction Card files at the National Baseball Hall of Fame library, a dataset that became available early in the twenty-first century, provides the primary source data we need to conduct reliable salary research.

The misnamed transaction card files (which actually contain limited transaction information) provide a wealth of financial compensation data. The cards were created by the American and National League offices. They are a collection of tens of thousands of individual index cards containing the details of individual player contracts as reported to the leagues for the 1911 through the 1987 seasons. When a contract was signed by a player and team, the contract was sent to the league office for approval. When approved, the league recorded all of the nonstandard information from the contract. That is, they recorded all of the information that was filled into the blanks (employer and employee name, salary, date of contract signing, etc.) as well as any changes (i.e., deleted clauses) or additions (bonuses, penalty clauses, etc.) to the contract. The information was then filed and the contract returned to the team. The Hall of Fame has a small collection of full contracts, both signed and blank. This allows for the comparison of the standard contract with the changes. For example, when a transaction card reads "clause seven deleted," we can look at a copy of the standard player contract for the year in question in order to see that clause seven gave the team the right to void the contract with ten days' notice.

The down side of using these transaction card files to study wages is that they represent the contracted amount of pay, but not necessarily the actual pay. This is where the team accounting books, as represented by the Yankee data, are truly the best source. The accounting books indicate the actual amount paid to the player by the team. This may differ from the contracted amount for a number of reasons. For example, the player may have been fined, sent back to the Minor Leagues and hence paid at a different rate, or traded but took a few (unpaid) days to report

One example will serve to illustrate this point. In 1925 Babe Ruth's contract called for him to receive $52,000 in salary. However, that year due to suspensions and fines, the Yankees actually only paid him $42,621. Given the paucity of team accounting records, the transaction card files are the best we can do for primary salary data in most instances.

Notes

Abbreviations
BM: *Baseball Magazine*
NYT: *New York Times*
OB: *Organized Baseball*.
TSN: *The Sporting News*

Introduction
1. National League and American Association of Professional Baseball Clubs, *Annual Meeting*, 92, 104.
2. "Baseball 'Trust,'" *Literary Digest*, December 7, 1912, 1090.
3. Fullerton, "Baseball—The Business and the Sport," 417.
4. Henry Fetter attributes the Yankees' dominance to a "new style of team management ... one in which spheres of authority and lines of responsibility were sharply demarcated, and owner, general manager, and field manager each had a distinct role to play in a carefully planned, entirely unsentimental model of organizational efficiency" (Fetter, *Taking on the Yankees*, 9).
5. Both the consumer price index and the implicit price deflator (used to calculate real, inflation-adjusted, GNP) exhibited double-digit rates of increase.

1. Baseball's Interminable Wars
1. Burk, *Never Just a Game*, 195–96; U.S. House of Representatives, *OB: Report*, 51; Haupert, Baseball Salary Database for Johnson's and Collins' salary information. Levitt, *Battle That Forged Modern Baseball*; Pietrusza, *Major Leagues*, 209–52; and Okkonen, *Federal League* are two useful sources for the history of the Federal League. The Federal League's experiences in battling an incumbent league were eerily similar to those of the All-America Football Conference, American Football League, and American Basketball Association. The American Football League was the only league to get all of its teams included in a merger with an incumbent league.

2. Thomas, *Walter Johnson*, 133–35; contract details from Haupert, Baseball Salary Database. According to historian Robert Burk, Johnson had tried to buy his own option for $1,000, so he could become a free agent. None of the other clubs made a serious offer for him, so he remained with the then-lackluster Senators (Burk, *Never Just a Game*, 182).

3. "Baseball Moguls See Dire Changes," NYT, April 14, 1919, 10.

4. "Bluffed Baseball Heads," NYT, April 4, 1919, 12.

5. U.S. House of Representatives, *OB: Report*, 56–57; "Claims of Federal League Owners to be Settled by OB," NYT, January 14, 1918, 13.

6. Seymour, *Baseball: Golden Age*, 243; "Claims Baltimore Club Was Ignored," NYT, June 12, 1917, 10.

7. Levitt, "Ed Barrow, the Federal League, and the Union League," 99. See also Lancaster, "Baltimore, a Pioneer in Organized Baseball," for a general history of professional baseball in Baltimore. See also Lynch, *Harry Frazee*, and Fountain, *Betrayal*, for accounts of the turmoil.

8. "New Baseball Rules Mean Fun for Fans," NYT, February 4, 1917, S1.

9. H. G. Salsinger, "Rival League for Detroit? Not Yet," TSN, December 14, 1916, 2; Joe Vila, "Third Major League Creates Enthusiasm among Magnates," TSN, November 16, 1916, 1.

10. U.S. House of Representatives, *OB: Report*, 57; "Called Federals a Joke," NYT, March 29, 1919, 10. Major League Baseball officials undoubtedly referred to the Federal League in uncomplimentary language, but what did the Baltimore officials expect—a visit from Welcome Wagon? When the All-America Football Conference challenged the NFL in 1945, then-NFL commissioner Elmer Layden quipped, "New league? Why they haven't even got a football," ("All America Bankroll," *Newsweek*, December 17, 1945, 89).

11. "Big Leagues Are Attacked in Suit," NYT, April 20, 1922, 23.

12. Paul Eaton, "Small Chance That Feds Will Fight On," TSN, December 16, 1920, 3.

13. "Baseball Is Victor in Trust Law Fight," NYT, May 30, 1922, 12.

14. "United States v. E. C. Knight Co.," http://www.oyez.org/cases/1851-1900/1894/1894_675, viewed April 2, 2014; Poggi, *Theater in America*, 17; Paul Eaton, "Baseball Leaders Bound Fed Case Shall Go to the Limit," TSN, April 24, 1919, 2; Joe Vila, "Landis Given All Powers Asked for to Keep Baseball Clean," TSN, December 16, 1920, 1.

15. "Future of Baseball Secure, Says Heydler," NYT, May 31, 1922, 25.

16. "Foreign Relations May Pinch Players," NYT, February 3, 1917, 10; "Peril to Baseball Lies in War Cloud," NYT, February 4, 1917, S1.

17. "Military Training for Ball Players," *NYT*, February 16, 1917, 12.

18. "President Tener of National League against Pooling of Players and Receipts," *NYT*, November 21, 1917, 14.

19. "Exemption Scheme Assailed by Tener," *NYT*, November 23, 1917, 9; "Ban Johnson Plans an Effort to Procure Exemption for Big League Players," *NYT*, November 22, 1917, 14. The industrialists realized that organizing a company-sponsored baseball team would enable them to reduce "excess profit" taxes and to provide morale-raising and distraction for their rank-and-file workers ("Taxes and Baseball Jumpers," *TSN*, December 2, 1920, 4). Other industrialists were content to arrange exhibition games between big league teams and semipro players; again the hope was to bolster worker morale. Sometimes the industrialists lost more than a game, as one lamented that the big league team came, it conquered, and it left signing some promising players (John Sheridan, "Back of the Home Plate," *TSN*, July 1, 1920, 4).

20. "National League Calls Upon Its Players to Join the Colors," *NYT*, December 19, 1917, 14.

21. "American League Makes No Changes," *NYT*, December 14, 1917, 10.

22. "Roster of Clubs in International League May Be Reduced to Six for Season of 1918," *NYT*, December 10, 1917, 12; "Big League Players Likely to Get No Training Trips," *NYT*, January 28, 1918, 10.

23. "League to Play Out Its Season," *NYT*, June 23, 1918, 27; "Big Leagues May Merge for Season," *NYT*, June 17, 1918, 14.

24. "Says League Will Quit," *NYT*, July 21, 1918, 17; "Ruppert in Favor of Continuing Game," *NYT*, July 21, 1918, 24.

25. "Topics of the Times: Baseball Is Declared Nonessential," *NYT*, July 22, 1918, 10; "American League Clubs to Continue," *NYT*, July 22, 1918, 8; "Baseball Reprieve Granted by Baker," *NYT*, July 27, 1918, 6; "Baseball Season Will Close Sept. 1," *NYT*, August 3, 1918, 6.

26. "Baker Approves a World's Series," *NYT*, August 23, 1918, 10. In an editorial in the *New York Times*, the writer pointed out that in recent years, "baseball has been 'honest,' in the sense that the players do their best to win," before worrying, "All too clearly, professional baseball has become a moneymaking scheme, and one as sordid and as ruthless as exists anywhere in the country" ("Topics of the Time: Baseball Will Not Be Missed," *NYT*, September 10, 1918, 12).

27. "Baseball Races Assured," *NYT*, November 20, 1918, 12.

2. The Rise of Landis

1. "Frazee Advocates New Commission," *NYT*, November 21, 1918, 12.

2. George Robbins, "Ban Johnson in Spotlight When Big Problems Arise," *TSN*, November 9, 1916, 1.

3. Bernstein, "George Sisler and the End of the National Commissioner," 95.

4. Quote in *NYT*, "Perry Case Causes Split of Leagues," July 10, 1918, 18; U.S. House of Representatives, *OB: Report*, 58; "Tener Steps Down as League Leader," *NYT*, August 7, 1918, 10; "Baseball War Is Ended," *NYT*, October 18, 1918, 14.

5. Graham, *New York Yankees*, 36. See also Lynch, *Harry Frazee*, 68-82, for a detailed discussion of the trade. Murdock has an account of the situation (Murdock, *Ban Johnson*, 167-74).

6. John Sheridan, "Back of the Home Plate," *TSN*, December 18, 1919, 6.

7. Burk, *Never Just a Game*, 227.

8. "Owners to Discuss Baseball Changes," *NYT*, October 18, 1920, 22.

9. "Ask Taft to Act as Baseball Head," *NYT*, November 24, 1918, 1; "Baker Offers Support," *NYT*, November 25, 1918, 14.

10. Both quotes in "Taft Gives Terms as Baseball Head," *NYT*, November 25, 1918, 14.

11. "Local Baseball Owner Adds Approval to the Selection of W. H. Taft as Leader of the Game," *NYT*, November 26, 1918, 12; "Baseball Tribunal Declined by Taft," *NYT*, December 1, 1918, 24; the *New York Times* ran several articles on this fiasco during late November and early December 1918.

12. "American League Inquiry Ordered," *NYT*, September 17, 1919, 25.

13. "National League Seeks to Confer with American on Joint Polity," *NYT*, December 12, 1918, 12.

14. "Frazee to Answer Johnson's Threat," *NYT*, December 16, 1918, 12.

15. "Boston Club Owners Defies Johnson to Force Him out of the American League," *NYT*, December 17, 1918, 14.

16. Joe Vila, "Prophets of Big Ban's Fall Made to Look Like Insects," *TSN*, December 19, 1918, 1.

17. "American League Inquiry Ordered," *NYT*, September 17, 1919, 25; "Johnson Case Postponed," *NYT*, August 16, 1919, 9.

18. "Peace Proposal with Strings," *TSN*, January 8, 1920, 4.

19. Joe Vila, "Yankees' Court Antics Get Small Notice from Scribes," *TSN*, February 5, 1920, 1.

20. "National League to Battle for One-Man Commission, Excluding Herrmann," *NYT*, December 14, 1918, 14; "Want Baseball Season to Open on May 1," *NYT*, December 13, 1918, 12.

21. "Hunt for Chairman Begins in Earnest," *NYT*, January 21, 1919, 10; "Baseball Solons Raise Admissions," *NYT*, February 12, 1920, 13; "Suit Halts Naming of New Chairman," *NYT*, March 1, 1919, 17.

22. Quote in "Selection at Joint Meeting," *NYT*, January 10, 1920, 12; "August Herrmann Resigns as Chairman of the National Baseball Commission," *NYT*, January 9, 1920, 18; "To Name Chairman at Joint Meeting," *NYT*, February 5, 1920, 11.

23. Lieb, *Detroit Tigers*, 162.

24. "Comment on Current Events in Sports: Baseball," *NYT*, November 1, 1920, 22; "Baseball," *NYT*, October 25, 1920, 24; Joe Vila, "Twelve-Club Proposal Falls Flat with New York Fans," *TSN*, October 28, 1920, 1.

25. "Baseball Trouble Near Settlement," *NYT*, November 11, 1920, 21; "Lasker Eleven Say Die Has Been Cast," *TSN*, November 11, 1920, 1.

26. "Players Belong to Clubs," *NYT*, November 10, 1920, 22.

27. "Baseball Conflict Shifts to Minors," *NYT*, November 10, 1920, 1.

28. George Robbins, "Ban Johnson in Spotlight When Big Problems Arise," *TSN*, November 9, 1916, 1; "Players Ask Place on the Commission," *NYT*, January 27, 1920, 17.

29. First quote in "Club Owners Are Still Far Apart," *NYT*, October 31, 1920, RE2; second quote in "War in Baseball," *NYT*, November 10, 1920, 12; see also "Renews Invitation to Joint Meeting," *NYT*, November 4, 1920, 20.

30. "Johnson Opposes Baseball Meeting," *NYT*, October 15, 1920, 22; "Baseball Inquiry Again Under Way," *NYT*, October 10, 1920, 21.

31. "Owners to Discuss Baseball Changes," *NYT*, October 18, 1920, 22.

32. Seymour, *Baseball: Early Years*, 319–20.

33. "War in Baseball," *NYT*, November 2, 1920, 12.

34. "Club Owners Vote for New League and Baseball War," *NYT*, November 9, 1920, 1.

35. Burk, *Never Just a Game*, 236.

36. "Comment on Current Events in Sports: Baseball," *NYT*, January 26, 1920, 8.

37. "Baseball Peace Declared: Landis Named Dictator," *NYT*, November 13, 1920, 1.

38. "It's Not So Much New Men," *TSN*, September 19, 1918, 4.

39. U.S. House of Representatives, *OB: Report*, 60.

40. *NYT*, "Landis Discusses Baseball Reform," November 29, 1920, 21.

41. "Judge Landis Is Eliminated from Chairmanship Contest," *NYT*, February 15, 1920, 20; "Judge McDonald Probable National Commission Head," *NYT*,

August 13, 1920, 15; "No Agreement on Judge M'Donald," *NYT*, August 14, 1920, 12. Note: Sometimes McDonald's name was spelled MacDonald.

42. U.S. House of Representatives, *OB: Report*, 58–59.

43. "Majors and Minors Reach Agreement," *NYT*, January 13, 1921, 16.

44. "Baseball Peace Declared; Landis Named Dictator," *NYT*, November 13, 1920, 1, 12.

45. Seymour, *Baseball: Golden Age*, 368.

46. "Possibilities in Judge Landis," *TSN*, February 12, 1920, 4.

47. "First American Dictator," *American Review of Reviews*, 95.

48. Given the *Sporting News*' lack of awe towards the judge, one wonders whether the editor chose the picture in a fit of whimsy.

49. "Landis Threatens to Quit Baseball," *NYT*, December 13, 1923, 26; Irving Vaughan, "Landis a Master of Strategy in Disposing of Opponents," *TSN*, December 20, 1923, 1.

50. "The Issue with Landis," *TSN*, December 27, 1923, 4; F. C. Lane, "An Open Letter to Commissioner Landis," *BM*, December 1924, 303.

51. "Another Peace Treaty," *NYT*, November 15, 1920, 13.

52. Voigt, *American Baseball*, 148; "Where the Prophets," *TSN*, October 11, 1923, 4.

53. Voigt, *American Baseball*, 148.

54. Francis Richter, "Casual Comment," *TSN*, June 21, 1923, 4.

55. Francis Richter, "Casual Comment," *TSN*, September 20, 1923, 4.

56. Irving Sanborn, "Should Owners Be Subject to Discipline 'For the Good of the Game?'" *BM*, August 1927, 391.

57. Francis Richter, "Casual Comment," *TSN*, January 13, 1924, 4; "$147,000 in Checks to Foley Endorsed by E. M. Fuller & Co.," *NYT*, June 12, 1923, 1, among the many articles in the *New York Times* during 1923 and other years.

58. Paul Eaton, "Can Landis Get O.B. Out of Trust Class?" *TSN*, November 25, 1920, 3; James Isaminger, "Baker Sure before Announcing Again," *TSN*, December 2, 1920, 1.

59. Quotes from "Scribbled by Scribes," *TSN*, December 2, 1920, 4; "Landis Defends Position," *NYT*, December 5, 1920, 1.

60. First quote in "Chicago Lawyer Attacks Landis," *NYT*, January 16, 1921, 10; second quote in "Palmer Rules No 'Crime' By Landis," *TSN*, February 17, 1921, 2; "Wants a Landis Inquiry," *NYT*, February 3, 1921, 5; "Landis Impeached by Welty in House," *NYT*, February 15, 1921, 1, 2.

61. "Landis Impeached by Welty in House," *NYT*, February 15, 1921, 2.

62. "Palmer Rules No 'Crime' By Landis," *TSN*, February 17, 1921. 2.

63. U.S. House of Representatives, *Conduct of Judge Kenesaw Mountain Landis*, baseball owner quote on 19, Federal Statute on 38, see also 4, 18.

64. Quote in "Buck Passed on Landis," TSN, March 10, 1921, 4; "Landis Impeached by Welty in House," NYT, February 15, 1921, 1, 2.

65. "Scribbled by Scribes," TSN, March 2, 1922, 4.

66. Quote in "Huston Launches Attack on Johnson," NYT, December 21, 1920, 20; "Johnson's Forces Rule A.L. Session," NYT, December 18, 1920, 17. Johnson biographer Eugene Murdock believes Johnson should have retired upon Landis's appointment as commissioner (Murdock, *Ban Johnson*, 226).

67. Both quotes from "Frazee Launches Attack on Johnson," NYT, December 23, 1920, 17.

68. Francis Richter, "Casual Comments," TSN, February 15, 1923, 4. Johnson later endorsed another plan for federal regulation ("Petition Asks U.S. Baseball Control," NYT, January 15, 1925, 17).

69. Joe Vila, "Politicians Would Control Baseball," TSN, January 14, 1926, 1; "Editorial Comment," BM, March 1926, 438. Politicians repeatedly proposed regulations during the 1920s ("Federal Control of Baseball Urged," NYT, January 1, 1927, 16; "Collier Explains Suggestion," NYT, January 16, 1925, 11).

70. "Johnson Is Shorn of Baseball Power," NYT, December 18, 1924, 26; "Johnson Founded American League," NYT, January 24, 1927, 12. The New York City assistant district attorney basically confirmed Landis's claim that without further evidence, O'Connell and Dolan were the only two proven to have been involved in the affair (Joe Vila, "Investigation Strangles Itself with Lack of Direct Evidence," TSN, February 12, 1925, 1; "O'Connell Keeps His Title," TSN, February 19, 1925, 4).

71. W. A. Phelon, "The Hectic Doings at the Big League Meetings," BM, February 1925, 409, 430; "Editorial Comment," BM, February 1925, 387–88. Phelon's description suggests that Shakespeare might have found Johnson a worthy subject. Several months later, American League owners continued their magnanimous conduct towards Johnson by granting him a $10,000-a-year increase in salary and a five-year extension of his contract in December ("Ban Johnson Gets $10,000 Pay Rise," NYT, December 10, 1925, 30). Murdock describes the humiliation of Johnson (Murdock, *Ban Johnson*, 207–211).

72. "National League Fights for Landis," NYT, February 4, 1926, 18; "Landis Pleased but Silent on a New Term of Ten Years," NYT, February 5, 1926, 17; "Loss of Landis Would Be Serious Blow, Says Comiskey; Scores Colleagues' Action," NYT, February 13, 1926, 21.

73. F. C. Lane, "Has Judge Landis Made Good?" BM, February 1925, 293–95, 428.

74. "Johnson Restored to Former Power," NYT, December 16, 1926, 31.

75. "Vote $65,000 Salary to Baseball Czar," NYT, December 17, 1926, 1.

76. "No Title," NYT, January 26, 1927, 1; "Final Showdown Seen Here," NYT, January 18, 1927, 19; "To Stick to Yanks, Barrow Declares," NYT, January 21, 1927, 10; "Mayor Walker May Head American League, But He Denies Receiving Formal Offer," NYT, April 23, 1927, 1; "Mayor Won't Take Baseball Job Now," NYT, April 24, 1927, 2.

77. "Verdict This Week on Cobb-Speaker," NYT, January 25, 1927, 16; see also Murdock, *Ban Johnson*, 218-221.

78. John Kieran, "Sports of the *Times*," NYT, January 22, 1927, 17.

79. *Literary Digest*, "When Ban Johnson Stept Down," March 19, 1927, 64, 66.

80. James Harrison, "Sports of the *Times*," NYT, April 27, 1927, 21. American League owners may have felt as the bandit Calvera laments near the end of *The Magnificent Seven*: "Generosity, that was my first mistake."

81. James Harrison, "Sports of the *Times*," NYT, May 1, 1927, S2; Irving Sanborn made a similar assessment, "Ban Johnson, the Man Who Created Modern Baseball," BM, October 1927, 491-93, 524.

82. "Ban Johnson Quits League Presidency," NYT, July 9, 1927, 8; "Status of Johnson May Come Up Today," NYT, July 8, 1927, 12; Murdock, *Ban Johnson*, 220-22.

83. "Keep Game a Game, Is Johnson's Plea," NYT, July 141, 1927, 17.

84. "Casual Comment," TSN, July 21, 1927, 4.

85. "Barnard New Head of American League," NYT, November 3, 1927, 31.

86. "Barnard Is Slated for League Head," NYT, November 1, 1927, 22.

87. "Editorial Comment," BM, February 1929, 386.

3. Baseball's Gambling Problem

1. Seymour, *Baseball: Early Years*, 87.

2. "Silver: I don't see tanking in the NBA," *Des Moines Register*, March 13, 2014, 5C; Thompson, "Hoop Dreams," 18, 20-21.

3. Quote in "New Baseball Rules Mean Fun for Fans," NYT, February 4, 1917, S1; "Labor Federation Egging on Players," NYT, January 14, 1917, S3.

4. W. A. Phelon, "Reds Seems to Have Beaten Garry to It," TSN, August 8, 1918, 6.

5. "The Breaks," TSN, September 19, 1918, 4.

6. "Launch Drive on Baseball Gamblers," NYT, May 25, 1920, 12; "Magistrate Fines Men," NYT, May 26, 1920, 12.

7. "Magistrate Fines Men," NYT, May 26, 1920; "Sues Yanks for $100,000," NYT, May 28, 1920, 14.

8. Wilfred Heinz, "Boss of the Behemoths," 46, 72, 74, 77.

9. Surdam, *Rise of the NBA*, 80–81.

10. "Big League Players Likely to Get No Training Trips," NYT, January 28, 1918, 10.

11. Quote in "Heydler Reserves Decision in Case," NYT, January 31, 1919, 12; "Heydler Will Hold Hearing for Chase," NYT, January 22, 1919, 8.

12. "Magee Sues Chicago Club," NYT, April 15, 1920, 13; Ginsburg, *Fix Is In*, 95. A jury ruled in favor of the Cubs ("Magee Loses Suit against the Cubs," NYT, June 10, 1920, 17).

13. "Cubs Ask Magee's Suit Be Dismissed," NYT, May 21, 1920, 11.

14. "Magee Testifies He Bet on Reds," NYT, June 9, 1920, 12; "Chase Denies Making Bet," NYT, June 10, 1920, 17; "Magee Suit Begun in District Court," NYT, June 8, 1920, 19. Magee claimed in the lawsuit trial that he stole second base ("Magee Testifies He Bet on Reds," NYT, June 9, 1920, 12).

15. "Scribbled by Scribes," TSN, June 17, 1920, 4; "In Justice to John Heydler," TSN, June 17, 1920, 4.

16. "Chase Barred from Parks," NYT, August 4, 1920, 19.

17. Weintraub, *House that Ruth Built*, 49; Cohen, "Rose Out, McGraw In: Why?" 7; "Swann Seeks Head of Baseball Plot," NYT, October 5, 1920, 1.

18. "Heydler Reserves Decision in Case," NYT, January 31, 1919, 12; Graham, *New York Giants*, 109–110.

19. First quote in W. A. Phelon, "For Good Cheer We Hand It to Phelon," TSN, September 5, 1918, 5; second quote in "Matty to Be Next Leader of Giants," NYT, February 8, 1919, 14; "Herrmann Blocks Hal Chase Trade," NYT, February 10, 1919, 14.

20. Most of Chase's contemporaries described him as one of the slickest fielders ever with a decent bat. The Thorn, Palmer, and Gershman *Total Baseball* encyclopedia though, numerically rates Chase as nothing special. As a hitter, Chase was impatient; he had but 276 walks and 7,417 at bats, making his on-base percentage a pallid .319. Billy Beane and SABR-metricians (Society of American Baseball Researchers) would shun Chase. The idea that he was one of the greatest players of his era seems questionable as do the claims that some of the White Sox were the best at their positions, aside from Joe Jackson, Eddie Collins, and Ed Cicotte.

21. Allen, *Cincinnati Reds*, 128. Allen thought that Chase's ball playing ability merited inclusion in the Hall of Fame, but of course, the player's shady character precluded such.

22. "So Much for Zimmerman," TSN, March 11, 1920, 4.

23. Joe Vila. "M'Graw One Mogul with Clean Skirts." TSN, November 11, 1920, 1.

24. "Hoyne Says 1920 Series Was About to be Fixed," *NYT*, October 2, 1920, 3; "Chase Accused in Affidavits," *NYT*, October 4, 1920, 8; "Jury to Indict Two in National League," *NYT*, October 6, 1920, 1.

25. "Benton Tells of Bribe Offer to Lose Game," *NYT*, September 24, 1920, 1; "Indict Two Gamblers in Baseball Plot; Men Named by Williams in Confession; Inquiry Here to Guard the 1920 Series," *NYT*, September 30, 1920, 1.

26. Tormey, "'The Old College Try,'" quote on 105. On the eve of the 1919 season, a reporter observed, "Harmony is one thing which the Cincinnati club for the last few seasons has lacked." But perhaps the managerial change bringing Pat Moran to the job helped the team mend its divisions ("Herrmann Blocks Hal Chase Trade," *NYT*, February 10, 1919, 14). An editorial in the *Sporting News* put it thusly: "The Reds won by a rather easy margin in a league that some of the harsher critics say is a wreck" ("Time and Space Wasted," *TSN*, October 2, 1919, 4).

27. Quote in Ginsburg, *Fix Is In*, 104; Asinof, *Eight Men Out*, 17, 24. A writer in the *Sporting News* said in March 1919, "Charley Comiskey has been accused of being niggardly with his players, but he can't be said to have been that when he dealt with Collins" ("Contract Should Be Preserved in Museum," *TSN*, March 13, 1919, 7).

28. John Sheridan, "Back of the Home Plate," *TSN*, December 15, 1921, 4.

29. "Bars Exhibition Games," *NYT*, October 16, 1917, 19.

30. Burk, *Never Just a Game*, 222.

31. "To Share Series Money," *TSN*, July 30, 1919, 16; "Plan New Division of Series Money," *NYT*, June 29, 1919, 18; "Commissioner's Determines World's Series," *TSN*, August 7, 1919, 2; "A Second Guess on the Strike," *TSN*, September 19, 1918, 4.

32. "Players Divide Spoils," *NYT*, September 13, 1918, 12; "Last Game for Players," *NYT*, October 5, 1919, 116; "Division of Spoils Occupies Players," *NYT*, October 1, 1921, 17.

33. "Majors' Joint Conference Turns Down War Economists," *TSN*, December 20, 1917, 3; Irving Sanborn, "Why Baseball's Welfare Demands a Revised World's Series," *BM*, January 1925, 344.

34. "To Suppress Gamblers," *NYT*, July 13, 1919, 18; "American League Inquiry Ordered," *NYT*, September 17, 1919, 25.

35. Cook, *1919 World Series*, 142.

36. See Surdam, *Ball Game Biz*, 37–38.

37. "Joy if Reds Win—But a Shock If They Do," *TSN*, October 2, 1919, 3.

38. "Analysis of Strength of White Sox and Reds Leaves World's Series Result in Doubt," *NYT*, September 21, 1919, 101. Umpire Billy Evans argued that Eddie Collins was the "greatest money ball player," and claimed, "If the Reds can silence the mental and physical batteries of the great second sacker, they will come pretty close to going over a winner" (Billy Evans, "Reds Must Stop Collins to Win," *NYT*, September 25, 1919, 23). Collins batted .226 and made two errors in the series.

39. "Backers of Reds Are Hard to Find," *NYT*, September 27, 1919, 19; "Much Betting on Game in Chicago," *NYT*, October 10, 1919, 14.

40. "Rumors Arouse Comiskey," *NYT*, October 11, 1919, 10.

41. "'National League Has Class'—Matty," *NYT*, October 12, 1919, 103. Cook repeated the Asinof anecdote that White Sox owner Charles Comiskey promised pitcher Ed Cicotte a raise or a bonus if he won thirty games (in the truncated 1919 season, although the alleged bonus may have been for the 1917 season). Cicotte reached twenty-nine wins and then allegedly did not get to start any more games. His disappointment supposedly inspired him to consort with gamblers to fix the series. Gene Carney believes Comiskey rewarded Cicotte for winning twenty-nine games in 1919 with a $3,000 bonus, although Carney characterizes the money as "hush money." Carney doubted the story of Comiskey's chicanery regarding a bonus, as he points out that Cicotte never claimed there was a bonus. In addition, Cicotte had opportunities to win thirty games in 1917, getting fairly regular starts through the end of the season. Charles Fountain too disputes the bonus legend (Cook, *1919 World Series*, 9; Asinof, *Eight Men Out*, 24; Carney, "Mysterious Mr. Cicotte," 93; Fountain, *Betrayal*, 148).

A simple check of box scores near the end of the 1919 season reveals the flaws in Cook's and other historians' claims regarding this agreement. Cicotte had won twenty-eight games in 1917, but had slumped to just twelve wins in 1918. Cicotte appeared to miss some starts in the middle of September 1919, but he started games on September 19, 24, and 28. He started the latter two games against the sixth-place St. Louis Browns. He lost the game on the twenty-eighth by a 10-2 score. If Comiskey was trying to bilk Cicotte of his thirtieth win, he did so in a rather bizarre fashion: two late-season starts against a mediocre club.

42. Asinof, *Eight Men Out*, 115-36. Fullerton's claims regarding a fix was prominently depicted in Sayles's *Eight Men Out*. Studs Terkel played Fullerton.

43. Koppett, *Essence of the Game*, 209-10, see also 214.

44. The *New York Times* ran many articles on this situation throughout December 1946 and January 1947; see, for instance, Alexander Feinberg, "'Fixer' Jailed Here for Bribe Offers to Football Stars," NYT, December 16, 1946, 1.

45. White Sox attendance rose from 627,186 to 833,492 between 1919 and 1920 (Thorn, Palmer, and Gershman, *Total Baseball*, 75). Part of the increase was due to the larger number of games played in 1920, but the trend was amplified by the increase in ticket prices in 1920.

46. "White Sox Players Accuse Teammates," NYT, October 4, 1920, 8; Brown, *Chicago White Sox*, 107.

47. "Cubs Are Named in Gambling Charges," NYT, September 5, 1920, S16; "Jury to Probe Charges," NYT, September 8, 1920, 19; Allen, *Cincinnati Reds*, 145–46; "Thirteen Indicted in Baseball Fixing," NYT, October 30, 1920, 6.

48. "Says 1919 World's Series Was Fixed," NYT, September 23, 1920, 12.

49. "Says Rothstein Will Be Called in Inquiry," NYT, September 25, 1920, 19.

50. Quote in "White Sox Would Not Dare Win, Rumor Says," NYT, September 24, 1920, 2; Lewis, *Cleveland Indians*, 117.

51. "New Witness Tells of Baseball Plot," NYT, September 28, 1920, 1.

52. "Eight White Sox Players Are Indicted on Charge of Fixing 1919 World Series; Cicotte Got $10,000 and Jackson $5,000," NYT, September 29, 1920, 1.

53. "Baseball Inquiry Will Go Through to End, Says Judge," NYT, October 1, 1920, 1.

54. "Delay Ball Inquiry, Seeking Witnesses," NYT, October 7, 1920, 4.

55. "Talks of Federal Control," NYT, October 2, 1920, 3; "Comment on Current Events in Sports: Baseball," NYT, November 8, 1920, 23.

56. "Question Brooklyn before the Series," NYT, September 30, 1920, 1; "Dodgers Cleared of Any Suspicion in Coming Series," NYT, October 3, 1920, 1.

57. "It's a Sweeping Flood, Now," TSN, October 7, 1920, 20. Today, of course, he would claim that his statements were "taken out of context."

58. "National League Favors a Change," NYT, October 8, 1920, 24.

59. Hugh Fullerton, "Baseball on Trial," 184.

60. "Comiskey Reviews Steps of His Probe," NYT, November 5, 1920, 23.

61. "Are the Fans Going to Fall?" TSN, December 2, 1920, 4.

62. "Ousted White Sox Players Forming Team of Their Own," NYT, April 9, 1921, 17.

63. "Editorial Comment," BM, June 1921, 290.

64. "Few Wagers Made on World's Series," NYT, October 6, 1920, 24; "Betting Is Brisk on Series Outcome," NYT, October 9, 1923, 18.

65. "Yankee Owners Give Praise to Comiskey and Offer Him Use of Their Whole Team," NYT, September 29, 1920, 1. Harry Frazee made a similar, if less grandiose offer. Loaning players was not unheard of in professional sports. The National Football League eventually had to outlaw such practices as the Pittsburgh Steelers loaning the New York Giants' football team a quarterback for a late-season game (NYT, "Redskins Protest Heller's Transfer," November 21, 1934, 25).

66. "Comiskey Gives $1,500 to Each Honest Player," NYT, October 5, 1920, 3.

67. W. A. Phelon, "Reds Get Chesty in Talking New Terms," TSN, January 8, 1920, 2; "Must Stamp Out Baseball Gambling," NYT, January 11, 1920, 92.

68. "Trial Date to Be Set," NYT, February 4, 1921, 18; "Baseball Plotters Flee from Country," NYT, April 27, 1921, 4; "Baseball Plot Confessions Gone," NYT, July 23, 1921, 10; "More Evidence against Ball Players Gone," NYT, July 24, 1921, 5. About the same time, Joe Jackson's attorney, James H. Price, announced that poor Joe Jackson might have to pay $1,200 income tax and penalty on the $5,000 he received from the gamblers ("Indicted White Sox Demand Particulars," NYT, February 15, 1921, 6).

69. "Ask Why Rothstein Was Not Indicted," NYT, August 2, 1921, 28.

70. "Purified Baseball," NYT, August 4, 1921, 11. This may explain why Comiskey paid his players a pro rata salary during the series, in addition to the players' losers' share of World Series money.

71. First quote in "The Moral Plane of the Fan," TSN, December 30, 1920, 4; second quote in "White Sox Players Are All Acquitted by Chicago Jury," NYT, August 3, 1921, 1, 3.

72. "Baseball Leaders Won't Let White Sox Return to the Game," NYT, August 4, 1921, 1.

73. "Movement Started to Clear Jackson," NYT, July 16, 1922, 23; "Composite Score of 1919 World's Series," NYT, October 10, 1919, 14.

74. "Editorial Comment," BM, April 1924, 486. Happy Felsch later won back pay and interest in a settlement of his lawsuit ("Felsch Gets His Back Pay," NYT, February 10, 1925, 17). Carney goes into great detail regarding the Milwaukee trial (Burying the Black Sox, 1-16 has a good summary of that case).

75. "James O'Brien, Stockbroker, Wins $100,000 Baseball Bet; Celebrates with Dinner," NYT, October 3, 1921, 1.

76. "Scribbled by Scribes," TSN, October 7, 1920, 5.

77. Quote in "Landis's Ire Aroused," NYT, June 21, 1921, 24; "Ultimatum to Gamblers," NYT, June 9, 1921, 20.

78. Rice quote in Thomas Rice, "There May Be More in Douglas Scandal," *TSN*, August 24, 1922, 3; Landis quote in "Douglas Barred from Baseball for Treachery," *NYT*, August 17, 1922, 1; Lardner, "That Was Baseball," 136.

79. "Illness of Douglas Halts Legal Fight," *NYT*, August 29, 1922, 19.

80. Ginsburg, *Fix Is In*, 191; see also Alexander, *John McGraw*, 256–66.

81. Graham, *New York Giants*, 154; "Banton Would Act on Baseball Bribe," *NYT*, January 16, 1925, 11; F. C. Lane, "A Review of the Recent Scandal," *BM*, December 1924, 299. J. C. Koford described O'Connell as not being bright. "As a matter of fact, his teammates looked on him as being nothing more or less than a dumb-bell. Jimmy had the rudiments of education that Joe Jackson lacked, but he had the same moronic tendency to believe the last thing told him." Another writer, though, painted a brighter picture of the player: "Jimmy O'Connell has many friends out here [Pacific Coast] who cannot understand his conduct at all. He must have changed a good deal since he was the idol of this circuit and one of the most sincere performers that ever played the game on the coast" (J. C. Koford, "Stove League Stories," *TSN*, October 16, 1924, 8; Les Coates, "Lane Should Have Cut Loose Sooner," *TSN*, October 9, 1924, 5).

82. "Time to Become Serious?" *TSN*, February 5, 1925, 3.

83. Ginsburg, *Fix Is In*, 191–93; John Sheridan, "Back of the Home Plate," *TSN*, October 9, 1924, 4; "The Black Sheep Flock Grows," *TSN*, October 9, 1924, 4; "Player-Share Plan Favored by Many," *NYT*, November 14, 1924, 23; Joe Vila, "Cozy Dolan Takes French Leave, Deserting Even His $100,000 Suit," *TSN*, November 20, 1924, 1.

84. Joe Vila, "O'Connell's Immunity Stand Fails to Deter Investigation," *TSN*, February 5, 1925, 1.

85. "Again We Have Silence," *TSN*, January 22, 1925, 4. F. C. Lane made a rather bizarre claim in *Baseball Magazine* in January 1925 while the O'Connell-Dolan situation was front page news: "I make the flat, unblushing claim that professional baseball is the cleanest, most honorable sport of which I have any knowledge. . . . There is more chicanery and cheap politics in the selection of many a humble pastor in a country pulpit than there is in the management of a Major League ball club" (F. C. Lane, "Why Need Baseball Apologize?," *BM*, January 1925, 353).

86. "League Head Acts on Scandal Charges," *NYT*, August 24, 1923, 7; Allen, *Cincinnati Reds*, 164. The *New York Times* ran several articles on the allegations, but the stories dwindled by mid September.

87. "Johnson Condemns Baseball Gambling," NYT, November 4, 1922, 18.

88. Quote in "Baseball Gambling Attacked by Landis," NYT, January 27, 1923, 10; "Scribbled by Scribes," TSN, January 4, 1923, 4. Landis later used a figure of less than 30 percent of the money received was paid out ("Landis Continues Fight on Gambling," NYT, April 24, 1923, 18).

89. "Landis Continues Fight on Gambling," NYT, April 24, 1923, 18.

90. Irving Sanborn, "The Slimy Trail of the Baseball Pool," BM, June 1923, 293–94; Irving Sanborn, "The Slimy Trail of the Baseball Pool, BM, July 1925, 293–94, 341.

91. "Baseball Scandal Up Again, with Cobb and Speaker Named," NYT, December 22, 1926, 1, 17.

92. Alexander, Ty Cobb, 180, 187; "Dutch Leonard to Pitch," NYT, August 2, 1924, 4.

93. "Baseball Scandal Up Again, with Cobb and Speaker Named," NYT, December 22, 1926, 17.

94. "Paid for Letters in Baseball Scandal," NYT, December 23, 1926, 1.

95. "Paid for Letters in Baseball Scandal," NYT, December 23, 1926, 1.

96. "Detroit Stands by Cobb," NYT, December 23, 1926, 16; Lieb, Detroit Tigers, 181.

97. Gay, "Unraveling the Cobb-Speaker Scandal," 130–31.

98. "Home Folks Back Cobb in Scandal," NYT, December 24, 1926, 1.

99. "Transcript of Main Testimony Taken in Baseball Scandal," NYT, December 24, 1926, 12; "Congress May Air Baseball Scandal," NYT, December 25, 1926, 8.

100. "Scribbled by Scribes," TSN, January 6, 1927, 4.

101. "Leonard Denies Receiving Money," NYT, December 29, 1926, 17; "Cobb and Speaker Cleared by Landis," NYT, January 28, 1927, 11.

102. "Boyd Scouts West Story," NYT, December 30, 1926, 16; "Lawyers for Stars Confer Today," NYT, December 31, 1926, 9; "Says Bet Was Made on Horse, Not Game," NYT, December 30, 1926, 16.

103. "The Week in Sports: Baseball," NYT, December 27, 1926, 13.

104. John Sheridan, "Back of the Home Plate," TSN, January 6, 1927, 4.

105. John Sheridan, "Men Accused by Leonard Silly Perhaps, But Criminals? No!" TSN, January 6, 1927, 3.

106. Francis Powers, "Cleveland Fandom Keen for New Dope," TSN, January 6, 1927, 1.

107. Francis Richter, "Casual Comment," TSN, January 6, 1927, 4.

108. "Johnson Accepts Landis Challenge," NYT, January 18, 1927, 19; there was a spate of articles in the New York Times during January.

109. "Cobb Incompetent, Johnson Asserts," *NYT*, January 20, 1927, 17.
110. James Harrison, "Ruppert Endorses Tactics of Landis," *NYT*, January 23, 1927, S1.
111. "Cobb and Speaker Cleared by Landis," *NYT*, January 28, 1927, 11; Gay, "Unraveling the Cobb-Speaker Scandal," 131. Cobb biographer Charles Alexander details the long-running animosity between Cobb and Navin resulting from the owner's refusal to pay a medical bill for Cobb and his refusal to purchase needed players to bolster Cobb's efforts to win a pennant (Alexander, *Ty Cobb*, 179).
112. James Harrison, "Speaker to Confer with Huggins Today," *NYT*, January 30, 1927, S1; "Mack Sees a 'Chance,'" *NYT*, January 31, 1927, 14; "Speaker Accepts Senators' Terms," *NYT*, February 1, 1927, 21; "Ty Cobb May Sign with Mack Today," *NYT*, February 8, 1927, 17. In the end, Cobb and Speaker proved to be expensive baubles. Mack released Cobb after the 1927 season, rueful that he could not afford to keep Cobb on at his high salary. He later re-signed Cobb for the 1928 season. Washington decided to move towards a youth movement after the 1927 season, so the team released Speaker. Speaker too performed his swan song with Connie Mack in 1928 (James Isaminger, "Mack Releases Ty to Reduce Payroll," *TSN*, October 10, 1927, 1; "Casual Comment," *TSN*, February 9, 1928, 4).
113. James Harrison, "Johnson Is Deposed by American League; Judge Landis Wins," *NYT*, January 24, 1927, 1, 12.
114. "Editorial Comment," *BM*, February 1927, 390.
115. "White Sox Bought Four Detroit Games in 1917, New Charge," *NYT*, January 2, 1927, 1, 14.
116. Irving Vaughan, "Chicago Feeds on, but Does Not Relish, Diet of Scandal," *TSN*, January 6, 1927, 1.
117. "Players Are Ready to Answer Risberg," *NYT*, January 5, 1927, 16.
118. James Harrison, "29 Baseball Men Confront Risberg, Deny His Charges," *NYT*, January 6, 1927, 1, 30. Gandil was a troubling character. He told reporters that Rowland lied about a story regarding his allowing Gandil to leave the club in September 1917 to meet a couple of friends in Philadelphia. Gandil said, "I never had any friends" ("Baseball Awaits Decision by Landis," *NYT*, January 9, 1927, S1).
119. "Landis Is Puzzled at Risberg's Aim," *NYT*, January 10, 1927, 29.
120. "Landis Exonerates Accused Players," *NYT*, January 13, 1927, 30. Landis's moratorium on gambling allegations was wise, as a couple of days later, Yankees and Giants officials had to deny allegation that the 1922 World Series was fixed ("Speaker to Await Landis's Next Step," *NYT*, January 15, 1927, 12).

121. "Editorial Comment," *BM*, March 1927, 439–40.
122. James Harrison, "Majors Would End Pact with Minors," *NYT*, December 16, 1927, 30; Burk, *Much More Than a Game*, 16–17.
123. Francis Richter, "Casual Comment," *TSN*, March 26, 1925, 4; "Baker Answers Charges," *NYT*, May 13, 1925, 19; "Court Orders Baker to Return 632 Shares of Phillies' Stock," *NYT*, June 27, 1925, 8.
124. "Hornsby and Moore Confer on 'Debts,'" *NYT*, January 11, 1927, 35; "Moore May Sue Hornsby," *NYT*, January 14, 1927, 17; Alexander, *Rogers Hornsby*, 139–41.
125. "$50,000,000 Value Placed on Majors," *NYT*, March 13, 1927, S.

4. The Financial Side of the Game

1. "Disclose Earnings of Detroit Club," *NYT*, February 3, 1920, 16.
2. "Estate of M'Keever Shows Club Value," *TSN*, January 3, 1929, 1.
3. "4,340,644 Saw N.L. Games in 1924, Gain of 220,827," *NYT*, December 10, 1924, 27.
4. U.S. House of Representatives, *OB: Report*, 91.
5. U.S. House of Representatives, *OB: Report*, 94.
6. Tax rate information from http://federal-tax-rates.insidebov.com/, viewed December 17, 2016, and www.taxpolicycenter.org/, viewed December 17, 2016. Gene Smiley and Richard Keehn suggest that the statistical evidence suggest that the "primary motive for the 1920s tax cuts was the desire to reduce income tax avoidance." Wealthy Americans parked their wealth into tax-exempt securities, while corporations delayed cash distributions of profits (dividends) until tax policies became favorable. The tax cuts made disbursing dividends more beneficial for stockholders (Smiley and Keehn, "Federal Personal Income Tax Policy," quote on 287, see also 288–92, 302).
7. "Hornsby and Moore Confer on 'Debts,'" *NYT*, January 11, 1927, 35. Breadon announced dividends of $51,000 following the team's 1928 pennant ("Cards Declare Dividend," *NYT*, October 17, 1928, 32).
8. "Scribbled by Scribes," *TSN*, December 22, 1921, 4; "John McGraw, the Financier," *TSN*, December 29, 1921, 4; "Senators Pay 40% Dividend, Re-elect Griffith President," *NYT*, January 7, 1925, 29; "Senators Pay 40 Percent.," *NYT*, January 6, 1926, 18. Two years later, the Senators were not as lucrative and no dividend was declared as the team used its earnings to buy more players (Paul Eaton, "Senator Divided Goes into Players," *TSN*, January 13, 1927, 2).
9. "Indians' Earnings Dropped $160,186 in 5-Year Period," *NYT*, July 8, 1926, 20.

10. "Baseball Business from the Inside," *Collier's*, March 25, 1922, 29; Haupert and Winter, "Yankee Profits and Promise, 197–214.

11. John Sheridan, "Back of the Home Plate," *TSN*, August 16, 1923, 4; "Macy's to Put Up 21-Story Building," *NYT*, February 9, 1922, 11; "Cut in Rail Income Laid to Coal Strike," *NYT*, May 7, 1923, 25.

12. U.S. House of Representatives, *OB: Report*, 103.

13. "Mack Growing Rich with Tail End Team," *TSN*, November 9, 1922; Surdam, *Wins, Losses, & Empty Seats*, 20–21. F. C. Lane observed that second-division teams could earn a profit, except that some owners "exaggerated the prestige of a winning club" (F. C. Lane, "Bigger and Better Baseball," *BM*, February 1930, 389).

14. U.S. House of Representatives, *OB: Report*, 98. Simple linear regression equations covering the 1920–30 seasons showed that win-loss percentage and a dummy variable for New York were both statistically significant at the 5 percent level or better:

$$\text{Attendance} = -376{,}360 + 1{,}877{,}586(\text{W-L Pct.}) + 219{,}746(\text{NY Dummy})$$
$$R^2 = .613.$$

$$\text{Net income} = -380{,}124 + 985{,}268(\text{W-L Pct.}) + 46{,}966(\text{NY Dummy})$$
$$R^2 = .525.$$

15. U.S. House of Representatives, *OB: Report*, 1,599–607.

16. Oscar Reichow, "Hot Dogs and Peanuts by Wholesale," *BM*, August 1919, 396, 426.

17. New York Public Library, New York Yankees Baseball Club Collection, Third Folder, 1915–38, Meeting of October 9, 1923.

18. "Clubs Will Limit Spring Training," *NYT*, December 18, 1918, 12.

19. F. C. Lane, "The Enormous Financial Hazards of Running a Major League Baseball Club," *BM*, January 1923, 42–45, 372–73; "National Leaguers Move for Peace," *NYT*, December 15, 1926, 23.

20. John Sheridan, "Back of the Home Plate," *TSN*, December 27, 1923, 4; Kieran, "Big-League Business," 17.

21. "Decision on Benton Is Left to Landis," *NYT*, February 14, 1923, 14; see also "National League to Reward Stars," *NYT*, February 13, 1924, 23; "The Burden of Transportation," *TSN*, March 10, 1921, 4.

22. Kieran, "Big-League Business," 16; Paul Eaton, "New Players Cost Senators $124,500," *TSN*, January 15, 1925, 1; "Scribbled by Scribes," *TSN*, April 16, 1925, 3; "Club Owners Plan to Reduce Squads," *NYT*, January 5, 1924, 17. Spring training was one of those discretionary expenses that owners could

easily jettison as they did during 1918, although transportation restrictions also affected their decision ("Clubs Will Train in South Again," NYT, December 25, 1918, 16).

23. Ernest Lanigan, "Where the Money Goes on a Ball Club," BM, May 1925, 556.

24. Haupert and Winter, "Pay Ball: Estimating the Profitability," 94, 97.

25. "Fuller Creditors on Stoneham Trail," NYT, September 5, 1923, 19; Murdock, *Ban Johnson*, 241. Many of the game's earlier owners were relatively small-scale brewers or saloon owners (especially in the American Association and Union Association of the 1880s), such as Chris von der Ahe (Burk, *Never Just a Game*, 69-70; Pietrusza, *Major Leagues*, 81-82, 176).

26. Damon Kerby, "Why Baseball Owners Choose Their Company," BM, June 1929, 317.

27. "This Time Huston Sells Out for Keeps," TSN, May 24, 1923, 1. Frank Graham details how Huston and Robinson were good buddies, drinking and hunting together during the off season (Graham, *New York Yankees*, 32).

28. "Sale of Yankees' Franchise Denied," NYT, October 11, 1922, 27; "Ruppert to Be Sole Owner of the Yankees," NYT, December 13, 1922, 30; "Ruppert Declares Huston Will Stay," NYT, January 6, 1923, 10; "Ruppert Completes Deal for Yankees," NYT, May 22, 1923, 15. Francis Richter recalled that when Huston and Ruppert paid $450,000 for the Yankees in 1915, many baseball men thought they had paid too much, especially since they needed to get a lease on the Polo Grounds (Francis Richter, "Casual Comments," TSN, January 4, 1923, 4).

29. "Editorial Comment," BM, September 1925, 438.

30. "American Positive in Declaration of Policy," TSN, December 19, 1918, 7.

31. "No Secret That Frazee Is Not Wanted Around," TSN, December 19, 1918, 7.

32. "Red Sox Park in Wrangle," NYT, February 10, 1920, 19; "Court Enjoins Frazee," NYT, February 17, 1920, 10; Lynch, *Harry Frazee*, 110-111.

33. H. G. Salsinger, "None of the Gloom Stuff for Detroit," TSN, January 10, 1918, 5; "Stone after Red Sox," NYT, December 7, 1921, 23.

34. "Yanks Win Battle over Chief Bender," NYT, January 5, 1919, 21. Establishing the "greatest team of all time" is a hobby for many fans and sportswriters. After the Yankees' fabulous 1927 season, sportswriter Colver Newton applied a crude statistical analysis to determine the greatest team ever. He concluded that the 1927 Yankees ranked no higher than sixth place, behind the Chicago Cubs of 1906-10 and Boston Nationals of 1891-98, and Philadelphia Athletics of 1910-14 (J. Newton Colver, "Are the Yankees the Strongest Club of Baseball History?" BM, January 1928, 361).

35. "Syndicate May Buy Red Sox Next Week," *NYT*, July 4, 1923, 10; "Red Sox Are Sold for Over Million," *NYT*, July 12, 1923, 15; Joe Vila, "Johnson Elated That Frazee Finally Is out of Baseball," *TSN*, July 19, 1923, 1. One of the most bizarre rumors ever floated in baseball surfaced a couple of weeks after Frazee sold the Red Sox. Someone claimed that Ruppert was going to sell Huston's half of the Yankees to none other than Harry Frazee. Ruppert immediately squelched the rumor ("Sale of Yankees Denied by Ruppert," *NYT*, July 18, 1923, 11; Francis Richter, "Casual Comment," *TSN*, August 2, 1923, 4).

36. "Scribbled by Scribes," *TSN*, March 7, 1923, 4.

37. "Fuchs Now Owns Braves," *NYT*, September 2, 1926, 19; Kieran, "Big-League Business," 16.

38. Thomas Rice, "Ask Ebbets Not to Quit Them in Pinch," *TSN*, August 30, 1923, 3.

39. "Heirs Will Elect New Head of Robins," *NYT*, May 1, 1925, 21; "Believe Ebbets Will Covers Robins' Sale," *NYT*, May 5, 1925, 23.

40. Kavanagh and Macht, *Uncle Robbie*, 146; "Death Takes Second Owner of the Robins," *NYT*, April 30, 1925, 1, 8; "E. J. McKeever Became Head of Robins upon Ebbet's Death," *NYT*, April 20, 1925, 15.

41. "Landis Peace Plea to Robins Fails," *NYT*, December 12, 1929, 41; "Brooklyn Retains Robinson as Pilot," *NYT*, February 5, 1930, 20.

42. Wayne Otto, "William Wrigley, Baseball's Wealthiest Magnate," *BM*, September 1922, 453–54; Francis Richter, "Casual Comment," *TSN*, November 5, 1925, 4; Gold, "'The Other' Veeck Revives the Cubs," 69. Wrigley later made a mistake in replacing McCarthy with Rogers Hornsby as manager a year after McCarthy had led the Cubs to the 1929 World's Series ("Red Sox Went Limit in Bid for M'Carthy," *TSN*, October 9, 1930, 2). The Yankees swept in and hired McCarthy, who led the club to great success in the late 1930s.

43. "Casual Corner," *TSN*, February 10, 1927, 4.

44. William Slocum, "New Yorkers Pleased at New Turn in Affairs of Giants," *TSN*, January 23, 1919, 1. Brush had died in 1912.

45. "Rickard Would Buy Control of Giants, Plans Arena Chain," *NYT*, March 4, 1927, 1, 7; "Rickard Expands on Bid for Giants," *NYT*, March 5, 1927, 9.

46. "New Owners Gain Control of Indians," *NYT*, November 16, 1927, 21; Lewis, *Cleveland Indians*, 164.

47. Henry Edwards, "Where Baseball Is a Millionaire's Hobby," *BM*, March 1928, 452.

48. "Now for the Test of It," *TSN*, April 5, 1917, 4; "Breadon Now in Charge," *NYT*, May 9, 1922, 26.

49. "$50,000,000 Value Placed on Majors," *NYT*, March 13, 1927, S3.

50. Henry Edwards, "Where Baseball Is a Millionaire's Hobby," *BM*, March 1928, 451–52.

51. "Editorial Comment," *BM*, September 1929, 434. Ban Johnson irritated St. Louis Cardinals owner Sam Breadon, when he claimed the Cardinals should be moved to Kansas City. Johnson, never one to keep his thoughts to himself, said: "St. Louis isn't large enough for two big league teams, and the Cardinals are slowly starving to death." Unfortunately for Johnson's reputation as a seer, the Cardinals won the pennant the following season ("Cards Starving, Says Ban," *NYT*, September 28, 1925, 15).

52. James Gould, "What's the Matter with St. Louis?" *BM*, August 1930, 399–400.

53. From InsideGov.com, http://federal-tax-rates.insidegov.com/, viewed December 17, 2016.

54. Quirk and Fort, *Pay Dirt*, 55; Haupert, "The Economic History of Major League Baseball." Prorating the value of a franchise based on the sale of a fraction of the total number of shares could distort the actual imputed value. A prospective owner, for instance, might pay a premium to acquire a controlling interest in a club.

55. Thomas, "Helene Britton," n.p.; "Gardner Seeking to Buy Cardinals," *NYT*, January 12, 1919, 30; "$50,000 to Revive Cards," *NYT*, May 23, 1918, 10; "Gets Option on Cardinals," *NYT*, March 6, 1917, 12; "Cardinals Plead for Loan," *NYT*, August 14, 1918, 6.

56. "Gaffney May Buy Braves," *NYT*, October 31, 1918, 14; "Believes Taft May Not Covet Position," *NYT*, November 30, 1918, 12.

57. "Baseball Owners Round Up Players," *NYT*, November 22, 1918, 10; "Yankees' Manager Planning Trades," *NYT*, November 29, 1919, 13.

58. "Baseball Leagues Will Clean House," *NYT*, December 8, 1918, 11; "Robins to Have No Rival," *NYT*, June 5, 1917, 8; "Report Commission Reduced to Pauper," *NYT*, December 10, 1918, 14. A few weeks later, a new rumor floated that Gaffney was now interested in the Red Sox and would have the team play in his Braves Field; in this way, he would have two teams playing in the stadium, spreading the overhead. What would happen to Fenway Park was left unstated. Baseball people thought that, with the war over and prosperity possibly returning, Gaffney might have a chance to turn a profit in Boston ("Gaffney Is Possible New Owner of Red Sox," *NYT*, December 23, 1918, 12).

59. "G. W. Grant Buys Braves," *NYT*, January 31, 1919, 12.

60. "Scribbled by Scribes," *TSN*, March 1, 1923, 4.

61. "Retiring Magnates Take Note," *TSN*, January 8, 1920, 2.

5. Getting Fans to the Ballpark

1. "Editorial Comment," BM, March 1926, 438.
2. "Editorial Comment," BM, September 1926, 440.
3. Irving Sanborn, "Forecasting a Baseball League of Nations." BM, April 1922, 776.
4. Cited by Barthel, *Baseball Barnstorming*, 105; "A New Division in Baseball," TSN, December 6, 1923, 4.
5. "Editorial Comment," BM, August 1928, 386; Irving Sanborn, "Does OB Need a Community Center?" BM, July 1924, 342.
6. "Editorial Comment," BM, September 1926, 440.
7. Irving Sanborn, "What Prohibition Hasn't Done for Baseball," BM, October 1920, 525.
8. Burk, *Never Just a Game*, 228.
9. Surdam and Brown, "Major League Baseball," unpublished paper, 30.
10. U.S. House of Representatives, OB: Report, 100.
11. Woolley, "Business of Baseball," 255.
12. "Herrmann to Quit Post as Chairman," NYT, December 11, 1919, 14.
13. "Throng of 38,600 at Polo Grounds," NYT, May 17, 1920, 19; "Yankees Play before 108,200 Fans in 5 Consecutive Days," NYT, June 6, 1920, 95; "Attendance Records Falling as Yankees Travel Around," NYT, July 6, 1920, 18; "Ruth Escapes When Auto Is Smashed," NYT, July 8, 1920, 17.
14. H. G. Salsinger, "Cobb Starts to Pick His Detroit Team," TSN, November 25, 1920, 2.
15. "Scribbled by Scribes," TSN, March 31, 1921, 4; John Sheridan, "Back of the Home Plate," TSN, March 31, 1921, 4; "Baseball in Good Condition—Heydler," NYT, July 14, 1921, 30.
16. "Braves Get Big Crowds," NYT, August 31, 1921, 18.
17. Thomas Rice, "Fans Quit National as Season Closes," TSN, September 14, 1922, 2.
18. Canes, "Social Benefits of Restrictions on Team Quality," 81–113.
19. "Another Record Smashed," NYT, April 20, 1923, 16.
20. "Giants Rout Cards before 42,000 Fans," NYT, May 21, 1923, 18.
21. "Yanks Win Title, 6–4 Victory Ends $1,063,815," NYT, October 16, 1923, 1, 16.
22. "The Baseball Strain," NYT, September 22, 1924, 18. Irving Sanborn, though, thought New York quite capable of sustaining large crowds, due to its "transient population which includes a steady proportion of amusement seeking visitors. Consequently a champion team always is a big attraction there even after all the native fans of Gotham become blasé over a surfeit of pennants"

(Irving Sanborn, "Clearing Up the Draft Muddle," BM, March 1927, 442; see also Irving Sanborn, "Baseball Becomes a Live Issue with the Younger Generation," BM, August 1928, 393-95).

23. Bert Walker, "Baseball Takes Rank with Huge Industries," TSN, January 1, 1925, 8.

24. Irving Sanborn, "Does Football Threaten Baseball's Supremacy?" BM, February 1928, 392.

25. Thorn, Palmer, and Gershman, *Total Baseball*, 75-76.

26. "Yankees Drew 2,500,000 Fans Last Season," NYT, January 4, 1928, 19. The number referred to in the headline included people gaining admittance on free passes.

27. John Sheridan, "Back of the Home Plate," TSN, February 3, 1921, 4.

28. "Barnard Has No Fear of Yankees Running Away with His League," TSN, February 2, 1928, 2; "Development of Prophecy," TSN, August 8, 1928, 4.

29. "Cubs Expect to Top Yanks' Best Gate," NYT, September 21, 1929, 15.

30. "Editorial Comment," BM, July 1930, 338; F. C. Lane, "Bigger and Better Baseball," BM, February 1930, 389.

31. Allen, *Cincinnati Reds*, 184; for rotation of holiday dates, see Thomas Rice, "Ask Ebbets Not to Quit Them in Pinch," TSN, August 30, 1923, 3; "National League Would Aid Pitcher," NYT, December 9, 1925, 32.

32. "Weeghman Verbally Pounded by Rickey for Offers to Hornsby," NYT, February 14, 1918, 13; "No More Juggling Dates," TSN, May 19, 1921, 4. An example of such team behavior occurred in 1921 when the Yankees refused to reschedule a late-season game with the Senators, who needed the game to have a chance to finish third and get World Series money. The Yankees did, however, agree to make up games with the St. Louis Browns as part of double-headers, straining the Browns' pitching staff (No title, TSN, October 6, 1921, 6; see also "A Wail from Cincy," TSN, May 22, 1924, 4 for an example of Branch Rickey's machinations).

33. "War May Curtail Baseball Season," NYT, October 23, 1917, 15; "American Sees No Need of Wartime Retrenchment," TSN, December 20, 1917, 3; "Suit Halts Naming of New Chairman," NYT, March 1, 1919, 17.

34. "Making the Best of It," TSN, October 8, 1922, 4; "Ban Johnson Gets $10,000 Pay Rise," NYT, December 10, 1925, 30. Because the National League had three teams without Sunday ball to the American League's two, it had more difficulty adjusting to a shorter season ("Majors Deadlocked on Baseball Dates," NYT, January 10, 1926, S1).

35. Ralph Davis, "One Might Think a Schedule All of It," TSN, October 31, 1918, 3.

36. "Majors Scheduled to Open on April 15," TSN, November 21, 1929, 5.
37. F. C. Lane, "Big Business in a Ball Park," BM, April 1929, 516; "Evers with Braves as They Head South," NYT, March 14, 1917, S2.
38. "Minors to Raise Prices," NYT, February 15, 1918, 6; "President Tener of National League against Pooling of Players and Receipts," NYT, November 21, 1917, 14, "Majors' Joint Conference Turns Down War Economists," NYT, December 20, 1917, 3; "American League Meets and Moguls Decide to Take Dimes and Nickels for Tax," NYT, February 15, 1918, 6. The question of who pays a tax befuddles most legislators and citizens. Typically, both consumers and producers share the tax, even though one party has the legal responsibility to remit the money to the government. What usually happens is that the overall price paid by the consumer increases, while the net amount the producers gets to keep decreases, leaving both parties worse off. In either event, fewer people will attend the games.
39. Ralph Davis, "Magnates Can Not Avoid Higher Rates," TSN, February 5, 1920, 3; Oscar Reichow, "Chicago All Excitement and Doubt as Magnates Gather," TSN, February 12, 1920, 1.
40. Haupert, Baseball Salary Database; James O'Leary, "Hank's Howl First Step toward Trade," TSN, February 5, 1920, 1.
41. "A Tax of Confiscation," TSN, April 26, 1917, 4.
42. "Leagues Protest against Tax Hike," NYT, January 19, 1919, 27. The government's zealousness in collecting taxes went out onto a limb—literally—when the Internal Revenue Service demanded 10 percent from people who sold seats on rooftops and treetops of buildings adjacent to ballparks. These seats were often sold for a nickel or a dime ("'Perchers' Must Pay Tax," NYT, May 26, 1918, E7).
43. Thomas Rice, "Minors Staked All on Bluff and Lost When It Was Called," TSN, January 23, 1919, 1. The Sporting News decried the government's decision to exempt admission prices paid to attend college games, since those were not profit-seeking institutions ("Is There No Justice?" TSN, February 7, 1924, 4).
44. "Ticket Tax Cut Starts Tomorrow," NYT, June 28, 1928, 17.
45. "Baseball Solons Raise Admissions," NYT, February 12, 1920, 13; Thomas Rice, "Ebbets a Victim of Politics and Spite," TSN, May 6, 1920, 3. Peter Craig's thesis on "Organized Baseball" is a splendid piece of research, especially for an undergraduate thesis. His table 9 on page 209 charts ticket prices between 1910 and 1950, including the effects of federal taxes (Craig, "Organized Baseball," 208-9).
46. "Defense Rests Case in Baseball Trial," NYT, July 29, 1921, 15.

47. "A Program for Landis," *TSN*, September 15, 1921, 4; "Baker Withdraws 'Tampering' Charge," *NYT*, February 15, 1922, 18.

48. John Sheridan, "Back of the Home Plate," *TSN*, October 13, 1921, 4; "25 Cents Added to Prices at Pittsburgh Baseball Park," *NYT*, March 1, 1926, 13.

49. Surdam, "New York Yankees Cope with the Great Depression," 824–25; New York Yankees Base Ball Club, Cash books.

50. U.S. House of Representatives, *OB: Report*, 97–98.

51. "Scribbled by Scribes," *TSN*, February 15, 1923, 4; advertisements in *TSN*, August 9, 1923, 10; June 18, 1925, 10; April 29, 1926, 10; and May 19, 1927, 10.

52. "School Children to See Chicago Ball Games Free," *NYT*, December 13, 1929, 32; "Explains Baseball Vote," *NYT*, July 21, 1927, 21; "Record of a 'Losing' Club," *TSN*, January 22, 1920, 4.

53. "Plan New Division of Series Money," *NYT*, June 29, 1919, 18; "Figures and Other Information on World's Series," *NYT*, October 1, 1919, 13; "World's Series to Start Oct. 4," *NYT*, September 22, 1924, 22.

54. "A Thought for the Future," *TSN*, June 10, 1920, 4. Pittsburgh owner Dreyfuss discovered that there was no law in the city against ticket resale at a markup ("Scalpers Draw Ire of the Pirate Fans," *NYT*, October 5, 1927, 18).

55. "Arrest Marquard for Speculating," *NYT*, October 10, 1920, 1; "Marquard's Days with Robins Ended," *NYT*, October 13, 1920, 21. Even American League president Ban Johnson found to his chagrin that his friends had succumbed to the ticket resale temptation; he had given out six hundred tickets to his friends and to people friendly to the American League, only to find out that twenty-four of the tickets had come into possession of scalpers ("Speaker to Await Landis's Next Step," *NYT*, January 15, 1927, S12).

56. "Yankees Set Rules for Series Tickets," *NYT*, September 20, 1926, 28; "Gougers Ask $50 for Set of Tickets," *NYT*, October 2, 1926, 12.

57. "Capital in Furor over World Series," *NYT*, October 3, 1924, 24; "U.S. to Aid Fight on Series Gougers," *NYT*, October 1, 1925, 24.

58. "Scribbled by Scribes," *TSN*, February 10, 1927, 4; "It Would Happen," *TSN*, March 3, 1927, 4.

59. "Casual Comment," *TSN*, October 20, 1927, 4.

60. "Yankee-Athletic Ticket Rush Brings Police Riot," *NYT*, September 7, 1928, 17.

61. "Extra Police Ready for Stadium Jam," *NYT*, September 8, 1928, 19.

62. "75,000 Requests Rejected for World's Series," *NYT*, October 3, 1928, 25; "Yankees Win Series, Total Receipts $777,290," *NYT*, October 10, 1928, 22. In comparison, the Giants and Yankees generated $722,000 in gate receipts

during the eight-game 1921 World's Series, held in the Polo Grounds before it was enlarged ("Record Making Series for Attendance and Receipts," TSN, October 20, 1921, 3). On the other hand, the 1925 series between Washington and Pittsburgh went the full seven games and generated $1,182,854 in gate receipts ("$1,182,854 World Series Gate, Pays $118,285 to Government," NYT, October 20, 1925, 1).

63. "U.S. to Get $80,000 Tax," NYT, October 10, 1928, 23; "Facts and Figures of the Big Classic," TSN, October 18, 1928, 3.

64. "The Conflicting Elements Opposed to Sunday Ball," *Sporting Life*, February 1897, 4.

65. "Sunday Ball May Yet be Played in Tebeau's Town," *Sporting Life*, April 30, 1898, 6; see "Court Frees Charles J. Harvey," NYT, April 27, 1917, 17 for two examples of upper-class attitudes; Joe Vila, "Landis Must Fight for His Principles," TSN, December 2, 1920, 2.

66. John Sheridan, "Back of the Home Plate," TSN, December 23, 1920, 4.

67. Jim Nasium, "This Business of Baseball," TSN, January 6, 1927, 5. If readers find this nom de plume weird, another writer sported the name Red Byrd—he covered the St. Louis Cardinals, of course.

68. Bevis, *Sunday Baseball*, 204, 241-42; Irving Sanborn, "The Pros and Cons of Sunday Baseball," BM, October 1926, 488.

69. Light, *Cultural History of Baseball*, 1997, 710.

70. "Ruppert Bids for Sunday Baseball," NYT, November 3, 1917, 12; "Ebbets in Court Today," NYT, August 28, 1917, 12; Thomas Rice, "Sunday Ball Live Issue in Brooklyn," TSN, November 1, 1917, 3.

71. Quote in "Herrmann Blocks Hal Chase Trade," NYT, February 10, 1919, 14; Muir quote in "Sunday Baseball Strongly Urged," NYT, March 6, 1919, 12; Paul Eaton, "Learn People Like a Pleasant Sunday," TSN, February 20, 1919, 3.

72. "Bar Sunday Double Bills," NYT, April 16, 1919, 10; "Sunday Baseball One Step Nearer," NYT, April 30, 1919, 17; "Advent of Sunday Baseball Draws 60,000 Persons to Polo Grounds and Ebbets Field," NYT, May 5, 1919, 14. An interesting consequence of Sunday ball was its effect on the National Football League; a prohibition on Sunday games would have hurt the NFL and thwarted a potential rival for sports supremacy.

73. Harry Williams, "Why the Giants Want Yankees Out," TSN, March 18, 1920, 8; Christy Mathewson, "Sunday Baseball as Matty Sees It," NYT, February 1, 1920, S2; New York Yankees Base Ball Club, Cash books. The Yankees' actual rent for 1919 and 1920 was $65,000; the rent increased to $100,000 for 1921 and 1922.

74. "Giants and Yanks Start Active War," *NYT*, January 6, 1923, 10.

75. "Heydler Advocates Conflicting Dates," *NYT*, January 7, 1923, S1; "Says Yankees Can't Prevent Conflicts," *NYT*, January 9, 1923, 29; Surdam, "What Brings Fans to the Ball Park?," 42.

76. "Carry Sunday Ball Protest to Ebbets," *NYT*, April 12, 1924, 11; "Sunday Ball Reformers Active," *NYT*, March 10, 1926, 37.

77. "Pastor Defends Sunday Baseball," *NYT*, October 22, 1924, 8.

78. "Editorial Comment," *BM*, June 1926, 336; "Editorial Comment," *BM*, June 1928, 290.

79. "Sunday Baseball Defended by Mack," *NYT*, August 20, 1926, 14. Given that the Athletics' stadium held roughly 28,000 people, paying an average of less than a dollar per ticket, it is difficult to see how the team lost that much revenue. In 1926 Shibe testified, the team drew 714,000, or about 9,000 per game without Sunday ball. In order for his contention to be true, the stadium would need to have been sold out for every Sunday game (and we haven't discussed the revenue the team would have lost via revenue sharing).

80. "Sunday Baseball Sustained in Court," *NYT*, August 22, 1926, S1; "Philadelphia Sees First Sunday Game," *NYT*, August 23, 1926, 10; "Sees Struggle for Athletics," *NYT*, March 15, 1933, 22. The *Sporting News'* account of the Sunday game took an ironic turn: "200 police men were dispatched to the park, with pistols protruding from their belts to 'keep order.' Of course, there was no order to keep. Aside from the inconvenience the rain brought, the 200 cops probably enjoyed the day more than any other Sunday they had put in during their years on the force" ("Sunday Ball in Philadelphia," *TSN*, August 26, 1926, 4). Mack claimed in 1927 that he had to release Ty Cobb because he could not afford to pay him; he argued that Sunday ball would have provided sufficient revenue to retain Cobb, "Cobb Not to Play for Mack in 1928," *NYT*, November 3, 1927, 31.

81. Surdam, *Wins, Losses, & Empty Seats*, 190–92; Bevis, *Sunday Baseball*, 239–41; "Boston Council Plays Politics, Delaying Sunday Sports Law," *TSN*, December 27, 1928, 1.

82. "Brooklyn to Lose Some Extra Dates," *TSN*, November 15, 1928, 2.

83. Sunday Baseball Jangle Had Been On for Six Weeks," *TSN*, February 14, 1929, 2.

84. Surdam, *Wins, Losses, & Empty Seats*, 349.

85. Surdam and Brown, "Major League Baseball," n.p.; U.S. House of Representatives, *OB: Hearings*, 1,610.

86. "Editorial Comment," *BM*, May 1924, 534; Haupert, Baseball Salary Database. Top golfers fell short of earning as much as Babe Ruth, but they still earned

more than many Major League players ("Golf vs. Baseball as a Paying Profession," *Literary Digest*, April 9, 1921, 68–69).

87. Paul Packard, "Gridiron vs. Diamond," BM, January 1922, 657; James Gould, "New Rules on the Gridiron," BM, December 1927, 308.

88. Irving Sanborn, "Does Football Threaten Baseball's Supremacy?" BM, February 1928, 391; James Gould, "The Grand Panorama of Intercollegiate Football," BM, January 1929, 349.

89. Clifford Bloodgood, "Professional Football Reports Progress," BM, December 1930, 313, 327.

90. "Yankees Make Offer for Service Game," NYT, January 4, 1923, 16; "Stadium Panic Has Kickback in Court," TSN, November 14, 1929, 3. John Kieran wrote that the Giants and Yankees used to compete for prestigious college games but later conspired to divide the games between them while maintaining a set price (John Kieran, "Big-League Business," 17).

91. New York Yankees Base Ball Club, Cash books.

92. Tom Swope, "Garry Herrmann Figuring on a Financial Touchdown," TSN, February 25, 1926, 3.

93. "Pro Football and Baseball," TSN, December 10, 1925, 4; Francis Richter, "Casual Comment," TSN, November 18, 1926, 6.

94. "Baseball and Parking Space," TSN, October 18, 1923, 4.

6. Making the Game More Popular

1. "Yanks Adopt Number System," TSN, January 31, 1929, 2; "Numbering the Players," TSN, January 31, 1929, 4; Morris, *A Game of Inches*, 465–66; "Editorial Comment," BM, June 1923, 296. *The Sporting News* waxed sarcastic about the owners' hesitance in providing such elementary information.

2. "Scribbled by Scribes," TSN, March 1, 1923, 4; John Foster, "No Help for the Bettors by Big League Magnates," TSN, March 8, 1923, 5; James Gould, "Why Not Make Official Scoring Really 'Official?'" BM, March 1930, 437–38.

3. Bob Hunter, "Lifting Curtain on Dodgers' Dream House in Fantasy Land," TSN, April 11, 1962, 25–26.

4. F. C. Lane, "The True Inside Dope on the Lively Ball," BM, September 1925, 441; "Much Betting on Game in Chicago," NYT, October 10, 1919, 14. In one ridiculous episode, the Phillies arrested an eleven-year-old boy for keeping a baseball hit into the bleachers; the municipal-court judge ruled that the boy acted with the same "natural impulse" of all boys and was not guilty of larceny ("Boy Who Got Ball in Stands Found Not Guilty of Larceny," NYT, July 20,

1923, 10). Today, of course, the boy's parents would probably sue the Phillies for having their child arrested. Owners weighed the favorable publicity and goodwill by allowing fans to take balls home versus the cost.

5. Kieran, "Big-League Business," 17. The economics of baseballs was interesting. Manufacturers provided balls to the league offices for free in return for being able to advertise that the company was the maker of the official ball. The league sold the balls to the individual clubs, with the funds financing the league ("Saving a Few Thousand Balls," *TSN*, May 17, 1928, 4). Ed Barrow claimed to be the first baseball executive to allow fans to keep balls hit into the stands: "I just got sick and tired of watching the ushers wrestling with the customers and building up a thousand dollars' worth of bad will over a two-dollar baseball" (Barrow, *My Fifty Years in Baseball*, 9).

6. Walter Hapgood, "'How to Get and Hold the Crowds,'" *TSN*, December 14, 1922, 4.

7. Bales, "Baseball's First Bill Veeck," 12; Al DeMaree, "Grand-Stand Girls," 22, 36. Roberts Ehrgott describes ladies' day (Ehrgott, *Mr. Wrigley's Ball Club*, 3-4).

8. Quote in "The Ladies, God Bless 'Em," *TSN*, May 23, 1929, 4.

9. "Bars Free Admission of Women to Games," *NYT*, July 6, 1929, 9; "Ladies' Days at Ball Games Found Successful in West," *NYT*, August 4, 1929, VII: 13; "Women Jam Park, Cash Fans Outside," *TSN*, July 31, 1930, 1; "Editorial Comment," *BM*, September 1930, 480.

10. Graham, *Brooklyn Dodgers*, 179; Surdam, *Wins, Losses, & Empty Seats*, 269-70.

11. Pietrusza, *Major Leagues*, 65.

12. Amusing since no umpires were ever killed in the line of duty; perhaps baseball could have issued the statement, "no umpires were injured during the playing of this game."

13. "Bottles Fly While Robins Break Even," *NYT*, August 12, 1920, 21.

14. "Giants and Braves Get an Even Break," *NYT*, August 16, 1920, 14; "Promises Workhouse Term to Curb Bottle Throwers," *NYT*, August 23, 1920, 15.

15. Francis Richert, "Casual Comments," *TSN*, July 27, 1922, 4.

16. "Yanks Beat Browns Before 30,000 Fans," *NYT*, September 17, 1922, 106; "Fan Declares Witt Was Not Struck by a Thrown Bottle," *NYT*, September 21, 1922, 25; "'Pop Bottle Mystery' Solver Is Lucky Fan," *NYT*, October 2, 1922, 21; Steinberg, "The 'Little World Series' of 1922," 9; "Throw Out the Pop Bottles," *TSN*, May 16, 1929, 4.

17. "Baseball Game in Detroit Ends in a Riot; 18,000 Rush Field; Game Forfeit to Yankees," *NYT*, June 14, 1924, 1.

18. "Meusel and Cole Indefinitely Suspended for Fight at Detroit; Ruth May Be Banned," NYT, June 15, 1924, 25; "Ruth and Meusel Fined $50 and $100," NYT, June 21, 1924, 9.

19. "44,000 Stop Battle as White Sox Lose," NYT, April 27, 1925, 10.

20. "Police Quell Riot as Pirates Win, 7–1," NYT, May 15, 1925, 14.

21. "13 Boys with Tickets Hurt at Yankee Stadium When Swarm of Ticketless Lads Storm Gates," NYT, July 3, 1925, 1.

22. George Robbins, "Chicago Fandom Forced to Accept One Thing as a Fact," TSN, November 28, 1918, 1.

23. "League Says Yanks Shall Have a Park," NYT, August 25, 1920, 17.

24. "Waiver Route Probable," NYT, August 5, 1922, 12.

25. "Washington Feels Pennant Is Won," NYT, September 22, 1924, 22; "Pirates Build for Series," NYT, September 20, 1925, S2; Ralph Davis, "Pirates Best Team Ever, Says Clarke," TSN, October 8, 1925, 1.

26. "Robins Lose Their Cage," NYT, August 9, 1918, 8; "Better Use for Ball Parks," TSN, October 31, 1918, 4.

27. "Discuss Ousting of Yanks," NYT, May 21, 1920, 11; "Hunt for Home Is Spared to Yanks," NYT, May 22, 1920, 19. The team considered a proposed lease of the Polo Grounds from the National Exhibition Company on February 27, 1915; the terms included a $55,000 rental fee (New York Public Library, New York Yankees Baseball Club Collection, Third Folder, 1915–38).

28. Weintraub, *House That Ruth Built*, 136.

29. "Yankee Ball Park Big Sports Arena," NYT, August 30, 1922, 20; "Scribbled by Scribes," TSN, November 29, 1923, 4; "Agreed against This Alliance," TSN, August 16, 1923, 4; "To Continue Bouts in Baseball Parks," NYT, November 25, 1922, 18; "Johnson Puts Ban on Bouts in Park," NYT, October 20, 1923, 13; "Rickard Arranges First Stadium Card," NYT, March 5, 1925, 16. F. C. Lane argued that what an owner, "does with his park in the meantime [apart from baseball games] appears to be his own affair." He disputed Johnson's authority to dictate what events could or could not be held within stadiums (F. C. Lane, "The Enlarged Polo Grounds' Park: Baseball's Most Famous Stadium," BM, April 1924, 522).

30. "Yankee Colonels Silent on Stadium," NYT, February 1, 1921, 12; Weintraub, *House That Ruth Built*, 41, 49; Sullivan, *Diamond in the Bronx*, xii–xiii.

31. Weintraub, *House That Ruth Built*, 137; New York Yankees Base Ball Club, Cash books. The *New York Times* reported a figure of $3.5 million ("Yankees' New Park Almost Completed," NYT, March 11, 1923, S1). The Yankees discussed

buying property in the Bronx with a price of $550,000 (New York Public Library, New York Yankees Baseball Club Collection, Third Folder, 1915–38, Meeting of March 31, 1921).

32. "An Experiment in New York," *TSN*, January 26, 1922, 4.

33. "Fans Interested in New Stadium," *NYT*, March 25, 1923, S1; "Yankee Stadium Seats Only 62,000," *NYT*, May 17, 1923, 15. The stadium's seating capacity fluctuated throughout the 1920s, reaching a high of 82,000, see Lowry, *Green Cathedrals*, 160.

34. Joe Vila, "Faults Are Found with New Ball Park of the Yankees," *TSN*, March 15, 1923, 1.

35. "To Enlarge Polo Grounds Stands," *NYT*, October 14, 1919, 20; "Enlarged Stands Will Seat 62,000," *NYT*, October 23, 1921, 96.

36. Lieb, *Detroit Tigers*, 173; K. W. Hall, "Work of Enlarging Navin Field Starts," *TSN*, August 10, 1922, 1.

37. Lowry, *Green Cathedrals*, 236; Paul Eaton, "Griff Showing His Confidence in Fans," *TSN*, December 8, 1921, 3; "Senators to Seat 35,000," *NYT*, August 22, 1923, 11; "Washington So Sure of World's Series That Bids for Seats Already Exceed Supply," *NYT*, July 4, 1925, 7.

38. "Cubs' New Single-Deck Stand Will Be Largest in Country," *NYT*, February 24, 1923, 8; "Red Sox Owners Will Spend $300,000 to Improve Grounds," *NYT*, December 2, 1923, S4; "New Stand at Pirates' Park Will Raise Capacity to 40,000," *NYT*, January 25, 1925, S2; "Reds to Construct $1,500,000 Stadium," *NYT*, April 29, 1925, 17; Lowry, *Green Cathedrals*, 66.

39. "Attitude of Cards Halts Ball's Plan," *TSN*, October 26, 1922, 1; "Phil Ball Weighs Top with Bottom," *TSN*, December 24, 1925, 1.

40. John Sheridan, "Back of the Home Plate," *TSN*, March 27, 1924, 4.

41. "Stadium for 80,000 New Home of Indians," *NYT*, November 17, 1927, 23; Lowry, *Green Cathedrals*, 73.

42. "Joshing versus Business in Baseball," *Literary Digest*, April 28, 1923, 76.

43. "Is Professional Baseball Sport?" *Literary Digest*, September 17, 1921, 50.

44. "This Our Latest Problem," *TSN*, April 27, 1922, 4; "Casual Comment," *TSN*, May 31, 1928, 4.

45. John Sheridan, "Back of the Home Plate," *TSN*, August 17, 1922, 4; New York Public Library, New York Yankees Baseball Club, Yankees Baseball Collection, "Minutes of a Special Meeting of the Board of Directors, October 24, 1939" and "Minutes of February 20, 1941 Meeting." Sheridan predicted an optimistic outcome from broadcasting home games.

46. "Radio Permit Denied by Giants' Officials," *NYT*, May 23, 1923, S2. For the continuing debate on radio during the Great Depression, see Surdam, *Wins, Losses, & Empty Seats*, 197–218.

47. "Radio and Printed Word," *TSN*, June 7, 1923, 4. For a more disinterested viewpoint, see Raymond Yates, "How Radio Magnifies the World's Series," *BM*, November 1925, 555–56.

48. Smith, *Baseless Fears*, 20–36; Bales, "Baseball's First Bill Veeck," 12; "Barnard Favors $50,000 Broadcasting Charge," *TSN*, December 5, 1929, 5.

49. "Admissions and Sport," *TSN*, October 25, 1928, 4; N. J. Abodaher, "Baseball via the Ether Waves," *BM*, November 1929, 552.

50. "Casual Comment," *TSN*, September 8, 1927, 4; "Radio, Press and Magnates," *TSN*, August 16, 1928, 4; Weintraub, *House That Ruth Built*, 300–301; James Gould, "Is the Radio Good for Baseball?" *BM*, July 1930, 341–42, 373–74.

51. Allen, *Cincinnati Reds*, 203.

52. "Advertisement," *TSN*, November 19, 1925, 7.

53. "Turn Thumbs Down on Twilight Game," *NYT*, July 2, 1918, 10.

54. Negro Leagues Baseball Museum, "eMuseum: Historical Timeline," http://www.nlbemuseum.com/history/timeline6.html, accessed December 11, 2016.

7. Not a Perfect Game

1. "To Speed Up Ball Games," *NYT*, July 26, 1924, 6; Irving Sanborn, "President Barnard Holds the Stop Watch," *BM*, June 1928, 301–3, 326–27; "Editorial Comment," *BM*, June 1928, 290, 326. Ban Johnson encouraged his owners to eliminate dead spots in ball games; he believed too much time was wasted arguing calls or engaging in dilatory behavior on the diamond. Some observers, though, defended the leisurely pace; baseball was unlike football and basketball with their emphasis on the clock ("Scribbled by Scribes," *TSN*, August 7, 1924, 4; "Stop-Watching Ball Games," *TSN*, March 29, 1928, 4). The average game length (not separated by league) was a little longer in 1921 than 1920, but the average trend was toward slower games (Lindholm, "Baseball Game Length."

2. F. C. Lane, "Is Base Stealing Doomed?" *BM*, June 1921, 297–302, 326; "The Hidden Risks in Base Stealing," *BM*, June 1922, 295–97; "What Are the Odds on the Base Stealers?" *BM*, June 1926, 307–8, 326. According to Baseball-Reference.com, American League players had a 73.9 percent rate of success in 2013; National League players had a 71.9 percent rate that season.

3. "Base Stealing Has Become a Lost Art," *TSN*, January 6, 1921, 3.

4. Quote in F. C. Lane, "The Faulty Foundation of Batting Averages," BM, January 1929, 349; John Ward, "How Big League Parks Distort Slugging Records," BM, September 1929, 450; Irving Sanborn, "The Big Barrier to Proposed Changes in Baseball Records," BM, July 1928, 343–44.

5. Irving Sanborn, "Some Needed Changes in the Baseball Records," BM, August 1922, 401–3, 421; J. C. Koford, "What We Can Learn from 'Total Bases,'" BM, June 1922, 309–10, 334, 336; "Scribbled by Scribes," TSN, August 2, 1923, 4.

6. "Baseball Season Is Record Maker," NYT, July 27, 1919, 21; "Home Run Epidemic Hits Major Leagues," NYT, May 24, 1921, 23.

7. Ed Murray, "The Home Run Angle," BM, October 1930, 509.

8. "Says Homers Due to Changes in Bat," NYT, July 19, 1925, S6; "Lively Controversy over the Lively Ball," Literary Digest, October 5, 1929, 81. One fan suggested that leagues limit bat thickness and length, but nothing resulted from this suggestion. By the 1950s and 1960s, such fabled home run hitters as Henry Aaron were using lighter bats and relying on their wrists to power the ball (F. C. Lane, "The Much Discussed Menace of the Lively Ball," BM, October 1929, 505).

9. Vincent, "How Rules Changes in 1920 Affected Home Runs," 19–22; F. C. Lane, "Should the Lively Baseball be Abolished?" BM, August 1925, 407–408.

10. "Passing of Trick Pitching," Literary Digest, October 6, 1928, 48–49, for a history of trick pitching; "American League Meets and Moguls Decide to Take Dimes and Nickels for Tax," NYT, February 15, 1918, 6; John Sheridan, "Back of the Home Plate," TSN, September 20, 1923, 4.

11. "Says Homers Due to Change in Bat," NYT, July 19, 1925, S6.

12. Quote in "Magnates Approve the 'Rabbit Ball,'" NYT, July 16, 1925, 15; "Says Homers Due to Change in Bat," NYT, July 19, 1925, S6; F. C. Lane, "The True Inside Dope on the Lively Ball," BM, September 1925, 439; Vincent, "How Rules Changes in 1920 Affected Home Runs," 21–22. Sportswriter Irving Sanborn was one of the reporters who subscribed to Professor Fales's findings (Irving Sanborn, "Is the 'Rabbit' Baseball's Most Famous Alibi?" BM, October 1925, 492).

13. "Says Tests Reveal Ball Is Not Lively," NYT, August 28, 1929, 22. The A. J. Reach Company improved baseballs late in 1925; the company used a cushioned cork center: "The center . . . is surrounded by black semi-vulcanized rubber, over which is vulcanized another cover of red rubber. This cushion of red rubber is supposed to take some of the liveliness out of the 'Jack Rabbit' which was in use until late in 1925" ("Scribbled by Scribes," TSN, January 7, 1926, 4).

14. "Telling Where All the Baseballs Go," *TSN*, December 30, 1920, 5.

15. "Used 46,164 Baseballs," *NYT*, December 9, 1925, 32: "National Leaguers Move for Peace," *NYT*, December 15, 1926, 23; "Scribbled by Scribes," *TSN*, April 16, 1925, 3.

16. Barthel, *Baseball Barnstorming*, 90.

17. John Sheridan, "Back of the Plate," *TSN*, August 7, 1924, 4; "Comment on Current Events in Sports: Baseball," *NYT*, April 2, 1923, 21.

18. F. C. Lane, "Should the Lively Baseball Be Abolished?" *BM*, August 1925, 407-8.

19. "Few Changes in Baseball Code," *NYT*, January 31, 1926, S1; "Editorial Comment," *BM*, January 1924, 344; "Dreyfuss Would Cut Homers to Doubles When 'Rabbit Ball' Goes over Short Fences," *NYT*, July 15, 1925, 12. Apparently the Boston Braves decided to erect bleachers close in to the playing field for the 1928 season in the hopes of increasing the number of home runs for its hitters. The plan backfired. In 1927 the Braves hit but 37 home runs; they bolstered their total to 52 the following season. Unfortunately, the team's pitchers went from yielding 43 home runs to 100 home runs in 1928 ("Casual Comment," *TSN*, May 17, 1928, 4).

20. "Survey Condemns Home-Run Epidemic," *NYT*, July 14, 1929, S5; "The Lively Controversy," *Literary Digest*, October 5, 1929, 79.

21. "Sweeping Changes in Baseball Code," *NYT*, February 10, 1920, 19; F. C. Lane, "The Erratic Career of the Base on Balls," *BM*, June 1925, 306; John Sheridan, "Back of the Home Plate," *TSN*, August 2, 1923, 4.

22. "American League Hits Heydler Plan," *NYT*, December 12, 1928, 39; "Baseball Season to End Week Later," *NYT*, December 14, 1928, 32; other articles on the subject appear in the days before and after this article.

23. "Scribbled by Scribes," *TSN*, December 20, 1928, 4.

24. "Let Us Be Logical," *TSN*, October 13, 1927, 4.

25. H. G. Salsinger, "Ruth Is Hero Where Once Cobb Reigned," *TSN*, August 5, 1920, 1.

26. "Critics Discuss What's to Be Done about the Fallen Ruth," *TSN*, November 2, 1922, 6; Francis Richter, "Casual Comments," *TSN*, July 6, 1922, 4.

27. *Literary Digest*, "What Is Babe Ruth Worth to the Yankees?" March 29, 1930, 40, 76.

8. The Stars Are Realigned

1. "'Inside Baseball'—From the Owner's View Point," *Literary Digest*, April 8, 1922, 46.

2. Quote in F. C. Lane, "The Winning Combination," BM, November 1928, 531; "An Army of A's and Still No Ball Team," TSN, January 6, 1921, 8.

3. New York Yankees Base Ball Club, "Players Purchased and Sold;" $20,000 on February 16 and $17,500 on July 7, 1916.

4. "Where Does the Failure Lie?" TSN, July 1, 1920, 4.

5. Lieb, *Boston Red Sox*, 139; the *Macmillan Baseball Encyclopedia* lists the price as $55,000, *Macmillan Baseball Encyclopedia*, 2,697.

6. Speaker demanded $10,000 of the $50,000 or $55,000 sale price from Lannin—not from Cleveland—and the owner acquiesced rather than lose the deal (Lewis, *Cleveland Indians*, 86). As a footnote, Harry Frazee eventually sold Sad Sam Jones to the Yankees, where he perked up.

7. "Bush and Schang Sold," NYT, December 15, 1917, 10; Lieb, *Boston Red Sox*, 160; Mack claimed that Strunk, Schang, and Bush "considered themselves so far superior to the young players on the club that harmony was impossible." But these three players were still young too, so his explanation seems odd ("Cubs and Red Sox Scattering Money," NYT, January 6, 1918, 27).

8. "Scribbled by Scribes," TSN, February 7, 1918, 4. Lynch's *Harry Frazee* provides a comprehensive discussion.

9. F. C. Lane, "Carl Mays' Cynical Definition of Pitching Efficiency," BM, August 1928, 390.

10. Quote in "Mays Injunction Hearing Is Delayed," NYT, September 6, 1919, 16; "Yankees Get Carl Mays," NYT, July 31, 1919, 6; "Yanks' Owners Are Sustained by Court," NYT, October 26, 1919, S7; Lieb, *Boston Red Sox*, 181. See also Lynch, *Harry Frazee*, 68–75.

11. New York Yankees Base Ball Club, "Players Purchased and Sold," July 31, 1919.

12. "Mays's Suspension Shock to Yankees," NYT, August 1, 1919, 18; "Discuss Mays Case Today," NYT, August 3, 1919, 17; "Comment on Current Events in the World of Sports," NYT, August 4, 1919, 18.

13. "Ruppert Answers Navin," NYT, October 11, 1919, 10.

14. "Owners of Yanks to Enjoin Johnson," NYT, August 4, 1919, 17. Throughout the remainder of the season, the *New York Times* and the *Sporting News* ran articles pertaining to the brouhaha.

15. Ball's quote in "War of Factions in American League," NYT, August 10, 1919, 18; "Injunction Issued against Johnson," NYT, August 7, 1919, 16; "Cleveland Stock Held by Johnson," NYT, September 5, 1919, 21. During the hearing, the Yankees' attorney suggested that it was dangerous to allow the president of the league to hold stock in a club in that league; the attorney ignored the fact

that Garry Herrmann, chairman of the National Commission, owned the Cincinnati Reds. Edward Woolley pointed out, though, that owners such as Charles Somers of Cleveland, floated loans to fellow owners during the American League's earliest years ("Mays Injunction Hearing Is Delayed," *NYT*, September 6, 1919, 16;Woolley, "Business of Baseball," 252).

16. "Two Clubs Accept Yanks' Invitation," *NYT*, August 8, 1919, 17; "Mays Case Nears Peaceful Ending," *NYT*, August 12, 1919, 16. Adding the volatile Mays to the White Sox's divisive atmosphere raised the specter of a ball club imploding.

17. Quote in "Yanks' Owners Are Sustained by Court," *NYT*, October 26, 1919, 87; "Owners of New York Yankees Start Suit against Ban Johnson for $500,000 Damages," *NYT*, February 3, 1920, 16.

18. "Comment on Current Events in Sports: No Third League in Sight," *NYT*, November 10, 1919, 14; "American League Directors Prepare for Legal Action against National Commission," *NYT*, November 20, 1919, 15; "New Board Gives Yankees a Shock," *NYT*, December 17, 1919, 20.

19. "American League Strife Is Ended," *NYT*, February 11, 1920, 18; "Ban Johnson's Retirement Predicted by Baseball Men as a Result of New Peace Terms," *NYT*, February 12, 1920, 13.

20. "American League Waives on Mays," *NYT*, December 4, 1923, 17; "Mays Sold to Reds; Big Bid for Hornsby," *NYT*, December 12, 1923, 26. Through no fault of his own, Mays' acquisition by the Reds' caused another controversy. All of the American League teams waived on Mays, as did all but two National League clubs—Cincinnati and Philadelphia. The Phillies disputed the Mays trade to the Reds and asked Landis to rescind the deal; for the Yankees, if the deal stood, they would receive $25,000, but if the Phillies' waiver claim was upheld, the Yankees would get just the $5,000 waiver price ("Landis Threatens to Quit Baseball," *NYT*, December 13, 1923, 26).

21. Lieb, *Boston Red Sox*, 178.

22. Lieb, *Boston Red Sox*, 185–87. An interesting coincidence regarding Scott was his streak of 1,307 consecutive games played; his streak ended on May 6, 1925; Lou Gehrig began his streak a week later ("Shortstop Everett Is Benched; Consecutive Game Record Ends at 1,307," *NYT*, May 7, 1925, 13).

23. New York Yankees Base Ball Club, "Players Purchased and Sold," July 25, 1922; "3-Team Deal Sends Peck to Senators," *NYT*, January 11, 1922, 30; "Yankees Get Dugan from the Red Sox," *NYT*, July 24, 1922, 17; Graham, *New York Yankees*, 80–81.

24. Frazee quote in "Dugan Deal Causes Storm of Protests," *NYT*, July 25, 1922, 24; "Yankees Get Dugan from the Red Sox," *NYT*, July 24, 1922, 17.

25. "Ban Johnson Calls Deal 'Regrettable,'" *NYT*, July 25, 1922, 24; Ira Irving, "The Mysteries of the Baseball 'Waiver' Rule," *BM*, September 1928, 448.

26. "Big Prices Doomed in Baseball Deals," *NYT*, February 1, 1918, 10; "Scribbled by Scribes," *TSN*, November 27, 1919, 4.

27. "Written Law Helpless Here," *TSN*, February 7, 1918, 4.

28. "Editorial Comment," *BM*, January 1924, 344.

29. John Sheridan, "Back of the Home Plate," *TSN*, February 16, 1922, 4; "Editorial Comment," *BM*, February 1923, 395.

30. "What Price Victory?" *TSN*, October 18, 1928, 4.

31. Stetson Palmer, "The Mystery of Chronic Losers," *BM*, July 1929, 357.

32. "Comment on Current Events in Sports: Baseball," *NYT*, December 26, 1921, 21.

33. "Scribbled by Scribes," *TSN*, January 26, 1922, 4.

34. "Senators Get Ruel from the Red Sox," *NYT*, February 11, 1923, S2.

35. "Ruth Bought by New York Americans for $125,000, Highest Price in Baseball Annals," *NYT*, January 6, 1920, 16; trade listed as January 3 in the *Macmillan Baseball Encyclopedia*, 2,681.

36. H. G. Salsinger, "Ruth Is Hero Where Once Cobb Reigned," *TSN*, August 5, 1920, 1. Frazee was paying a higher rate of interest to Ruppert for the Fenway loan than Ruppert was paying to Frazee on the four installments of the Ruth purchase (due to the mortgage being long term and the purchase price being short-term loans). And since Ruppert held the mortgage on Fenway, this was essentially a zero-risk deal for the colonel. So even if this was a baseball deal, it effectively reduced the net price paid by Ruppert for Ruth (Haupert, personal note; he has a copy of the deal).

37. Quote in "No Connection with Club," *NYT*, December 2, 1920, 18; "Records Give New View of Ruth Deal," *NYT*, November 27, 1920, 17.

38. "The New York-Boston Case," *TSN*, December 2, 1920, 4; During the 1951 congressional hearings, committee members questioned then-commissioner Ford Frick regarding the series of trades between the Red Sox and Yankees (U.S. House of Representatives, *OB: Report*, 61).

39. Graham, *New York Yankees*, 47.

40. Weintraub, *House That Ruth Built*, 222; "Ruth Wants $15,000," *NYT*, February 10, 1920, 19. The canard that Frazee needed money to finance *No, No, Nanette* is palpably false. The musical did not debut until 1925. Sportswriter Frederick Lieb, no fan of Frazee's, wrote that Frazee told him, "The Ruth deal was the only way I could retain the Red Sox." Frazee's baseball manager, Edward Barrow, warned Frazee not to sell Ruth, saying, "You can't do this to me,

Harry. Why, Ruth is the biggest attraction in baseball" (Lieb, *Boston Red Sox*, 182–83).

41. Quote in "Babe Ruth Accepts Terms of Yankees," NYT, January 7, 1920, 22; "Transfer of Contract Does Not End Story of Ruth Deal," TSN, January 15, 1920, 5. See Lynch, *Harry Frazee*, 106-29 for a detailed examination of the deal.

42. "Comment on Current Events in Sports: Ruth as a Gothamite," NYT, January 12, 1920, 11; New York Yankees, Cash books.

43. Thomas Rice, "What Babe Ruth at $125,000 Means in Turnstile Count to New York Yankees," TSN, January 15, 1920, 3.

44. Haupert and Winter, "Pay Ball: Estimating the Profitability," 96; Haupert and Winter, "Yankee Profits and Promise" for a fuller accounting of Ruth's effects upon the team's finances.

45. "Transfer of Contract Does Not End Story of Ruth Deal," TSN, January 15, 1920, 5.

46. "Yanks Cannot Buy Sisler," NYT, October 14, 1920, 20.

47. Quote in "M'Quillan Deal Comment Is Mild," NYT, August 1, 1922, 22; "Nehf Comes to Giants," NYT, August 2, 1919, 11; "Player Transfers in Major Leagues," NYT, August 3, 1919, 18. The $100,000 price for McQuillan is also discussed in Francis Richter, "Casual Comment," TSN, August 17, 1922, 4; Graham, *New York Giants*, 114, 135. If the Giants really paid $100,000 for McQuillan, they must have had money to burn; the pitcher went 6-6 for the Giants during the latter part of 1922 and only 15-14 in 1923.

48. Lieb and Baumgartner, *Philadelphia Phillies*, 146; Graham, *New York Giants*, 119.

49. "Scribbled by Scribes," TSN, February 16, 1922, 4.

50. "Scribbled by Scribes," TSN, June 16, 1921, 4; "M'Graw Gets Groh in Deal with Reds," NYT, December 7, 1921, 23; "Groh Reinstated; Cannot Be Traded," NYT, June 10, 1921, 19; Allen, *Cincinnati Reds*, 156.

51. Ritter, *Glory of Their Times*, 214.

52. Lieb and Baumgartner, *Philadelphia Phillies*, 157-58.

53. "Call Big Leagues to Join Session," NYT, December 5, 1917, 12.

54. "Written Law Helpless Here," TSN, February 7, 1918, 4. The author of this book is surprised that the editorialist used the phrase, "making an ass of himself."

55. "National League Takes Firm Stand," NYT, December 10, 1919, 14; the American League owners enacted similar legislation, see "American Leaguers Busy," NYT, February 11, 1920, 18; "Weeghman Obtains Alexander and Killefer for Cubs, Paying $50,000 in Big Baseball Deal," NYT, December 12, 1917, 16.

Weeghman also acquired Dode Paskett and Lefty Tyler from the Phillies and Braves respectively to bolster his pennant-winning Cubs ("Cubs and Red Sox Scattering Money," NYT, January 6, 1918, 27).

56. "Big Offer for Hornsby," NYT, December 23, 1919, 10; "Giants May Deal over Rickey's Head," TSN, January 29, 1920, 2; "Hornsby Not on Market," NYT, June 13, 1920, 24; "Denies $500,000 Offer by Cubs for Hornsby," NYT, November 6, 1924, 15; "Record Offer for Hornsby Declined," NYT, December 30, 1920, 19.

57. "Leagues Prepare to Assist Landis," NYT, November 30, 1920, 19.

58. "Rickey Comes Here to Trade Hornsby," NYT, November 10, 1923, 11.

59. "Hornsby to Remain a Card," NYT, November 11, 1926, 29.

60. "Breadon Reported Ready to Trade Hornsby; Giants and Cubs Loom as Leading Bidders," NYT, December 16, 1926, 31.

61. James Harrison, "Giants Get Hornsby; Trade Big Surprise," NYT, December 21, 1926, 1, 26; Joe Vila, "John M'Graw Weaving Strong Fabric on Giant Pennant Loom," TSN, February 17, 1927, 1.

62. John Kieran, "Sports of the *Times*," NYT, April 2, 1927, 15; "Hornsby Meeting Called Tomorrow," NYT, April 7, 1927, 17. At first rumors floated that Charles Stoneham would reimburse Breadon for the difference in value attached to the 1,167 shares; another exciting rumor was that Al Jolson, entertainer par excellence, would purchase Hornsby's shares ("St. Louis Aroused over Hornsby Deal," NYT, December 22, 1926, 17; "Al Jolson Makes Offer to Buy Hornsby's Stock in the Cards," NYT, December 28, 1926, 14).

63. "M'Graw Is Booming Stock of Cardinals," NYT, March 6, 1927, S1, S3; Graham, *New York Giants*, 172. There were many articles in the *New York Times* and the *Sporting News* regarding the contretemps.

64. "Hornsby Accepts $100,000 for Stock," NYT, April 10, 1927, S1.

65. "Hornsby Is Traded 'For Good of Giants,'" NYT, January 11, 1928, 32; Graham, *New York Giants*, 176.

66. Joe Vila, "Vila Sums Up Why Hornsby Departed," TSN, January 19, 1928, 3; "$70,000 Suit Filed against Hornsby," NYT, January 28, 1927, 11. Alexander discusses Hornsby's gambling lawsuit (Alexander, *Rogers Hornsby*, 142-44).

67. "Editorial Comment," BM, March 1928, 438; "Hornsby Deal Made 'To Avoid Conflict,'" NYT, January 12, 1928, 34." The Braves would eventually get Babe Ruth for a few months in 1935; the results were disappointing.

68. Irving Vaughan, "Cub Fans See Flag Coming with Rajah," TSN, November 15, 1928, 1

69. F. C. Lane, "The Amazing Hornsby Deal," BM, March 1928, 435.

9. Competitive Balance

1. Quirk and Fort, *Pay Dirt*, 244–46; Scully, *Business of Major League Baseball*, 87–93.

2. Quirk and Fort, *Pay Dirt*, 247; Scully, *Business of Major League Baseball*, 89–91.

3. John Sheridan, "Back of the Home Plate," TSN, September 7, 1922, 4. Sheridan voiced similar complaints in 1920, denigrating the National League champion Brooklyn club: "the playing standard of baseball has declined as far as the great old National League is concerned.... The playing standard of the American League has not declined as far as the playing standard of the National League" (John Sheridan, "Back of the Home Plate," TSN, December 2, 1920, 4).

4. Coase, "Problem of Social Cost," 1–44; Rottenberg, "Baseball Players' Labor Market," 242–56. In the reserve-clause era, it was rare for an owner to release a player from his contract outright, unless his perceived future value was zero. Otherwise, he would sell the player contract to another MLB team or a Minor League team. Since player contracts were essentially perpetual, it was usually only when a player's expected value was zero that his contract would be terminated rather than sold for at least some scrap value.

5. Thomas Rice, "Searchers for Pitchers Can Get in Touch with Robinson," TSN, June 16, 1921, 3.

6. Surdam, "What Brings Fans to the Ball Park?" 40–41.

7. "Old Stars Dirt Cheap Compared to Modern," TSN, December 22, 1921, 8.

8. H. G. Salsinger, "Navin Sees Merit in Griff's Reforms," TSN, January 9, 1919, 5.

9. Barrow, *My Fifty Years in Baseball*, 56.

10. "President Tener of National League Puts Quietus on Resignation Rumor," NYT, December 18, 1917, 19.

11. "Huggins Trades Five Players to Get Pratt for the Yankees," NYT, January 23, 1918, 6; "Sisler Deal Still Brewing," NYT, December 25, 1917, 18.

12. Ira Irving, "The Mysteries of the Baseball 'Waiver' Rule," BM, September 1928, 447–48; "Landis Announces a Plan to Strengthen Weaker Teams," NYT, November 13, 1923, 17; "Gehrig Leaves Yanks to Play under Option with Hartford," NYT, April 15, 1924.

13. Oscar Reichow, "Kid Gleason Thinks White Sox Are Given Shabby Treatment," TSN, December 23, 1920, 1.

14. Stoney McGlinn, "What's Wrong with the Athletics?" BM, November 1927, 542. Mack was reviled for selling all of his star players, with one writer bemoaning,

"How long will Mack be permitted to burlesque baseball in Philadelphia? He is no longer playing good faith with Philadelphia fans or with fans of the other American League cities. If he does not care to play big league ball let him get out and have some one [*sic*] take over the club" ("Who Should Call Mack Burlesquer?" *TSN*, February 28, 1918, 4).

15. "Editorial Comment," *BM*, July 1927, 363.

16. "Ball to Rebuild the Browns; Sisler Not in Four to Stay," *NYT*, July 27, 1927, 18.

17. Sparks, *Frank "Home Run" Baker*, 174.

18. "Pipp and Lewis Send in Contracts as Huggins Begins Roundup of Yankees," *NYT*, February 25, 1919, 12.

19. "Huggins Retained to Manage Yanks," *NYT*, October 29, 1920, 22; Graham, *New York Yankees*, 64. Spatz and Steinberg hail the hiring of Barrow and describe how manager Miller Huggins and Barrow specialized in their roles (Spatz and Steinberg, *1921: The Yankees, The Giants*, 51-55).

20. Joe Vila, "Huggins Drives Official Spike in Trade Rumors Naming Yanks," *TSN*, November 17, 1927, 1.

21. Surdam, *Wins, Losses, & Empty Seats*, 137; Levitt, *Ed Barrow*, 304; see also Armour and Levitt, *Pursuit of Pennants*, for a general discussion. Fetter, too, claims that the Yankees used superior management techniques (Fetter, *Taking on the Yankees*, 9-12).

22. "Yanks Bound to Win Now," *TSN*, February 10, 1921, 3.

23. Lewis, *Cleveland Indians*, 107; "Assembling a Winner," *NYT*, October 5, 1920, 19.

24. Johnson's signing, http://sabr.org/bioproj/person/0e5ca45c; Paul Eaton, "Griff Shows Faith in Game's Future," *TSN*, February 2, 1922, 3; Paul Eaton, "Griffith Bids High for Future Honors," *TSN*, September 14, 1922, 3; Paul Eaton, "New Players Cost Senators $124,500," *TSN*, January 15, 1925, 1; "Griffith Balances Books and Finds New Men Cost $154,750," *TSN*, January 16, 1930, 1.

25. William Killefer, "Rebuilding a Major League Ball Club," *BM*, September 1923, 440.

26. Harry Neilly, "How a Poor Baseball Franchise Became a Gold Mine," *BM*, May 1927, 574, see also 557.

27. James Gould, "Considering the Cardinals," *BM*, November 1928, 533-34.

28. James Gould, "The Ever-Changing Cardinals," *BM*, February 1929, 393-94.

29. Surdam, "Coase Theorem," 207–10. The effects of integration on the distribution is an interesting question.

30. Surdam, "Coase Theorem," 208.

31. Warren Brown, "They Come High in San Francisco," BM, August 1922, 407.

32. "Shortsighted Boys," TSN, December 20, 1928, 4; Francis Richter, "Casual Corner," TSN, December 4, 1924, 4; "Baseball Players Who Are Sold," *Literary Digest*, December 6, 1924, 73–74; "Not Good Business," TSN, November 4, 1926, 4.

33. "Bill Seeks Tax of 90 Per Cent. On Sales of Baseball Players," NYT, February 3, 1925, 26.

34. Ford Sawyer, "The Price of a Rookie," BM, June 1923, 305.

35. F. C. Lane, "A Twenty-Two Thousand Dollar Gamble," BM, October 1914, 50.

36. "Giants Give Seven Men for Earl Smith," TSN, January 9, 1919, 5.

37. "Yanks Buy Many Players," NYT, August 21, 1919, 12.

38. Quote in "Scout Reports on Minor Stars Vary," TSN, January 5, 1922, 7; "Giants Pay $75,000 for Young Player," NYT, December 8, 1921, 27; George Berto, "Kepper Has More Trades in Prospect," TSN, December 29, 1921, 6.

39. Joe Vila, "Johnson Elated That Frazee Finally Is out of Baseball," TSN, July 19, 1923, 1.

40. Ford Frick, "Crosses of Gold in Baseball," BM, May 1925, 570.

41. John Sheridan, "Back of the Home Plate," TSN, December 22, 1921, 4. Sheridan made a fanciful estimate: he assumed that Rogers Hornsby was worth twenty times O'Connell's value, or $1.5 million. He thought Hornsby should get 6 percent of his value in yearly salary, so he deduced that Hornsby should have gotten $90,000 a year in salary, far in excess of his actual salary.

42. George Berto, "Kepper Has More Trades in Prospect," TSN, December 29, 1921, 6.

43. "Baseball Business from the Inside," *Collier's*, March 25, 1922, 16.

44. Eugene Karst, "What Will He Hit in the Majors?" BM, March 1929, 441–42.

45. "White Sox Give $100,000 and Two Players for Coast Star," NYT, May 30, 1922, 19.

46. Warren Brown, "They Come High in San Francisco," BM, August 1922, 407.

47. W. A. Phelon, "Sixth Place Best in Sight for the Reds," TSN, September 1, 1921, 2.

48. Allen, *Cincinnati Reds*, 168.

49. First quote in "M'Graw in Denial of Cannon Claim," NYT, November 1, 1922, 24; second quote in Joe Vila, "Jack Bentley Was Bought by John M'Graw for His Own Use," TSN, November 9, 1922, 1.

50. "Obdurate Dunn May Come Off His Perch," *TSN*, December 14, 1922, 1; "Brooklyn Offers $100,000 for Boley," *NYT*, April 28, 1923, 10; "Bid for Boley Refused," *NYT*, May 30, 1923, 11.

51. Charles Foreman, "Orioles Weather a Tough Trip Abroad," *TSN*, August 2, 1923, 3; Honig, *Baseball When the Grass Was Real*, 64.

52. "Landis Is Firm on Meeting Date," *NYT*, December 6, 1922, 25; "Athletics Buy Strand," *NYT*, December 12, 1923, 20; "Mack Makes Still Another Big Deal," *TSN*, December 20, 1923, 1.

53. "Groves [*sic*] Sale Confirmed," *NYT*, October 17, 1924, 25; Charles Foreman, "Dunn-Mack Instalment Plan Revealed by Groves' Purchase," *TSN*, November 6, 1924, 6; James Isaminger, "Connie Mack Gets First Choice Any Time Jack Dunn Unloads," *TSN*, December 23, 1920, 1. When Dunn died, some observers were shocked to discover that Mack did not, in fact, own any shares in the Baltimore club (Don Riley, "Baltimore Interests Go Begging for Buyer," *TSN*, November 22, 1928, 5).

54. "Given to Portland," *TSN*, November 20, 1924, 1; "Athletics Give Orioles $50,000 for Earnshaw," *NYT*, May 29, 1928, 19.

55. "Big Deal Depends upon One Player," *NYT*, December 19, 1922, 26; Joe Vila, "Vila Has an Idea of Why Deal for Jakey May Fell Through," *TSN*, January 18, 1923, 1.

56. Joe Vila, "They Should All Star if Prices Paid Count," *TSN*, March 8, 1923, 7; "Detroit Jumps into Big Money to Beat Off Rival Major Bidding," *TSN*, December 13, 1928, 1; Lieb, *Detroit Tigers*, 189; Lewis, *Cleveland Indians*, 163.

57. Lieb, *Pittsburgh Pirates*, 189; Parker, *Big and Little Poison*, 35.

58. Graham, *Brooklyn Dodgers*, 87.

59. "Landis Not Certain Peace Will Prevail," *NYT*, December 14, 1923, 25; Francis Richter, "Casual Comment," *TSN*, December 27, 1923, 4.

60. "Louisville Star Bought by Giants," *NYT*, January 6, 1924, 51; "Sale of Baldwin Upheld by Landis," *NYT*, January 29, 1924, 14.

61. "Editorial Comment," *BM*, March 1926, 438.

62. Francis Richter, "Casual Comment," *TSN*, September 16, 1926, 4.

63. Levitt, *Ed Barrow*, table 8, no pagination.

64. "Lary and Reese Are Bought by Yankees," *NYT*, January 5, 1928, 35; "What Strategy Prompted Yanks to Purchase Lary," *NYT*, January 8, 1928, XI:3.

65. J. Newton Colver, "Future Keystone of the Yankee's Infield," *BM*, April 1928, 499; Barrow, *My Fifty Years in Baseball*, 181.

66. F. C. Lane, "Ed Barrow, 'The Power behind the Throne,'" *BM*, February 1927, 395-96. As early as 1917, the Yankees reportedly employed more scouts than

any other team in baseball ("Labor Federation Egging on Players," NYT, January 14, 1917, S3).

67. *Literary Digest*, "Is the American Boy Quitting Baseball?" July 12, 1930, 34; "The Case of Baseball," TSN, March 26, 1925, 4. John Sheridan asked in 1923: "What will be the effect of the growth of golf clubs in the small towns [which produced many ballplayers]?" (John Sheridan, "Back of the Home Plate," TSN, October 18, 1923, 4).

68. Irving Sanborn, "Baseball Becomes a Live Issue with the Younger Generation," BM, August 1928, 393; Riess, *Touching Base*, 182.

69. John Sheridan, "Back of the Home Plate," TSN, November 29, 1923, 4.

70. "Editorial Comment," BM, June 1928, 290; Irving Sanborn, "A Vision of Professional Baseball in the Future," BM, May 1928, 541; F. C. Lane, "Bigger and Better Baseball," BM, February 1930, 388.

71. "Heydler Urges Major Leagues to Develop Own Young Players in Training School," NYT, October 28, 1923, S1.

72. "A Few Words for the Scout," TSN, February 28, 1918, 4.

73. Surdam, *Run to Glory and Profits*, 178–79; Al Hirshberg, "The Celtics' Cinderella Star," *Sport*, January 1962, 51–52, 70–71. Player Al Bridwell recalled that Cincinnati Reds owner Garry Herrmann came to watch his team play. Herrmann was interested in Bridwell's teammate, but Bridwell had a good game. Herrmann made a snap judgment and signed the youngster on the spot (Ritter, *Glory of Their Times*, 120).

74. "Two More Scouts Join Yank Staff," NYT, December 16, 1925, 31.

75. Riess, *Touching Base*, 176; Riess, *City Games*, 89; Burk, *Never Just a Game*, 223–24.

76. Ford Frick, "Bachelor of Arts vs. Artist of Baseball," BM, October 1927, 497.

77. Clifford Harvey, "From College Campus to Major Diamond," BM, June 1929, 297; Ralph Brewer, "Look at These College Boys," BM, February 1930, 394.

78. Clifford Harvey, "From College Campus to Major Diamond," BM, June 1929, 297; Ralph Brewer, "Look at Those College Boys," BM, February 1930, 394; Clifford Harvey, "The College Man in Big League Baseball," BM, March 1927, 455, 469; Ford Frick, "Bachelor of Arts vs. Artist of Baseball," BM, October 1927, 497.

79. Lee Douthit, "The College Player in Big League Baseball," BM, March 1930, 448; "What Hurts College Player," TSN, May 9, 1922, 2.

80. Ford Frick, "Bachelor of Arts vs. Artist of Baseball," BM, October 1927, 498.

81. Wallace, "College Men in the Big Leagues," 490.

82. "Scribbled by Scribes," TSN, November 11, 1926, 4.

83. "Scribbled by Scribes," TSN, February 26, 1925, 5; "Scribbled by Scribes," TSN, November 11, 1926, 4.

84. U.S. House of Representatives, OB: Report, 153–54.

85. Quote in "Favors Fewer Players," NYT, December 6, 1917, 10; "Baseball Leagues Will Clean House," NYT, December 8, 1918, 11; "Limit Again Twenty-Five," NYT, May 14, 1919, 23. Some observers attributed the American League's dominance in World's Series play to that league's higher limit on active players compared with the National League's rule.

86. "Financing Minor Leagues," TSN, November 13, 1930, 4; Kieran, "Big-League Business," 154.

87. National League of Professional Base Ball Clubs, Constitution, 1933, no page numbers.

88. "Who Says Communism?" TSN, March 31, 1921, 4.

10. Owners versus Players

1. "Knabe Testifies for Feds," NYT, March 27, 1919, 10; "Begin Baseball Trial," NYT, March 26, 1919, 12.

2. "In Restraint of the Baseball Trade," NYT, April 15, 1919, 10.

3. "Fans and Players Need Not Worry," NYT, April 15, 1919, 12.

4. Pietrusza, Major Leagues, 99–126 provides a quick overview of the league.

5. Burk, Never Just a Game, 178–209 provides a good account.

6. "What Purpose in Fultz's Activity?" TSN, November 16, 1916, 4.

7. "Players' Requests Denied," NYT, January 6, 1917, 10. The other three concessions demanded included permission for players to sign new contracts immediately after they were unconditionally released; money for traveling expenses to and from training camps; and notification in full of National Board findings in grievance hearings and a chance to reply ("Baseball Players Will Strike Unless Demands on Minor Leagues Are Met," NYT, January 12, 1917, 10).

8. "Fraternity Unjust, Says John K. Tener," NYT, January 13, 1917, 8.

9. Johnson's quote in "League Heads Plan to Oppose Players," NYT, January 17, 1917, 10; Fultz's quote in "It Is Players' Union against Owners' Union," NYT, January 19, 1917, 9.

10. "Club Owners See Fraternity Break," NYT, January 20, 1917, 8; "Fraternity Admits Nine More Leagues," NYT, January 23, 1917, 10.

11. "Meeting in Chicago Today," NYT, January 16, 1917, 11; "Labor Federation Egging on Players," NYT, January 14, 1917, S3.

12. "Players May Have to Pet White Rats," NYT, January 30, 1917, 10; "Fraternity Has No Union Charter Yet," NYT, January 28, 1917, S1.

13. "Eddie Collins States Stand," *NYT*, January 18, 1917, 8; "Big Leagues Sever Fraternity Bonds," *NYT*, January 18, 1917, 8. Warren Tormey argues that Collins represented a new breed of ballplayers, one whose behavior and interests were antagonistic to the likes of Chick Gandil, Swede Risberg, and other White Sox players. He believes Collins accepted and manifested the growing middle-class management ethos (Tormey, "'Old College Try,'" 98–111).

14. "Comment on Current Events in Sports," *NYT*, January 15, 1917, 6.

15. Quote in "Not Opposed to Players," *NYT*, February 8, 1917, 13; "Jennings Predicts Champions in 1917," *NYT*, January 28, 1917, S4.

16. "Players Can Accept Terms Says Fultz," *TSN*, February 1, 1917, 1.

17. "Owners Declare Strike Is Broken," *NYT*, February 13, 1917, 13; "Says Stars Have Signed," *NYT*, February 9, 1917, 9. Barney Dreyfuss leveled a different criticism at the Players' Fraternity; he believed it caused "altogether too much handshaking in the game. Baseball is a fighting, scrappy game, and that is what the public wants to see. Nowadays . . . [a player] puts his arm around the rival first baseman and asks him how much salary he gets" ("Club Owners Dear to Players' Body," *NYT*, February 14, 1917, 6).

18. "Baseball Skies Cleared by Action Taken at New York," *TSN*, February 22, 1917, 3; "Fultz Calls Off Baseball Strike," *NYT*, February 15, 1917, 9; "Players May Now Sign," *NYT*, February 18, 1917, S5.

19. "Military Training for Ball Players," *NYT*, February 16, 1917, 12; "American League Meets and Moguls Decide to Take Dimes and Nickels for Tax," *NYT*, February 15, 1918, 6.

20. "Baseball Players' Union Progressing," *NYT*, August 17, 1922, 17. The reader may pardon the author for the following: It appeared that baseball unionization became a case of "loose cannons," as in addition to Ray Cannon, the owners appointed Judge Robert Cannon as the players' legal advisor in the 1960s, before the ascension of Marvin Miller. The owners' action in selecting Judge Cannon was an apparent violation of labor law (Miller, *Whole Different Ball Game*, 8).

21. "Cannon versus Cannon," *TSN*, September 14, 1922, 4.

22. "Not to Antagonize Baseball Owners," *NYT*, October 13, 1922, 25; Francis Richter, "Casual Comment," *TSN*, November 2, 1922, 4.

23. "Says Frank Frisch Is Union Nominee," *NYT*, December 16, 1922, 20; Burk, *Much More Than a Game*, 6.

24. Ty Cobb, "What Baseball Should Do for Its Own," *BM*, February 1923, 393–94.

25. "Aids Baseball Veterans," *NYT*, October 26, 1923, 20; Irving Sanborn, "Does OB Need a Community Center?" *BM*, July 1924, 341; "Home for Aged Players," *NYT*, January 20, 1917, 8.

26. Burk, *Much More Than a Game*, 25; Dick Kerr, "Should There Be Forced Arbitration of Salary Disputes?" *BM*, January 1926, 353, 374.

27. "Scribbled by Scribes," *TSN*, April 12, 1923, 4; "The News from Milwaukee," *TSN*, April 12, 1923, 4; "Evers with Braves As They Head South," *NYT*, March 14, 1917, S2.

28. "New Baseball Rules Mean Fun for Fans," *NYT*, February 4, 1917, S1–S2.

29. U.S. House of Representatives, *OB: Report*, 54.

30. U.S. House of Representatives, *OB: Report*, 54.

31. U.S. House of Representatives, *OB: Report*, 53.

32. Burk, *Never Just a Game*, 200.

33. U.S. House of Representatives, *OB: Report*, 55.

34. "Let the Reserve Clause Rest," *TSN*, November 16, 1920, 4.

35. Joe Vila, "Coming Week May Show If Pirates Are to Be Counted In," *TSN*, May 19, 1921, 1.

36. Franklin Wilson, "Baseball Can't Afford to Close Door of Opportunity," *TSN*, November 22, 1923, 5.

37. U.S. House of Representatives, *OB: Report*, 131; Surdam, *Run to Glory and Profits*, 218.

38. U.S. House of Representatives, *OB: Report*, 129.

39. U.S. House of Representatives, *OB: Report*, 119, 128.

40. U.S. House of Representatives, *OB: Report*, 49.

41. U.S. House of Representatives, *OB: Report*, 135.

42. "Ban Johnson Plans an Effort to Procure Exemption for Big League Players," *NYT*, November 22, 1917, 14; "New Draft Order May Free Players," *NYT*, June 3, 1918, 12.

43. "Daubert's Claim Is Denied," *NYT*, October 6, 1918, 30; "Contract Should be Preserved in Museum," *TSN*, March 13, 1919, 7.

44. Mack quote in "Says Players Are Not Free Agents," *NYT*, December 26, 1918, 8; "Cobb to Quit Baseball," *NYT*, December 17, 1918, 14.

45. "Leagues Face Big Problem," *NYT*, October 9, 1918, 12.

46. "May Bar Deserters," *NYT*, December 12, 1918, 12.

47. "Irish Meusel Released," *NYT*, September 17, 1926, 14. In 1929, Landis declared some lesser-known players to be free agents because of their club officials'

manipulations of the player-movement rules ("Landis's Order Makes Nine Men Free Agents," NYT, March 17, 1929, XII:5).

48. "M'Innis and Smith Balk on Big Trade," NYT, December 22, 1921, 19; "McInnis Loses Salary Claim for $10,000 against Red Sox," NYT, January 10, 1924, 24.

49. "Players and Automobiles," TSN, April 18, 1929, 4; "Joshing versus Business in Baseball," *Literary Digest*, April 28, 1923, 74, 76. No real badgers were involved in "badger baiting."

50. Burk, *Much More Than a Game*, 13.

51. "Landis Declares Kauff Ineligible," NYT, April 8, 1921, 21.

52. "Kauff Loses Injunction Suit," TSN, January 26, 1922, 6.

53. "Jim Vaughn Ineligible," NYT, August 10, 1921, 19; "Dick Kerr Comes Back," TSN, August 13, 1925, 4.

54. "Sale of Yankees' Franchise Denied," NYT, October 11, 1922, 27; "Comment on Current Events in Sports: Baseball," NYT, October 24, 1921, 23; "Ruth Is Suspended; Fined Series Money," NYT, December 6, 1921, 25. Landis later supported revising the rule to allow World's Series participants to barnstorm ("Baseball Decision Soon to Be Made," NYT, June 28, 1922, 19).

55. First quote in "Let the Player Get This Straight," TSN, October 27, 1921, 2; second quote in "Scribbled by Scribes," TSN, November 3, 1921, 4.

56. Thomas Rice, "Wherein Magnates Are at Fault Again," TSN, October 27, 1921, 2; "Scribbled by Scribes," TSN, August 19, 1926, 4.

57. "Ruth Makes Debut as Vaudeville Star," NYT, November 4, 1921, 24; "Ruth Top-Liner on Keith Circuit," NYT, October 28, 1921, 24; "Babe Ruth Warmly Greeted in Debut on New York Stage," NYT, November 15, 1921, 25.

58. New York Yankees Base Ball Club, Cash books; "Baseball: Yesterday's Results," NYT, May 20, 1922, 16; "Scribbled by Scribes," TSN, December 15, 1921, 4.

59. "Ruth Must Apply for Reinstatement," NYT, May 18, 1922, 24; "Judge Landis Talks on Ruth's Status," NYT, May 19, 1922, 21.

60. Quote in "Ruth Fined $200; Loses Captaincy," NYT, May 27, 1922, 1; "Ruth in Row with Umpire and Fan at Polo Grounds," NYT, May 26, 1922, 1; "Ruth's Suspension to Cost Him $1,500," NYT, June 22, 1922, 20.

61. New York Yankees Base Ball Club, Cash books.

62. "Ruth Sees Ruppert; Waves Olive Branch," NYT, September 2, 1925, 27; "Baseball," NYT, September 7, 1925, 9; "Ruth Fined $5,000, Costly Star Banned for Acts Off Field," NYT, August 30, 1925, 3. There were quite a few other articles during the week. Ruth's marriage was unraveling at the time, and Mrs. Ruth was rumored to be ready to file a $100,000 suit for separate maintenance ("If Huggins Stays, I Quit, Says Ruth," NYT, August 31, 1925, 11).

63. "Huggins Accepts Ruth's Apology, but Ban Still Remains; Babe May Play Tomorrow," *NYT*, September 6, 1925, S1.

64. Francis Richter, "Casual Comment," *TSN*, May 11, 1922, 4.

65. Allen, *Cincinnati Reds*, 155.

66. "Shocker Settles Case with Browns," *NYT*, January 19, 1924, 9.

67. Francis Richter, "Casual Comment," *TSN*, April 12, 1923, 4; "Finding Work for Landis," *TSN*, February 22, 1923, 4.

68. Thomas Rice, "Need of 12-Month Contract Apparent," *TSN*, November 6, 1916, 4.

69. "Baseball Players Should Be Licensed, Declares Ban Johnson, Favoring Bill," *NYT*, January 21, 1923, S1.

70. "Heydler Absolves Pirate Dissenters," *NYT*, August 18, 1926, 16; "Heydler Will Act in Pittsburgh Case," *NYT*, August 17, 1926, 19; "The Week in Sports: Baseball," *NYT*, August 16, 1926, 13.

71. John Sheridan, "Back of the Home Plate," *TSN*, August 26, 1926, 4.

72. "The Week in Sports: Baseball," *NYT*, August 23, 1926, 12; "Frisch Quits Giants, Angered by M'Graw," *NYT*, August 22, 1926, S1 and S2.

73. Quote in "McGraw Opens Way to Return," *NYT*, August 23, 1926, 10; "Frisch Fined $500; Ordered to Report," *NYT*, September 3, 1926, 10. In a weird parallel, Frisch's St. Louis counterpart, Rogers Hornsby, was suspended for missing a game after the club physician cleared him to play. Sam Breadon suspended and fined Hornsby ("Cards Suspend Hornsby," *NYT*, September 28, 1923, 8).

74. "Scribbled by Scribes," *TSN*, May 19, 1927, 4; "The Cobb Incident," *TSN*, May 19, 1927, 4.

75. "National Lays Down War Rules for Player," *TSN*, March 21, 1918, 5; "Owners Fined, Not Players," *NYT*, December 10, 1917, 12.

76. "53 Players Placed on List of Outlaws," *NYT*, January 9, 1924, 27.

11. Highly Paid but Exploited Players

1. "Want Players Fined for Reporting Late," *NYT*, December 10, 1925, 30.

2. John Sheridan, "Back of the Home Plate," *TSN*, March 3, 1921, 4; "This Matter of Salaries," *TSN*, January 23, 1930, 4. For baseball's use of bonus clauses, see Haupert, "Bonus Clauses and the Standard Player Contract," 109–15.

3. "Players May Learn of Debt He Owes to Baseball Scribes," *TSN*, February 15, 1917, 7.

4. "Johnson to Renew Offer for Oakland," *NYT*, January 4, 1925, S1. See appendix 2.

5. "Scribbled by Scribes," *TSN*, April 9, 1925, 4.

6. "Editorial Comment," *BM*, April 1927, 486.

7. Fullerton, "Earnings in Baseball," 743, 747.

8. Quote in "Jennings Predicts Champions in 1917," *NYT*, January 28, 1917, S4; "Baseball Magnates Will Plan Defense against Threatened Strike Today," *NYT*, January 15, 1917, 6.

9. Tener quote in "New Baseball Rules Mean Fun for Fans," *NYT*, February 4, 1917, S1–S2; "Baseball Salaries Still at Top Notch," *NYT*, February 25, 1917, 74.

10. "Alexander Signs for Year," *NYT*, February 22, 1917, 12; "John M'Graw to Manage Giants Five Years More at Highest Salary Paid in Baseball," *NYT*, March 26, 1917, 12.

11. Quote in "Agreement by Players at the Root of Holdouts in Big Leagues," *NYT*, February 19, 1918, 10; Henry Edwards, "Ban Johnson's Part Is with Baseball," *TSN*, November 1, 1917, 2; "Red Sox to Refuse Help for Holdouts," *NYT*, February 26, 1918, 10.

12. "Salaries to Come Down," *NYT*, December 22, 1918, 25.

13. "National Lays Down War Rules for Players," *TSN*, March 21, 1918, 5.

14. "Players Must Be Able to Use Brush," *TSN*, August 8, 1918, 3; "Baseball Players," *TSN*, April 8, 1920, 8.

15. "National League Salary Reduction May Cause Strike of Baseball Players," *NYT*, January 16, 1919, 10; "Clubs Adopt Plan for Season Limit," *NYT*, January 18, 1919, 8, James Isaminger, "Isaminger Knocks Salary Limit Idea," *TSN*, January 23, 1919, 1.

16. "Scribbled by Scribes," *TSN*, December 19, 1918, 4.

17. "Better Salaries for All the Giants in Announcement of President Stoneham," *NYT*, January 24, 1910, 12.

18. Veeck, *Hustler's Handbook*, 256–57; *NYT*, "American League Makes No Changes," December 14, 1917, 10; Seymour quotes slightly different figures, *Baseball: Golden Age*, 334, although he claims Comiskey paid Cicotte a $2000 bonus in 1917.

19. "Stars May Testify at Baseball Trial," *NYT*, July 8, 1921, 15.

20. Francis Richter, "Casual Comment," *TSN*, April 19, 1923, 4. Gene Carney believes that Happy Felsch spread the story that Comiskey granted the Black Sox pay raises for 1920 as "hush money" in order to help Joe Jackson in his lawsuit against the owner for back pay (Carney, "Mysterious Mr. Cicotte," 94).

21. Burk, *Never Just a Game*, 233.

22. Ritter, *Glory of Their Times*, 143–44.

23. "Scribbled by Scribes," *TSN*, March 3, 1921, 4; Oscar Reichow, "Chicago Takes Rest after All Its Recent Big Doings," *TSN*, January 27, 1921, 1; "Dick Kerr Must Serve His Year of Penance, Says Landis," *NYT*, December 14, 1922, 29.

24. "Scribbled by Scribes," *TSN*, January 26, 1922, 4; Francis Richter, "Casual Comment," *TSN*, March 23, 1922, 4.

25. "Baseball Salaries and Ring Purses," *TSN*, December 30, 1920, 5. Daniel clearly minimized the ardor and risk of being in the ring with a heavyweight contender. The congressional committee listed Cobb's and Walter Johnson's early salaries and showed the effect of the Federal League upon their salaries (U.S. House of Representatives, *OB: Hearings*, 1091).

26. John Kieran, "Sports of the *Times*," *NYT*, February 10, 1927, 19; "$52,000 Ruth Offer a Mere Formality," *NYT*, February 11, 1927, 25. Cobb's contract with the Athletics was for $50,000 with a reputed $10,000 signing bonus; Cobb also had a potential $15,000 bonus if the team won the pennant. Tris Speaker reportedly received $30,000, although the press reported his salary as $40,000 ("Babe's New Score Is Made in Pay," *NYT*, March 6, 1927, 14; Haupert, Baseball Salary Database).

27. "Is It the Verdict of the Fan?" *TSN*, February 2, 1928, 4.

28. "Editorial Comment," *BM*, June 1930, 290.

29. "Third Sacker Heinie Groh," *TSN*, June 16, 1921, 3; W. A. Phelon, "Moran Ask Every Red to Toe Scratch," *TSN*, January 12, 1922, 3.

30. "Roush to Ask $54,000 for 3 Years; Wants to Come Here," *NYT*, January 6, 1922, 21; "Dilly-Dally Costs Reds a Lot of Money," *TSN*, February 14, 1924, 6.

31. "Cincinnati Man Would Raise General Fund to Pay Roush," *NYT*, March 2, 1923, 12; "Reds' Directors Vote against Paying Roush over $15,000," *NYT*, April 5, 1923, 15; "Edd Roush Accepts Terms with Reds," *NYT*, April 15, 1923, S1; Stinson, *Edd Roush*, 167.

32. "Higher Rank for Mr. Ebbets," *NYT*, March 31, 1923, 12; "Zack Wheat Signs with the Robins," *NYT*, March 31, 1923, 9. Wheat received $8,300 for each season, 1921–23.

33. "Not Money but Discipline," *NYT*, April 15, 1923, 18.

34. James Isaminger, "Grant Shows That It's Not All Dollars," *TSN*, April 21, 1923, 6.

35. "Evers with Braves as They Head South," *NYT*, March 14, 1917, S2; "Hornsby Demands $25,000; St. Louis Offers $15,000," *NYT*, February 10, 1922, 19; "Hornsby Signs for 3 Years, Salary More than $20,000," *NYT*, February 8, 1925, S2.

36. "Hornsby to Receive $80,000 for 2 Years," *NYT*, January 9, 1927, S1; "Braves Will Pay Hornsby $121,800," *NYT*, March 2, 1928, 31.

37. "Scribbled by Scribes," *TSN*, February 7, 1924, 3; "Frisch Sought $25,000," *NYT*, March 5, 1925, 17.

38. Parker, *Big and Little Poison*, 80–81.

39. "Editorial Comment," *BM*, May 1929, 530, 575.

40. John Sheridan, "Back of the Home Plate," *TSN*, September 1, 1927, 4.

41. Eig, *Luckiest Man*, 195; "Yanks Sign Gehrig to 3-Year Contract," *NYT*, January 7, 1928, 9.

42. "Editorial Comment," *BM*, May 1929, 530; "$25,000 for Vance; His Terms Are Met," *NYT*, March 15, 1929, 21; "Robins Sign Vance at $20,000 for Year," *NYT*, March 7, 1928, 20.

43. "Dazzy Vance Balks at Ten-Day Clause," *NYT*, March 5, 1925, 17; "Dazzy Vance Signs 3-Year Contract," *NYT*, March 11, 1925, 14.

44. "Connie Mack Spent $700,000 to Produce a Winning Club," *TSN*, January 30, 1930, 3. The congressional committee report of 1952 shows an Athletics payroll of almost $250,000, but this may have included coaches' salaries (U.S. House of Representatives, *OB: Report*, 1,610). According to reporters, Charles Ebbets discovered that winning a pennant had long-term repercussions. His Dodgers payroll remained high for several seasons, as stars from that team continued to draw salaries well above their 1920 ones. By 1925 despite a now-lackluster team, Ebbets's team reportedly had a greater payroll than any team in baseball aside from the Yankees. Then again, some of the Dodgers' payroll went to players—Dazzy Vance and Jack Fournier—who had not been on the 1920 team ("Scribbled by Scribes," *TSN*, March 19, 1925, 4).

45. Ritter, *Glory of Their Times*, 245.

46. Charles Foreman, "Jack Dunn Just like Every Manager When Winter Comes," *TSN*, November 8, 1293, 5; see also Franklin Wilson, "Baseball Can't Afford to Close Door of Opportunity," *TSN*, November 22, 1923, 5; Honig, *Baseball When the Grass Was Real*, 66.

47. Honig, *Baseball When the Grass Was Real*, 66; see also Franklin Wilson, "Baseball Can't Afford to Close Door of Opportunity," *TSN*, November 22, 1923, 5.

48. "Scribbled by Scribes," *TSN*, January 8, 1920, 4; "Babe Ruth Comes High," *NYT*, January 18, 1919, 8; "Three Big Stars Still Holdouts," *NYT*, March 18, 1919, 12; "Ruth Demands $20,000," *NYT*, December 25, 1919, 18.

49. "Scribbled by Scribes," *TSN*, April 9, 1925, 4.

50. "Editorial Comment," *BM*, April 1930, 482. H. G. Salsinger believed that if Ruth concentrated on getting base hits instead of home runs, "you would

probably see the greatest batter of all time . . . he would run up a batting average that would dazzle you." In addition to his potentially higher batting average, Salsinger lauded Ruth as "one of the smartest players I ever saw. Did you ever see Ruth make the wrong play?" (H. G. Salsinger, "What Determines a Ball Player's Value?" BM, May 1924, 542).

51. John Sheridan, "Back of the Home Plate," TSN, February 24, 1927, 4.

52. "Babe Ruth's $210,000 for Three Years of Swat," *Literary Digest*, March 19, 1927, 61.

53. "Editorial Comment," BM, April 1922, 778.

54. "Ruth and Ruppert Compromise When Babe Signs for Two Years," TSN, March 13, 1930, 1. According to another article, Ruth would lose $10,246 in federal taxes each year ("Ruth's Salary Cut $10,246 Each Year by U.S. Income Tax," NYT, March 11, 1930, 30).

55. "A Bird in the Hand," TSN, September 23, 1926, 4.

56. Parker, *Big and Little Poison*, 100.

57. F. C. Lane, "What the Ball Players Do in Winter," BM, March 1922, 732; "What Babe Ruth Does with His Money," *Literary Digest*, October 5, 1929, 78.

58. Jake Daubert, "Why Business Is Bad for a Ball Player," BM, September 1922, 441–42.

59. "Scribbled by Scribes," TSN, August 5, 1926, 4; "A Question of Salary," TSN, August 5, 1926, 4.

60. U.S. House of Representatives, OB: *Hearings*, 1,610.

61. Levin, et al., *Commissioner's Blue Ribbon Panel on Baseball*, 61, 65, 69, 73, 77.

62. U.S. House of Representatives, OB: *Report*, 109; Surdam, *Postwar Yankees*, 72; Levin, et al., *Commissioner's Blue Ribbon Panel on Baseball*, 61, 65, 69, 73, 77; Burk, *Much More Than a Game*, 23. Player salaries as a proportion of net nominal gross operating income rose sharply in 1933, compared with 1929 and 1939, due to the precipitous drop in revenues. In the American League: 1929—35.2 percent; 1933—65.9 percent; 1939: 40.8 percent. In the National League: 1929—29.9 percent; 1933—55.7 percent; 1939—32.4 percent (U.S. House of Representatives, OB: *Hearings*, 1,602-3, 1,606-7, and 1,610).

63. Brown, Gabriel, and Surdam, "Pay Structure of the New York Yankees, 1919–1941," 458.

64. New York Yankees Base Ball Club, contract Books; "Bob Meusel Fails to Come to Terms," NYT, March 6, 1925, 17; see also Michael Haupert, "Bonus Clauses and the Standard Player Contract," 109-15.

65. "Away with the Bonus System," TSN, December 8, 1921, 8; "Bonus Contracts," TSN, February 27, 1930, 4; Francis Richter, "Casual Comment," TSN, Decem-

ber 14, 1922, 4. Pitcher Dutch Ruether got a contract with bonus clauses for winning fifteen and twenty games ("$2,000 Bonus for Ruether If He Wins Twenty Games," NYT, March 15, 1923, 23). The hurler had his only twenty-win season in 1922; he won but ten games the year before, so owner Charles Ebbets was hedging his bets for 1923.

66. "They Come High," NYT, March 7, 1922, 11. There were other articles during the subsequent weeks detailing Ruth's contract and alleged bonus; it appeared that T. L. Huston was the owner responsible for insinuating that Ruth had such a bonus clause. Ruth did receive a share of exhibition game receipts. Haupert, "Bonus Clauses and the Standard Player Contract," 109–15.

67. Burk, *Much More Than a Game*, 25.

68. James Gould, "Why Not Make Official Scoring Really 'Official?'" BM, March 1930, 437, 471.

69. "Not in Our 'Industry,'" TSN, January 22, 1920, 4; "Fault in Mack's Philanthropy," TSN, January 17, 1918, 4.

70. Ralph Davis, "Pirates Won't Cut In on Profits Again," TSN, January 5, 1922, 3.

71. "Scribbled by Scribes," TSN, April 6, 1922, 4.

72. Seymour, *Baseball: Golden Age*, 190. Thomas Barthel relates a story of a Cuban team beating the world's champion Athletics in 1910, whereby the Cubans boasted they were the "world's champions." Baseball owners undoubtedly shuddered when Jack Johnson beat a white man for the heavyweight boxing title (Barthel, *Baseball Barnstorming*, 59, 100, 105).

73. "May Discipline Red Sox," NYT, October 6, 1918, 30. The owners' fears reflected that of Walt Disney and McDonald's in their zealous protection of their companies' good names and understandably so. When Disney released *Fantasia* for a second run in the late 1960s, disturbing rumors arose that many of the patrons found it a remarkable light show conducive to getting high on drugs and speculated whether the creators of the movie had been high. Clearly this was not in Disney's interests (Alan Brien, "London: A Prolonged Cultural Siesta," NYT, June 15, 1970, 48).

74. "Ruth Defies Landis, May Be Suspended," NYT, October 17, 1921, 1.

75. "The Barnstorming Issue," TSN, November 2, 1922, 4; Ralph Davis, "No More Fall Trips If Mags Have Way," TSN, December 7, 1922, 3.

76. "Scribbled by Scribes," TSN, September 20, 1923, 4.

77. "Let the Player Get This Straight," TSN, October 27, 1921, 4.

78. Barthel, *Baseball Barnstorming*, 106.

12. The Minor Leagues' Bumpy Ride

1. "Shift of Minors to Major Control Silent but Sure," *TSN*, January 12, 1928, 5.
2. "Baseball Leagues Will Clean House," *NYT*, December 8, 1918, 11.
3. U.S. House of Representatives, *OB: Hearings*, 992.
4. John Sheridan, "Back of the Home Plate," *TSN*, October 18, 1923, 4.
5. Burk, *Much More Than a Game*, 28.
6. "Orioles May Withdraw," *NYT*, December 10, 1918, 14; "Minor Leagues Demand Restriction of Draft on Their Players by Majors," *NYT*, January 6, 1919, 10.
7. Sec Taylor, "Nebraska Offers a New Idea," *TSN*, April 5, 1928, 7; Welles Roberts, "Minor League Baseball in 1940?" *BM*, October 1930, 492; U.S. House of Representatives, *Organized Professional Team Sports*, 841-42; "Heinemann Has Plan to Help Weaker clubs," *TSN*, November 11, 1920, 3; "This Is Not League Ball," *TSN*, December 1, 1921, 4.
8. "Sexton Points Way to Strict Economy," *TSN*, December 7, 1921, 73.
9. "M. H. Sexton Pleads with Minors to Get on Business Basis," *TSN*, December 8, 1921, 4, 8; "Minor Income and Outgo," *TSN*, March 1, 1928, 4. Sexton's league, the Mississippi Valley League, Class D, tried something new: "to start operations on an expense basis calculated to match what receipts should be—if receipts fall down then expenditures will be cut accordingly." Sexton would have final approval on individual player salaries and all expenditures ("So Good It's Doubtful," *TSN*, March 2, 1922, 4).
10. Sec Taylor, "Mounting Cost of Running Team Is Not Met by Revenue Derived, Writes Sec Taylor," *TSN*, December 8, 1927, 1.
11. "Why Start on the Player?" *TSN*, October 8, 1922; "Minors to Talk Gate Rates," *TSN*, November 23, 1922, 7.
12. "Minor League Club Values," *TSN*, January 15, 1925, 4; "Block Purchases the Newark Club," *NYT*, September 8, 1927, 30.
13. Chick Foreman, "Orioles Widen Gap in 'Race' for Flag," *TSN*, June 29, 1922, 3; "The Ultimatum to Jack Dunn," *TSN*, July 13, 1922, 4. One fan wrote to a local newspaper and suggested that the Orioles and Philadelphia Athletics merge. The Athletics, long the dregs of the American League, would, in fact, get some of Dunn's star players (Chick Foreman, "International Has No Sign of Ambition," *TSN*, July 20, 1922, 3).
14. Noll, "Economics of Promotion and Relegation in Sports Leagues," 169-203.
15. Jack Dunn, "A Minor Leaguer's View of the Draft Problem," *BM*, April 1923, 503, 521.

16. U.S. House of Representatives, *OB: Report*, 142.

17. U.S. House of Representatives, *OB: Report*, 145.

18. U.S. House of Representatives, *OB: Report*, 106.

19. Irving Sanborn, "Baseball's Biggest Problem—The Draft," *BM*, March 1928, 439.

20. "Fraternity Is under Ban," *NYT*, February 16, 1917, 12.

21. "Fifteen Players Drafted by Majors," *NYT*, October 10, 1923, 17; "Records Show Major Draft Is Not Respector [*sic*] of Ages," *TSN*, November 20, 1924, 6.

22. "23 Minors Drafted by Major Leagues," *NYT*, October 10, 1925, 11; "25 Minor Leaguers Drafted by Majors," *NYT*, October 2, 1926, 12.

23. Irving Sanborn, "How the Chaos in the Draft Laws Helps New York," *BM*, October 1924, 486.

24. "Landis Puts Ban on Drafting by Clubs from Own Farms," *NYT*, October 23, 1930, 31.

25. "Minor Leagues May War," *NYT*, November 1918, 14.

26. "Heydler Outlines New Plan for World Series Receipts," *NYT*, January 11, 1919, 14.

27. "Scribbled by Scribes," *TSN*, February 22, 1923, 4; Charles Foreman, "Six Straight Pennants: A New World's Record!" *BM*, October 1924, 505.

28. "A Job for Moses," *TSN*, November 27, 1919, 4.

29. Quote in "The Logic of the Draft," *TSN*, December 23, 1920, 4; "Scribbled by Scribes," *TSN*, December 23, 1920, 4.

30. "Minors in Clash with Big Leagues," *NYT*, January 16, 1919, 10; Bruce Dudley, "Class AA Leaguers Do Not Live Up to Pledge," *TSN*, January 6, 1921, 8.

31. "Cincinnati Reds May Get Daubert," *NYT*, January 20, 1919, 12; "Stallings Seeks a Trade to be Relieved of Herzogs' $10,000 Contract," *NYT*, January 28, 1919, 10.

32. "Comment on Current Events in Sports: Minor Chords in Baseball," *NYT*, November 3, 1919, 10; "Players Ask Place on the Commission," *NYT*, January 27, 1920, 17.

33. Burk, *Much More Than a Game*, 28.

34. "Scribbled by Scribes," *TSN*, January 27, 1921, 4; Morganson [no first name], "Toronto Fans Grow Sour as Leafs Fall," *TSN*, August 16, 1923, 3; "Late Events Not Cheering to Opponents of Draft," *TSN*, January 25, 1923, 3; "The International Comes Back," *TSN*, December 4, 1924, 4.

35. "Coast Ball League Is Ready to Fight," *TSN*, December 15, 1921, 20; "Scribbled by Scribes," *TSN*, December 29, 1921, 4.

36. "Declare Big League Draft Rule Illegal," *TSN*, January 10, 1923, 26; "Landis Supports Stand of Majors," *TSN*, January 11, 1923, 26; "Majors Agree to $7,500 Draft Plan," *TSN*, January 8, 1922, 119; "Draft Is Rejected by International," *TSN*, February 14, 1922, 23.

37. "$10,000 Draft Limit Is New Plan Offered," *TSN*, October 24, 1923, 16; "Two Leagues Vote to Restore Draft," *TSN*, December 14, 1923, 25.

38. John Sheridan, "Back of the Plate," *TSN*, September 4, 1924, 4; Burk, *Much More Than a Game*, 31–32.

39. Lipman, *Mr. Baseball*, 69; Mann, *Branch Rickey*, 108.

40. Burk, *Much More Than a Game*, 35; Ralph Davis, "Pittsburg Fancies Its Turn Has Come," *TSN*, December 16, 1920, 3; U.S. House of Representatives, *OB: Report*, 44–45.

41. U.S. House of Representatives, *OB: Report*, 62–64.

42. John Sheridan, "Back of the Home Plate," *TSN*, June 16, 1927, 4.

43. John Sheridan, "Back of the Home Plate," *TSN*, May 3, 1928, 4; "Casual Comment," *TSN*, December 1, 1927, 4. Ira Irving was somewhat more optimistic about the Cardinals' experiences with their farm system, citing the key players on the 1926 team that had been developed on Cardinals' farm clubs (Ira Irving, "The 'Chain Store' Idea Invades Baseball," *BM*, June 1928, 315).

44. John Sheridan, "Back of the Home Plate," *TSN*, February 2, 1928, 4; John Kieran, "Big-League Business," 150.

45. Surdam, *Wins, Losses, & Empty Seats*, 148–49, 343, table 29.

46. John Sheridan, "Back of the Home Plate," *TSN*, December 23, 1926, 4; John Sheridan, "Back of the Home Plate," *TSN*, June 16, 1927.

47. "Editorial Comment," *BM*, September 1930, 434.

48. U.S. Congress, *OB: Report*, 64–65; "Landis Swings the Big Stick," *TSN*, March 21, 1929, 4.

49. U.S. Congress, *OB: Report*, 64–65; "Major League Ownership," *TSN*, May 23, 1929, 4; "Editorial Comment," *BM*, June 1929, 290.

50. "Chain Store Curb Likely to Be Asked," *TSN*, April 4, 1929, 1; Barrow, *My Fifty Years in Baseball*, 8; "Yankees Take Over Syracuse," *TSN*, December 13, 1928, 5.

51. Ira Irving, "The Far-Reaching Results of 'Farm' Baseball," *BM*, January 1929, 345–46.

52. U.S. House of Representatives, *OB: Report*, 108.

13. Baseball and Ethnic Diversity

1. "Baseball Field the Real Melting Pot," *TSN*, April 26, 1917, 4.

2. "The Challenge to the Jew," TSN, September 15, 1921, 4.

3. "Dick Kinsella Finds That $100,000 Jew," TSN, September 6, 1923, 1; "Editorial Comment," BM, June 1928, 290; Joe Vila, "La Zerre, Lizziera or Li Zerri! No, It's Not the Mussolini Yell," TSN, December 31, 1925, 1. The latter article, in addition to discussing McGraw's signing of Cohen, mangled Tony Lazzeri's name.

4. "Scribbled by Scribes," TSN, August 2, 1923, 4; F. C. Lane, "Why Not More Jewish Ball Players?," BM, January 1926, 341, 372–73.

5. Frederick Lieb, "Baseball—The Nation's Melting Pot," BM, August 1923, 394.

6. C. P. Huntington, "Is Japan Ready for Professional Baseball?" BM, August 1928, 492; "Baseball and Brotherhood," TSN, January 25, 1923, 4.

7. Armando Marsans and Dolf Luque were Cuban pioneers in Major League Baseball, see Enders, "Armando Marsans," and Bjarkman, "Dolf Luque." Enders believes it likely that Marsans was Castilian without African descent.

8. Irving Sanborn, "Forecasting a Baseball League of Nations," BM, April 1922, 775–77.

9. Oliver Arata, "The Colored Athlete in Professional Baseball," BM, May 1929, 555–56; Burk, Much More Than a Game, 33.

10. "Editorial Comment," BM, June 1921, 290. David Pietrusza describes Lawson's ideas in greater detail in Major Leagues, 255.

14. Hilldale and the Negro Leagues

Portions of this chapter are taken from Haupert, "Ed Bolden: Black Baseball's Great Modernist," 61–72; Haupert and Winter, "Old Fellows and the Colonels," 79–92.

1. Lomax, Black Baseball Entrepreneurs, 210–12.

2. White, History of Colored Base Ball, 143.

3. Lanctot, Fair Dealing and Clean Playing, 66.

4. Haupert and Winter, "Old Fellows and the Colonels," 83.

5. Lanctot, Fair Dealing and Clean Playing, 22.

6. Hogan, Shades of Glory, 142.

7. Bill Cash-Lloyd Thompson Collection.

8. Bill Cash-Lloyd Thompson Collection.

9. Haupert and Winter, "Old Fellows and the Colonels," 81–84.

10. Lomax, Black Baseball Entrepreneurs, 34–36.

11. Hogan, Shades of Glory, 14.

12. Hogan, Shades of Glory, 67.

13. Haupert, "William Hulbert and the Birth of the National League," 87–89; Haupert and Winter, "Building a League One Dollar at a Time," 148–63.

14. They played 123 and 139 games respectively in 1918 and 1919.

15. Bill Cash-Lloyd Thompson Collection.

16. Lanctot, *Fair Dealing and Clean Playing*, 62.

17. The Negro League Baseball Players Association (http://www.nlbpa.com/the _teams.html) lists eighty different teams that participated in eleven professional leagues between 1887 and 1950 and an additional twenty-seven independent clubs. Thirty-five of those teams played in at least two different leagues, twenty changed leagues twice, and another eight teams participated in four or more different leagues during this time period. Among those leagues which folded during a league season were the League of Colored Baseball Clubs (1887), the Middle States League (1899), the Eastern Colored League (1928), the first Negro National League (1931), and the East-West League (1932).

18. Haupert and Winter, "Yankee Profits and Promise," 197–214.

19. When it opened, Yankee Stadium had a capacity of 58,000. When the Yankees abandoned the Polo Grounds at the conclusion of the 1922 season, that stadium had a seating capacity of 34,000, which was expanded to 55,000 for the 1923 season. The total capacity of the Polo Grounds could exceed 34,000 by roping off the outfield for standing room patrons.

20. Haupert and Winter, Yankee Financial Records.

21. The standard arrangement for the use of Yankee Stadium was for the renters to cover all operating costs and pay a percentage of the gate to the Yankees.

22. Wright, *Old South, New South*, 149, 184.

23. The data for 1922 are only available through July 22.

24. Bill Cash-Lloyd Thompson Collection.

25. Bill Cash-Lloyd Thompson Collection.

26. The white National League also had stability problems in its early years. In the first decade of its existence twenty different franchises were members at one time or another, with only Chicago and Boston surviving the entire decade.

27. Lomax, *Black Baseball Entrepreneurs*, 242–45.

28. Lomax, *Black Baseball Entrepreneurs*, 176.

29. Lanctot, *Fair Dealing and Clean Playing*, 92.

30. Lanctot, *Fair Dealing and Clean Playing*, 93.

31. Lanctot, *Fair Dealing and Clean Playing*, 93.

32. Lomax, *Black Baseball Entrepreneurs*, 260.

33. Lomax, *Black Baseball Entrepreneurs*, 181.

34. Lomax, *Black Baseball Entrepreneurs*, 110.

35. Lomax, *Black Baseball Entrepreneurs*, 130.

36. Lomax, *Black Baseball Entrepreneurs*, 135.

37. Bill Cash-Lloyd Thompson Collection.

38. Lanctot, *Fair Dealing and Clean Playing*, 200.

39. Lanctot, *Fair Dealing and Clean Playing*, 210.

40. Lanctot, *Fair Dealing and Clean Playing*, 210–13.

41. Lanctot, *Fair Dealing and Clean Playing*, 214–15.

Appendix 1

1. Michael Haupert interview with Clifford Kachline, June 2003, Cooperstown, New York.

2. A lackluster season for Ruth is a career year for most players. In 1922 Ruth batted .315 with 35 home runs and 90 RBIs in 110 games.

Appendix 2

1. D. J. Simons and C. F. Chabris, *What People Believe about How Memory Works: A Representative Survey of the U.S. Population*, 2011. PLoS ONE 6(8): e22757. doi:10.1371/journal.pone.0022757.

Bibliography

Archival Sources

Bill Cash-Lloyd Thompson Collection. Afro-American Historical and Cultural Museum, Philadelphia PA.

Haupert, Michael. Professional Baseball Salary Database. National Baseball Hall of Fame, Cooperstown NY.

Haupert, Michael, and Kenneth Winter. Yankee Financial Records. National Baseball Hall of Fame, Cooperstown NY.

National Baseball Hall of Fame, Cooperstown NY. New York Yankees Base Ball Club. Cash books, general ledger, and contract books, 1915–1944. Denoted as New York Yankees Base Ball Club.

New York Public Library. New York Yankees Baseball Club Collection, 1913–1950.

Published Sources

Alexander, Charles. *John McGraw*. New York: Viking, 1988.

———. *Rogers Hornsby: A Biography*. New York: Henry Holt, 1995.

———. *Ty Cobb*. New York: Oxford University Press, 1984.

Allen, Lee. *The Cincinnati Reds*. 1984. Reprint, Kent OH: Kent State University Press, 2006.

Armour, Mark, and Daniel Levitt. *In Pursuit of Pennants: Baseball Operations from Deadball to Moneyball*. Lincoln: University of Nebraska Press, 2015.

Asinof, Eliot. *Eight Men Out: The Black Sox and the 1919 World Series*. 1963. Reprint, New York: Pocket Books, 1979.

Bales, Jack. "Baseball's First Bill Veeck." *The Baseball Research Journal* 42, no. 2 (Fall 2013): 7–16.

Barrow, Edward. *My Fifty Years in Baseball*. New York: Coward-McCann, 1951.

Barthel, Thomas. *Baseball Barnstorming and Exhibition Games, 1901–1962: A History of Off-Season Major League Play*. Jefferson NC: McFarland, 2007.

Bernstein, Sam. "George Sisler and the End of the National Commission." *The National Pastime: A Review of Baseball History* 23 (2003): 92–96.

Bevis, Charles. *Sunday Baseball: The Major Leagues' Struggle to Play Baseball on the Lord's Day, 1876-1934.* Jefferson NC: McFarland, 2003.

Bjarkman, Peter. "Dolf Luque." *SABR Biography Project.* http:/sabr.org/bioproj /person/29c1fec2.

Brown, Kenneth, Paul Gabriel, and David Surdam. "An Inquiry into the Pay Structure of the New York Yankees: 1919-1941." *Eastern Economic Journal* 38, no. 4 (Fall 2012): 449-59.

Brown, Warren. *The Chicago White Sox.* 1952. Reprint, Kent OH: Kent State University Press, 2007.

Burk, Robert. *Much More Than a Game: Players, Owners, and American Baseball Since 1921.* Chapel Hill: University of North Carolina Press, 2001.

——. *Never Just a Game: Players, Owners, and American Baseball to 1920.* Chapel Hill: University of North Carolina Press, 1994.

Canes, Michael. "The Social Benefits of Restrictions on Team Quality." In *Government and the Sports Business*, edited by Roger Noll, 81-113. Washington DC: Brookings Institution, 1974.

Carney, Gene. *Burying the Black Sox: How Baseball's Cover-Up of the 1919 World Series Fix Almost Succeeded.* Washington DC: Potomac Books, 2007.

——. "The Mysterious Mr. Cicotte." In *Mysteries from Baseball's Past: Investigations of Nine Unsettled Questions*, edited by Angelo Louisa and David Cicotello, 90-107. Jefferson NC: McFarland, 2010.

Charles River Editors. *The Black Sox Scandal: The History and Legacy of America's Most Notorious Sports Controversy.* Seattle WA: CreateSpace Independent Publishing Platform, 2015.

Coase, Ronald. "The Problem of Social Cost." *Journal of Law and Economics* 3, no. 1 (1960): 1-44.

Cohen, Eliot. "Rose Out, McGraw In: Why?" *The Baseball Research Journal* 20 (1991): 6-7, 50.

Cook, William. *The 1919 World Series: What Really Happened?.* Jefferson NC: McFarland, 2001.

Craig, Peter. "Organized Baseball: An Industry Study of $100 Million Spectator Sport." BA thesis, Oberlin College, 1950.

DeMaree, Al. "Grand-Stand Girls." *Collier's* 81, no. 22 (June 2, 1928): 22, 36.

Dodd, Don. *Historical Statistics of the United States: Two Centuries of the Census, 1790-1990.* Westport CT: Greenwood Press, 1993.

Ehrgott, Roberts. *Mr. Wrigley's Ball Club: Chicago and the Cubs during the Jazz Age.* Lincoln: University of Nebraska Press, 2013.

Eig, Jonathan. *Luckiest Man: The Life and Death of Lou Gehrig*. New York: Simon & Schuster, 2005.

Enders, Eric. "Armando Marsans." SABR *Biography Project*. http://sabr.org/bioproj /person/f2c0b939.

Fetter, Henry. *Taking on the Yankees: Winning and Losing in the Business of Baseball*. 2003. Reprint, New York: W. W. Norton, 2005.

"The First American Dictator." *American Review of Reviews* 77, no. 1 (January 1928): 95–96.

Fountain, Charles. *The Betrayal: The 1919 World Series and the Birth of Modern Baseball*. New York: Oxford University Press, 2016.

Fullerton, Hugh. "Baseball—The Business and the Sport." *American Review of Reviews* 63, no. 4 (April 1921): 417–20.

———. "Baseball on Trial." *New Republic* 26, no. 307 (October 20, 1920): 183–84.

———. "Earnings in Baseball." *North American Review* 229, no. 6 (June 1930): 743–48.

Gay, Timothy. "Unraveling the Cobb-Speaker Scandal." *Mysteries from Baseball's Past: Investigations of Nine Unsettled Questions*, edited by Angelo Louisa and David Cicotello, 120–35. Jefferson NC: McFarland, 2010.

Ginsburg, Daniel. *The Fix Is In: A History of Baseball Gambling and Game Fixing Scandals*. Jefferson NC: McFarland, 1995.

Gold, Eddie. "'The Other' Veeck Revives the Cubs." *The Baseball Research Journal* 25 (1996): 69–70.

Graham, Frank. *The Brooklyn Dodgers: An Informal History*. 1945. Reprint, Carbondale: Southern Illinois University Press, 2002.

———. *The New York Giants: An Informal History of a Great Baseball Club*. 1952. Reprint, Carbondale: Southern Illinois University Press, 2002.

———. *The New York Yankees: An Informal History*. 1943. Reprint, Carbondale: Southern Illinois University Press, 2002.

Haupert, Michael. "Bonus Clauses and the Standard Player Contract." *Baseball Research Journal* 36 (2007): 109–15.

———. "The Economic History of Major League Baseball." https://eh/net /encyclopedia/the-economic-history-of-major-league-baseball. No date posted. Viewed April 3, 2016.

———. "Ed Bolden: Black Baseball's Great Modernist." *Black Ball* 5, no. 2 (Fall 2012): 61–72.

———. "William Hulbert and the Birth of the National League." *Baseball Research Journal* 44, no. 1 (Spring 2015): 83–92.

Haupert, Michael, and Kenneth Winter. "Building a League One Dollar at a Time: The Story of the Immediate Success of the American League." In *The Cooperstown Symposium on Baseball and American Culture, 2007–08*, edited by William Simons, 148–63. Jefferson NC: McFarland, 2009.

——. "The Old Fellows and the Colonels: Innovation and Survival in Integrated Baseball." *Black Ball* 1, no. 1 (Spring 2008): 79–92.

——. "Pay Ball: Estimating the Profitability of the New York Yankees, 1915–1937." *Essays in Economics and Business History* 21 (Spring 2003): 89–102.

——. "Yankee Profits and Promise: The Purchase of Babe Ruth and the Building of Yankee Stadium." In *The Cooperstown Symposium on Baseball and American Culture*, edited by William Simons, 197–214. Jefferson NC: McFarland, 2003.

Heinz, Wilfred. "Boss of the Behemoths." *Saturday Evening Post* 228, no. 23 December 3, 1955, 46, 72, 74, 77.

Hogan, Lawrence. *Shades of Glory*. Washington DC: National Geographic, 2006.

Honig, Donald. *Baseball When the Grass Was Real*. 1975. Reprint, New York: Berkley Medallion Books, 1977.

Kavanagh, Jack, and Norman Macht. *Uncle Robbie*. Cleveland OH: Society for American Baseball Research, 1999.

Kieran, John. "Big-League Business." *Saturday Evening Post* 202, no. 48 (May 31, 1930): 16–17, 149–50, 154.

Koppett, Leonard. *The Essence of the Game Is Deception: Thinking about Basketball*. Boston: Sports Illustrated Book, 1973.

Lamb, William. *Black Sox in the Courtroom: The Grand Jury, Criminal Trial and Civil Litigation*. Jefferson NC: McFarland, 2013.

Lancaster, John. "Baltimore, A Pioneer in Organized Baseball." *Maryland Historical Magazine* 35, no. 1 (March 1940): 32–55.

Lanctot, Neil. *Fair Dealing and Clean Playing: The Hilldale Club and the Development of Black Professional Baseball, 1910–1932*. Jefferson NC: McFarland, 1994.

Lardner, John. "That Was Baseball: The Crime of Shufflin' Phil Douglas." *New Yorker* 32, no. 12 (May 12, 1956): 136–58.

Levin, Richard, George Mitchell, Paul Volcker, and George Will. *The Report of the Independent Members of the Commissioner's Blue Ribbon Panel on Baseball Economics*. July 2000, http://www.mlb.com/mlb/downloads/blue_ribbon.pdf.

Levitt, Dan. "Ed Barrow, the Federal League, and the Union League." *The National Pastime: A Review of Baseball History* 28 (2008): 97–103.

Levitt, Daniel. *The Battle That Forged Modern Baseball: The Federal League Challenge and Its Legacy*. Chicago: Ivan R. Dee, 2012.

———. *Ed Barrow: The Bulldog Who Built the Yankees' First Dynasty*. Lincoln: University of Nebraska Press, 2008.

Lewis, Franklin. *The Cleveland Indians*. 1949. Reprint, Kent OH: Kent State University Press, 2006.

Lieb, Frederick. *The Boston Red Sox*. 1947. Reprint, Carbondale: Southern Illinois University Press, 2001.

———. *The Detroit Tigers*. 1946. Reprint, Kent OH: Kent State University Press, 2008.

———. *The Pittsburgh Pirates*. 1948. Reprint, Carbondale: Southern Illinois University Press, 2003.

Lieb, Frederick, and Stan Baumgartner. *The Philadelphia Phillies*. 1948. Reprint, Kent OH: Kent State University Press, 2009.

Light, Jonathan. *The Cultural History of Baseball*. Jefferson NC: McFarland, 1997.

Lindholm, Scott. "Baseball Game Length: A Visual Analysis." January 29, 2015. http://www.beyondtheboxscore.com/2015/1/29/7921283/baseball-game-length-visual-analysis. Viewed December 20, 2016.

Lipman, David. *Mr. Baseball: The Story of Branch Rickey*. New York: G. P. Putnam's Sons, 1966.

Lomax, Michael. *Black Baseball Entrepreneurs, 1902–1931*. Syracuse NY: Syracuse University Press, 2014.

Lowry, Philip. *Green Cathedrals: The Ultimate Celebration of All 271 Major League and Negro League Ballparks Past and Present*. Reading MA: Addison-Wesley Publishing, 1992.

Lynch, Michael. *Harry Frazee, Ban Johnson and the Feud That Nearly Destroyed the American League*. Jefferson NC: McFarland, 2008.

The Macmillan Baseball Encyclopedia, 10th Edition. New York: Macmillan, 1996.

Mann, Arthur. *Branch Rickey: American in Action*. Boston MA: Houghton, Mifflin, 1957.

Miller, Marvin. *A Whole Different Ball Game: The Inside Story of Baseball's New Deal*. 1991. Reprint, New York: Fireside Book, 1992.

Morris, Peter. *A Game of Inches: The Stories behind the Innovations That Shaped Baseball: The Game on the Field*. Chicago: Ivan R. Dee, 2006.

Murdock, Eugene. *Ban Johnson: Czar of Baseball*. Westport CT: Greenwood Press, 1982.

National League and American Association of Professional Baseball Clubs. *Annual Meeting of the National League and American Association of Professional Baseball Clubs, December 10 to 14, 1901*. No publisher, 1901.

National League of Professional Base Ball Clubs. *Constitution and Playing Rules of the National League of Professional Baseball Clubs*. New York: American Sports Publishing Company, 1933.

Noll, Roger. "The Economics of Promotion and Relegation in Sports Leagues: The Case of English Football." *Journal of Sports Economics* 3, no. 2 (May 2002): 169–203.

Okkonen, Marc. *The Federal League of 1914–1915: Baseball's Third Major League.* Garrett Park MD: Society for American Baseball Research, 1989.

Parker, Clifton. *Big and Little Poison: Paul and Lloyd Waner, Baseball Brothers.* Jefferson NC: McFarland, 2003.

Pietrusza, David. *Major Leagues: The Formation, Sometimes Absorption and Mostly Inevitable Demise of Eighteen Professional Baseball Organizations, 1871 to Present.* Jefferson NC: McFarland, 1991.

Poggi, Jack. *Theater in America: The Impact of Economic Forces, 1870–1967.* Ithaca NY: Cornell University Press, 1968.

Pomrenke, Jacob. *Scandal on the South Side: The 1919 Chicago White Sox.* Phoenix AZ: Society for American Baseball Research, 2015.

Quirk, James, and Rodney D. Fort. *Pay Dirt: The Business of Professional Team Sports.* Princeton NJ: Princeton University Press, 1992.

Riess, Steven. *City Games: The Evolution of American Urban Society and the Rise of Sports.* Urbana: University of Illinois Press, 1989.

———. *Touching Base: Professional Baseball and American Culture in the Progressive Era.* 1983. Rev. ed., Urbana: University of Illinois Press, 1999.

Ritter, Lawrence. *The Glory of Their Times: The Story of the Early Days of Baseball Told by the Men Who Played It.* New York: Macmillan, 1966.

Rottenberg, Simon. "The Baseball Players' Labor Market." *Journal of Political Economy* 64, no. 3 (1956): 242–56.

Scully, Gerald. *The Business of Major League Baseball.* Chicago: University of Chicago Press, 1989.

Seymour, Harold. *Baseball: The Early Years.* New York: Oxford University Press, 1960.

———. *Baseball: The Golden Age.* New York: Oxford University Press, 1971.

Smiley, Gene, and Richard Keehn. "Federal Personal Income Tax Policy in the 1920s." *Journal of Economic History* 55, no. 2 (June 1995): 285–303.

Smith, Lowell. *Baseless Fears: Professional Baseball's Wary Relationship with Radio, 1921–1934.* Master's thesis, University of Nebraska–Lincoln, 1995.

Sparks, Barry. *Frank "Home Run" Baker: Hall of Famer and World Series Hero.* Jefferson NC: McFarland, 2006.

Spatz, Lyle, and Steinberg, Steve. *1921: The Yankees, the Giants, and the Battle for Baseball Supremacy in New York.* Lincoln: University of Nebraska Press, 2010.

Steinberg, Steve. "The 'Little World Series' of 1922." *The National Pastime: A Review of Baseball History* 28 (2008): 7-14.

Stinson, Mitchell. *Edd Roush: A Biography of the Cincinnati Reds Star.* Jefferson NC: McFarland, 2010.

Stout, Glenn. *The Selling of the Babe: The Deal That Changed Baseball and Created a Legend.* New York: Thomas Dunne Books, 2016.

Sullivan, Neil. *The Diamond in the Bronx: Yankee Stadium and the Politics of New York.* New York: Oxford University Press, 2001.

Surdam, David. *The Ball Game Biz: An Introduction to the Economics of Professional Team Sports.* Jefferson NC: McFarland, 2010.

———. "The Coase Theorem and Player Movement in Major League Baseball." *Journal of Sports Economics* 7, no. 2 (May 2006): 201-21.

———. "The New York Yankees Cope with the Great Depression: An Examination of Team Financial Records, 1929-39." *Enterprise & Society* 9, no. 4 (December 2008): 816-40.

———. *The Postwar Yankees: Baseball's Golden Age Revisited.* Lincoln: University of Nebraska Press, 2008.

———. *The Rise of the National Basketball Association.* Urbana: University of Illinois Press, 2012.

———. *Run to Glory and Profits: The Economic Rise of the NFL during the 1950s.* Lincoln: University of Nebraska Press, 2013.

———. "What Brings Fans to the Ball Park? Evidence from New York Yankees' and Philadelphia Phillies' Financial Records." *The Journal of Economics* 35, no. 1 (2009): 35-48.

———. *Wins, Losses, & Empty Seats: How Baseball Outlasted the Great Depression.* Lincoln: University of Nebraska Press, 2011.

Surdam, David, and Kenneth Brown. "Major League Baseball and the Rise of Leisure in America, 1920-41." Unpublished paper.

Thomas, Henry. *Walter Johnson: Baseball's Big Train.* Lincoln: University of Nebraska Press, 1995.

Thomas, Joan. "Helene Britton." SABR Bioproject, http://sabr.org/bioproj/person/ecd910f9. Viewed April 3, 2016.

Thompson, Derek. "Hoop Dreams." *The Atlantic.* April 2014, 18, 20-21.

Thorn, John, Pete Palmer, Michael Gershman, and David Pietrusza. *Total Baseball: The Official Encyclopedia of Major League Baseball.* 6th ed. New York: Total Sports, 1999.

Thorn, John, Pete Palmer, and Michael Gershman. *Total Baseball: The Official Encyclopedia of Major League Baseball.* 7th ed. Kingston NY: Total Sports, 2001.

Tormey, Warren. "'The Old College Try'; Eddie Collins and the 1919 Black Sox." *Baseball and Social Class: Essays on the Democratic Game That Isn't*, edited by Ronald Kates and Warren Tormey, 98–111. Jefferson NC: McFarland, 2012.

U.S. Department of Commerce, Bureau of the Census. *Historical Statistics of the United States: Colonial Times to 1970, Bicentennial Edition*, 2 parts. Washington DC: Government Printing Office, 1975.

U.S. House of Representatives. *Conduct of Judge Kenesaw Mountain Landis: Hearings before the Committee on the Judiciary*. House Serial 25. Statement of Hon. Benjamin F. Welty, M. C. Washington DC: Government Printing Office, 1921.

———. *Organized Baseball: Hearings before the Subcommittee on the Study of Monopoly Power of the Committee of the Judiciary*. House Report No. 2002, 82nd Cong., 1st Sess. Washington DC: Government Printing Office, 1952.

———. *Organized Baseball: Report of the Subcommittee on Study of Monopoly Power of the Committee on the Judiciary Pursuant to H. Res. 95. Documents and Reports*. House Report no. 2002, 82nd Cong., 1st sess. Washington DC: Government Printing Office, 1952.

———. *Organized Professional Team Sports: Hearings before the Antitrust Subcommittee of the Committee on the Judiciary*. Serial no. 8, 85th Cong., 1st sess.. Washington DC: Government Printing office, 1957.

Veeck, Bill. *The Hustler's Handbook*. New York: Simon & Schuster, 1965.

Vincent, David. "How Rules Changes in 1920 Affected Home Runs." *The Baseball Research Journal* 35 (2007): 19–22.

Voigt, David. *American Baseball: From the Commissioners to Continental Expansion*. 1970. Norman: University of Oklahoma, 1983.

Wallace, Francis. "College Men in the Big Leagues." *Scribners* 82, no. 4 (October 1927): 490–95.

Weintraub, Robert. *The House That Ruth Built*. New York: Little, Brown, 2011.

White, Sol. *History of Colored Base Ball*. 1907. Reprint, Lincoln: University of Nebraska Press, 1995.

Woolley, Edward. "The Business of Baseball." *McClure's Magazine* 39, no. 3 (July 1912): 241–56.

Wright, Gavin. *Old South, New South: Revolutions in the Southern Economy Since the Civil War*. New York: Basic Books, 1986.

Index

Aaron, Henry, 343n8

Adams, Babe, 214

advertising, 85, 100, 134, 265; and promotions, 122–23; as revenue source, 259, 266, 267

African American players, 3–4, 93, 186, 235, 252, 255–56, 257, 278; salaries of, 259–60, 266, 271, 273, 274, 300. *See also* Hilldale baseball club (Hilldale Daisies); Negro Leagues

alcohol abuse, 60, 93–94

Alexander, Charles, 326n111

Alexander, Dale, 183–84

Alexander, Grover Cleveland, 52, 85, 158, 160, 164, 168, 176, 249; salary of, 220, 222

Allen, Lee, 46, 62, 101, 134, 319n21

Altrock, Nick, 93

American Association, 10, 109, 123, 246, 329n25; and gambling, 41; and profit-sharing for players, 234, 238–39

American Federation of Labor (AFL), 198

American League, 35–36, 160, 263, 268; and attendance, 77–78, 95, 99, 127, 288; competitive balance within the, 23, 165–67, 170–75,

192–93, 293–94; and the designated hitter proposal, 143; and fan behavior, 123; finances of the, 21; and gambling, 24–25, 36–37, 49–50, 64–66, 67–69; governance of the, 16–17, 18–20, 21–22, 23–25, 33–38, 55, 68–69, 83, 150–51; and Kenesaw Mountain Landis, 26, 33, 34–35, 36, 65, 67–69; and length of seasons, 15, 20, 101–2; and the National Commission, 16–17, 18, 21–22, 23–24; and the National League, 16–17, 18, 25, 50, 68, 99, 137, 139, 195, 350n3; and player movement, 56, 148–58, 170–71, 346n20; and profitability, 73–74, 75, 77–78, 280, 281; and revenue sharing, 192–93; and salaries of players, 195, 198–99, 204–5, 221, 222, 224–25, 363n62; and scheduling, 20, 101–2, 111; style of play in the, 136–38, 139, 143, 290–92; and Sunday games, 333n34; and World War I, 15. *See also* Johnson, Ban; National League

American Legion amateur baseball, 187

American Negro League, 269, 273. *See also* Negro Leagues

Andrews, Ivy, 185

anti-Semitism, 253, 254. *See also* racism

antitrust lawsuits, Federal League, 2, 8–9, 32, 203, 205; and the Baltimore Federal League club, 9–13, 22, 32, 75, 200, 201, 203; and the reserve clause, 7, 194, 201, 203

Arata, Oliver, 255

Asinof, Eliot, 47, 48, 321nn41–42

Attell, Abe, 45, 57

attendance, 1, 72, 92–94, 96, 98–99, 129, 233, 288–89; and the American League, 77–78, 95, 99, 127, 288; and Babe Ruth, 81, 95, 97, 99–100, 126, 127, 164, 192, 211; and city size, 94, 96, 286–87; at the Colored World Series, 271, 272; declines in, 8, 54, 73, 97–98, 99, 100, 115, 133, 146, 147, 148, 157, 164, 229; and doubleheaders, 96, 100–101, 126; and exhibition games, 97; and the Hilldale Daisies, 272, 274; increases in, 87, 95, 97, 99–100, 104, 115, 119, 157, 223, 322n45; in the Minor Leagues, 240; and the National League, 95, 97, 99, 100, 249, 288; and office workers, 96, 134; and pennant races, 1, 51, 97–98, 99, 100, 104, 169–70; and profitability, 3, 5, 73, 77–78, 85, 86, 157; and race, 92–93, 252, 253; and radio, 132, 133–34; and revenue sharing, 192, 193; and scheduling, 96, 100–102, 110–11, 112–13, 114–16; and style of play, 95–96; and Sunday games, 110–11, 112–13, 114–16, 337n79; and ticket prices, 98, 102–8, 119, 322n45; of women, 87, 122–23, 134; at the World Series, 98, 106, 107, 108, 126–27; and World War I, 8, 94–95

Austrian, Alfred S., 24, 25, 53, 54

Averill, Earl, 183–84

Bagby, Jim, 175

Baker, Frank, 81, 147, 153, 173

Baker, Newton, 15

Baker, William, 90, 114, 153, 158–60

Baldwin, Howard, 184

Ball, Philip, 83, 87, 151, 155, 172, 271; and Ban Johnson, 26, 155; and gambling, 43; and Sportsman's Park, 127, 130

ballpark experience, 3, 120–22, 126–30, 132; and concessions, 78, 81, 105, 108, 121, 123–25, 128, 260, 261, 264, 266; and fan behavior, 3, 37, 87, 92, 110, 123–25; and gambling, 40, 41–42, 49–50, 57, 59; and ladies' days, 37, 122–23; and night ball, 116, 134–35; and promotions, 122–23. *See also* stadiums

Baltimore Federal League. See antitrust lawsuits, Federal League

Baltimore Orioles (1901–1902), 10, 263. *See also* New York Yankees

Baltimore Orioles (Minor League), 181–83, 229, 240, 244, 353n53; antitrust suit of the, against Major League Baseball, 9–13, 22, 32, 75, 200, 201, 203

Bancroft, Dave, 158

Barber, Red, 134

Barnard, E. S., 37, 38, 100

barnstorming, 48, 144, 207, 209–10, 231, 234–36, 358n54; and basketball, 254; and the Negro Leagues, 260. *See also* exhibition games

Barrow, Edward ("Ed"), 36, 82, 129, 149, 170, 173, 174, 186, 339n5, 351n19; and the Boston Red Sox,

84, 156, 173, 347n40; and farm teams, 250–51; as International League president, 197

Barry, Jack, 147

Barry, Thomas J., 155

Barthel, Thomas, 141, 236, 364n72

baseballs, 140–41, 343nn12–13; cost of, 79, 121, 265, 338n4, 339n5

base stealing, 3, 136, 137–38, 277, 292, 342n2. *See also* style of play

basketball, 40–41, 42, 188, 189, 235, 254

Beall, Walter, 185

Bell, Bert, 42

Bender, Charles ("Chief"), 8, 147

Bennett, Eddie, 174

Bentley, Jack, 181, 184–85

Benton, Larry, 158

Benton, Rube, 47, 182, 213

The Betrayal (Fountain), 47

betting. *See* gambling

Bigbee, Carson, 214

Bishop, Max, 182, 229

Bissell, Herbert, 202, 203

blacklisting, player, 7, 27, 11, 56, 71, 224. *See also* rights, player

black players. *See* African American players

Black Sox in the Courtroom (Lamb), 47

The Black Sox Scandal (Rivers), 47

Black Sox World Series scandal. *See* World Series gambling scandal

Block, Paul, 240

blue laws, 110, 111–12, 114, 115, 263, 266. *See also* Sunday games

Bodie, Frank ("Ping"), 305

Bohne, Sammy, 62

Bolden, Edward W., 258, 266, 267, 268, 274, 278; and the American Negro League, 269, 273; breakdown of, 272–73; business reputation of, 262–63; and the Eastern Colored League (ECL), 258, 260, 268, 270–73; and league membership, 263, 269–70; and player movement, 259, 269, 271; as promoter, 258, 261–63, 273. *See also* Hilldale baseball club (Hilldale Daisies)

Boley, Joe, 172, 182, 229

Boston Braves, 2, 18, 142, 146, 153, 199, 254–55, 293, 295, 344n19; and attendance, 95, 97, 115, 164, 288; and Braves Field, 90, 91, 115, 289, 331n58; franchise value of the, 84, 89, 90–91, 240, 285; pennant wins of the, 90, 165; and player trades with the New York Giants, 91, 158–64, 178; and profitability, 74, 90–91, 281, 282; and revenue sharing, 192, 296; and salaries of players, 226, 227; and Sunday games, 114, 115

Boston Red Sox, 49, 130, 147, 154, 165–66, 295, 331n58; and attendance, 73, 95, 96, 115, 148, 157, 288; and Babe Ruth, 18, 77, 83–84, 95, 146, 148, 155–58, 164, 230, 347n36, 347n40; and Fenway Park, 83–84, 115, 130, 155, 173, 289, 331n58, 347n36; franchise value of the, 83–84, 154–55; pennant wins of the, 148, 156, 167; and player trades with the New York Yankees, 18, 77, 83–84, 95, 146, 18, 149–53, 155–58, 164, 173, 230, 347n36, 347n40; and profitability, 73–74, 77, 83–84, 280, 281; and revenue sharing, 193; and salaries of players, 232; and Sunday

Boston Red Sox (*continued*)
games, 114, 115; win-loss records of the, 166, 171, 172, 293; World Series wins of the, 148

boxing, 1, 34, 116, 129, 224, 254; and stadium rentals, 78, 117, 118, 127, 128, 264

Boyer, Clete, 152

Bradley, Alva, 38, 87

Branom, Dud, 172

Braves Field, 90, 91, 115, 289, 331n58. *See also* stadiums

Breadon, Sam, 87, 90, 108, 121, 130, 161–63, 327n7, 331n51, 349n62, 359n73; and advertising, 100; and the farm system, 76

Bridwell, Al, 354n73

Briggs, Otto, 260, 267

Brigham, H. H., 52

Britton, Helene, 90, 170

Brooklyn Dodgers, 104, 123, 174–75, 184, 257, 293, 295; and attendance, 96, 97, 111, 112, 115, 228, 288; and Ebbets Field, 85, 97, 121, 123–24, 289; franchise value of the, 85; mascot of the, 174; and profitability, 73, 281, 282; and revenue sharing, 192, 296; and salaries of players, 228, 362n44; and Sunday games, 111, 112, 113, 115; and the World Series, 54, 56, 175

Broun, Heywood, 28

Brouthers, Dan, 170

Brush, John, 86

Brush Stadium. *See* Polo Grounds

Burk, Robert, 19, 95–96, 202–3, 208, 223, 232–33, 238, 312n2

Burke, Jimmy, 158

Burns, George, 159

Burns Detective Agency, 304

Burying the Black Sox (Carney), 47

Bush, Joe ("Bullet"), 147, 148, 152, 306, 345n7

Caldwell, Slim, 175

Callahan, Edward J., 72

Cannon, Raymond ("Ray"), 58–59, 199–200, 356n20

Cannon, Robert, 356n20

Cantrell, Guy, 250

Carey, Max, 214

Caribbean leagues, 260

Carney, Gene, 47, 321n41, 323n74, 360n20

Caveney, Jimmy, 180

Chapman, Ray, 141, 149, 175

Charleston, Oscar, 273

Chase, Hal, 55, 56, 60, 202, 213, 319nn20–21; and gambling, 23, 33, 43–46, 47, 59

Chicago Cubs, 9, 80, 126, 167–68, 187, 215, 243, 277, 293, 330n42; and attendance, 86, 95, 100, 130, 288; and gambling, 43, 52, 319n12; and ladies' days, 122; pennant wins of the, 41, 85, 176; and player movement, 153, 158, 160, 164, 176, 183, 295, 348n55; and profitability, 78, 85–86, 100, 281, 282; and radio, 133; and revenue sharing, 192, 296; and salaries of players, 13, 232; and ticket prices, 105, 106; and Wrigley Field, 42, 100, 126, 130, 289

Chicago White Sox, 47–48, 51–52, 65, 156, 180, 183, 289, 295; and attendance, 51, 54, 96, 97, 104, 125,

Elberfeld, Kid, 170
Eller, Hod, 140
equipment: baseballs, 79, 121, 140–41,
265, 338n4, 339n5, 343nn12–13; bats,
139, 343n8
Essick, Bill, 188
Evans, Billy, 141, 321n38
exhibition games, 210, 229, 234, 236,
313n19; and African American
players, 255, 261–62, 263, 267, 275;
and attendance, 97; and the Hilldale Daisies, 261–62, 263, 267, 272;
and revenue, 80, 81, 261–62, 263,
267, 272, 275; and scheduling, 101–2,
209. *See also* barnstorming
expenses, 216, 232, 328n22; and
baseball costs, 79, 121, 265, 338n4,
339n5; in the Minor Leagues, 239;
transportation costs, 79–80, 220,
239, 261, 270. *See also* revenue;
salaries, player

Faber, Urban ("Red"), 50, 172
Fales, Harold, 140–41, 343n12
Fallon, William J., 45, 61
fan behavior, 337n80; and foul balls,
121, 338n4, 339n5; and gambling at
the ballpark, 40, 41–42, 49–50; and
rowdiness, 3, 37, 92, 110, 122, 123–25,
144. *See also* ballpark experience
farm systems, 75, 174, 176, 177, 247–51,
277, 367n43. *See also* Minor Leagues
Farrell, Frank, 82
*Federal Baseball Club v. National
League. See* antitrust lawsuits,
Federal League
Federal League, 1, 99, 146, 165, 173,
311n1, 312n10; antitrust lawsuits

of the, against MLB, 2, 7, 8–13, 22,
32, 75, 194, 200, 201, 203, 205; and
player movement, 7–8, 9, 147, 166,
178, 191; and profitability, 7; and
the reserve clause, 194–95, 201,
202; and salaries of players, 8, 147,
166, 195, 196, 199, 202, 219–20, 221,
224, 225, 361n25; and stadiums, 7, 9
Felsch, Happy, 200, 223, 299, 323n74,
360n20
Fenway Park, 115, 130, 289, 331n58;
mortgage on, 83–84, 155, 173,
347n36. *See also* stadiums
Ferrell, Wes, 143
Fetter, Henry, 311n4
Fewster, Chick, 153
Filchock, Frank, 51
Fisher, Ray, 212–13
football, 189, 204, 235, 311n1, 312n10,
323n65, 336n72; college, 74, 116–18,
264, 338n90; and gambling, 42, 51;
and scouting systems, 187–88; and
stadium rentals, 78, 102, 117–18,
127, 129, 264
Forbes Field, 59, 130, 289. *See also*
stadiums
Ford, Henry, 253
Foreman, Charles, 244
Fort, Rodney, 88, 89, 167
Foster, Rube, 258, 259, 267–68, 269–72,
273, 275, 278
Fountain, Charles, 47, 321n41
Fournier, Jack, 362n44
Foxx, Jimmy, 229
franchise values, 13, 85, 87, 154–55,
329n28, 331n54; in the Minor
Leagues, 10, 240; and movement,
27, 90–91; and profitability, 3,

integration, 3–4, 93, 269, 277; of Cuban and Latin players, 252, 254–55, 256, 368n7. *See also* African American players

Intercity Baseball Association, 262

International League, 10, 21, 122, 180, 182, 240; and the draft, 246; and World War I, 197, 237. *See also* Minor Leagues

Irving, Ira, 367n43

Jackson, Joe, 47, 53, 56, 57, 58–59, 160, 319n20, 323n68, 360n20; salary of, 219, 222, 223, 229

Jackson, Travis, 185

Jewish players, 253–54

Johnson, Arnold, 155

Johnson, Ban, 19–20, 21, 22, 23, 24, 27, 127, 142, 331n51; achievements of, 35, 37, 38, 215, 263; and African American players, 235; and American League owners, 17, 18–19, 20–21, 23–24, 25, 26, 31, 33–38, 68–69, 82, 84, 148–49, 150–52, 154, 317n71; and antitrust lawsuits, 9, 10, 11; and Charles Comiskey, 18–19, 21, 23–24, 25, 33, 36, 38, 46, 53, 56, 57, 151; and the Cleveland Indians, 21, 151, 155, 345n15; and the Cobb-Speaker affair, 36, 64, 65, 66, 67–69; and fan behavior, 123, 125, 215; and federal regulation, 34, 317n68; and franchise movement, 10, 90; and gambling, 24–26, 33–34, 36–37, 44, 46, 50, 52–53, 55, 57, 61, 62, 64, 65, 66, 67–69, 222; and Garry Herrmann, 16, 22; and Harry Frazee, 18, 20–21, 23–24, 33–34, 83,

84, 148, 150–51, 154; and Kenesaw Mountain Landis, 26, 27, 29, 34, 36–37, 38, 61–62, 65–66, 67–69, 317n66; and length of games, 342n1; and licensing of players, 34, 214; and the Major League Advisory Board, 35–36; and the Mays trade, 150–52; and the media, 25–26; and player movement, 8, 18–19, 21, 150–52, 153, 155, 170–71; and the Players' Fraternity, 197, 199; resignation of, 36, 37–38, 68–69, 317n66; and salaries of players, 8, 222; salary of, 36, 37, 38, 317n71; and stadium rentals, 128, 340n29; and suspensions of players, 21–22, 37, 125, 150–52, 211, 215, 219; and ticket resale, 335n55; and the World Series gambling scandal, 24–26, 52–53, 55, 57, 222; and World War I, 14, 15

Johnson, Byron Bancroft. *See* Johnson, Ban

Johnson, George, 267

Johnson, Judy, 259–60, 269, 273, 274

Johnson, Syl, 179–80

Johnson, Walter, 4, 91, 143, 166, 175, 240, 312n2; salary of, 8, 218, 219, 222, 361n25

Jones, Bobby, 116

Jones, Percy, 164

Jones, Sam ("Sad Sam"), 148, 152, 306, 345n6

Jonnard, Claude, 250

Kachline, Clifford, 303–4

Kamm, Willie, 172, 180

Kansas City Monarchs, 135, 271, 275. *See also* Negro Leagues

Lewis, Duffy, 152, 173
Lewis, Harry, 54
licensing, player, 34, 213–14. *See also* rights, player
Lieb, Frederick, 23, 149, 152, 254, 306, 347n40
Lomax, Michael, 262
Long, Herman, 170
Longworth, Nicholas, 54
Lowry, Philip, 130
Lundy, Dick, 261
Luque, Dolf, 254–55, 368n7
Lynn, Byrd, 51–52
Lyons, Ted, 172

Mack, Connie, 64, 81, 180, 198, 206, 225, 234, 277, 345n7; and Ban Johnson, 19, 37–38; and player movement, 18, 146–47, 152, 172, 188, 215; and player sales, 8, 77, 81, 146–47, 172, 351n14; and profitability, 77, 82; and purchase of Minor League players, 172, 177, 178, 180, 182–83, 185, 353n53; and salaries of players, 166, 178, 224, 229, 234, 326n112, 337n80; and Sunday games, 111, 114–15
Mack, Stubby, 183
Mackey, Biz, 273
Magee, Lee, 33, 43–44, 59, 172–73, 213; lawsuits of, 43, 319n12, 319n14
Maguire, Freddie, 164
Major League Advisory Board, 35–36
Mann, Arthur, 247
Mann, Leslie, 59–60
Marbury, William L., 194
Maris, Roger, 152, 153
Marquard, Rube, 106–7, 175, 178

Marsans, Armando, 254, 368n7
Mathewson, Christy, 44, 45, 46, 51, 91, 188, 220
May, Jakie, 181
Mays, Carl, 18, 19, 21–22, 33, 83, 149–52, 346n16, 346n20
McCaffery, James, 90
McCarthy, Joe, 86, 243, 330n42
McCarthy, William H., 45
McClellan, Hervey, 51–52
McDonald, Charles A., 19, 27, 52, 53–54
McGraw, Bob, 150
McGraw, John, 47, 86, 91, 127, 128, 129, 200; and the Baltimore Orioles (Major League), 10; and gambling, 31, 43, 45, 46, 59–62; and Hal Chase, 43, 45, 46; and Jewish players, 253–54; and the O'Connell-Dolan scandal, 60–61; and player movement, 45, 60, 68, 152, 178, 179, 188, 225, 253–54; and player trades with the Boston Braves, 91, 158–59, 160–64, 178; and purchase of Minor League players, 60, 179, 181, 183–85; race track ownership of, 31, 45; and Rogers Hornsby, 159, 160–63; and salaries of players, 225; salary of, 220; and style of play, 136, 138, 142; and suspensions of players, 46, 60, 214–15
McInnis, Stuffy, 147, 148, 207
McKechnie, Bill, 214
McKeever, Edward, 85, 111
McMahon, Eddie, 258
McMahon, Jess, 258
McManus, Charles, 102
McNamee, Graham, 134
McNeely, Earl, 175

National Commission (*continued*)
  sole commissioner, 19–20, 21, 22, 25, 26–30, 33; and player movement, 17–18, 151; and World Series players' payments, 49, 107, 108. *See also* Landis, Kenesaw Mountain
National League, 11, 13, 35, 90, 160, 184, 200, 235; and the American League, 16, 18, 25, 50, 68, 99, 137, 139, 167–68, 195, 350n3; and attendance, 85, 95, 97, 99, 100, 249, 288; and cash trades, 153; competitive balance within the, 165, 166–68, 293–94; and the designated hitter proposal, 143; and expenses, 79, 141, 220; and fan behavior, 123; farm clubs in the, 250; formation of the, 263; and gambling, 40, 41, 44, 55, 59, 61; governance of the, 2, 19, 21, 22, 25, 55, 85, 160; and Kenesaw Mountain Landis, 26, 33, 35, 61, 213; and length of seasons, 20, 95, 101; and the National Commission, 16–17, 18, 19, 22, 23–24; and player movement, 153, 160–61, 163, 213, 346n20; and profitability, 74, 85, 281, 282; and revenue sharing, 191–92, 296; revenues in the, 73–74, 77–78, 191–92, 296; and salaries of players, 195, 219–21, 222, 226–27, 232, 234, 363n62; and scheduling, 20, 101, 102, 109, 113, 333n34; style of play in the, 137–38, 139, 142–43, 160, 290–92; and Sunday games, 109, 113, 333n34; volatility in the, 268, 278, 369n26; and World War I, 14–15. *See also* American League

Navin, Frank, 22, 23, 129, 206, 250, 326n111; and salaries of players, 204–5, 224
Neale, Alfred ("Greasy"), 47
Nebraska State League, 239. *See also* Minor Leagues
Negro American League, 269. *See also* Negro Leagues
Negro Leagues, 4, 78, 275, 278; and barnstorming, 260; and the Colored World Series, 260, 261, 269, 271, 272; and the Eastern Colored League (ECL), 258, 260, 268, 270–73, 275; and exhibition games, 261–62, 263, 267, 272, 275; and the Negro National League (NNL), 267–68, 269–72, 275; and night ball, 135; outlaw baseball in, 270; and player movement, 259; and profitability, 261, 265–67, 269; and revenue, 261, 263, 269; and salaries of players, 259–60, 266, 271, 273, 274, 300; and scheduling, 260–61, 262, 263–64, 266, 267; stability of the, 264, 267–69, 272, 369n17; and ticket prices, 260; and umpires, 261, 268, 272, 273. *See also* Hilldale baseball club (Hilldale Daisies)
Negro Leagues Baseball Players Association, 369n17
Negro National League (Greenlee), 269
Negro National League (NNL), 258, 267–68, 269–72, 275, 369n17. *See also* Negro Leagues
Negro Southern League, 269. *See also* Negro Leagues
Nehf, Art, 158, 189–90

Neilly, Harry, 176

newspaper coverage, 131, 132–33, 134; and baseball pools, 62; and salaries of players, 217–19, 220, 226, 230. *See also* media

New York Giants, 2, 31, 123, 132, 167, 193, 277, 285, 293; and attendance, 78, 95, 96, 98, 99, 112–13, 115, 127, 129, 192, 288; and Jewish players, 253–54; and the O'Connell-Dolan scandal, 34, 59–62, 67, 70, 317n70; pennant wins of the, 165; and player movement, 3, 44, 153, 167, 175, 176–77, 188, 207, 225, 227, 243, 253–54, 295; and player purchases from the Minor League, 179, 181, 184–85, 186, 348n47; and player trades with the Boston Braves, 91, 158–59, 160–64, 178; and the Polo Grounds, 95, 97, 98, 104, 112–13, 118, 124, 127, 128, 129, 151, 264, 289, 336n73, 340n27, 369n19; and profitability, 76, 78, 86, 281, 282; and revenue sharing, 192, 296; and salaries of players, 49, 220, 221, 227; and stadium rentals, 117–18, 127, 128, 338n90; and stadium sharing, 102, 112–13, 127, 128, 151, 264; and style of play, 136, 138, 142; and Sunday games, 111, 112–13, 115; and suspension of players, 208–9; and ticket prices, 104, 105; and the World Series, 34, 49, 98, 127, 335n62

New York Yankees, 3, 56, 124, 177, 251, 303–6, 329n34; and attendance, 95, 96, 97, 98, 99–100, 111–13, 115, 126, 127, 132, 134, 157, 211, 212, 233, 264, 288, 332n22, 333n26; comparison of the, with the Hilldale Daisies, 263–65, 301; detectives hired by the, to trail players, 303, 304–5; dominance of the, 2, 3, 100, 154, 165, 170, 171, 173–74, 193, 277, 311n4; and franchise value, 80–81, 82–83, 87, 127, 285, 329n28; and ladies' days, 123; lawsuit of, against Ban Johnson, 151–52; mascot of the, 174; pennant wins of the, 59, 83, 99–100, 147, 154, 157, 165, 174; and player movement, 18, 149–53, 155, 171, 173–74, 295; and player trades with the Boston Red Sox, 18, 77, 83–84, 95, 146, 18, 149–53, 155–58, 164, 173, 230, 347n36, 347n40; and profitability, 74, 75, 76–77, 78, 80–83, 87, 128, 157, 264, 280, 281, 284–85, 301; and purchase of Babe Ruth, 3, 77, 83–84, 95, 146, 148, 155–58, 164, 230, 264, 347n36, 347n40; and purchase of Minor League players, 179, 185–86; and radio, 132, 133; and revenue, 78, 81, 117–18, 128, 157, 211, 212, 233, 264–65, 282–83, 338n90, 369n21; and revenue sharing, 192–93, 296–98; and salaries of players, 81, 228, 229–31, 232–33, 305–6; and scheduling, 263, 333n32; scouting system of the, 186, 188, 353n66; and stadium sharing, 102, 112–13, 127, 128, 151, 264, 336n73, 340n27; and style of play, 136–37, 142; and Sunday games, 111–13, 115; and ticket prices, 102, 105, 107, 108, 305–6; win-loss records of the, 165, 171, 172–73, 293, 328n14; and the World Series, 157, 335n62. *See also* Yankee Stadium night ball, 116, 134–35, 277. *See also* innovations

O'Connell, Jimmy, 142, 179, 324n81; gambling scandals of, 34, 60–62, 67, 70, 317n70
O'Connor, Leslie, 211, 250
O'Doul, Lefty, 143, 153, 229
Olson, Ivan, 47
on-base percentage, 138–39, 174. *See also* style of play
organized crime, 42, 54–55. *See also* gambling
O'Toole, Marty, 178
Ott, Mel, 138
outlaw baseball, 208, 209, 212–13, 215; in the Negro Leagues, 270

Pacific Coast League, 44–45, 78, 122–23, 180, 181, 207, 335n62; and the draft, 246; and franchise values, 240. *See also* Minor Leagues
Paige, Satchel, 260
Palmer, Alexander Mitchell, 32
Paskett, Dode, 348n55
Passon, Harry, 274
Pattison, Jimmy, 243
Peckinpaugh, Roger, 143, 175, 306
Pennock, Herb, 147, 152
Pepper, George Wharton, 11, 36, 194
Perritt, Pol, 43
Perry, Scott, 17, 18
Pershing, John, 25
Phelon, W. A., 57, 317n71
Philadelphia Athletics, 3, 289; and attendance, 96, 99, 100, 114, 115, 146, 147, 229, 288, 337n79; pennant wins of the, 146, 166; and player movement, 18, 177, 295, 351n14; and player sales, 8, 77, 81, 146–47, 351n14; and profitability, 77, 280, 281; and purchase of Minor League players, 180, 182–83, 185; and salaries of players, 224, 229, 362n44; and Sunday games, 114–15, 337nn79–80; win-loss records of the, 166, 171, 172, 293
Philadelphia Phillies, 2, 52, 60, 153, 165, 177, 289, 295, 338n4; and attendance, 95, 96, 115, 288; pennant wins by the, 90, 158, 165; and player sales, 158–60; and profitability, 74, 89–90, 281, 282; and revenue sharing, 192, 296; and Sunday games, 114, 115; win-loss records of the, 166, 167, 293
Piercy, William ("Bill"), 209, 306
Pillette, Herman, 179–80
Pittsburgh Pirates, 105, 108, 127, 166, 214, 293; and attendance, 94, 96, 111, 114, 115, 130, 249, 288; and Forbes Field, 59, 130, 289; pennant wins of the, 159–60, 249; and player movement, 17–18, 153, 178, 184, 295; and profitability, 281, 282; and revenue sharing, 296; and salaries of players, 227–28, 232, 234; and the World Series, 335n62
Plank, Eddie, 8, 147, 188
"platoon" baseball, 141–42. *See also* style of play
player movement, 2, 3, 4, 10–11, 17–19, 164, 295, 348n55, 357n47; in the American League, 56, 148–58, 170–71, 346n20; and Babe Ruth, 77, 83–84, 95, 146, 148, 155–58, 164,

230, 347n36, 347n40; and blacklisting, 7, 11, 56; and competitive
balance, 168-86, 193; and demo-
tion to the Minor Leagues, 171; and
the draft, 10-11, 88, 175, 177, 181,
185, 238, 241-47, 248, 251; and the
Federal League, 7-8, 9, 147, 166,
178, 191; and free agency, 68, 168,
169, 205, 206-7, 232, 312n2, 357n47;
and the National League, 153, 160-
61, 163, 213, 346n20; in the Negro
Leagues, 259; and player sales, 3, 8,
60, 75, 77, 79, 81, 146-48, 155-60,
166, 172-76, 345n6, 348n47, 351n14;
and purchases of Minor League
players, 3, 60, 172, 175, 177-86, 193,
224, 240, 241-42, 243-44, 247-48;
and the reserve clause, 4, 7, 8, 11,
12, 168, 169, 195, 203, 350n4; and
roster limits, 190-91, 245; and
sources of new players, 186-90;
and star players, 163-64, 168-70,
173-77, 193; statistical analysis of,
176-77; and suspensions, 18, 21-22,
56, 150, 208; and trades between
the Braves and Giants, 91, 158-59,
160-64, 178; and trades between
the Red Sox and Yankees, 18, 77,
83-84, 95, 146, 18, 149-53, 155-58,
164, 173, 230, 347n36, 347n40. *See
also* contracts, player; rights, player;
salaries, player
player sales. *See* sales, player
Players' Fraternity, 196-99, 356n17.
    See also rights, player
Players' National League of 1890, 195.
    See also rights, player
Poles, Spottswood, 260, 267

Polo Grounds, 95, 104, 128, 151,
340n27; and capacity, 97, 98, 129,
264, 289, 369n19; fan behavior at
the, 124; and rental revenue, 112-13,
118, 127, 336n73. *See also* stadiums
Pomrenke, Jacob, 47
pools, baseball, 62-63. *See also* gambling
population, 94, 96, 253, 286-87. *See
also* city size
Pratt, Derrill, 171
Price, James H., 323n68
Pride of the Yankees (film), 92-93
profitability, 3, 5, 74-75, 301; and
the American League, 73-74, 75,
77-78, 280, 281; and attendance,
3, 5, 73, 77-78, 85, 86, 157; of the
Boston Braves, 74, 90-91; of the
Boston Red Sox, 73-74, 77, 83-84;
of the Brooklyn Dodgers, 73; of the
Chicago Cubs, 78, 85-86, 100; of
the Chicago White Sox, 74, 104;
of the Cincinnati Reds, 74; of the
Cleveland Indians, 74, 76; and
concessions, 78, 81, 105; of the
Detroit Tigers, 73, 74; and dividend
payments, 76, 281-82, 327nn7-8;
and expenses, 79-80; and the
Federal League, 7; of the Hilldale
Daisies, 261, 265-67, 273, 301; in
the Minor Leagues, 241; and the
National League, 74, 85, 281, 282;
in the Negro Leagues, 261, 265-67,
273; of the New York Giants, 76,
78, 86; of the New York Yankees,
74, 75, 76-77, 78, 80-83, 87, 128,
157, 264, 284-85, 301; of the
Philadelphia Athletics, 77; of the

profitability (*continued*)
Philadelphia Phillies, 74, 89–90; and revenue, 5, 73–78; and salaries of players, 79, 81; of the St. Louis Browns, 74, 76; of the St. Louis Cardinals, 75, 76, 90, 327n7; and Sunday games, 3, 80, 116; and tax rates, 75–76, 89; and ticket prices, 81; of the Washington Senators, 76, 86, 89, 327n8; and World War I, 79. *See also* revenue
Prohibition, 94, 128, 132
Prudhomme, Johnny, 183–84
Pyle, C. C., 118

Quigley, Ernie, 123–24
Quinn, Bob, 84, 114
Quinn, Jack, 306
Quirk, James, 88, 89, 167

racism, 3–4, 10, 93, 253, 254–55, 256, 259–60, 274, 364n72; and anti-Semitism, 253, 254; and sports-writers, 253, 254. *See also* African American players
radio, 3, 5, 78, 131–34, 135, 174, 205, 277, 341n45. *See also* innovations; media
railroad travel, 79–80. *See also* trans-portation costs
Raschi, Vic, 305
Rawlings, Johnny, 47, 159
Raymond, Bugs, 59
receipts, gate. *See* gate receipts
recreation expenditures, 5, 74–75, 280. *See also* economy, American
Reese, Jimmy, 185–86
relegation and promotion, 240–41. *See also* Minor Leagues

Replogle, R. A., 52
reserve clause, 4, 7, 8, 12, 350n4; and competitive balance, 11, 168, 169, 170; in the Negro Leagues, 259, 272; and rights of players, 194–95, 200, 201, 202–5, 244; and salaries, 194, 195, 202, 216, 217, 222–23, 350n4. *See also* rights, player
revenue, 92–94, 217, 282–83; from advertising, 259, 266, 267; and broad-casting rights, 78, 132, 133, 174; from concessions, 78, 81, 105, 108, 121, 128, 260, 261, 264, 266, 282–83; and exhibition games, 80, 81, 261–62, 263, 267, 272, 275; and gate receipts, 2, 78, 81, 92, 104, 106, 107–8, 132, 157, 211, 212; and marginal revenue product of players, 217, 233; in the Negro Leagues, 261, 263, 269; and profit-ability, 5, 73–77, 81; salaries as per-centage of, 232–33; sharing, 191–93, 238–39, 296–98; and stadium rentals, 78, 117–18, 127, 128, 255, 257, 264–65, 267, 269, 270–71, 336n73, 369n21. *See also* profitability; ticket prices
revenue sharing, 296–98; and compet-itive balance, 191–93; in the Minor Leagues, 238–39. *See also* revenue
Rhyne, Hal, 184
Rice, Grantland, 210
Rice, Thomas, 60, 97, 104, 157, 169, 210, 213; on Sunday games, 111, 112–13
Richardson, Hardy, 170
Richter, Francis, 34, 67, 124, 185, 223
Rickard, Tex, 83, 86, 118, 128
Rickey, Branch, 17–18, 161, 166, 182; and the farm system, 247–48, 249, 250

Riess, Steven, 186
rights, player, 194–95, 200, 215, 355n7; and blacklisting, 7, 11, 27, 56, 71, 224; exploitation of, 216–26, 233, 236; in football, 204; and free agency, 168, 169, 205, 206–7, 232; and involvement in baseball governance, 24, 201; and licensing, 34, 213–14; in the Minor Leagues, 196–97; and penalties for holding out, 212, 216, 219, 220, 224, 225; and public opinion, 198; and the reserve clause, 194–95, 200, 201, 202–5, 244; and suspensions, 195, 207–15, 219, 224, 359n73; and the ten-day release clause, 8, 194, 200, 201–2, 204, 205–6, 228; and unionization, 4, 24, 195–201, 215, 356n17, 356n20. *See also* player movement; salaries, player
Ring, Jimmy, 47, 162
Ringling, John, 83
Risberg, Swede, 36–37, 65, 57, 68, 69–71, 223, 299
Rivers, Charles, 47
Robertson, Gene, 185
Robinson, Jackie, 93, 255, 257
Robinson, Wilbert, 82, 85, 329n27
Robison, Stanley, 90
roster limits, 190–91, 199, 220, 245, 355n85
Rothstein, Arnold, 45, 253
Rottenberg, Simon, 168, 169
Roush, Edd, 47, 159, 160, 162, 212, 222, 225–26
Rowe, Jack, 170
Rowland, Clarence ("Pants"), 69, 70, 326n118

Ruether, Walter ("Dutch"), 175, 363n65
rule changes, 26–27, 48, 49, 142–43, 160; and ball club stock ownership, 162–63; and barnstorming, 209–10, 358n54; and the draft, 245; pitching, 140, 141; and price limits on Minor League stars, 184; and punishments for betting, 71, 72
Ruppert, Jacob, 20, 22, 33, 56, 95, 212, 306; and Ban Johnson, 18, 33, 68, 150–52; and Harry Frazee, 153, 155–56, 173, 330n35, 347n36; and innovations, 174; New York Yankees purchase of, 80–81, 82–83, 87, 127, 329n28; and player purchases, 77, 80, 147, 150–51, 155–58, 160, 172–73, 185–86, 347n36; and profitability, 76–77, 80–81; and salaries of players, 72, 169, 190, 228, 233, 305; and Yankee Stadium construction, 82, 117, 128
Russell, Allan, 150
Ruth, Babe, 4, 120, 143, 160, 168–69, 174, 193, 254, 304–5, 358n62, 352n50; and attendance, 81, 95, 97, 99–100, 126, 127, 164, 192, 211; and barnstorming, 144, 209–10, 231, 235–36; and Bob Meusel, 179, 209; and fan behavior, 125; and gambling on horse races, 71–72; and gate receipts, 81, 157, 192, 211, 212; home runs hit by, 1, 136, 139, 156, 228, 230, 233, 370n2; popularity of, 72, 81, 97, 127, 139, 144–45, 229; purchase price of, 77, 155, 156, 157, 173, 183, 264, 347n36; salary of, 139, 144–45, 156, 157, 218, 225,

Tener, John, 10, 14–15, 18, 19, 201; on gambling, 41; and the Players' Fraternity, 197, 198; on salaries of players, 219–20

Tenney, Fred, 156

Terkel, Studs, 321n42

Terry, Bill, 185

Terry, Ralph, 152

Thomas, Fay, 185

Thomas, Fred, 148

Thorn-Palmer Total Baseball Rating (TBR) system, 176–77

Thorpe, Jim, 116

ticket prices, 81, 106, 124, 334n45; and attendance, 98, 102–8, 119, 322n45; increases in, 102–3, 104–5, 107, 305–6; in the Minor Leagues, 240; in the Negro Leagues, 260; and resale, 106–7, 335nn54–55; and revenue sharing, 191; and salaries of players, 103, 198; and Sunday games, 112, 115; and war taxes, 103–4, 105, 106, 108, 334n38, 334n42; World Series, 98, 106–8, 126–27. *See also* revenue

Tierney, James J., 132

Toole, John Conway, 20, 21, 22

Tormey, Walter, 48, 356n13

trades, player. *See* player movement

transportation costs, 79–80, 220; for the Hilldale Daisies, 261, 270; and the Minor Leagues, 239. *See also* expenses

Traynor, Pie, 142

Tyler, Lefty, 348n55

Uhle, George, 175

umpires, 123–24, 215; in the Negro Leagues, 261, 268, 272, 273

union, players', 4, 24, 195–201, 215, 356n17, 356n20. *See also* rights, player

Vance, Dazzy, 179, 184, 228, 362n44

Vaughan, Irving, 70

Vaughan, Manning, 215

Vaughn, Jim, 209

Veeck, William, Sr., 43, 52, 86, 101, 122, 176, 222

Vila, Joe, 21–22, 50, 99, 110, 181; on gambling, 46, 61; on Harry Frazee, 20–21; on Miller Huggins, 173; on the reserve clause, 203; on Yankee Stadium, 129

Virginia League, 239. *See also* Minor Leagues

Von der Ahe, Chris, 109–10, 128, 329n25

Waddell, Rube, 182

Wagner, Honus, 160

Wagner, Robert F., 21, 149, 151

Walberg, Rube, 229

Walker, Bert, 218, 230

Walker, James (Senator), 22

Walker, James J., 34, 36

Walsh, Christy, 144–45, 304

Waner, Lloyd, 142, 227–28, 231

Waner, Paul, 142, 184, 227–28, 231

Ward, John Montgomery, 195

Washington Senators, 11, 80, 90, 91, 175–76, 285, 295, 326n112; and attendance, 99, 115, 127, 288; and Clark Griffith Stadium, 129–30, 289; pennant wins of the, 76, 86, 139, 166, 175; and profitability, 76, 86, 89, 280, 281, 327n8; sale of the,

Washington Senators (*continued*)
89; and Sunday games, 111; win-
loss records of the, 166, 293; and
the World Series, 34, 127, 333n32,
335n62

Weaver, Buck, 53, 58, 299

Weeghman, Charles, 13, 126, 160, 176,
191, 280, 348n55

Weintraub, Robert, 128, 156

Weiss, George, 174, 251

Wells, Willie, 255

Welsh, Jimmy, 163

Welty, Benjamin, 32

Wera, Julian, 185

West, Fred O., 64, 66

Wheat, Zack, 160, 172, 174–75, 222,
226, 229

White, Jim, 170

White, Sol, 257–58, 268

Williams, Claude ("Lefty"), 51, 224, 299

Williams, Cy, 139

Williams, Harry, 112

Williams, Joe ("Smokey"), 261

Williams, Ken, 139

Wilson, Franklin, 204

Wilson, Hack, 243

Wilson, Rollo, 273

Winter, Kenneth, 77, 81–82, 157

Witt, Whitey, 124–25

Wood, Joe ("Smoky Joe"), 63–64, 66,
71, 143, 206

Wood, Leonard, 25

Woodruff, Harvey, 22

Woolley, Edward, 345n15

World Series, 23, 34, 61, 148, 157,
174–75, 321n38, 326n20; and attendance, 98, 106, 107, 108, 126–27;
and barnstorming rules, 48, 144,
209–10, 235–36; gate receipts at the,
106, 107–8, 335n62; and interleague
series proposals, 49; players' shares
of the receipts from, 48–49, 54, 56,
65, 107, 108, 151, 223, 323n70; radio
broadcasts of the, 133; and scheduling, 101; and stadium capacity,
126–27; and ticket prices, 98, 106–8,
126–27; and World War I, 15, 313n26.
See also World Series gambling
scandal

World Series, Colored, 260, 261, 269,
271, 272. *See also* Negro Leagues

World Series gambling scandal, 1, 40,
47–51, 54, 253; aftermath of the,
51–52, 53–59, 69–71, 97; attempted
cover-up of the, 46, 55; and governance of Major League Baseball,
23, 24–25, 27, 28, 30, 48–49, 55; grand
jury investigation of the, 52–53; and
public opinion, 55–56, 57–58; and
the Risberg-Gandil scandal, 36–37,
69–71; and salaries of players, 56,
58–59, 222–24, 299, 321n41, 360n20;
suspensions of players involved in
the, 30, 31, 53, 56, 58, 208, 209; trial
regarding the, 57–58. *See also* Chicago
White Sox; gambling; World Series

World War I, 1, 4–5, 13–15, 127, 197,
242, 253, 313n19; and attendance,
8, 94–95; and ball production, 140;
and length of seasons, 1, 8, 14–15,
79, 94–95, 101, 220; and the Minor
Leagues, 205, 237–38, 243; and
roster limits, 191, 220; and salaries
of players, 8, 13, 205–6, 220–21, 222;
and Sunday games, 111; and taxes
on sports admissions, 103–4, 105,

www.ingramcontent.com/pod-product-compliance
Lightning Source LLC
Chambersburg PA
CBHW020339100426
42812CB00029B/3188/J